her works is called "Illustrator's Commentary" rather than "Author's Commentary." All titles of books containing illustrations by the artist being profiled are highlighted in boldface type.

Indexes

A **Cumulative Author Index** lists all of the authors who have appeared in *CLR* with cross-references to the biographical, autobiographical, and literary criticism series published by the Gale Group. A complete list of these sources is found facing the first page of the Author Index. The index also includes birth and death dates and cross-references between pseudonyms and actual names.

A **Cumulative Nationality Index** lists all authors featured in *CLR* by nationality, followed by the number of the *CLR* volume in which their entry appears.

A **Cumulative Title Index** lists all author titles covered in *CLR*. Each title is followed by the author's name and corresponding volume and page numbers where commentary on the work is located.

Citing *Children's Literature Review*

When writing papers, students who quote directly from any volume in the Literary Criticism Series may use the following general format to footnote reprinted criticism. The first example pertains to material drawn from periodicals, the second to material reprinted from books.

Cynthia Zarin, "It's Easy Being Green," *The New York Times Book Review* (November 14, 1993): 48; excerpted and reprinted in *Children's Literature Review,* vol. 58, ed. Deborah J. Morad (Farmington Hills, Mich: The Gale Group, 2000), 57.

Paul Walker, *Speaking of Science Fiction: The Paul Walker Interviews,* (Luna Publications, 1978), 108-20; excerpted and reprinted in *Children's Literature Review,* vol. 58, ed. Deborah J. Morad (Farmington Hills, Mich: The Gale Group, 2000), 3-8.

Suggestions are Welcome

In response to various suggestions, several features have been added to *CLR* since the beginning of the series, including author entries on retellers of traditional literature as well as those who have been the first to record oral tales and other folklore; entries on prominent illustrators featuring commentary on their styles and techniques; entries on authors whose works are considered controversial; occasional entries devoted to criticism on a single work or a series of works; sections in author introductions that list major works by and about the author or illustrator being profiled; explanatory notes that provide information on the critic or work of criticism to enhance the usefulness of the excerpt; more extensive illustrative material, such as holographs of manuscript pages and photographs of people and places pertinent to the careers of the authors and artists; a cumulative nationality index for easy access to authors by nationality; and occasional guest essays written specifically for *CLR* by prominent critics on subjects of their choice.

Readers who wish to suggest new features, topics, or authors to appear in future volumes, or who have other suggestions or comments are cordially invited to call, write, or fax the Managing Editor:

Managing Editor, Literary Criticism Series
The Gale Group
27500 Drake Road
Farmington Hills, MI 48331-3535
1-800-347-4253 (GALE)
Fax: 248-699-8054

ISSN 0362-4145

volume 71

Children's Literature Review

Excerpts from Reviews,
Criticism, and Commentary
on Books for Children
and Young People

Jennifer Baise
Editor

Rebecca Blanchard, Thomas Ligotti
Associate Editors

GALE GROUP
THOMSON LEARNING

Detroit • New York • San Diego • San Francisco
Boston • New Haven, Conn. • Waterville, Maine
London • Munich

STAFF

Library of Congress Catalog Card Number 76-643301
ISBN 0-7876-4577-X
ISSN 0362-4145
Printed in the United States of America

10 9 8 7 6 5 4 3 2 1

Contents

Preface vii

Acknowledgments xi

Preface

Literature for children and young adults has evolved into both a respected branch of creative writing and a successful industry. Currently, books for young readers are considered among the most popular segments of publishing. Criticism of juvenile literature is instrumental in recording the literary or artistic development of the creators of children's books as well as the trends and controversies that result from changing values or attitudes about young people and their literature. Designed to provide a permanent, accessible record of this ongoing scholarship, *Children's Literature Review* (*CLR*) presents parents, teachers, and librarians—those responsible for bringing children and books together—with the opportunity to make informed choices when selecting reading materials for the young. In addition, *CLR* provides researchers of children's literature with easy access to a wide variety of critical information from English-language sources in the field. Users will find balanced overviews of the careers of the authors and illustrators of the books that children and young adults are reading; these entries, which contain excerpts from published criticism in books and periodicals, assist users by sparking ideas for papers and assignments and suggesting supplementary and classroom reading. Ann L. Kalkhoff, president and editor of *Children's Book Review Service Inc.,* writes that "*CLR* has filled a gap in the field of children's books, and it is one series that will never lose its validity or importance."

Scope of the Series

Each volume of *CLR* profiles the careers of a selection of authors and illustrators of books for children and young adults from preschool through high school. Author lists in each volume reflect:

- an international scope

- representation of authors of all eras

- the variety of genres covered by children's and/or YA literature: picture books, fiction, nonfiction, poetry, folklore, and drama

Although the focus of the series is on authors new to *CLR,* entries will be updated as the need arises.

Organization of the Book

A *CLR* entry consists of the following elements:

- The **Author Heading** consists of the author's name followed by birth and death dates. The portion of the name outside the parentheses denotes the form under which the author is most frequently published. If the author wrote consistently under a pseudonym, the pseudonym will be listed in the author heading and the author's actual name given in parentheses on the first line of the biographical and critical information. Also located here are any name variations under which an author wrote, including transliterated forms for authors whose native languages use non-roman alphabets. Uncertain birth or death dates are indicated by question marks.

- A **Portrait of the Author** is included when available.

- The **Author Introduction** contains information designed to introduce an author to *CLR* users by presenting an overview of the author's themes and styles, biographical facts that relate to the author's literary career or critical responses to the author's works, and information about major awards and prizes the author has received. The introduction begins by identifying the nationality of the author and by listing genres in which s/he has written for children and young adults. Introductions also list a group of representative titles for which the author or illustrator being profiled is best known; this section, which begins with the words "major works include," follows the genre line of the introduction. For seminal figures, a listing of major works about the author follows when appropriate, highlighting important biographies about the author or illustrator that are not excerpted in the entry. The centered heading "Introduction" announces the body of the text.

■ **Criticism** is located in three sections: **Author Commentary** (when available) **General Commentary** (when available), and **Title Commentary** (commentary on specific titles).

The **Author Commentary** presents background material written by the author or by an interviewer. This commentary may cover a specific work or several works. Author commentary on more than one work appears after the author introduction, while commentary on an individual book follows the title entry heading.

The **General Commentary** consists of critical excerpts that consider more than one work by the author or illustrator being profiled. General commentary is preceded by the critic's name in boldface type or, in the case of unsigned criticism, by the title of the journal. *CLR* also features entries that emphasize general criticism on the oeuvre of an author or illustrator. When appropriate, a selection of reviews is included to supplement the general commentary.

The **Title Commentary** begins with the title entry headings, which precede the criticism on a title and cite publication information on the work being reviewed. Title headings list the title of the work as it appeared in its first English-language edition. The first English-language publication date of each work (unless otherwise noted) is listed in parentheses following the title. Differing U.S. and British titles follow the publication date within parentheses. When a work is written by an individual other than the one being profiled, as is the case when illustrators are featured, the parenthetical material following the title cites the author of the work before listing its publication date.

Entries in each title commentary section consist of critical excerpts on the author's individual works, arranged chronologically by publication date. The entries generally contain two to seven reviews per title, depending on the stature of the book and the amount of criticism it has generated. The editors select titles that reflect the entire scope of the author's literary contribution, covering each genre and subject. An effort is made to reprint criticism that represents the full range of each title's reception, from the year of its initial publication to current assessments. Thus, the reader is provided with a record of the author's critical history. Publication information (such as publisher names and book prices) and parenthetical numerical references (such as footnotes or page and line references to specific editions of works) have been deleted at the discretion of the editors to provide smoother reading of the text.

■ A complete **Bibliographical Citation** of the original essay or book precedes each piece of criticism.

■ Selected excerpts are preceded by brief **Annotations,** which provide information on the critic or work of criticism to enhance the reader's understanding of the excerpt.

■ Numerous **Illustrations** are featured in *CLR*. For entries on illustrators, an effort has been made to include illustrations that reflect the characteristics discussed in the criticism. Entries on authors who do not illustrate their own works my include photographs and other illustrative material pertinent to their careers.

Special Features: Entries on Illustrators

Entries on authors who are also illustrators will occasionally feature commentary on selected works illustrated but not written by the author being profiled. These works are strongly associated with the illustrator and have received critical acclaim for their art. By including critical comment on works of this type, the editors wish to provide a more complete representation of the artist's career. Criticism on these works has been chosen to stress artistic, rather than literary, contributions. Title entry headings for works illustrated by the author being profiled are arranged chronologically within the entry by date of publication and include notes identifying the author of the illustrated work. In order to provide easier access for users, all titles illustrated by the subject of the entry are boldfaced.

CLR also includes entries on prominent illustrators who have contributed to the field of children's literature. These entries are designed to represent the development of the illustrator as an artist rather than as a literary stylist. The illustrator's section is organized like that of an author, with two exceptions: the introduction presents an overview of the illustrator's styles and techniques rather than outlining his or her literary background, and the commentary written by the illustrator on his or

Guide to Gale Literary Criticism Series

For criticism on	Consult these Gale series
Authors now living or who died after December 31, 1999	*CONTEMPORARY LITERARY CRITICISM (CLC)*
Authors who died between 1900 and 1999	*TWENTIETH-CENTURY LITERARY CRITICISM (TCLC)*
Authors who died between 1800 and 1899	*NINETEENTH-CENTURY LITERATURE CRITICISM (NCLC)*
Authors who died between 1400 and 1799	*LITERATURE CRITICISM FROM 1400 TO 1800 (LC)* *SHAKESPEAREAN CRITICISM (SC)*
Authors who died before 1400	*CLASSICAL AND MEDIEVAL LITERATURE CRITICISM (CMLC)*
Authors of books for children and young adults	*CHILDREN'S LITERATURE REVIEW (CLR)*
Dramatists	*DRAMA CRITICISM (DC)*
Poets	*POETRY CRITICISM (PC)*
Short story writers	*SHORT STORY CRITICISM (SSC)*
Black writers of the past two hundred years	*BLACK LITERATURE CRITICISM (BLC)* *BLACK LITERATURE CRITICISM SUPPLEMENT (BLCS)*
Hispanic writers of the late nineteenth and twentieth centuries	*HISPANIC LITERATURE CRITICISM (HLC)* *HISPANIC LITERATURE CRITICISM SUPPLEMENT (HLCS)*
Native North American writers and orators of the eighteenth, nineteenth, and twentieth centuries	*NATIVE NORTH AMERICAN LITERATURE (NNAL)*
Major authors from the Renaissance to the present	*WORLD LITERATURE CRITICISM, 1500 TO THE PRESENT (WLC)* *WORLD LITERATURE CRITICISM SUPPLEMENT (WLCS)*

Children's
Literature
Review

Acknowledgments

The editors wish to thank the copyright holders of the excerpted criticism included in this volume and the permissions managers of many book and magazine publishing companies for assisting us in securing reproduction rights. We are also grateful to the staffs of the Detroit Public Library, the Library of Congress, the University of Detroit Mercy Library, Wayne State University Purdy/Kresge Library Complex, and the University of Michigan Libraries for making their resources available to us. Following is a list of the copyright holders who have granted us permission to reproduce material in this volume of *CLR*. Every effort has been made to trace copyright, but if omissions have been made, please let us know.

COPYRIGHTED EXCERPTS IN *CLR*, VOLUME 71, WERE REPRODUCED FROM THE FOLLOWING PERIODICALS:

The ALAN Review, v. 21, Winter, 1994; v. 22, Fall, 1994; v. 22, Winter, 1995. Reproduced by permission.—*America's Graphic Design Magazine,* v. 52, January, 1998. Reproduced by permission by permission of author.—*ANQ,* v. 3, January, 1990. Copyright © 1990 Helen Dwight Reid Educational Foundation. Reproduced with permission of the Helen Dwight Reid Educational Foundation, published by Heldref Publications, 1319 18th Street, NW, Washington, DC 20036-1802.— *Booklist,* v. 81, June 15, 1985; v. 82, April 15, 1986; v. 82, May 1, 1986; v. 83, September 15, 1986; v. 83, February 15, 1987; v. 83, March 1, 1987; v. 84, September 15, 1987; v. 84, April 1, 1988; v. 94, April, 1988; v. 84, June 1, 1988; v. 84, July, 1988; v. 85, September 15, 1988; v. 85, January 15, 1989; v. 86, September 1, 1989; v. 87, July, 1991; v. 88, December 1, 1991.; v. 88, January 15, 1992; v. 88, April 15, 1992; v. 88, June 1, 1992; v. 921, June 1, 1992; v. 89, September 1, 1992; v. 89, October 15, 1992; v. 89, November 1, 1992; v. 89, April 15, 1993; v. 89, July, 1993; v. 89, August, 1993; v. 90, September 15, 1993; v. 90, October 15, 1993; v. 90, March 1, 1994; v. 90, June 1, 1994; v. 90, August, 1994; v. 91, November 1, 1994, v. 91, December 1, 1994; v. 91, July, 1995; v. 91, August, 1995; v. 92, December 1, 1995; v. 92, February 1, 1996; v. 92, May 1, 1996; v. 92, July, 1996; v. 93, March 1, 1997; v. 93, March 15, 1997; v. 93, June 1, 1997; v. 93, July, 1997; v. 94, January 1, 1998; v. 95, November 1, 1998; June 1, 1999; v. 95, July, 1999; v. 96, April 15, 2000. Copyright © 1985, 1986, 1987, 1988, 1989, 1991, 1992, 1993, 1994, 1995, 1996, 1997, 1998, 1999, 2000 by American Library Association. Reproduced by permission.—*Bulletin of the Center for Children's Books,* v. 39, April, 1986. Copyright © 1986 by The University of Chicago. Reproduced by permission./v. 47, June, 1994. Copyright © 1994 by The Board of Trustees of the University of Illinois. Reproduced by permission.—*Bulletin of the Center for Children's Books,* v. 41, June, 1985; v. 39, April, 1986; v. 40, November, 1986; v. 40, July-August, 1987; v. 41, January, 1988; v. 42, October, 1988; v. 42, July, 1989; v. 44, March, 1991; v. 44, June, 1991; v. 45, September, 1991; v. 45, May, 1992; . 46, July-August, 1993; v. 47, June, 1994; v. 48, October, 1994; v. 48, July-August, 1995; v. 50, May, 1997; v. 51, September, 1997; v. 52, January, 1999. Reproduced by permission.—*CM Magazine,* v. 17, January, 1989; v. 18, March, 1990; v. 19, October, 1991; v. 19, November, 1991; v. V, October 2, 1998; v. VI, January 7, 2000; v. VIII, October 20, 2000. Reprinted from CM Magazine by permission of The Society of Management Accountants of Canada.—*Emergency Librarian,* v. 21, May-June, 1994. Reproduced by permission.—*The Five Owls,* v. 3, September-October, 1988; v. 4, September-October, 1989; v. 5, September-October, 1990. Reproduced by permission.—*The Horn Book Magazine,* v.lxvi March-April, 1990; v. lxvi, November-December, 1990; v. lxvii, January-February, 1991; v. lxvii, March-April, 1991; v.lxvii, July-August, 1991; v. lxvii, November-December, 1991; v. lxvii, July-August, 1992; v. lxviik, November-December, 1992; v. lxx, January-February, 1994; v.lxx, November-December, 1994; v. lxxi, January-February, 1995; v. lxxi, July-August, 1995; v. lxxi, September-October, 1995; v. lxxii, September-October, 1996; v. lxxiii, May-June, 1997; v. lxxiii, September-October, 1997; v. lxxiv, March-April, 1998; v. lxxiv, May-June, 1998; v. lxxiv, July-August, 1998; v.lxxiv, September-October, 1998; v.lxxv, May, 1999; v. lxxv, September, 1999; v. lxxvi, January, 2000; v. lxxvi, September, 2000. Copyright © 1990, 1991,1992, 1994, 1995, 1997, 1998, 1999, 2000 by Horn Book Inc. Reproduced by permission.—*Instructor,* v. 107, October, 1997. Reproduced by permission of Scholastic Inc.—*Journal of Youth Services in Libraries,* v. 11, Summer, 1998. Copyright © 1998 by the American Library Association. Reproduced by permission.—*Kirkus Reviews,* v.lxiii, September 15, 1990; v. lviii, October 15, 1990; v. lviii, December 15, 1990; v. lix, February 1, 1991; v. lix, June 15, 1991; v. lix, September 1, 1991; v. lix, December 1, 1991; v. lx, April 1, 1992; v.lx, April 15, 1992; v. lx, November 15, 1992; v. lx, September 15, 1992; v. lxi, April 1, 1993; v. lxi, July 1, 1993; v. lxii, February 15, 1994; v. lxii, April 15, 1994; v. lxii, July 15, 1994; v. lxiii, December 15, 1994; v. lxiv, April 15, 1996; v. lxiv, May 1, 1996; v. lxiv, September 1, 1996; v. lxv, February 1, 1997; v.lxv, August 15, 1997; v. lxvi, April 15, 1998. Copyright © 1990, 1991, 1992, 1993, 1994, 1996, 1997, 1998 The Kirkus Service, Inc. All rights reserved. Reproduced by permission of the publisher, Kirkus Reviews and Kirkus Associates, L.P.— *KLIATT,* v. 31, May, 1997; v. 32, July, 1998. Copyright © 1997, 1998 by KLIATT. Reproduced by permission.—*Library Journal,* v. 124, February 15, 1999. Copyright © 1999 by Reed Publishing USA. Reproduced by permission.—*The Na-*

COPYRIGHTED EXCERPTS IN *CLR*, VOLUME 71, WERE REPRODUCED FROM THE FOLLOWING BOOKS:

PHOTOGRAPHS AND ILLUSTRATIONS APPEARING IN *CLR*, VOLUME 71, WERE RECEIVED FROM THE FOLLOWING SOURCES:

Aliki
1929-

(Full name Aliki Liacouras Brandenberg) American author/illustrator of picture books and nonfiction; reteller and illustrator of picture books, fiction, and nonfiction.

Major works include *Three Gold Pieces: A Greek Folk Tale* (1967), *Corn Is Maize: The Gift of the Indians* (1976), *Digging Up Dinosaurs* (1981), *A Medieval Feast* (1983), *William Shakespeare & the Globe* (1999).

For further information on Aliki's life and works, see *CLR,* Volume 9.

INTRODUCTION

Aliki is a versatile author whose books are both entertaining and informative. Writing for a preschool through middle school audience, she is widely known for her nonfiction on scientific and historical subjects, easy-reading biographies of prominent American and European figures, fiction that is often amusing and sensitive, and adaptations of Greek folktales. Her works contain concise language and detailed illustrations that range from jovial cartoons to painting in the style of illuminated manuscripts. Warmth and enthusiasm permeate Aliki's books as she invests many of them, including her nonfiction titles, with a playful sense of humor. Critics applaud Aliki for creating books that are exceptional both visually and textually. Praised for her thorough research, simplicity, and attention to detail, Aliki is also appreciated for the appealing humor and engaging qualities of her books. She is considered an author whose unique approaches provide children with enjoyable learning experiences.

BIOGRAPHICAL INFORMATION

Born in Wildwood Crest, New Jersey, while her parents were on vacation, Aliki grew up in Philadelphia and Yeadon, Pennsylvania. Aliki showed an early interest in drawing during her preschool years, and while in kindergarten she drew a portrait of her family and Peter Rabbit's family, both of which included three girls and a boy, and received the attention of her teacher who predicted that Aliki would one day become an artist. Aliki continued to draw throughout her childhood, and, upon graduation from high school, she attended the Philadelphia Museum School of Art. After graduating from college in 1951, Aliki worked in advertising and display, painted murals, taught art and ceramics, and created her own line of greeting cards. In 1956, she embarked on a trip to Greece, her parents' homeland, to learn more of her heritage, and visited other European countries as well. While in Italy, she met Franz Brandenberg, a children's book author. The couple married in 1957 and moved to Brandenberg's native Switzerland where Aliki worked as a freelance artist. Fascinated by the life of Swiss national hero William Tell, Aliki researched, wrote, and illustrated her first book, *The Story of William Tell*, which was published in 1960. That same year, Aliki and Brandenberg moved to New York City, where she began illustrating the works of other authors, including her husband. While she was creating the pictures for a volume of publisher Thomas Y. Crowell's "Let's-Read-and-Find-Out" series of science books for children, she was inspired to write and illustrate *My Five Senses* (1962), an original book for the series which would later include much of her nonfiction. In 1977, Aliki moved with her family to England, where she and Franz have continued their careers as children's book writers.

MAJOR WORKS

Aliki has written a variety of nonfiction books, including biography, history, and science. Her biographies include portraits of such figures as William Tell, Johnny Appleseed, George Washington Carver, William Penn, King Louis XIV, and William Shakespeare. Noted for their accurate detail, these works present a generalized approach to their subjects without sacrificing character or atmosphere. All her works begin with her own personal interest in a subject, which she then devotedly researches over an extended period of time. Her meticulous research yields an engaging distillation of her subject matter; she is praised for addressing complex subjects and conveying the information to children and young readers in a very accessible manner. In several of her historical works, Aliki blends history with another area of interest. For example, in *Corn Is Maize: The Gift of the Indians*, Aliki combines history with science to explicate the significance of corn in America. In her acclaimed work *A Medieval Feast*, she integrates history with sociology to re-create what a feast would have been like in the year 1400. In her science books, she explicates such topics as dinosaurs, fossils, mammoths, mummies, and food. Aliki explains complex facts and processes simply so that young readers can learn effortlessly about the burial rites of ancient Egypt or how a dinosaur skeleton is assembled. Perhaps Aliki's most popular science books have dinosaurs as their subject matter. The humor in such works as *My Visit to the Dinosaurs* and *Digging Up Dinosaurs* infuses a great deal of human interest into the study of dinosaurs.

In addition to her nonfiction works, Aliki is noted for fiction picture books that are often inspired by her own experiences and those of her two children. She engages the reader through simple text and imaginative illustrations. In such works as *Christmas Tree Memories, June 7!* and *Those Summers*, Aliki captures the essence of her childhood through the portrayal of vivid family memories. In *The Two of Them*, Aliki presents a powerful generational tale of mutual love that was inspired by her own father. Employing a reverse chronological sequence and a dual point of view, Aliki tells the poignant story of an immigrant child in *Marianthe's Story: Painted Words, Spoken Memories*. Also significant in her body of works are Aliki's retellings of Greek folktales, written in a direct, colloquial style. In her versions of Greek myth and folktales, she also has introduced new and less typical information to readers, as in her award-winning *Three Gold Pieces*, in which she retells the story of a submissive Greek peasant and the meager pay he receives for ten years of hard work.

Intrinsic to the text of her works are Aliki's illustrations, which vary from book to book and range from comic book style drawings and word bubbles to elaborate frieze pictures and faux illuminated manuscript. Observers note that Aliki's illustrations both complement and amplify her texts. Utilizing such mediums as gouache, pen and ink, and watercolor, she creates a variety of pictures to match the format and mood of her books. A childlike, primitive style characterizes Aliki's early works, which are drawn simply and colored brightly. Later books, such

as the Greek folktale *Three Gold Pieces*, present readers with more dramatic, often opulent illustrations. With *My Visit to the Dinosaurs*, Aliki introduces an illustrative technique that helps distinguish her informational books—the inclusion of running commentaries, often in speech balloon style, that comment on the main text. Frequently presented as conversations between children and other characters, these voice-bubbles provide an entertaining, human reaction to the subject under discussion while supplying clarification and new knowledge. Perhaps her most successful illustrations are those that depict a fifteenth-century royal banquet in *A Medieval Feast*. Modeling her watercolor paintings on actual tapestries and illuminated manuscripts, Aliki is acclaimed for capturing the beauty of her sources without losing her artistic individuality.

While Aliki's works are noted for their conciseness, which makes them enduringly popular among her preschool to middle school audience, their simplicity belies the experience and research that underlies each work. Aliki commented to *St. James Guide to Children's Writers*, "Much of my work involves intricate and time-consuming research—made doubly difficult because I both write and illustrate. I spend long hours at my desk. Some books take three years to complete. That is why I call what I do 'hard fun.' But I love the challenge of a new idea, and finding out something I don't know about a subject—or even myself."

AWARDS

Aliki is the recipient of numerous awards, including the Boys' Clubs of America Junior Book Award in 1968 for *Three Gold Pieces: A Greek Folk Tale*; the New York Academy of Sciences Children's Science Book Award in 1977 for *Corn Is Maize: The Gift of the Indians*; the Dutch Children's Book Council Silver Slate Pencil Award and the Garden State Children's Book Award both in 1981 for *Mummies Made in Egypt*; Omar's Book Award in 1986 for *Keep Your Mouth Closed, Dear*; the Prix du Livre pour Enfants in 1987 for *Feelings*; the World of Reading Readers' Choice Award in 1989 for *The Story of Johnny Appleseed*; the Pennsylvania School Librarians Association Award in 1991 in recognition of outstanding contributions in the field of literature; the Garden State Children's Book Award in 1996 for *My Visit to the Aquarium*; the Honor Book Award and the *Boston Globe-Horn Book* award in 1999 for *William Shakespeare and the Globe*; and the Jane Addams Peace Prize in 1999 for *Marianthe's Story*.

GENERAL COMMENTARY

Raymond, Allen

SOURCE: "Aliki: 55 Books and Counting," in *Teaching PreK-8*, Vol. 30, No. 1, September, 1999, pp. 56-8.

Last May *Teaching PreK-8* spent the better part of a day interviewing the delightfully stunning woman we all know as Aliki—her first name—in the New York offices of HarperCollins, one of her publishers (the other publisher is Greenwillow). The next day she flew back to London, where Aliki and her husband, Franz Brandenberg (a native of Switzerland), have been living for the last 20 years.

Aliki, who has a grand sense of humor, was born in the United States of Greek parents who moved here shortly before her birth. Thus, as she tells it, "I was born very Greek—but in Philadelphia."

Blessed with unusual artistic talent in both art and music (she has a lovely voice), Aliki began attending art school when only 11 years old, culminating in her graduation from the Philadelphia College of Art.

A ROSE BY ANY OTHER NAME . . . ?

She began her career in advertising art, married Franz and moved to Switzerland where she and her new husband lived for three years, before moving to New York and then to London.

She wrote her first book, *The Story of William Tell*, while living in Switzerland. That's when she first decided to use Aliki, and thus did her new career begin.

She intimated that using Aliki on those first few books came about almost by accident. Her maiden name is Liacouras, and Aliki Liacouras Brandenberg seemed a bit long. "It might fall off the page," she said with a chuckle.

On the other hand, she felt uncomfortable with just Aliki . . . "it seemed pretentious," she commented. Her publisher, however, liked "Aliki" and came up with the clincher: "The name," she was told, "is already in all of the card catalogs." That did it . . . and Aliki, it is.

PASSION FOR PERFECTION.

In our conversation with Aliki she used "hard" and "difficult" interchangeably to characterize the effort that went into books she has written, illustrations she has painted, research she has done, layouts she has planned and bright ideas she has brought to the printed page.

Why so much difficulty? Chalk it up to Aliki's passion for perfection, as well as her insatiable desire to know everything about whatever she's working on, including facts and figures that don't end up in her books.

For instance, it took visits to nine zoos and countless hours of research—plus three years—to create *My Visit to the Zoo* (1997). And it was only after visits to 11 aquariums and immersion in 35 textbooks that *My Visit to the Aquarium* (1993) was completed.

Somehow, in spite of the time Aliki spends on each book, she has still managed to be the author and/or illustrator of at least 55 books . . . and counting.

Talent seems to run in Aliki's family, by the way. One sister has written several cookbooks; another sister is a musician and actress; her brother is president of Temple University in Philadelphia.

Same thing with Aliki's children. Her son, Jason, is a filmmaker and her daughter, Alexa, is the author of two books, with a third on the way. Enough talent for one family? Not quite. Aliki's husband, Franz Brandenberg, has written many books which Aliki illustrated.

BEHIND THE SCENES.

When Aliki visits schools, she delights students with behind-the-scenes stories that kids rarely hear, like being inspired to write *Mummies Made in Egypt* (1979) after seeing a mummified cat.

Even her correspondence with students has that special touch. "When children write to me they may type their letters, but not sign them. I tell them to sign, because their soul is in their signature, not in the keys they push."

SEARCHING FOR CLUES.

In her latest book, *William Shakespeare & the Globe* (1999), Aliki writes, "William Shakespeare is a mystery. Little is known about him—not even the exact day he was born, or what he looked like . . . we search for clues . . . and we find some in his own plays and poems. We have to guess the rest." But hers were educated guesses, based on her three years of research.

THE CROWNING TOUCH.

As the book transports its readers back 400 years, the many historically accurate, beautifully detailed illustrations on every page tell their own stories, helping to make this book a treasure, not only for kids, but for adults, too.

The crowning touch is the addition, on the bottom of almost every one of the book's gorgeous pages (art by Aliki, of course) of an appropriate Shakespearean quotation which, through her exhaustive research, meshes beautifully with the story being told on that particular page. It's indeed a wonderful touch.

But then, one almost expects the unusual, "the wonderful touch," from Aliki. It's a part of her persona. Whether writing books, illustrating books—or both— she exudes a joy and confidence that says, "Yes, I can do that, and it will be beautiful."

And it is.

TITLE COMMENTARY

DINOSAURS ARE DIFFERENT (1985)

Publishers Weekly

SOURCE: A review of *Dinosaurs Are Different,* in *Publishers Weekly,* Vol. 227, No. 20, May 17, 1985, p. 118.

Most of Aliki's gang is there, yelling for stragglers to catch up with them and their parents, at a natural history museum. "All those teeth!" says one little girl, but it's the bones that really tell the kids how dinosaurs differed from each other. Readers of the favorite author/illustrator's new Let's-Read-And-Find-Out Science book share the information gained from the formidable skeletons and reconstructions of prehistoric beasts. Vividly colored pictures as well as the children's ongoing remarks make education fun. On each page, the scientific names of the animals and their orders are set forth. At the top of one list is the ancestor of the Archosauria (ruling reptiles), rarely found in children's books. In the crowd of various ages and ethnic backgrounds and guards alert to tots temporarily lost, there is the artist herself at work, accompanied by her husband and frequent collaborator, Fritz Brandenberg, and their children, testifying to the book's authenticity. (4-8)

Stefan Kanfer

SOURCE: A review of *Dinosaurs Are Different,* in *Time,* Vol. 126, December 23, 1985, p. 62.

Of all the giant creatures that ever walked the earth, none have more enduring fascination for children than the dinosaurs, possibly because no grownup has

ever seen them either. In *Dinosaurs Are Different* (Crowell), Aliki accurately re-creates the monsters, as a group of children wander around the drawings. When it is pointed out that Anatosauruses had more than 1,400 teeth, one onlooker remarks, with the good sense that runs through the book, "It's a good thing they didn't have to brush them."

JACK AND JAKE (1986)

The Bulletin of the Center for Children's Books

SOURCE: A review of *Jack and Jake,* in *The Bulletin of the Center for Children's Books,* Vol. 39, No. 8, April, 1986, p. 142.

"They said 'Jack is hungry,' when it's Jake who cried. They said 'Jack is wet,' but it's Jack they dried." Nobody, except their big sister, can tell these identical twins apart. While the rhyming text bemoans the mix-up, the pictures show the difference: Jack and Jake may look alike, but they enjoy different things. Jack likes trucks, sports, roughhousing (he's the first to crawl); Jake likes flowers, reading, and stuffed animals (he's the first to talk). This is a clever idea, though young children will probably need help understanding it, and Aliki's bright paintings of the pudgy twins (there's one physical difference—Jack's hair is always disheveled) have a nice, casually off-beat humor. However, active/passive stereotyping of the twins' personalities is shallow, undermining Aliki's implicit moral that the real differences between people are inner, rather than superficial.

Ilene Cooper

SOURCE: A review of *Jack and Jake,* in *Booklist,* Vol. 82, No. 16, April 15, 1986, p. 1214.

Ages 4-6. When Jack and Jake are born no one can tell the twins apart. The unnamed narrator, the boys' older sister, chronicles the way parents, grandmother, friends, and relatives mix up the twins. Even as the boys grow older, the confusion remains; it is up to their sister to set everyone straight. "Jack does things and says things that only Jack could / Jake finds things that only Jake would." Each boy has his own distinct personality that others would notice, their sister says, if only they paid proper attention. The extended joke goes on a little too long, but children should respond to the inherent humor of the confusing situations. Aliki's black-bordered drawings are inhabited by lively cartoon characters and executed in perky watercolors that have immediate appeal. The ballooned conversations that appear in each scene do not integrate easily with the captions, which may cause a problem when reading the book aloud.

HOW A BOOK IS MADE (1986)

Denise M. Wilms

SOURCE: A review of *How a Book Is Made,* in *Booklist,* Vol. 83, No. 2, September 15, 1986, p. 121.

Ages 5-8. Aliki's bright, cheery pictures combine with her relatively minimal text to explain how picture books are made. Cat people fill all of the roles, which include not only the author/artist figure but also the editor and a staff of assorted production and salespeople whose abilities and energies contribute to the finished product. Little cartoon vignettes play out the action, allowing the author to introduce a slight story line that implies some of the emotions and hard work that go into the phases of book production. The information flows smoothly and simply until the portion explaining color separation and full-color printing. Here the concepts may be beyond the range of younger children. That's not to say they won't catch the general drift of things; the information is surprisingly complete and rendered with more than a little dose of affection and humor.

Zena Sutherland

SOURCE: A review of *How a Book Is Made,* in *The Bulletin of the Center for Children's Books,* Vol. 40, No. 3, November, 1986, p. 41.

Yes, there are other good books on how a book is made, but probably none better for younger readers; since the comic-strip format and the step-by-step illustrations (line and wash) make the information easily accessible. Most books about book production emphasize manufacturing procedures although they do not neglect creative input; here there is full attention paid to author and illustrator and to all of the staff at a publishing house. Aliki's explanation of such procedures as color separation or stages in production of the printed and bound book are clear, though the level of information varies enough that adult explanation will be required for the technical parts. Also mentioned: the sales force, the reviewers, the librarians, and the bookstore clerks. Ultimately, the book, via library or bookstore, reaches children.

Stefan Kanfer

SOURCE: A review of *How a Book Is Made,* in *Time,* Vol. 129, January 5, 1987, p. 81.

For the curious of any age, Aliki shows **How a Book Is Made** (Crowell). Here the author—and every other professional from editor to printer—is a cat. Except for this trifling departure from reality, every detail is absolutely accurate. With affection and whimsy, Aliki takes the reader from the day of inspiration to the fretful submission to the publisher, the text changes, the choice of typeface, the compelling and intricate business of color separation, the binding, the selling and, finally, that most curious of all processes, reviewing. In this case the judgment is an encouraging purr: Happy New Year.

WELCOME LITTLE BABY (1987)

Publishers Weekly

SOURCE: A review of *Welcome Little Baby,* in *Publishers Weekly,* Vol. 231, No. 6, February 13, 1987, p. 91.

This beautiful little book is the perfect gift for a new baby and his or her family. Accomplished author/artist Aliki tenderly depicts a newborn and its family's first experiences. "Welcome to our world, little baby," the text begins. "We've been waiting for you." The story evokes all the warm feelings new parents and their loved ones have toward babies. Aliki's illustrations show everyday events that will interest older children, while toddlers will be drawn to the prominently displayed faces of the baby and its mother. All ages.

Denise M. Wilms

SOURCE: A review of *Welcome Little Baby,* in *Booklist,* Vol. 83, No. 13, March 1, 1987, pp. 1010-11.

Ages 2-5. As the title suggests, this is written to a newborn child. Its spare text celebrates the complete innocence of a tiny baby and the wondrous newness of the world this child will be experiencing and exploring. "Welcome to our world, little baby. We've been waiting for you. You're very small and all you want is to eat, to sleep, and to feel warm. . . . You will grow and grow and find the world around you.

You'll see it. You'll smell it, and feel it, too." Aliki's airy pictures—breezy, whimsical line drawings in pastel pencil shades—are fresh and springlike, suggesting the joy and delight associated with a new life. Humorous touches in facial expressions or in activities keep this from being oversentimental. It's a nice preview for siblings still waiting for the new baby; children already coping with a newborn may not feel so welcoming!

Lucy Young Clem

SOURCE: A review of *Welcome Little Baby*, in *School Library Journal*, Vol. 33, No. 10, June/July, 1987, p. 75.

PreS-Gr 2—Here's a different sort of "new baby" book, a warm, tender greeting for a little one. Simple prose combined with charming pictures in the soft, bright colors of spring express the wonder and promise of a new life. Sweet without being saccharine, the text describes the small world of an infant and the way in which that sphere will expand as the baby discovers "things you didn't know when you were born." Impressionistic illustrations in crayon and ink follow the text; mother and child are shown at home and visiting the park, experiencing the sights and sounds around them. This is not a book about sibling relationships, as the focus is almost entirely on baby and mother, with the father appearing on the last page as part of the family. For this reason, the book would be a lovely gift for a new mother, but may not have much appeal to young children. *Welcome Little Baby* is just that—a welcome that expresses the miracle of birth and growth.

📖 *OVERNIGHT AT MARY BLOOM'S* (1987)

Publishers Weekly

SOURCE: A review of *Overnight at Mary Bloom's*, in *Publishers Weekly*, Vol. 232, No. 7, August 14, 1987, p. 101.

It's been too long since our last sojourn *At Mary Bloom's,* but she's back, and her latest episode is just as irresistible and sprightly as the first one. A little girl receives an invitation for an overnight visit and accepts immediately. Mary Bloom, who clearly has not lost her sense of childhood fun, presides over a cozy and wonderful home. Complete with a cuddly

baby, two sheepdogs, a cat, an owl, a rabbit, a skunk, mice, gerbils, hamsters, a monkey and a talking crow named Lucas, a visit with Mary Bloom's a kid's idea of adventure, creative play and independence. Aliki's now-familiar technique of full color with ink outline conveys the fun and excitement of every kid's sleepover dream. Ages 4-8.

Pamela Miller Ness

SOURCE: A review of *Overnight at Mary Bloom's*, in *School Library Journal*, Vol. 34, No. 1, September, 1987, p. 158.

PreS-Gr 2—Children who delighted in the gentle warmth and frolicsome chaos of Aliki's *At Mary Bloom's* (Greenwillow, 1983) will certainly welcome this sequel, in which the narrator describes a fun-filled overnight with her neighbor Mary Bloom, Mary's baby, and their extraordinary menagerie. Aliki depicts the magical chemistry between a child and a very special adult who is not a relative. Mary Bloom can turn even daily routines like tossing salad, walking the dogs, and preparing for bed into activities that give her young friend as much pleasure as playing "Dress Up . . . Hide and Seek and Make a Loud Rumpus." Aliki's full-page illustrations create setting, characters, and mood and will immediately draw children into the action. Cartoon-like in style (many including snippets of conversation in balloons), the figures are outlined in black ink and lightly shaded in soft primary hues with watercolor, crayon, and colored pencil. Mary Bloom's is a colorful, joyous, magical world, infinitely inviting and accessible to a child's imagination. This is an excellent choice for adults to share with toddlers at bedtime or in small group story hours, for preschoolers to savor the illustrations on their own, and for beginning readers to read independently or aloud to a young sibling.

Denise M. Wilms

SOURCE: A review of *Overnight at Mary Bloom's*, in *Booklist*, Vol. 84, No. 2, September 15, 1987, p. 140.

Ages 3-6. "Come spend the night," says Mary Bloom to her young friend, and the excited child packs her bags as quickly as she can. As in *At Mary Bloom's,* plenty happens, here in the company of the cheerful grown-up who relishes her young visitor. The pair fixes a meal, picnics on the rug, cleans up, and then tends to Mary Bloom's pet menagerie. Afterward, they play games, walk the dogs, and get ready for bed. When morning comes, there's a definite sense that more enjoyment is on the way. The text is quite spare; it's the cheerful pictures that convey the story's energy and fun. Mary Bloom should be every child's friend.

DINOSAUR BONES (1988)

Publishers Weekly

SOURCE: A review of *Dinosaur Bones,* in *Publishers Weekly,* Vol. 232, No. 24, December 11, 1987, p. 63.

The latest Let's-Read-and-Find-Out Science Book is written in the lively and informative style of Aliki's **Digging Up Dinosaurs** and **Dinosaurs Are Different,** with the added personal perspective of **My Visit to the Dinosaurs.** Here Aliki helps children understand that our knowledge of dinosaurs began less than 200 years ago, when Mary Ann Mantell discovered fossilized dinosaur teeth in a pile of rocks near an English quarry. The major findings of other scentists are included as well. Aliki has a perfect sense of just which details will most delight her readers: dinosaur footprints, a banquet held inside a life-size dinosaur model. Full-color illustrations of curious, questioning people and their discoveries make a treasure hunt of this fact-filled volume. Ages 4-8.

Zena Sutherland

SOURCE: A review of *Dinosaur Bones,* in *The Bulletin of the Center for Children's Books,* Vol. 41, No. 5, January, 1988, p. 81.

Gr. K-3. In a companion volume to three earlier books about dinosaurs, Aliki explains how, based on discoveries of fossil remains and the rock strata in which they were found, scientists have been able to classify species and assign them chronological niches. The text is written simply and clearly, and the cartoon-style drawings give additional information through captions and comments-in-balloons. An index-chart gives habitats and geological periods, and the text gives, in addition to facts about scientific history, a sense of the way knowledge is gathered, sifted, organized, and perennially questioned.

Cathryn A. Camper

SOURCE: A review of *Dinosaur Bones,* in *School Library Journal,* Vol. 34, No. 8, April, 1988, p. 93.

PreS-Gr 2—There's nothing intrinsically wrong with this latest Aliki contribution to dinomania; it's just that it all seems a bit familiar. Some of the information appears to be culled from Aliki's earlier (and admittedly, drabber) books. Other pages seem similar in content to Aliki's more recent volumes. Still, she has managed to provide a simplified explanation of the history of paleontology in a format that even preschoolers will comprehend. She reiterates much basic information about the separation of the continents, earth's time periods, and how scientists reconstruct dinosaurs from fossilized bones. Little information is provided about more recent dinosaur discoveries. Like the text, the illustrations in this book are reminiscent of other recent Aliki books on prehistoric life. Overall, this is a good book, but one which may duplicate information available in others.

DIGGING UP DINOSAURS (1989)

Cathryn A. Camper

SOURCE: A review of *Digging Up Dinosaurs,* in *School Library Journal,* Vol. 35, No. 7, March, 1989, p. 173.

PreS-Gr 2—The most notable change in this revision is the pictures: bright crayon-colored drawings have replaced the drab gray and green illustrations of the earlier edition. The hand-lettered captions and the dialogue in balloons have been slightly enlarged, making them easier to read. Textual changes are slight; Brontosaurus is now called Apatosaurus and some pages have been combined to streamline the book. Although the 1981 edition already depicted both men and women and people of diverse ethnic backgrounds, it's nice to be greeted by a smiling female paleontologist on the cover of the new edition. There's not much new information here, but the packaging is certainly more timely and appealing.

AUNT NINA, GOOD NIGHT (1989)

Publishers Weekly

SOURCE: A review of *Aunt Nina, Good Night,* in *Publishers Weekly,* Vol. 235, No. 26, June 30, 1989, p. 103.

A delightful bedtime tale, this third book about Aunt Nina looks at the bedtime delaying tactics of a group of nieces and nephews. They have come to Aunt Nina's house to spend the night, but when it comes time for lights out, the children repeatedly find reasons they cannot sleep. When the nephews miss the nieces, Aunt Nina tucks them all into her own bed. When they miss their parents, she lets them call home. She lets them visit their pets, reads to them and even starts a pillow fight. Only when the children cry, "We miss Aunt Nina," and she crawls into bed with them does the household finally settle down for the night. The repetitive language and lovable characters will soothe any child's passage to sleep; Aliki's pictures are full of children with rosy cheeks and striped pajamas, sharing joyous moments with an aunt they obviously adore. The watercolors are as perfect as the sentiments, embellishing each frame of the story with touches of humor and tenderness. Ages 3-up.

Denise Anton Wright

SOURCE: A review of *Aunt Nina, Good Night,* in *School Library Journal,* Vol. 35, No. 13, September, 1989, p. 222.

PreS-K—Aunt Nina is young, single, and has no children of her own, so naturally she dotes upon her six nieces and nephews. In this, the third book about Aunt Nina, she has invited the children to spend the night at her house. Of course, spending the night with their beloved aunt and being all together is so exciting that the children delay going to sleep as long as possible. Eventually Aunt Nina climbs into the large bed with the children, and the last illustrations show them sleeping peacefully with the cat asleep at the foot of the bed. The book consists mostly of the brief conversations between Aunt Nina and the children, including the repeated, gentle command, "Lights out!" Across from each page of Brandenberg's text are Aliki's large colored pencil and watercolor illustrations detailed with black pen. The warm browns, greens, and blues welcome readers into the loving world of Aunt Nina's home. Reinforcing this feeling are the soft, rounded, plump lines of everything connected with Aunt Nina: her chairs, bed, comforter, and pillows. Even the characters have a roundness to them. This reassuring picture book is ideal for sharing aloud with younger children, either individually or in a group setting. While the subject matter makes it a natural for bedtime, children will enjoy visiting Aunt Nina any time of the day.

📖 THE KING'S DAY: LOUIS XIV OF FRANCE (REV. ED., 1989)

Publishers Weekly

SOURCE: A review of *The King's Day: Louis XIV of France,* in *Publishers Weekly,* Vol. 236, No. 4, July 28, 1989, p. 221.

Life at the court of Versailles boggles the mind: Louis XIV had, among other things, a garden containing four million tulips, and an everyday supper consisted of some 40 dishes! Tidbits like this abound in Aliki's new book, in which she chronicles a day in the life of this 17th-century monarch. Her thorough research never overwhelms the seamless telling, although some details won't suit every reader: an entire page is devoted to the monarch's mistresses and the many offspring they bore him. Some of the pages seem crowded; perhaps a more generous design, allowing for more white space, would have been more effective. Nevertheless, the book presents an intriguing glimpse of the splendor and extravagance of the Sun King's court. Ages 7-11.

Deborah Abbott

SOURCE: A review of *The King's Day: Louis XIV of France,* in *Booklist,* Vol. 86, No. 1, September 1, 1989, p. 63.

Gr. 2-5. Once again Aliki works her magic as she did in *A Medieval Feast* presenting an in-depth portrait of a fascinating slice of history. This time her subject is Louis XIV of France, about whom little is written for children. Aliki's trademark, writing a simple story in a picture-book format accompanied by elaborate color drawings, allows her books to be read at two different levels. Between each illustration and the straightforward text is a caption that reveals the more-sophisticated details that older readers relish. Children will gain insight into the self-centered complexity of the absolute monarch through the presentation of the elaborate daily rituals of rising, attending mass, eating, holding court, and going to bed. The thousands of servants, the immense meals, and the grandeur of Louis' costumes and palaces, such as Versailles, are aptly depicted in delicate lines and luxurious colors. Both the text and the captions are sprinkled with French words, defined on the last page beneath the chronology of the Sun King's life.

Irvy Gilbertson

SOURCE: A review of *The King's Day: Louis XIV of France*, in *The Five Owls*, Vol. 4, September/October, 1989, p. 8.

Through text and inviting illustrations, Aliki describes a typical day in the life of King Louis XIV of France. Muted full color pictures, many almost an entire page in size, show carefully detailed work and an interesting use of white space throughout. Below each illustration, yet within the border of the picture, is italicized wording that expounds on the easily read, larger print text elsewhere on the page. The italicized type figuratively suits the elaborate reign of the Sun King and the illustrations expand the comprehension of the text. Beginning readers will enjoy reading the large type and looking at the pictures. Older readers will be challenged by the italicized type and the detail of the images. A handsome dust jacket introduces us to King Louis XIV and we follow him from page to page in this correlated picture-story. The book has a definite beginning, middle, and end. In the beginning we learn about the King and where he lived. The middle emphasizes his daily routine. The Sun King's day consisted of dressing in the morning, (Lever), attending chapel, conducting affairs of state, dinner (Petit Couvert), afternoon outings, evening entertainment, supper (Grand Couvert), and finally going to bed (Coucher). The last page provides a chronology of King Louis XIV and definitions of French words found within the text. Following ***Mummies Made in Egypt*** and ***A Medieval Feast*** (both Crowell), this picture-story focuses on the seventeenth century and is Aliki's third history book for young children. The constraint of consistently presenting one character in a variety of fresh images that are intriguing and accessible to children has been met with skill and good taste.

Shirley Wilton

SOURCE: A review of *The King's Day: Louis XIV of France*, in *School Library Journal*, Vol. 35, No. 14, October, 1989, p. 99.

Gr 2-5—As she did in ***A Medieval Feast*** (Crowell, 1983), Aliki draws upon prints and pictures from art history and incorporates facts about real people and places to introduce young people to a high period of Western history. In this case the "moment" she recreates is a day at the royal court of Versailles. Pictures of Louis XIV and his court are framed by a narrow gold border; many of the illustrations have inscriptions underneath in the manner of 17th-century engravings. The text, in bolder print, adds facts and explanations to the descriptive pictures. Color is the most striking element in Aliki's drawings. The richness of the king's costumes, his wigs, lace, red stockings, and high-heeled shoes are echoed by the attire of his courtiers. The pictures vary in size and placement, leading readers' eyes through the events of the king's day, from the royal rising ritual to the final ceremonial "coucher" or going-to-bed. The spectacular size of the palace of Versailles and the crowded events of court life, all centering on the elaborately costumed figure of Louis XIV, capture the spirit of absolute monarchy in a form that will surely appeal to curious children in this age of democracy and the common man. The book contains a brief chronology and a list of French words, but with no guide to pronunciation. Never mind—it is the pictures that tell the story.

Mary M. Burns

SOURCE: A review of *The King's Day: Louis XIV of France*, in *The Horn Book Magazine*, Vol. 66, No. 2, March/April, 1990, p. 217.

If Robin Leach ever decided to broaden his scope to include historical personages in his examination of "Lifestyles of the Rich and Famous," then certainly Louis XIV of France would be a prime subject. After all, few other monarchs—if any—could match his claim to the audacious sobriquet "Sun King." By narrowing her focus to a typical day in Louis's long reign, Aliki has effectively produced a fascinating presentation of the elaborate rituals that kept the courtiers busy with minutiae while insulating Louis from the great masses of common folk. The illustrations vary from double-page spreads, such as a group portrait of the principal players in the court drama, including Louis's mistresses, to an epigrammatic series depicting the various stages in the king's *lever*—his "getting-up ritual." In the latter, Aliki includes some deliciously intimate details that make the concept of absolute monarchy vividly concrete, such as the picture of two noblemen who "were honored to empty the royal chamberpot"! As in her other glimpses into history, she employs two narrative strands: one, set in large type, provides an overview; the other, set in smaller type, offers more detailed explanation. Her concern is with the trappings of absolute monarchy rather than its ultimate effect on the course of history. Thus, there is no mention of the sufferings of the peasants, the economic problems resulting from Louis's many wars, or the ambitions of a developing middle class. However, she cleverly inserts hints into the text which suggest that, with a less able ruler, this centralization of power might be in jeopardy. Thus, the book could be used with older readers as a pictorially engrossing introduction to this period of French history, with younger readers as an easily grasped glimpse into another era, or with potential travelers as preparation for a tour of Versailles. Furthermore, with the current interest in finding biographical material for the lower grades, this book certainly offers a well-researched, thoughtfully conceived, and appealing alternative to the plethora of "shrink lives" concocted by lesser talents to fill a need for supplementary curriculum materials.

MY FIVE SENSES (REV. ED., 1990)

Denise L. Moll

SOURCE: A review of *My Five Senses,* rev. ed., in *School Library Journal,* Vol. 36, No. 1, January, 1990, pp. 92-3.

PreS-Gr 1—A young boy learns about the world around him through the use of his senses in this revision of the popular title. Text changes are minimal, a total of four word substitutions in all. In a couple of instances the changes serve to bring the text up-to-date: "bird" replaces "eggbeater" in reference to sounds heard, while "baby powder" gives way to "soap" for scent. The other two substitutions, "frog" for "bird" as an object viewed, and "water" for "raindrops" in touch seem more arbitrary. But it is the new look of the book that is most striking. Illustrations are now more refined, and in full color, in contrast to the abstract, black-and-white, green-and-blue drawings in the original. The content of many of the pictures is the same, but this time the boy and his sister are of a more ambiguous race; sporting dark hair, brown eyes, and a deep skin tone, they could represent any of a number of cultures. In all, this is well worth considering, either as a new purchase or a replacement title.

FOSSILS TELL OF LONG AGO (REV. ED., 1990)

Denia Lewis Hester

SOURCE: A review of *Fossils Tell of Long Ago,* rev. ed., in *School Library Journal,* Vol. 36, No. 7, July, 1990, p. 66.

K-Gr 3—In this revised edition, Aliki has revamped the previous four-color edition with lively full-color illustrations, also adding the pointed, conversational observations of children as they make discoveries along with readers. In clear, precise language, she explains how dinosaur tracks are cast in mud, how insects trapped in sticky tree sap harden into amber, and how fossils of tropical plants are found in very cold places. The children populating these pages are boys and girls of every color, on foot or in wheelchair, all of them active observers with scientific curiosities; they are apparently making these discoveries in a museum, marveling and enjoying the bits of history cast in stone. The book closes with a suggestion for creating a one-minute fossil by making a clay imprint of a hand, letting it dry, and burying it for someone to find a million years from now. School and public libraries will want to replace the old edition with this one.

MANNERS (1990)

Kirkus Reviews

SOURCE: A review of *Manners,* in *Kirkus Reviews,* Vol. 58, October 15, 1990, p. 1451.

Aliki makes a tart lesson in etiquette smoothly palatable—in a comprehensive assortment of good and bad behavior that's presented with such generous good humor that few children will feel preached at. Aliki offers quick takes on ordinary situations where kindness and a little common sense make life pleasanter for everyone; comic-strip scenarios unfold, and multiracial children act out positive and negative responses, while readers are given samples of appropriate, courteous phrases to use in typical situations. Lively illustrations add relevant details and comical distractions. The Goops may be funnier, but Aliki's polite children and pint-sized boors should make their point while amusing the picture-book set.

Mary Lou Budd

SOURCE: A review of *Manners,* in *School Library Journal,* Vol. 36, No. 11, November, 1990, p. 101.

K-Gr 3—From the engaging jacket to the final endpaper, and in a lighthearted, humorous manner, children can see the cartoonlike depictions of the acceptable behavior, with the boorish counteraction similarly depicted for purposes of comparison. Well organized into succinct areas, the book is cleanly formatted and presents colorful images to engage browsers. That "Manners are WORDS and ACTIONS that show others you CARE" is paramount. Readers will revel in the sheer fun of it all and will surely gain personal insights. Younger children will be better served by individual rather than group presentation because of some of the pictures' small, informative details. Peggy Parish's *Mind Your Manners* (Greenwillow, 1978) or Norah Smaridge's rhythmic *Manners Matter* (Abingdon, 1980; o.p.) can't compete with the cheerful, broad-based treatment this offers, nor will they spark as much interest in and discussion of a universal issue—to think of others before one's self. Culture, gender, and age are well represented, also contributing to the book's wide appeal.

Diane Roback and Richard Donahue

SOURCE: A review of *Manners,* in *Publishers Weekly,* Vol. 237, No. 45, November 9, 1990, p. 57.

This popular and prolific author-artist here examines an important topic for children—good manners: how to achieve them and how to maintain them. Every page brims with etiquette tips, expressed by small-sized figures drawn in Aliki's customarily cheery style. If there is a problem here, it is one of excess: the do's and don'ts fly by so thick and fast that readers may have difficulty grasping them. A lack of organization may further confuse the book's users. The subjects are broached in no discernible order, and text is presented willy-nilly in captions under pictures and in cartoon-style balloons. One page bears the heading "Ouch," and depicts two girls strolling down the street as another girl approaches. The copy above the picture reads, "Here comes Alexa. / Let's ignore her," while two tiny birds below—they and several animal friends make pertinent and impertinent asides throughout—say "bad manners and bad feelings" and "Is Alexa going to go home and cry?" Cause and effect seem to be missing here, and the main issue glossed over. Though certainly well-intentioned, this book may prove more chaotic than constructive. Ages 5-up.

📖 *MY FEET* AND *MY HANDS* (1990)

Christine A. Moesch

SOURCE: A review of *My Feet* and *My Hands,* in *School Library Journal,* Vol. 36, No. 11, November, 1990, pp. 101-02.

PreS-Gr 1—Aliki's colorful, multiethnic illustrations help present the subjects of feet and hands in a clear, concise manner. In *My Feet,* children are shown run-

ning, jumping, and hopping in bare feet and in all sorts of footwear. The text covers anatomy of the foot, footprints, being ticklish, and even activities to try with the feet (like drawing). The text of *My Hands* is essentially the same as the original edition, with added sentences about bones, disabilities, and even veins. The illustrations are much improved, bright and updated, with minorities and handicapped children well represented, performing activities such as drawing, clapping, and talking in sign language. Mention is made in this edition about left-handedness and the difference between children's and adults' hands. Both texts are simple and straightforward, without being condescending. Two fine introductions to human anatomy.

Carolyn K. Jenks

SOURCE: A review of *My Feet,* in *The Horn Book Magazine,* Vol. 66, No. 6, November/December, 1990, p. 763.

In this colorful beginning science book, a multiethnic group of children examines the parts and functions of feet. The simple, lively text calls attention to a part of the body often taken for granted: "I am lucky I have two feet that work well. My friend doesn't. There are many things she can't do. But with her crutches she can walk as fast as I can."

📖 *CHRISTMAS TREE MEMORIES* (1991)

Carolyn Phelan

SOURCE: A review of *Christmas Tree Memories,* in *Booklist,* Vol. 87, No. 21, July, 1991, p. 2048.

Ages 4-7. Aliki fashions a picture book based on family reminiscences. When a father, a mother, and two children gather before the tree on Christmas Eve, their handmade ornaments bring back memories of old times, family, and friends, as in "Remember we made 'stained-glass' cookies in kindergarten, and the mice escaped and ate most of them up." Warm, full-color artwork separates present from past, with the flashbacks in full-page illustrations on the right and the current scenes in small frames on the left-hand pages. While it's doubtful that kids will find someone else's Christmas memories as riveting as their own, Aliki provides a pleasant tale that could inspire some ornament making.

Kirkus Reviews

SOURCE: A review of *Christmas Tree Memories*, in *Kirkus Reviews*, Vol. 59, September 1, 1991, p. 1165.

Sharing a bedtime snack on Christmas Eve, a dark-eyed family of four reminisces about their tree ornaments, each laden with family history: a walnut cradle made during the Christmas baking, origami from the museum, a starfish Santa that recalls a summer trip, gifts from near and dear, and more. Each double spread shows the family by their tree and also depicts their happily remembered experiences, all in Aliki's comfortably realistic style. Off to bed at last, they leave snacks for Santa and for Nefi. A warm evocation of the value of family tradition.

Publishers Weekly

SOURCE: A review of *Christmas Tree Memories*, in *Publishers Weekly*, Vol. 238, No. 41, September 13, 1991, p. 78.

A family of four sits by the tree on Christmas Eve and strings memories like cranberries and popcorn. Over the years this brood has made corn husk wreaths, starfish Santas, pine cone angels and walnut cradles with the help of extended family and friends. In this holiday fantasyland where everyone smiles despite blizzards and illness, there are no fights over toys or disappointments of any kind. Each family member has a voice, though at times it is unclear who is speaking—parent or child. "We made spool figures the time we had chicken pox. We made a tent over our beds, and you brought us hot soup and sage tea." (Aliki's portrayal is warm and cozy—perhaps a bit too much so—with a Norman Rockwellesque patina over the proceedings. Homey illustrations reflect the warmth and closeness of her text, although flashbacks to earlier seasons may prove confusing. A few members of the multiracial cast have unclear facial characteristics that vary from picture to picture. Ages 4-8.

School Library Journal

SOURCE: A review of *Christmas Tree Memories*, in *School Library Journal*, Vol. 37, No. 10, October, 1991, pp. 26-7.

PreS-Gr 2—A quiet story of a family whose memories are stirred by handmade ornaments that hang on their Christmas tree. As the family gathers to admire the tree's beauty, they remember how and when each of these special decorations was made. Painted in Aliki's readily recognizable style, the book begins and ends with page-encompassing illustrations on two double-page spreads showing the tree and the people around it. In the middle of the book, the brief text is accompanied by vignettes on one page facing a bordered full-page illustration opposite it. The story is spare, but the deftly blended text and illustrations spark feelings that are warm, full, and rich. A wonderful book for families to share throughout the holiday season.

Carolyn K. Jenks

SOURCE: A review of *Christmas Tree Memories*, in *The Horn Book Magazine*, Vol. 67, No. 6, November/December, 1991, p. 719.

On Christmas Eve a family of four pauses in its holiday anticipation for an evening of reminiscing. When a bell is rung, the children know it is the signal to join their parents in the family's cozy, Christmas-filled living room. There is a plate of cookies and a pitcher of milk on the table—but the centerpiece of the room is the tree, whose candles shine brightly and whose branches hold ornaments, each of which comes with a story that everyone helps to tell. Scenes from the stories are depicted in the full-page illustrations done in watercolor, ink, and pencil crayons. The pictures show a loving, active family throughout the year, enjoying life with extended family, friends, and schoolmates. The book is a beautiful portrayal of one family's Christmas tradition of sharing memories—gifts which are there as they have been for years, to be received and appreciated again.

THE LISTENING WALK (1991)

Christine A. Moesch

SOURCE: A review of *The Listening Walk*, in *School Library Journal*, Vol. 37, No. 7, July, 1991, p. 64.

K-Gr 2—In this revised edition of the 1961 title, a father and child take a walk together and listen to the sounds around them. The text has been streamlined and updated, and Aliki has completely replaced her previous black-and-white sketches with colorful, lively illustrations of multiethnic people in contemporary settings. The writing is concise and to the point without being choppy, and the overall effect is unhurried and relaxed. Young readers (or listeners) will enjoy the book, both as a story and as a jumping-off point for their own walks.

📖 *I'M GROWING!* (1992)

Hazel Rochman

SOURCE: A review of *I'm Growing!*, in *Booklist*, Vol. 88, No. 16, April 15, 1992, p. 1532.

Ages 3-6. In her latest entry in the excellent "Let's-Read-and-Find-Out Science Book" series, Aliki's bright, clear, realistic illustrations show a smiling child who's delighted that he's growing bigger ("My shirt won't button. My jeans are too short"). Some basic concepts of physiology are explained in a straightforward, simple text with playful pictures of the Hispanic boy, his extended family, and his friends. People develop, they change, they age. They grow in height and weight. Their hair never stops growing. Inside, too, there are changes, in brain, heart, and other organs. This entertaining concept book celebrates individual differences while it acknowledges every child's longing to be big and strong.

Zena Sutherland

SOURCE: A review of *I'm Growing!*, in *The Bulletin of the Center for Children's Books*, Vol. 45, No. 9, May, 1992, p. 229.

Dark and handsome, strong Hispanic faces are the visual focus of Aliki's bright paintings, in a book with a direct and simple text narrated by a small (but growing) boy. The continuous text is logically arranged, moving from clothes that don't fit any longer to the fact that growth is continuous in youth, and on to such pertinent matters as individual growth patterns, changes visible or internal, and a healthful regimen that contributes both to growing and to good physical condition. There's also a reassuring message about comparative size and its lack of importance. This is a worthy addition to a pioneer series of high quality.

Denise L. Moll

SOURCE: A review of *I'm Growing!*, in *School Library Journal*, Vol. 38, No. 6, June, 1992, p. 106.

PreS-Gr 1—A brief examination of the human growth process, detailed by a young boy who has outgrown his clothing. The discussion includes obvious topics such as bones, muscles, teeth, plus internal organs. Growth rates and dwarfism are touched on, along with mention of the role of energy and food in the process. The text, and the context, are almost too simplistic; there are no explanations offered, just statements of fact. The vibrant illustrations are done in pen-and-ink, watercolor, and colored-pencil. The narrator and his family have dark skin, hair, and eyes, but their ethnic origin isn't specified. Patricia Pearce's *See How You Grow* (Barron's, 1988) offers more information for the same age group. All in all, an attractive but marginal effort.

📖 *MILK FROM COW TO CARTON* (REV. ED., 1992)

Kay Weisman

SOURCE: A review of *Milk from Cow to Carton*, rev. ed., in *Booklist*, Vol. 89, No. 5, November 1, 1992, p. 514.

Ages 5-8. This revision of **Green Grass and White Milk** (1974) features all new, full-color artwork rendered in watercolor, ink, and pencil crayons. With the exception of a few minor grammatical changes, the text has remained the same. The author has added a brief mention of the quality control procedures used by dairies and has redrawn the chart depicting how milk is processed, making it much easier to follow. She also includes a more complete explanation of how cheese is made. Unfortunately, four pages describing how to make yogurt have been eliminated. An excellent primary-level introduction to dairy science, this title in the "Let's-Read-and-Find-Out Science" series is comparable to Gibbons' *The Milk Makers*.

📖 *COMMUNICATION* (1993)

Jody McCoy

SOURCE: A review of *Communication*, in *School Library Journal*, Vol. 39, No. 4, April, 1993, p. 104.

Gr 2-4—Aliki introduces readers to many forms of communication, the reasons to practice them, and some of the barriers that may be encountered in the process. Unfortunately, despite her spirited, colorful cartoons, the text bogs down as simple explanations are cluttered with not-so-simple exceptions and commendable, but confusing, bibliotherapy. The difficulty of communicating feelings is clearly related to the subject, but its inclusion here clouds the clarity of sender-message-receiver-feedback. Verbal and written communication share space with braille (depicted as visual not tactile so one wonders how a blind person can feel a dark spot on a page) and sign for the deaf. Nonverbal communication is touched upon along with animal communication, pen pals, use of puppets, greeting cards, and miscommunication as in the game of gossip. The vivid illustrations represent a variety of ethnic groups and a wealth of emotional textures. An adequate collection of tidbits with little if any competition at this level, *Communication* has many possible applications in an educational setting or a parent and child may read it together. Youngsters may enjoy the illustrations and grasp a point or two, but it is unlikely that independent readers will seek it out.

Stephanie Zvirin

SOURCE: A review of *Communication,* in *Booklist,* Vol. 89, No. 16, April 15, 1993, p. 1512.

Ages 5-9. As Aliki has more than 40 picture books to her credit, her bright, cartoonlike characters, outlined in black, are familiar to many youngsters by now. She uses them again in her latest book, which concentrates on the ways we express ourselves. Written with her usual good humor and aplomb, the text considers not only the telling and listening aspects of person-to-person exchange, but also the importance of responding. Aliki relies on various combinations of handwritten and typeset text, large drawings, and cartoon strips to introduce some of the ways communication is accomplished—writing, speaking, braille—and to offer a glimpse at the subtle, emotional aspects of interchange: one series of drawings depicts a mother and child using puppets to help them deal with a difficult subject; another shows a story becoming distorted when it's told, retold, and told again; and still another demonstrates the importance of voicing angry feelings. The bright colors and varied page layouts provide plenty to keep readers interested and involved, while the perceptive text offers much to think about. A first-rate book, ideal for generating classroom or parent-child "communication."

📖 *MY VISIT TO THE AQUARIUM* (1993)

Publishers Weekly

SOURCE: A review of *My Visit to the Aquarium,* in *Publishers Weekly,* Vol. 240, No. 31, August 2, 1993, p. 79.

A-fish-ionados of big-city aquariums will recognize familiar watery environments within these splendidly illustrated pages. Based on several specific aquariums, Aliki's mega-museum features a three-story kelp jungle, a muggy tropical rain forest and a coral reef. More standard attractions include tide pools, freshwater tanks and, of course, the dark, glassed-in hall where sharks meet humans in eerie silence. The author/artist's characteristically skillful watercolors and varied compositions smoothly manage a flood of information. But, in contrast to the bountiful, unrestrained illustrations, the hardworking narration dulls colorful details. A few tidbits, however, successfully bait the hook: anchovies prefer to swim by the hundreds in a small round tank, "packed in tight, moving in never-ending circles"; a diver feeds fish "so they will not be tempted to eat each other." Some adult intervention may be necessary to extract the full value of the teeming text, but this book will enrich both the preparation for and memories of trips to an aquarium. An endnote stresses the need to preserve the environment. Ages 4-8.

Elizabeth Bush

SOURCE: A review of *My Visit to the Aquarium,* in *Booklist,* Vol. 90, No. 4, October 15, 1993, p. 444.

Ages 5-8. A young boy enthusiastically shares tidbits of information about aquatic life as readers join him on a tour of the aquarium. Fish facts, selected for their child-appeal and delivered in a brisk, conversational tone, are neatly organized by marine environment. As each fish is described within the boy's narration, it is also identified in an illustration by clear, unobtrusive script. The aquarium's inventive displays (based on those in several actual aquariums) vie with the fish for center stage. Visitors pass through a glass tunnel teeming with tropical fish, gape at a three-story kelp forest tank, and touch the fish in a shallow tide pool. The dominant blues and greens of Aliki's watercolors are not only cool and inviting; they also provide visual continuity amid the riot of brightly colored fish. Readers who delight in Aliki's attention to detail will not be disappointed. Watch for the marvelously varied expressions on visitors' faces and for our young guide's souvenir from the aquarium bookshop—a copy of *My Visit to the Aquarium.*

Frances E. Millhouser

SOURCE: A review of *My Visit to the Aquarium,* in *School Library Journal,* Vol. 40, No. 1, January, 1994, pp. 102-03.

PreS-Gr 2—Children and adults of various ages, races, and physical abilities tour a public aquarium and are treated to a look at many of the world's marine creatures. The language is almost lyrical, and its lilting quality imparts a feeling of journeying underwater to discover fish, crustaceans, mollusks, and more. Readers and viewers will be equally entertained, as Aliki uses watercolors, ink, and pencil crayons on waterboard for this excursion. The sense of motion is amplified in the colorful pictures as children run, point, and photograph their favorite species, shrink from the shark tank (seen from the shark's point of view), and reach into the touchable tide pool exhibit. Different sized illustrations add to the visual variety, and the creatures are labeled in script, enticing readers to linger over the pages. Whimsical touches—the docent is wearing bright fish earrings, and the last page features this book being sold at the aquarium gift store—add to a story alive with color and action.

📖 THE GODS AND GODDESSES OF OLYMPUS (1994)

Publishers Weekly

SOURCE: A review of *The Gods and Goddesses of Olympus,* in *Publishers Weekly,* Vol. 241, No. 32, August 8, 1994, p. 434.

Despite her vibrant art and her valiant attempt to simplify her material, Aliki's (*A Medieval Feast*; *My Visit to the Aquarium*) Whirlwind tour of Olympus doesn't manage to untangle the labyrinthine legends of the mythical past. Her book falls into two sections, the first breezing through traditional Greco-Roman theogony. Some of her truncated accounts may mystify the target audience: "Cronus married his sister Rhea, and they had many children. But Cronus was afraid that one of them might overthrow him just as he had overthrown his father. So as each child was born he swallowed it." By the time Cronus regurgitates his offspring, who join with Zeus to rule the universe, Aliki moves on to a series of page-long profiles of various deities. The two halves of the book just don't hang together. On the other hand, the art, which is generously interspersed with the text, provides consistency. Bountiful details adapted from Greek vase paintings and sculpture fill Aliki's stylized pencil drawings. Washes of gouache paints and colored pencils imbue the compositions with a distinctly Mediterranean sunniness. Ages 4-8.

Patricia Dooley (Green)

SOURCE: A review of *The Gods and Goddesses of Olympus,* in *School Library Journal,* Vol. 40, No. 9, September, 1994, p. 203.

K-Gr 3—There's tough competition in the mythology game these days, but Aliki's fans will welcome her introduction to these famous Greeks. After the Uranus-Gaea, Cronus-Rhea background is sketched, the occupants of the 12 golden thrones are each described, along with Hades (underground), Hestia (hearth-bound) and Eros (hovering). The author outlines the deities' characters and attributes, sometimes including a brief incident from their lives, but these are sketches, not stories, of the gods and their otherworldly realm. The copious and colorful illustrations are, a note claims, based on antique models, but their unsophisticated style recalls the D'Aulaires' *D'Aulaires' Book of Greek Myths* (Doubleday, 1980). Libraries possessing that book, or Leonard Everett Fisher's *The Olympians* (Holiday, 1984), might choose Marcia Williams's *Greek Myths for Young Children* (Candlewick, 1992) because of its stronger narrative interest.

Carolyn Phelan

SOURCE: A review of *The Gods and Goddesses of Olympus,* in *Booklist,* Vol. 91, No. 5, November 1, 1994, p. 502.

Gr. 2-4, younger for reading aloud. This large-format book provides a quick, brightly illustrated introduction to the ancient Greek gods and goddesses. Beginning with Gaea, Uranus, and the Titans, Aliki chronicles the rise and fall of Cronus and the defeat of the Titans by the new gods (Zeus and company), whom she introduces individually. The latter section, which comprises two-thirds of the book, will prove useful in libraries as a clear, simple overview of the more familiar gods and goddesses. The artwork varies in quality from the well-imagined scenes showing Gaea growing out of "a dark space named Chaos" to the awkward and slightly comical look of the scenes in which Cronus swallows his children and disgorges them. A Greek dramatist might have advised that those actions should take place offstage, to be reported by the players. While not a source for storytellers, this will prove useful in libraries with a demand for basic information on the gods and goddesses at the primary-grade level.

TABBY: A STORY IN PICTURES (1995)

Publishers Weekly

SOURCE: A review of *Tabby: A Story in Pictures,* in *Publishers Weekly,* Vol. 242, No. 20, May 15, 1995, p. 71.

A girl and her father visit an animal shelter at the start of this cheerful if thin wordless book by the author of the more successful *My Visit to the Dinosaurs* and *How a Book Is Made.* The pair takes home a wide-eyed kitten—Tabby—who is subsequently shown lapping up a bowl of milk, sleeping in a basket by the girl's bed, peering out the window as she and her friends build a snowman, and exploring the garden in springtime while the child plays alongside a smiling newborn. Later, with summer in full bloom, a tiny kitten creeps under the garden wall to frolic with Tabby. Finally, this kitten, its young owners, the girl and, of course, Tabby, celebrate Tabby's first birthday. Aliki's warmly hued, appealingly childlike art hints at the tenderness between girl and pet, but many of her compositions seem static and bland. Unfortunately, this volume lacks the whimsy and dimension that—in the best wordless stories—encourage creative interpretation. Ages 3-6.

Annie Ayres

SOURCE: A review of *Tabby: A Story in Pictures,* in *Booklist,* Vol. 91, No. 21, July, 1995, p. 1882.

Ages 3-6. The engaging cover pictures a perky kitten standing atop the bottom of a happy little Hispanic girl who is sprawled (and surely giggling) upon the floor. Opening this book, young children can "read" the wordless story of a kitten's first year. Beginning in the fall when the kitten is adopted from the animal shelter, Aliki's crisp and colorful illustrations follow the kitten through the seasons of the year as it grows and explores the world with the little girl. Brimming with simple stories of family and friends, growth and change, Tabby is a warmly winsome, wordless picture book.

Hanna B. Zeiger

SOURCE: A review of *Tabby: A Story in Pictures,* in *The Horn Book Magazine,* Vol. 71, No. 4, July/August, 1995, p. 446.

This wordless story begins on an autumn day when a coffee-skinned, round-cheeked little girl and her father approach an animal shelter. Inside, the little girl happily chooses a gray-and-white-striped kitten to bring home. There they are greeted by a smiling pregnant mother and twin friends from next door. We see the kitten being fed, cleaning herself, using a litter box, and sleeping in a basket next to the girl's bed. The season changes to winter, and the kitten perches on the back of the chair where the girl holds a newborn baby. In summer, the flowers and leaves in the garden are in full bloom; while the girl looks at a book, the baby dozes while sitting in a stroller. Sharp-eyed readers will see a tiny, white kitten as it pokes its head under the fence that separates the neighbors' yards. As the two kittens become friends, the twins next door frantically and tearfully search for their kitten, who is soon returned to them. When autumn comes again, the little girl delivers an invitation to her neighbors, and a turn of the page reveals a festive birthday party for Tabby, the cat. Using colorful, expressive pictures, Aliki tells a story that will delight preschoolers who understand visual clues long before they can read words.

Claudia Cooper

SOURCE: A review of *Tabby: A Story in Pictures,* in *School Library Journal,* Vol. 41, No. 8, August, 1995, p. 114.

PreS-Gr 1—In this warm, glowing wordless book, Aliki captures a kitten's first year, from her fall adoption at the animal shelter to her first birthday party. Delightful seasonal vignettes reveal not only Tabby's developmental progress but also the growing responsibilities assumed by her young owner. With the onset of winter, a new baby is added to the family. Summer finds a new kitten next door who, with his twin owners, is invited to share in the fall birthday of the now fully grown Tabby. Full-color mixed-media illustrations in a small format invite individual or lap "reading."

BEST FRIENDS TOGETHER AGAIN (1995)

Hazel Rochman

SOURCE: A review of *Best Friends Together Again,* in *Booklist,* Vol. 91, No. 22, August, 1995, p. 1954.

Ages 3-8. As a companion to all those books about children having to move away from their friends, here's a story of joyful reunion. At the end of Aliki's *We Are Best Friends* (1982), Peter had to move, and he had to part from his best friend, Robert. Now, in this upbeat sequel, Peter comes back for a visit. Aliki's clear, lovely pictures in pen, watercolor, and colored pencil show the friends a little uncertain at first ("Will he still like me?"). Some things have changed, but soon they play and talk together, like old times. Peter meets Robert's new friend, and when they go to fly a paper airplane in the park, all the kids welcome Peter back. Although the best friends must part again, it will be fun to look forward to the next visit and fun to remember. Like Viorst's Alexander, this gentle picture book will comfort all those who cannot bear to say goodbye.

Virginia Opocensky

SOURCE: A review of *Best Friends Together Again*, in *School Library Journal*, Vol. 41, No. 9, September, 1995, p. 167.

PreS-Gr 1—Peter and Robert, introduced in *We Are Best Friends* (Greenwillow, 1982), are together again. As the boys look forward to Peter's two-week visit, they are both excited and a little apprehensive about how the other might have changed. All concern soon vanishes and they enjoy all the things they used to do. "They were as happy as only old friends can be." In natural conversation, the youngsters remember past shared experiences and compare new friends. Neighborhood children also welcome Peter back in a great reunion. Watercolor and colored-pencil illustrations are bright and joyous. A simple, reassuring story for friends everywhere.

Maria B. Salvadore

SOURCE: A review of *Best Friends Together Again*, in *The Horn Book Magazine*, Vol. 71, No. 5, September/October, 1995, p. 584.

Robert cannot wait for Peter's visit. Even though Peter has moved away, the boys still consider themselves best friends. But Robert worries, too. Will Peter be the same? Will he still like Robert? When Peter finally arrives, the boys soon learn that although some things have changed—like Robert's room—the warmth and fun of their longtime friendship remain intact. They share the familiar as well as many new things they have learned from new friends. Peter's two-week visit is over too quickly, but he and Robert part knowing that visits are fun to anticipate—"and fun to remember. . . . Just like friends." The childlike pleasure of friendship and the joy of a reunion are

captured in Aliki's straightforward text and enhanced by crisp, bright, uncluttered, and carefully formatted illustrations. Open space and simple borders are effectively used to move the story to its satisfying conclusion. Readers will again empathize with the characters first introduced in *We Are Best Friends* (Greenwillow).

📖 *MOMMY'S BRIEFCASE* (1995)

Publishers Weekly

SOURCE: A review of *Mommy's Briefcase*, in *Publishers Weekly*, Vol. 242, No. 35, August 28, 1995, p. 112.

Taking a leaf from *The Jolly Postman*, Low and Aliki follow a working mother through her day, interspersing six briefcase-like pockets among their book's cheery, detail-packed pages. Rhyming couplets recount Mommy's routine at the Stuff Bear Co.: "My secretary types a letter. 'What's the address, please?' / I find it in my address book. It's listed with the B's." Meanwhile, kids can remove related paraphernalia from Mommy's briefcase—in this case, glasses and address book. A cardboard sandwich and apple serve as lunch on the run, while a change purse displays the coins used "to buy a cold drink from the juice machine." Other items include the morning paper (the *Newsy Times*, with headlines and pictures but no copy) a desktop picture of Mommy's offspring, etc. Aliki's animal cast is perky and personable, though she leans heavily on puns in background art: the *Times* includes a Meaosic section and Meous and Views column, while one of the company's models is pictured as a Cossack, or "Rushin' Bear." Still, many amusing touches make this book a candidate for repeated readings and a playful introduction to the working world. Ages 3-5.

📖 *WILD AND WOOLLY MAMMOTHS* (REV. ED., 1996)

Melissa Hudak

SOURCE: A review of *Wild and Woolly Mammoths*, rev. ed., in *School Library Journal*, Vol. 42, No. 2, February, 1996, p. 92.

K-Gr 3—This revision of a popular title (1977) provides a fascinating glimpse of woolly mammoths and the cave dwellers who hunted them. The text has been revamped and is more complex than in the earlier edition, with many interesting additions and sidebars reflecting new archaeological discoveries. The book is now geared to a second or third grade reading level, but would still make a fascinating read-aloud for younger children. The format has been enlarged, allowing for a more attractive, less cramped layout. The illustrations are beautifully done in watercolor and pencil and allow the mammoth to appear a realistic, yet almost mythical creature, which suits its extinct status. Overall, a good book has been transformed into an even better one.

Carolyn Phelan

SOURCE: A review of *Wild and Woolly Mammoths,* rev. ed., in *Booklist,* Vol. 92, No. 11, February 1, 1996, p. 933.

Ages 5-8. This revision of **Wild and Woolly Mammoths** (1977) seems better than the original in every way: the wording is more precise, the information is updated, the text reads more smoothly, the format is larger, and the ink-and-pastel illustrations are more colorful and dramatic. Even the new chart showing types of mammoths is well designed and quite informative. An excellent update.

THOSE SUMMERS (1996)

Kirkus Reviews

SOURCE: A review of *Those Summers,* in *Kirkus Reviews,* Vol. 64, May 1, 1996, p. 684.

This warm and accessible memoir of Aliki's childhood days at the beach with her extended family is a tone poem that vividly reflects a wealth of detail. All the senses are elicited through fine wordsmithing, from the stickiness of wet sand on the skin to the smells of saltwater taffy, barnacles, and seaweed. There's a dark side to the sunny picture: a brief mention of a child who drowned in the undertow, an incident that (true to the child's world) receives less ink than the terror of listening to the Shadow on the radio at night. In contrast to the excellent text, the pictures—though pleasant in every way—are almost irrelevant; Aliki (**My Visit to the Aquarium**, 1993, etc.) paints what has already been amply evoked in the magic of her words.

Susan Dove Lempke

SOURCE: A review of *Those Summers,* in *Booklist,* Vol. 92, No. 17, May 1, 1996, p. 1511.

Ages 4-8. Aliki rhapsodizes over her childhood memories of long days playing at the seashore: "We'd dive into the waves and dive out of the waves and get tumbled over and knocked down, and we'd splash and choke on salt water from laughing too much." She covers the pleasures of sand castles, sandy sandwiches, walking on the boardwalk at night, and listening to The Shadow on the radio with cousins. The text is unsentimental but loving, and the illustrations are suffused with joy, capturing children as both exuberant and awkward. Aliki's memory may have failed her in only one regard: the sand on the beach never seems to stick to the children. A book that gives grown-ups the chance to reminisce, this will make an especially pleasant reading choice in the dark of winter.

Publishers Weekly

SOURCE: A review of *Those Summers,* in *Publishers Weekly,* Vol. 243, No. 23, June 3, 1996, pp. 82-3.

Told this vividly, tales of carefree childhood summers can warm the heart in any season. Children as well as parents will willingly accompany Aliki's (**Mummies Made in Egypt; Christmas Tree Memories**) animated narrator back in time as she shares her memories of seaside vacations in "the big shady house we shared with our relatives." Choosing emblematic details, the author evokes the beach's timeless diversions: the cousins stay in the water so long that "our fingers puckered and our lips turned dark as blueberries"; they "roll in the hot sand like fish cakes." The energetic kids bound into the waves, but their cautious mothers "tiptoed in as if the sea were made of broken glass." Stylized pictures depict an exuberant extended family in constant motion. The golden-toned faces of children and adults alike are unusually expressive, whether conveying the thrill of being tossed by the surf or the benign terror of listening to the Shadow's voice cackle on an old-fashioned radio. An ebullient paean to summers by the sea. Ages 4-8.

Judith Gloyer

SOURCE: A review of *Those Summers,* in *School Library Journal,* Vol. 42, No. 8, August, 1996, p. 115.

K-Gr 2—Aliki offers vivid memories of childhood summers spent at the ocean with her cousins, parents, aunts, and uncles. The family engages in activities that are common to any beach outing—building sand castles, swimming, and drawing pictures in the sand. Little touches tie the story to times past—collecting seashells in rubber bathing caps and listening to "The Shadow" on the radio in the dark. What makes this title stand out is Aliki's gift of language: "We oozed droplets of liquid sand between our fingers"; "We stayed in [the water] so long, the shadows changed direction." The pictures are colorful and filled with grownups and children. What comes through is the close feeling of family. A delightful glimpse of a cherished childhood.

HELLO! GOOD-BYE! (1996)

Ilene Cooper

SOURCE: A review of *Hello! Good-Bye!*, in *Booklist*, Vol. 92, No. 21, July, 1996, p. 1827.

Ages 4-7. The title sums it up. This is a book about greetings around the world and the way simple words can have many meanings. "Hello" is an introduction, a welcome, a spectacular welcome. It can be said in different ways ("good-morning," "howdy"). It can even be said without words (a wave or the shake of a hand.) It can be loud or soft or take on many moods. The same is true of "good-bye," although that is often more difficult to say than "hello." Using her signature artwork, appealing in its childlike simplicity, Aliki shows in full-page boxes and cartoonlike strips all the many moods of greetings. Occasionally, she stretches the concept a little—"peek-a-boo" is not really a playful "hello," nor do you see many kids in baseball caps saying "toodle-oo"—but children should enjoy the ruminations anyway and perhaps mull over the different feelings these words evoke.

Publishers Weekly

SOURCE: A review of *Hello! Good-Bye!*, in *Publishers Weekly*, Vol. 243, No. 34, August 19, 1996, p. 66.

Aliki's drawings have a sweet, childlike quality, and here her text mirrors the inventive simplicity of her art. The entire book consists of permutations of "hello" and "good-bye": she demonstrates how the two words are used in other cultures and languages, in a variety of settings and in contexts that range from friendly to hostile to sad (for example, two forlorn children stand before an empty rocking chair as the caption reads, "A good-bye that lasts forever hurts the most"). Dialogue balloons animate panel art and shade the meaning of the text; e.g., accompanying

the statement "A hello can be embarrassing" is a picture of a red-faced boy clutching a slingshot before a broken window as a homeowner confronts him: "Hello, young man." The lively design, featuring as many as nine panels on a page, offsets the sometimes static quality of the writing. All told, kids will be entertained by Aliki's ingenuity. Ages 4-up.

Susan Garland

SOURCE: A review of *Hello! Good-Bye!*, in *School Library Journal*, Vol. 42, No. 9, September, 1996, p. 170.

K-Gr 3—Aliki has outdone herself with this fine concept book. Vivid cartoons rendered in watercolors and colored pencils show plenty of action and accurately reflect the concise text that explains the many ways to say "hello" and "goodbye." While entertaining readers, the author offers vocabulary by providing synonyms, and then explains that sometimes words are not necessary if gestures are used. Illustrations of people from far-away lands in traditional dress are found throughout. This engaging picture book makes a good read-aloud, but it is a better choice to sit and read one-on-one in order to mine all the gold nuggets to be found on each page. A winner!

Kirkus Reviews

SOURCE: A review of *Hello! Good-Bye!*, in *Kirkus Reviews*, Vol. 64, September 1, 1996, p. 1318.

A wry, informative look at the almost endless possibilities of greetings and farewells, for they are "a beginning and an end." Through a combination of jaunty illustrations and factual text, youngsters travel the wide world to experience universal moments of arrivals and departures. As with her earlier nonfiction (**Manners**, 1990, etc.), Aliki selects just-right, relevant examples that will resonate with young readers: A fanfare, a "Howdy!," a "Drive safely," an "Auf wiedersehen," a "Yoo-Hoo!," a bow, a hug, and a curtsy are a few of her choices. She goes from the easy good-byes (to a bad-mannered visitor) to the most difficult ones (two children huddle near a starkly empty rocking chair), conveying tremendous emotional range in very few pages. The illustrations, organized in storyboard form, effectively combine information with scenes of children involved in verbal and nonverbal salutations and leave-takings all over the world, further reducing the subject to its essentials. In all, the book will be something of a revelation to children and adults alike. Starred Review.

📖 MY VISIT TO THE ZOO (1997)

Lauren Peterson

SOURCE: A review of *My Visit to the Zoo*, in *Booklist*, Vol. 93, No. 21, July, 1997, p. 1820.

Ages 4-7. A young girl touring a large "conservation park" acts as guide and narrator of this story, sharing information about the animals and their native countries and introducing the concept of zoos as sanctuaries for endangered species. In a conversational tone, she talks about the lifestyles, eating habits, and unique characteristics of the animals she encounters. Captions provide some additional information, and basic animal identification is achieved through unobtrusive labels appearing alongside each animal picture. Youngsters also learn something about diverse areas of the world such as tropical rain forests and the African plains. Aliki does a nice job of depicting these colorful locales, as well as capturing the bustling, cheerful mood of the crowded zoo on a bright summer day. Good preparation for a school field trip; use the book after returning to reinforce learning.

Publishers Weekly

SOURCE: A review of *My Visit to the Zoo*, in *Publishers Weekly*, Vol. 244, No. 33, August 11, 1997, p. 402.

This fact-packed book's opening lines ("I didn't really want to visit the zoo. I had been to one that made me feel sad") set Aliki's (*My Visit to the Aquarium*) direct and responsible tone as she leads readers on yet another lively learning expedition. A girl discovers that this zoo (a composite of several actual sites), unlike others she's visited, allows its residents to roam as they would in the wild. The text is arranged around and within Aliki's cheerful illustrations, and introduces a broad range of animals, each labeled with its species and native region. Some (like 'the Great Apes' and 'the Great Cats') are united in double-page spreads, while others (like animals indigenous to the tropical rain forest) are arranged in a photo album-style grid. The animals are rendered in

varying degrees of detail: some are stunning likenesses (such as the lowland gorilla or orangutans), while others are stiff and less convincing (e.g., the cheetah or petting zoo animals). Nuggets of animal facts convey information in a credible childlike voice ("I thought a koala was a bear, but it is a marsupial"). Avoiding a preachy tone, Aliki deftly imparts her dual missive about the importance of both preserving animals' natural habitats and, for animals in captivity, supporting those zoos that serve as sanctuaries. Ages 4-up.

Kirkus Reviews

SOURCE: A review of *My Visit to the Zoo*, in *Kirkus Reviews*, Vol. 65, August 15, 1997, p. 1302.

Aliki (*Hello! Good-Bye!*, 1996, etc.) starts this fine picture book on the endpapers, which feature a tropical greenhouse with a host of labeled butterfly and hummingbird species. The simple first-person narration is by a girl who reluctantly accompanies her cousin to the zoo. She's been to other zoos where the animals seemed sad, but this zoo is different—the animals move about freely in naturalistic habitats. Aliki stresses the important role such zoos play in protecting and preserving endangered species in the fact-filled zoological tour that follows. A world map on the final page shows where each animal of the 80 species mentioned comes from and notes whether it is endangered or vulnerable. The main text moves along smoothly, and for those interested, more detailed information appears in picture captions. The colored pencil illustrations, though somewhat stylized, are lively and give readers a good working knowledge of each animal's appearance and the habitat in which it lives.

Margaret A. Bush

SOURCE: A review of *My Visit to the Zoo*, in *The Horn Book Magazine*, Vol. 73, No. 5, September/ October, 1997, p. 589.

Orangutans and a white crocodile are joined by dozens of other mammals, birds, and reptiles in this well-populated zoo. As in her earlier visit to the aquarium, Aliki begins with a child narrator and a large busy overview followed by tours of many different exhibits. Here two cousins find that this modern zoo is like a large variegated park. "There were houses where the animals could sleep and eat, and outdoor habitats where they roamed free, as they would in the wild." Text and detailed scenes shift comfortably between bits of information about particular animals and the functions of zoos in animal care and conservation. Aliki makes vigorous use of crayon along with her customary pen and watercolor drawings, adding texture and energy to pleasantly homey portraits of animals and people. Tours of the primate house, rain forest, open plains, and many other venues include large open scenes with labeled animals and small framed segments of information complementing the narrative. A few pages group small individual pictures of several species. From the jacket view featuring tigers, chimpanzees, and a panda, through the lush rain forest habitat on the endpapers, every page invites lingering enjoyment. Zoo fans of all ages will appreciate the *Visit.*

Jean Craighead George

SOURCE: A review of *My Visit to the Zoo,* in *Natural History,* Vol. 106, No. 11, December/January, 1996/1997, p. 8.

In *My Visit to the Zoo,* author-artist Aliki (HarperCollins), whose many other sparkling nature books include *My Visit to the Aquarium* and *My Visit to the Dinosaurs,* takes two children almost literally by the hand on an informative tour of a zoological park. Fascinating tidbits of information turn up in the text and are illustrated in mini-sidebars and boxes. By this means, children may pick up some basic taxonomy ("A gibbon is an ape, because apes have no tail"), natural history ("Koalas are nocturnal"), and environmental consciousness ("The condor was saved from extinction"). The book's major emphasis, like that of most zoos these days, is on conservation.

📖 *MARIANTHE'S STORY: PAINTED WORDS / SPOKEN MEMORIES* (1998)

Publishers Weekly

SOURCE: A review of *Marianthe's Story: Painted Words/Spoken Memories,* in *Publishers Weekly,* Vol. 245, No. 29, July 20, 1998, p. 219.

In perhaps her most personal work to date, Aliki presents two equally moving sides to Marianthe's story, the first as a new arrival to a foreign America, and the second the explanation of why she came. A third-person narrative describes the girl's first days of school; Man struggles with English until she realizes

that art translates to all languages. One day, as Mari prepares to tell her story through her paintings, the sympathetic teacher announces that "there is more than one way to tell a story. Someday Man will be able to tell us with words." Readers then flip the book over to begin the second installment, for which Man capably uses words to explain her background. Here Man's first-person narration recounts her early years in the old country, where extended family and community pulled together to grow food and to weather such tragedies as war and famine. Like her character, Aliki spins her tale gracefully in two media, placing words and art in impressive balance, and inventively incorporates a reverse-chronological sequence to fill in the details. Aliki takes an artistic leap, as she paints her characters with a range of extraordinarily expressive faces in close-up portraits, and effectively employs a changeable palette from the dusty grays of troubled past times to the chipper hues of a contemporary classroom. In an America comprised of immigrants, many youngsters facing the same sea changes as Mari will likely find her a stalwart companion, and those with a Man in their lives may gain a newfound respect for the strength it takes to make the journey. Ages 5-up.

The Horn Book Magazine

SOURCE: A review of *Marianthe's Story: Painted Words/Spoken Memories,* in *The Horn Book Magazine,* Vol. 74, No. 5, September/October, 1998, p. 595.

The story of a young immigrant girl from an unnamed country is told in a pair of back-to-back picture books. The first, **Painted Words,** describes Marianthe's adjustment to her American school; the second, **Spoken Memories** (arrived at by flipping the book over), allows the girl to tell her own story of why she and her mother came to this country. This sequencing is smart, allowing readers to get to know Marianthe the way her classmates do, as a new girl unable at first to speak a word of English, hearing her classmates' and teacher's words as "sputters and coughs," and only able to communicate through her paintings. In the second story Marianthe, now able to speak English, describes her idyllic homeland, a war, a famine, the death of her baby brother, and her father leaving to prepare for them all a better life in America. The absence of Marianthe's father in the first story is not explained; similarly, the fact that her homeland is not named is more distracting than universalizing (although the eastern Mediterranean is suggested by the flora and foods). Enhanced by the album-like design, Aliki's colored-pencil and crayon drawings are warm and expansive, giving heart to the somewhat purposive text. Marianthe herself is a solid presence in almost every picture: secure in the embrace of her family back home; solemn, initially scared, in Mr. Petrie's classroom; relaxed and confiding in a windblown scene where she's hanging out wash with her mother; happy at the center of her classmates when she can finally tell her story.

Diane S. Marton

SOURCE: A review of *Marianthe's Story: Painted Words/Spoken Memories,* in *School Library Journal,* Vol. 44, No. 10, October, 1998, p. 86.

K-Gr 3—These two carefully written stories, combined in one book, show the difficulties a child faces when coming to a new land and the unique heritage each one of us has. In **Painted Words** Marianthe, or Mari, starts school knowing no one and unable to speak or understand the language. She expresses herself and her feelings through her art. She shares her experiences and new knowledge with her mother, who provides the girl with warm reassurance. Finally the day comes when Mari is able to stand before the class with her paintings and tell her story with her new words, "page by painted page." Flip the book over for **Spoken Memories.** It is Mari's turn to tell her class what her life was like in her native land. The setting is a small, poor village, probably in Greece, but it could be anywhere. In simple, understated language, Aliki has captured the emotions and experiences of many of today's children. Colored-pencil and crayon illustrations in soft primary and secondary colors reinforce the mood of the text. Sometimes the art occupies a page by itself; sometimes the space is shared with text. The occasionally oversized heads and wide eyes of the children in otherwise realistic drawings lend a childlike and endearing quality. An illuminating book for all collections that serve youngsters from other lands.

Lauren Freedman

SOURCE: "Children's Literature: What's on the Horizons," in *Reading Horizons,* Vol. 39, No. 3, January/February, 1999, pp. 231-33.

In this beautiful picture book, Aliki offers the reader, through the character of Marianthe, a somewhat autobiographical narrative in two parts. In *One,* we learn about Mari's experiences as a new immigrant

starting a new life in America at a new school. Through drawing and painting, she communicates with her new teacher and classmates and begins to understand the ". . . sticks and chicken feet, humps and moons" of written English and the ". . . sputters, coughs and whispering wind" of spoken English. She makes friends and through the wise words of her mother deals well with the children who are not yet able to be friends. In *Two,* Marianthe shares with her classmates the story of her birth in her native country and the whys of her family's eventual move to America. Aliki's dedication reads, "For those dedicated, unsung teachers who change and enrich lives."

WILLIAM SHAKESPEARE & THE GLOBE (1999)

Kirkus Reviews

SOURCE: A review of *William Shakespeare & the Globe,* in *Kirkus Reviews,* 1 May 1999, p. 718.

For Aliki (**Marianthe's Story,** 1998, etc.), the story of the Globe Theatre is a tale of two men: Shakespeare, who made it famous, and Sam Wanamaker, the driving force behind its modern rebuilding. Decorating margins with verbal and floral garlands, Aliki creates a cascade of landscapes, crowd scenes, diminutive portraits, and sequential views, all done with her trademark warmth and delicacy of line, allowing viewers to glimpse Elizabethan life and theater, historical sites that still stand, and the raising of the new Globe near the ashes of the old. She finishes with a play list, and a generous helping of Shakespearean coinages. Though the level of information doesn't reach that of Diane Stanley's *Bard of Avon* (1992), this makes a serviceable introduction to Shakespeare's times while creating a link between those times and the present; further tempt young readers for whom the play's the thing with Marcia Williams's *Tales from Shakespeare* (1998).

The Horn Book Magazine

SOURCE: A review of *William Shakespeare & the Globe,* in *The Horn Book Magazine,* Vol. 75, No. 3, May, 1999, p. 348.

From the table of contents, in which chapters are labeled as acts and scenes, to the additional material at the back, Aliki's enthusiasm and respect for her subject is in clear evidence. Relevant quotes from Shakespeare's plays are placed throughout the book, which provides a fine introduction to both bard and theater through a logically organized and engaging text, plenty of detailed illustrations with informative captions, and a clean design. Following her description of Shakespeare's life and death, Aliki brings readers into the present with an introduction to Sam Wanamaker, the American actor and director responsible for the rebuilding of the Globe Theatre in London. Wanamaker died in 1993, four years before the new Globe opened, but Aliki proposes that "he lives on in the Globe playhouse he dreamed for us, just as Will lives on in his immortal plays." All's well that ends well—an appropriate conclusion for both topic and audience. As with Shakespeare, there's something here for every mood: history, biography, theater, and architecture commingle, with comedy, tragedy, romance, and poetry playing bit parts. Appended are a list of Shakespeare's works, a chronology, and a surprising list of words and expressions (including horn-book!) said to be invented by Shakespeare.

Publishers Weekly

SOURCE: A review of *William Shakespeare & the Globe,* in *Publishers Weekly,* Vol. 246, No. 22, May 31, 1999, p. 91.

William Shakespeare may get top billing in the title of this picture book, but the emphasis within is less certain. Aliki (***Mummies Made in Egypt***) doesn't investigate Shakespeare as a personality; dividing her work into five "acts," she focuses more on Elizabethan culture, dramatic conventions and living conditions, then shifts to Sam Wanamaker and the process of renovating the Globe in the 20th century. Aliki employs serviceable, almost pedestrian statements to convey the history, stretching occasionally toward cleverness. Of the open-ceilinged Globe, she comments, "When it rained, [the audience] knew it." The material on Wanamaker's restoration sheds light on the process by which the new Globe was built ("The first and only thatched roof in London since 1666"), although the character of Sam, with whom readers are meant to identify, remains bland. Pages are loaded with small panel illustrations of characters and historic figures in exaggerated poses. They capture a jolly theatrical spirit (nearly everyone in the quaint colored-pencil pictures wears a gentle smile), yet the many crowd scenes do not repay scrutiny. Unlike Diane Stanley's work in *Bard of Avon*, these pictures

give only a broad idea of the historical context. Quotations from the bard populate the margins, and numerous appendixes provide facts. The wide range of information here makes this book a useful introduction to Elizabethan theater, despite its disparate themes and generalized pictures. All ages.

Carolyn Phelan

SOURCE: A review of *William Shakespeare & the Globe,* in *Booklist,* July 1, 1999, p. 1824.

Gr. 4-7. Aliki takes on an ambitious project and completes it with a pervasive sense of history and fine sense of style. Her obvious love of Shakespeare and his theater shines through in the warmth of the presentation as well as her meticulous attention to illustrative detail. The many scenes of life in Elizabethan England will be absorbing to children, but some of Aliki's most sensitive work can be seen in her miniature portraits of key historical figures. Quotations from the plays appear throughout the book, in the front matter, in the margins, and as an unofficial epilogue. These short phrases bring Shakespeare's voice to the book, and the text itself demonstrates a good sense of what to include and exclude as it details what is known and surmised about the writer's life. Framing the central story is the tale of Sam Wanamaker (1919-1993), an actor and director whose ambition was to rebuild the Globe. Thus, the book goes beyond Shakespeare himself to introduce the team of people who worked, researched, raised money, and built a replica of the Globe, where performances bring the playwright's words to life in something very like their original setting. Students looking for an introduction to Shakespeare and his playhouse will find this an excellent starting place.

The Horn Book Magazine

SOURCE: A review of *William Shakespeare & the Globe,* in *The Horn Book Magazine,* Vol. 76, No. 1, January, 2000, p. 50.

"O wonderful, wonderful, and most wonderful wonderful! / and yet again wonderful, / and after that, out of all whooping!" Shakespeare ever provides the words. As audience, we applaud the ingenious drama that Aliki presents as introduction to both the playwright Shakespeare and the Globe Theater in which his plays were first performed. With meticulous attention to every detail, this impeccably researched picture book marries Shakespeare's tale to that of

Sam Wanamaker, who appears hundreds of years later, and an ocean away, with dreams first to visit the Globe, and, seeing it commemorated only as a now-forgotten plaque on a wall, to rebuild it. All told, Aliki brings alive for readers of all ages Shakespeare's life, his times, his plays, his actors, his theater, his words—now our theater, our words.

📖 *ALL BY MYSELF!* (2000)

The Horn Book Magazine

SOURCE: A review of *All by Myself!*, in *The Horn Book Magazine*, Vol. 76, No. 5, September, 2000, p. 545.

The mantra of young children everywhere is acted out with gusto in this enthusiastic picture book that zips along with a little boy as he goes about his day. From the moment our independent hero leaves his bed, he is in motion, scrubbing his ears, brushing his teeth, wrestling out of his jammies and into his school clothes. Succinct rhyming descriptions of his actions set the brisk pace: "Pull up the blue jeans, button and zip. / On with the socks, and now for a flip." Aliki leaves ample white space for the boy to perform these feats and lets his dog and cat make more frequent appearances than his parents, furthering the satisfying impression that he is accomplishing everything on his own. But even the most self-sufficient among us needs help sometimes, and the boy's mother is just the right person to step in when it's "time to stop." At bedtime, her arm encircles her young son as she reads to him on his bed, effectively reining in his energy—for the time being.

Sharon R. Pearce

SOURCE: A review of *All by Myself!*, in *School Library Journal*, Vol. 46, No. 9. September, 2000, p. 184.

PreS-Gr 1—Just as the title implies, this jubilant story shows and tells about a child doing all sorts of things independently. "Right shoe, / left shoe. / Tie, / comb, / done! / Breakfast's ready, / pour, / crunch, / yum!" The boy goes through a typical day, getting dressed, going to school, visiting the library, practicing his violin, helping with dinner, and getting ready for bed. Aliki's colorful illustrations closely match the moods and energy levels of a five- or six-year-old. The youngster's dog and cat have almost as much personality as he has. The text has hand-printed appearance, large and easy to read. The back cover features a chart labeled, "What can you do all by yourself?" with verbs such as wash, brush, button, zip, tie, pour, build, and write. A good choice for story-hours and beginning readers.

Publishers Weekly

SOURCE: A review of *All by Myself!*, in *Publishers Weekly*, Vol. 247, No. 34, August 21, 2000, p. 71.

A perky preschooler (or kindergartner) files solo through his daily routine in this upbeat offering, which begins with a wake-up visit from the boy's pet cat. As the child washes up, gets dressed, eats breakfast, plays at school, goes to the library, etc., he is pictured on his own. Only in frames depicting his drop-off at and pickup from school and at bedtime do his parents appear. The parents' limited role reinforces the book's celebration of children's independence, even if it sometimes presents a skewed perspective of age-appropriate autonomy. The text is simple and the picture clues are ample, but the verse's rhythm and rhyme scheme are intermittently forced (e.g., "Right shoe, left shoe. Tie, comb, done! Breakfast's ready, pour, crunch, yum!"). Aliki's (*William Shakespeare & the Globe*) brightly hued, unadorned art convincingly conveys the protagonist's high energy and enthusiasm. A cheerful if minor addition to the author/artist's oeuvre. Ages 3-6.

Additional coverage of Aliki's life and career is contained in the following sources published by the Gale Group: *Contemporary Authors* **Vols. 1-4 R;** *Contemporary Authors New Revision Series,* **Vols. 4, 12, 30;** *Major Authors and Illustrators for Children and Young Adults; St. James Guide to Children's Writers;* **and** *Something about the Author,* **Vols. 2, 35, 75, 113.**

Ellen Conford
1942-

American author of books for children and young adults.

Major works include *Impossible, Possum* (1971), *Dear Lovey Hart, I Am Desperate* (1975), *The Alfred G. Graebner Memorial High School Handbook of Rules and Regulations* (1976), *Hail, Hail Camp Timberwood* (1978), *Lenny Kandell, Smart Aleck* (1983), *I Love You, I Hate You, Get Lost* (1994).

For further information on Conford's life and works, see *CLR,* Volume 10.

INTRODUCTION

An author of children's picture books and novels for middle-graders and young adults, Conford is the creator of the "Jenny Archer" series and other novels for early readers. Praised for her fast-paced, humorous style, colorful characters, and contemporary dialogue, Conford usually places a suburban female protagonist in situations of love and conflict, a situation familiar to most of her readers. Conford's books tend to be upbeat and optimistic, written to entertain and amuse. According to Conford, "I don't write to pound home a message, or to teach a lesson, or to convert kids to a particular point of view. I want to write books that are fun to read, books that will help children to realize that there is such a thing as reading for pleasure, and that books do not merely inform and teach, but amuse."

BIOGRAPHICAL INFORMATION

The daughter of Harry and Lillian (Pfeffer) Schaffer, Conford was born March 20, 1942, in New York City. She attended Hofstra College (now Hofstra University) from 1959 to 1962. It was there she met David H. Conford, a poet and professor of English, whom she married on November 23, 1960. She began her career writing stories and poems published in *Reader's Digest* and other periodicals. Conford started writing for children when she was unable to find suitable reading material for her young son. The result was the picture book *Impossible, Possum*, published in 1971.

MAJOR WORKS

Impossible, Possum centers on a young possum named Randolph who is unable to hang by his tail. With the help of his sister Geraldine, Randolph overcomes his problem. Two other books for young children continued the possum story. In *Just the Thing for Geraldine* (1974) Randolph's older sister finds her talent for juggling more appealing than the feminine activities her parents promote, and in *Eugene the Brave* (1978) young Eugene must overcome his fear of the dark, essential for a nocturnal animal.

At the suggestion of her editor, Conford began writing books for middle-grade readers. *Dreams of Victory* (1973) is the story of Victory Benneker, a daydreaming sixth grader, who dreams of being the president of the United States after losing the class election. When chosen to be Litter in the class play, Victory dreams of becoming a famous actress. Victory eventually discovers that her imagination is her hidden talent. Jane Langton commented in the *New York Times Book Review*, "Any young reader who, like Victory Benneker, does not have the longest, blondest hair in the class or who is apt to be given the part of Litter in the pollution play will love her dreams." This book is representative of Conford's subsequent stories featuring female protagonists growing up in middle-class suburbia, written in a fast-paced, first-person narrative.

Conford followed up this novel with three more novels for middle-graders. *Felicia the Critic* (1973) is the story of Felicia Kershenbaum, a young girl not afraid to criticize others, including a policeman, the butcher, and ultimately the President of the United States. Diana L. Spirt says in her *Introducing More Books: A Guide for the Middle Grades,* "The relationship between freely giving your opinions and upsetting others' feelings is explored here as a vital part of getting along well in your family." *Me and the Terrible Two* (1974) features Dorie Kimball, a sixth-grade girl whose best friend and next-door neighbor has moved to Australia. Her new neighbors include the twins Haskell and Conrad, two boys Dorie is determined to dislike and who constantly harass her. When Dorie and Haskell are assigned to work together on a school project their great success leads to adoration and friendship. According to Ethel L. Heins, commenting in *The Horn Book Magazine*, "The book is appealingly full of school happenings, zippy repartee, and plenty of preadolescent witticisms." In *The Luck of Pokey Bloom* (1975) ten-year-old Pokey wants to win something, and thus constantly enters mail-in contests. Pokey is also troubled by her older brother Gordon, who becomes moody and distant as he transitions into adolescence with a case of puppy love. In the end, Pokey wins a transistor radio, and Gordon recovers from his infatuation.

With the publication of *Dear Lovey Hart, I Am Desperate*, Conford began to write for young adults. Freshman Carrie Wasserman, alias Lovey Hart, writes an advice column for the school newspaper. The column is a success and boosts circulation until some flip answers to serious problems cause the readers to revolt. Carrie's father, the school guidance counselor, is also not pleased. Her sister reveals Lovey's true identity, and Carrie offers an apology in the final column. In a review by Barbara Ellerman in *Booklist*, she stated, "A potentially corny story is whipped into shape with humorous situations, funny dialogue, and perceptive first person narrative." Carrie returns for her sophomore year in *We Interrupt This Semester for an Important Bulletin* (1979). A year older, Carrie turns to serious reporting in an attempt to impress her boyfriend and editor Chip. When Chip falls for the beautiful Southerner, Prudie Tuckerman, Carrie puts everything into her investigative reporting. While investigating the school lunch program, Carrie plants a tape recorder in the office of the supervisor. The recorded conversation sounds like evidence of misdoings and the paper runs the story. Once again Carrie and the paper are in trouble, as the accusations prove groundless. Prudie turns out to be faithless, and Chip and Carrie barely retain their jobs on the paper. A *Horn Book* contributor commented that "the fast funny dialogue, the characterization of Prudie as femme fatale, and Carrie's self-mocking . . . [attitude towards] her problems make the book light and amusing."

In another work for teen-age readers, *The Alfred G. Graebner Memorial High School Handbook of Rules and Regulations*, the chapters correspond loosely to passages from a handbook, but the protagonist in the story constantly runs into situations not covered by the rules. These include falling madly in love with a teacher and what to do when an upperclassman makes a pass. Sheila Salmon remarked in *Children's Book Review Service*, "Conford is able to blend what could be, and often is, stereotypical material into a fresh, fast-paced story." *Hail, Hail, Camp Timberwood* provides a fictionalized account of Conford's years at camp. Thirteen-year-old Melanie Kessler experiences first love and self-discovery her first summer away from home. Melanie makes friends easily but has a tougher time riding horses and overcoming her fear of the water. She also falls in love with Steve Tepper. Conford says her story "deals with the joys and anxieties of a girl spending her first summer 'on her own' and finding—as I did—that one of the people she gets to know most intimately is herself."

In a departure from her earlier work, *Lenny Kandell, Smart Aleck* features a male protagonist and a historical setting. Conford read newspapers and magazines and utilized her knowledge of old movies to set the story in 1946. Eleven-year-old Lenny dreams of becoming a comedian. His one-liners amuse his friends but not his teachers. Lenny falls for the beautiful Georgina, has to avoid the school bully after accidentally tripping him, and must confront the death of his father. Kathleen Garland noted in *School Library Journal,* "Children looking for a funny story will find it here—and will probably want to try out some of Lenny's jokes on their friends."

Ten-year-old Jenny Archer is the protagonist in Conford's best-known series of novels for younger readers. Jenny encounters adventures and unexpected problems with her best friend Wilson Wynn and her dog Berkley. In *A Job for Jenny Archer* (1988) Jenny sets out to earn enough money to buy her mother a fur coat. *A Case for Jenny Archer* (1988) finds her alerting the police to a gang of thieves. In 1999 Conford introduced a new heroine for early graders in *Annabel the Actress Starring in Gorilla My Dreams.* A follow-up in 2000, *Annabel the Actress Starring in Just a Little Extra,* depicted the would-be actress Annabel winning a bit part in a television movie that is being filmed in her hometown.

AWARDS

Impossible Possum won a Best Books of the Year citation from *School Library Journal* in 1971. *Just the Thing for Geraldine* was chosen for a Children's Books of International Interest citation in 1974. Also in 1974, Conford won a Library of Congress Children's Book of the Year citation for *Me and the Terrible Two.* She was awarded Books of the Year citations from the Child Study Association of America in 1975 for *The Luck of Pokey Bloom* and *Dear Lovey Hart, I Am Desperate. The Alfred G. Graebner Memorial High School Handbook of Rules and Regulations* garnered a Best Books for Young Adults citation from the American Library Association (ALA) in 1976. *Hail, Hail Camp Timberwood* was chosen for the Surrey School Award and the Pacific Northwest Young Reader's Choice Award in 1981 and the California Young Reader's Medal in 1982. In 1983, *Lenny Kandell, Smart Aleck* received a Best Books of the Year citation from *School Library Journal* and a Parents' Choice Award. Conford also received Parents' Choice Awards for *Why Me?* in 1985 and *A Royal Pain* in 1986. *If This Is Love, I'll Take Spaghetti* was chosen the South Carolina Young Adult Book Award winner for 1986-87 and given the South Dakota Prairie Pasque Award for 1989.

TITLE COMMENTARY

A ROYAL PAIN (1986)

Publishers Weekly

SOURCE: A review of *A Royal Pain,* in *Publishers Weekly,* Vol. 229, No. 17, April 15, 1986, p. 84.

Conford returns to the theme used to such success in *A Silver Crown*: one morning a girl wakes up to discover she's really a queen. Or, in teenager Abby Adams's case, heir to the throne of a tiny European country named Saxony Coburn. There was an unfortunate switch of babies, and Abby is whisked off to Saxony Coburn to take her rightful place as Princess Florinda XIV. It's all a great lark for Abby, especially after she meets Geoffrey, a reporter, and it's love at first sight for both. The party abruptly ends when Abby learns that there are some things a princess can never do. Falling in love with a commoner is one of them, especially when the princess has been betrothed to Prince Casimir. When Abby protests, her new parents decide to marry her on her 16th birthday, only three weeks away. Abby's solution is to become a "royal pain," so she'll be sent home. It's all meant to be a silly, comic romp, but Conford never quite pulls the joke off, because her characters are not very believable, and the "surprise" ending is no surprise. (12-up).

THE THINGS I DID FOR LOVE (1987)

Publishers Weekly

SOURCE: A review of *The Things I Did for Love,* in *Publishers Weekly,* Vol. 232, No. 7, August 14, 1987, pp. 105-06.

From the moment Stephanie asks herself, in the form of a school project, "Why do fools fall in love?" her own personal life becomes fraught with disaster and mishap. Her platonic relationship with Jon seems headed for more turbulent waters; Trevor, the kind of boy a parent dreams of for a daughter, starts to put the moves on her; and Bash takes her on motorcycle rides where more than the turns are scary. It's three against one, and while Stephanie figures out just who it is she loves, readers will have a fine time trying to outguess Conford's fast moves and broadly comic scenes. Despite a bit of a cliché regarding Bash (the tough dropout with the heart of gold dates back at least to James Dean), this book will help lift the back-to-school blues. Ages 11-up.

Katharine Bruner

SOURCE: A review of *The Things I Did for Love,* in *School Library Journal,* Vol. 34, No. 5, January, 1988, p. 84.

Gr 7-10—The title is sufficient to ensure this book's initial popularity. Moreover, Conford's empathetic depiction of adolescent confusion and her deftly humorous narration will guarantee it continued momentum. Stephanie, 16, is smart and thoughtful but klutzy. At five feet nine, she considers herself the "incredible hulk," doomed to be dateless. Spurred by a required research project for her psychology class, she determines to investigate the what and why of Love. Best friend Amy disappoints Steffie by falling so hard for a mohawk-haired motorcyclist that her I.Q. falls 40 points. Then Trevor, the high school's Don Juan, surprises Steffie by turning her interview with him into a suave come-on. Steady but unromantic friend Jon disturbs her with his jealousy. But most of all, Steffie dismays herself when she falls for the unlikely Bash, a leather-jacketed school dropout. With two loves aflame, she abandons the research project, "preferring experience to analysis," eventually concluding that, "There is absolutely nothing rational about love." Laced with pithy observations, tense moments of crisis, and lively dialogue, this well-realized agony of love should be an applauded addition to most collections.

📖 *A JOB FOR JENNY ARCHER* (1988)

Martha Rosen

SOURCE: A review of *A Job for Jenny Archer,* in *School Library Journal,* Vol. 34, No. 8, April, 1988, p. 79.

Gr 2-4—Welcome, Jenny Archer! Join Adler's "Cam Jansen" (Viking), Hurwitz's "Nora and Teddy" (Morrow), and Giff's "Kids of the Polk Street School" (Dell). This initial offering by Conford in a proposed series of first "chapter books" about Jenny; her best friend, Wilson Wynn; and her very large and friendly black dog, Barkley, will disappear so quickly from the library's fiction shelves that it might be wise to order duplicates. Conford's witty, humorous style is in evidence from the first page, when readers learn that Jenny isn't really poor; she just has "rich ideas." The subsequent chapters describe Jenny's scheme to raise enough cash to buy her mother a fur coat. These include a neighborhood dog-training business and her attempts, almost too successful, to sell the Archer's house without her parents' knowledge. Independent money-making is a theme popular with older readers in books such as Pfeffer's *Kid Power* (Watts, 1977), Van Leeuwen's *Benjy in Business* (Dial, 1983), and Springstubbs' *Eunice Gottlieb and the Unwhitewashed Truth About Life* (Delacorte, 1987). Younger readers will be entertained by Jenny's bright ideas and the unanticipated problems she creates. The further adventures of this feisty heroine will be eagerly awaited by all.

Denise M. Wilms

SOURCE: A review of *A Job for Jenny Archer,* in *Booklist,* Vol. 84, No. 15, April 1, 1988, p. 1341.

Gr. 2-4. Jenny Archer wants to buy her mother a fur coat for a birthday present so "when she wears it, she won't feel poor." To do that, however, she needs money. While Jenny's not adverse to working, her money-making schemes fall flat, and with her mother's birthday fast approaching, she's forced to realize that a small gift from the heart is what will make her mother the happiest. A light story that moves quickly, this has a nice feel for the way young children think, as well as mischievous sense of humor. It's right on target for readers who are easing away from picture books and into easy chapter books. Ten black-and-white illustrations will help in the transition.

Publishers Weekly

SOURCE: A review of *A Job for Jenny Archer,* in *Publishers Weekly,* Vol. 233, No. 17, April 29, 1988, p. 77.

In another entry in the Springboard Book line, Jenny takes her mother's wish for a fur coat—and the impossibility of her getting one—as a measure of their poverty. She resolves to earn the money for a coat herself, by inventing odd jobs to do for neighbors. But neither pet-training, baby-sitting, nor an attempt at a career in real estate (selling her own house) brings the hoped-for results she hopes for. A light lesson in the value of family love over material possessions, Conford's story is at its best when depicting the affinity between Jenny and her best friend Wilson.

With witty line drawings, the book should inspire other young entrepreneurs and remind them that sometimes it's okay to fail. Ages 7-9.

☐ *THE GENIE WITH THE LIGHT BLUE HAIR* (1988)

Publishers Weekly

SOURCE: A review of *The Genie with the Light Blue Hair,* in *Publishers Weekly,* Vol. 234, No. 24, December 9, 1988, p. 67.

Jean, 15, politely thanks her aunt and uncle for their birthday present to her: an ugly, tarnished lamp with a fat blue candle inside. That night when a storm causes the lights to go out, the lamp proves not only useful, but nothing short of miraculous. Arthur, a blue genie, emerges as soon as the candle is lit. Once Jean accepts that Arthur is indeed a genie, she begins to make wishes. Arthur, however, is slightly confused, which is why Jean's wishes end up badly: she is grounded, becomes a contestant on "Name That Poison," falters on homework assignments, finds herself the daughter of the man she loves and turns into an infamous writer. When Jean and Arthur finally discover and resolve a major mix-up, Jean's life returns to normal—only she has learned something that changes her attitude about herself. This light, humorous novel will amuse readers who enjoy a deft blending of fantasy and reality. Ages 12-up.

Maria B. Salvadore

SOURCE: A review of *The Genie with the Light Blue Hair,* in *School Library Journal,* Vol. 35, No. 6, February, 1989, p. 100.

Gr 6-9—For her 15th birthday, practical, shy Jeannie Warren is given a lamp by her aunt and uncle. The teapot-shaped "candlestick" which holds a blue candle reminds Jeannie's ten-year-old pain-in-the-neck brother, Richie, of Aladdin's magic lamp. When an unusual thunderstorm knocks out the electricity, Jeannie lights the lamp from which emerges a genie who closely resembles Groucho Marx—cigar and all. The magical results temporarily turn Jeannie's orderly world topsy-turvy, until it is discovered that the genie was intended to serve Aunt Jean. Things are righted, of course, when the genie goes to its rightful mistress. Jeannie narrates this fast-paced, humorous, and highly-readable tale that is filled with characters

who are not fully drawn but who are plausible nonetheless. Readers are likely to identify with Jeannie's lack of self-confidence and her pangs of growing up.

☐ *A CASE FOR JENNY ARCHER* (1988)

Ilene Cooper

SOURCE: A review of *A Case for Jenny Archer,* in *Booklist,* Vol. 85, No. 10, January 15, 1989, pp. 868-69.

Gr. 2-4. While waiting for camp to begin, Jenny Archer reads Missy Martin mysteries. She wishes she could be a detective like Missy and when new neighbors move in across the street, Jenny eyes them suspiciously. Maybe they're kidnappers, holding the little girl they say is their daughter hostage. Or perhaps the many paintings in their house are stolen goods—there's been a recent theft at the art museum. One evening when she's home with a babysitter, Jenny sees a truck pull up at the neighbors'. It's probably part of some nefarious plot, Jenny figures, and phones the police. There's a plot all right, but it's designed by real burglars who are trying to break into the house. Jenny has inadvertently saved the day, becoming the detective she's always wanted to be—sort of. Short, snappy, fun to read, and dotted with nicely conceived pencil illustrations, this fits in well with the other books in the Springboard series, which is designed to introduce readers to chapter books.

Joanne Aswell

SOURCE: A review of *A Case for Jenny Archer,* in *School Library Journal,* Vol. 35, No. 7, March, 1989, pp. 156, 158.

Gr 2-4—It's summer vacation and Jenny Archer is bored. A trip to the library supplies her with not only an armful of Missy Martin mysteries, but an idea toward a summer occupation as well. After all, if Missy can rid the world of dangerous criminals, why can't Jenny? In true sleuth fashion, Jenny, her friend Wilson, and Barkley, the dog, undertake an investigation that alerts the police to some local thugs trying to make off with the neighbors' furniture in a fake moving van. The crime is thwarted, thanks to Jenny Archer, a real-life junior detective. This lots-of-fun advanced easy reader contains eight chapters, all about three pages long, with large, clear print, and lots of white space. Its familiar but never dull vocabulary and simple sentence structure present an ideal next-up book for primary grade readers who've outgrown the easies. The children here are lively, the adults funny, wise, and supportive. The plot cleverly follows standard mystery story conventions, such as the faithful sidekick and the use of disguises, and neatly transfers the actions and conclusions of the fictional Missy to those of the real Jenny. A minor flaw is that the illustrations fail to capture the spirit of the adventure. Any library in need of a well-written adventure that will take readers by the hand and lead them to a place where book fantasies are allowed to come true shouldn't be without this playful mystery.

JENNY ARCHER, AUTHOR (1989)

Roger Sutton

SOURCE: A review of *Jenny Archer, Author*, in *The Bulletin of the Center for Children's Books*, Vol. 42, No. 11, July, 1989, p. 271.

Gr. 2-4. Like *A Job for Jenny Archer*, this overextends a mildly funny misunderstanding into a somewhat amusing situation. After her teacher has praised her composition, Jenny is more than eager to tackle the next writing assignment, an autobiography, "the story of your life." Jenny's own limited experience ("She was only a kid. She didn't have a story to tell yet. She'd hardly even had a life yet") causes her to imagine a more interesting life history, in ten chapters, one for each year, including such drama as the time she met her evil twin, Horrible Hortense, in an elevator in the Empire State Building. Mrs. Pike is less than pleased, at first, and it seems awfully unlikely that a girl of Jenny's age would not understand that an autobiography was supposed to be *true*. But Mrs. Pike comes around, the value of imagination is given its due, and Jenny gets a gold star. Good for her.

WHAT'S COOKING, JENNY ARCHER? (1990)

Carolyn Jenks

SOURCE: A review of *What's Cooking, Jenny Archer?*, in *School Library Journal*, Vol. 36, No. 1, January, 1990, p. 103.

Gr 2-4—In this fourth book about the enterprising Jenny Archer, she finds herself in the catering business. A creative cooking television show and

Jenny's friends convince her that she can compete successfully with the lunches in the school cafeteria. As the days go by, however, the young entrepreneur discovers the harsh realities of food prices, time constraints, and customers who are picky eaters. This easy-to-read, humorous story concerns itself with realistic, everyday happenings at school. Jenny is ambitious but light-hearted, and her open-minded mother fortunately has a good sense of humor. By the end of the story, Jenny has given up her lunch business, but is looking hopefully ahead with plans for the *Jenny Archer Cookbook*. Entertaining, light fare.

JENNY ARCHER TO THE RESCUE (1990)

Jana R. Fine

SOURCE: A review of *Jenny Archer to the Rescue*, in *School Library Journal*, Vol. 36, No. 10, December, 1990, pp. 74-5.

Gr 2-4—Jenny Archer is back, and this time she plans on being a real live heroine. There's only one problem: she doesn't know how to handle emergencies. With the help of her parents, she learns about safety and rescue treatment and, armed with a first-aid kit, she is ready for anything. When her two-year-old cousin visits, Jenny invents a game called "Accident," and practices her bandaging techniques with disastrous results. Ten short chapters advance the plot and are supplemented by black-and-white drawings. Jenny's actions are realistic and positive as she learns valuable information on first aid and emergency treatment. Readers will identify with the need to be recognized for something they can do and will enjoy her attempts to become someone out of the ordinary. Although not as fast paced as previous books in this transitional series, Conford blends first aid with fun, offering a story that children can read on their own.

Kirkus Reviews

SOURCE: A review of *Jenny Archer to the Rescue*, in *Kirkus Reviews*, Vol. 58, December 15, 1990, p. 1736.

Conford sticks to her proven formula in this fifth "Springboard Book" about the irrepressible Jenny. Jenny's latest enthusiasm, inspired by a news article about a "Young American Hero," is first aid. Her parents maintain their customary bemused stance, buying Jenny a first-aid kit and commenting gently on her futile efforts to find someone to rescue, which culminate in the usual discouraging disaster. After calling the fire department to put out a harmless trash fire, Jenny moves on to her next interest: becoming a Nobel Prize-winning scientist. Though the pattern is becoming worn, Jenny herself is still an endearing character in this reliable series of easily read chapter books.

📖 *LOVING SOMEONE ELSE* (1991)

Connie Tyrrell Burns

SOURCE: A review of *Loving Someone Else,* in *School Library Journal,* Vol. 37, No. 6, June, 1991, p. 122.

Gr 6-9—When Holly Campion's filthy rich father suffers enormous financial losses in a hostile company takeover, the shallow, superficial 17-year-old foregoes a summer of shopping to work as a companion to two eccentric and elderly sisters who live on Harmony Island. Her hope is to earn enough money to attend Sarah Lawrence; she is far too snotty to attend the local community college. Holly, who judges people solely by their wealth, falls obsessively in love with their nephew Avery, ignoring the intentions of a nice "townie," Pete. The plot is featherweight, the characterizations lack credence, and the ending is too pat. Holly's sudden realization that money isn't everything seems as trivial as her previous motivations.

Kirkus Reviews

SOURCE: A review of *Loving Someone Else,* in *Kirkus Reviews,* Vol. 59, June 15, 1991, p. 786.

After her family's fortune collapses, Holly goes to work for the nutty, elderly Brewster sisters. Earning money for college by working as a domestic companion, she is expected to perform duties others have always done for her. Holly has good intentions but no skills; still, she is determined to stick it out, if only for the frequent contact with the Brewsters' handsome, wealthy nephew Avery: Holly hopes to marry him and save her family. Conford offers plenty of humor, but the utter predictability makes the high jinks feel worn. No, Holly doesn't get Avery, but a poorer boy named Pete; and, yes, she does become less materialistic. Worthy ideals, to be sure, but all part of the formula.

Publishers Weekly

SOURCE: A review of *Loving Someone Else,* in *Publishers Weekly,* Vol. 238, No. 28, June 28, 1991, p. 102.

Conford's (*If This Is Love, I'll Take Spaghetti*; the "Jenny Archer" series) latest YA novel is a delectable treat, packed with humor, drama and the trials of adolescent infatuation. Holly is devastated when her father, a successful business executive, loses his job. The repercussions are wide-spread, but what disturbs Holly the most is that she'll have to attend a local community college instead of the prestigious (and expensive) school that had accepted her. Determined not to let this happen, Holly accepts a well-paying position as a companion/housekeeper to two elderly sisters. What sustains her throughout the heretofore unknown experience of menial labor is the passion she feels for Avery, the sisters' rich, handsome, older (around 30) nephew. From Holly's witty first-person narrative to the artfully developed conclusion, this book is top-notch—and especially timely in its portrayal of a family adjusting to financial difficulties. Ages 10-up.

Stephanie Zvirin

SOURCE: A review of *Loving Someone Else,* in *Booklist,* Vol. 87, No. 21, July, 1991, pp. 2039-40.

Gr. 7-12. With her usual delicious flair for comedy, Conford delivers a simple story about a girl who comes to understand what it means to have responsibility for someone else. Seventeen-year-old Holly Campion jokes that her greatest talent is shopping, but when her family suddenly finds itself in financial difficulties, it's to work, not the mall, she must go. An advertisement for a live-in companion draws her to the home of the eccentric Brewster sisters, Birdie and Blossom. They will pay her well despite her lack of experience. But what really convinces Holly to take the job is a look at their attractive, wealthy nephew, whom she thinks might be just the one to pull her out of the money doldrums. However, it's questionable whether she can survive the sisters' vegetarian diet, Blossom's Esperanto lessons, and the Friday night séances long enough to attract him. On top of that, what about townie Pete, who wants to be more than just her friend? Dry humor and clever characters make this a breezy read.

Zena Sutherland

SOURCE: A review of *Loving Someone Else,* in *The Bulletin of the Center for Children's Books,* Vol. 45, No. 1, September, 1991, pp. 4-5.

Gr. 6-9. Looking forward to the expensive college of her choice, Holly is depressed by her father's financial collapse; she decides to take a summer job to earn college money. The job, acting as helper-companion to two elderly sisters, seems unattractive until their debonair nephew shows up. Instantly smitten, Holly stays on, hoping for a relationship with Mr. Charming. She is, in a spoofy pattern that will be familiar to paperback romance fans, the object of instant interest to the nice boy-next-door type, while *he* is considered by the snobbish Other Girl to be her property. There's some diversity in the characters of the odd, elderly Brewster sisters—shades of *Arsenic and Old Lace*—but the tongue-in-cheek tone does not quite rescue the story from formula clichés.

📖 *CAN DO, JENNY ARCHER* (1991)

Maggie McEwen

SOURCE: A review of *Can Do, Jenny Archer,* in *School Library Journal,* Vol. 37, No. 12, December, 1991, pp. 80, 84.

Gr 2-3—A bored Jenny listens as Mrs. Pike announces the ground rules for a school contest. The class collecting the most cans will win the opportunity to use a new camcorder and star in its own movie production. Jenny is excited by the prospect, especially since the student who gathers the most cans will direct the film. Her severe case of contest-fever strains her relationship with best friend Beth, who is also competing. Further problems occur when Jenny's clever plans to win fail. But Beth, seeing Jenny's discouragement, secretly signs over her cans to her friend; that act brings Jenny to her senses and leaves her feeling like a winner. Through a feisty main character, Conford touches on typical childhood experiences with humor and sensitivity, and lightly handles the theme of overcompetitiveness. Readers will readily identify with Jenny's unbridled enthusiasm, the amusing situations she encounters, and the lessons she learns. A simple plot, minimal characterization, and an uncluttered format add further appeal for readers just moving into novels. The "Jenny Archer" books are similar to Sheila Greenwald's "Rosy Cole" series (Little) in content and format. The latter,

however, is slightly more difficult and has a more fully realized heroine. Jenny would be an excellent precursor to that series or to the "Ramona" (Morrow) books.

Carolyn Phelan

SOURCE: A review of *Can Do, Jenny Archer,* in *Booklist,* Vol. 88, No. 7, December 1, 1991, p. 702.

Gr. 2-4. Jenny, the heroine of several beginning chapter books by Conford, competes in a school contest to collect the most tin cans for recycling. The prize? The chance to direct a movie with the new video equipment the school will get for all that tin. The catch? In her race to win, Jenny plows through her friends' chances and their feelings, until her guilt and loneliness catch up to her. With more than a little humor to leaven the lessons, this should prove as popular as the other books in the series. Full-page drawings lighten the book visually, making it all the more accessible to students at this reading level.

Kirkus Reviews

SOURCE: A review of *Can Do, Jenny Archer,* in *Kirkus Reviews,* Vol. 59, December 1, 1991, p. 1531.

The school is buying video equipment with the proceeds from a scrap metal drive, and the student who collects the most cans will get to direct the first film! Suddenly discovering that she's always wanted to make movies, Jenny springs into action—plundering her neighbors' recycling bins, nagging her sitter and parents to buy more canned goods, even recruiting everyone in her grandparents' apartment building. It's not that easy—classmate Beth has turned from best friend to rival, and even the indomitable Jenny is temporarily discouraged when two big bags of her cans are inadvertently thrown away. Though little Wilson Wynn is the surprise contest winner, Jenny regains both friend and self-confidence by the end. A generous number of amiable b&w illustrations echo this light story's cheerful humor. Sixth in a popular series.

📖 *DEAR MOM, GET ME OUT OF HERE!* (1992)

Stephanie Zvirin

SOURCE: A review of *Dear Mom, Get Me Out of Here!,* in *Booklist,* Vol. 89, No. 4, October 15, 1992, p. 417.

Gr. 6-9. Here's another entry in this fall's surprisingly rich lineup of slapstick comedies. Thirteen-year-old Paul Tanner's nightmares come true when he discovers his new boys' school is a dismal place where teachers are as weird as—if not weirder than—the kids. His roommate, Orson Autrey, is convinced he can fly; the gym teacher holds checkers practice outside in a snowstorm; one boy keeps a pet rooster; and there's a janitor who's incapable of fixing anything. With his parents in Europe, however, there's little chance Paul can escape anytime soon. Things look up a bit when he spots Barbara Catalina, stepdaughter of Mr. Pickles, the school's headmaster. The problem is getting her to notice him. That's solved when classmate Chris, a budding journalist with an imaginative reporting style, decides Pickles is a mass murderer and enlists Paul (images of a grateful Barbara swirling in his brain) to help him prove it. A slight yarn, but with enough sassy comebacks, wacky characters, and broadly comic encounters to keep readers well entertained.

Cindy Darling Codell

SOURCE: A review of *Dear Mom, Get Me Out of Here!,* in *School Library Journal,* Vol. 38, No. 11, November, 1992, p. 119.

Gr 6-9—In a hurry to catch a plane for Switzerland, Paul Tanner's parents dump him at a boarding school they have never personally inspected. Had they stayed, they would have observed some highly unusual events. Paul's roommate keeps trying to fly from the roof and paints a glow-in-the-dark woman on the ceiling. When Chris, the school paper's editor, isn't printing total lies, he's breaking into the office files to do research. The coach's idea of sport is playing checkers on the hockey field during a blizzard. The food is of indefinite origin, but definitely gross. When Chris decides the headmaster is a deranged murderer in hiding, Paul isn't convinced, but he sees little to lose in helping his friend. At worst, he might be expelled from a school he hates. After several narrow escapes, the evidence piles up against Pickles, and Chris decides to expose him during the Founder's Day play. Conford is at her best in describing the casual, humorous absurdities that exist in many school situations. Her *The Alfred G. Graebner Memorial High School Handbook of Rules and Regulations* (Little, 1976) has become an anthem for students treading through the paradoxes created by a large, dim-witted educational bureaucracy. It is a tribute to this writer's exceptional skill that the ridiculous boarding school happenings of her newest novel seem quite plausible. Even rather large plot twists are made

reasonably digestible with the help of likable characters; perfect pacing; and smooth, comical dialogue. Not deeply thematic, this one's for fun!

Kirkus Reviews

SOURCE: A review of *Dear Mom, Get Me Out of Here!* in *Kirkus Reviews,* Vol. 60, November 15, 1992, p. 1440.

A lightweight farce with a daffy but resourceful cast and a surprise climax. When 13-year-old Paul's parents take an extended business trip, they leave him at ramshackle Burnside Academy, where, as roommate Orson says, "the strange meet the deranged." Introduced to quirky classmates and even quirkier teachers, headed by sinister Dudley Pickles, Paul wants out, but his frantic letters go unanswered. When a TV show about wanted criminals convinces Chris Bishop—writer, editor, publisher, and printer of the *Burnside Banner*—that Pickles is actually maniacal family killer Dwight Popper, Paul joins the surreptitious investigation, meanwhile chasing the headmaster's beautiful but oblivious stepdaughter. Inspired by Hamlet, the boys decide to force Pickles into the open with a dramatized version of the murder, presented at the Founder's Day celebration. Amazingly, it works. Chris is right—or nearly: it turns out that it isn't Pickles who's the culprit but his twin Bucky, Burnside's custodian. "Evil twin brother," says Orson in disgust. "That is so trite." Send Conford fans who enjoy this on to Gordon Korman's books.

Publishers Weekly

SOURCE: A review of *Dear Mom, Get Me Out of Here!,* in *Publishers Weekly,* Vol. 239, No. 50, November 16, 1992, p. 64.

Conford, the author of such upbeat novels as ***Dear Lovey Hart, I Am Desperate*** and ***You Never Can Tell,*** succeeds once again. When Paul first comes to Burnside Academy, he thinks he has stepped into a nightmare. Broken windows, frigid bathrooms and inedible meals are just the beginning. But school somehow seems bearable when Orson, Chris and Wendell befriend Paul; when the boys begin speculating about their headmaster's sordid past, Burnside actually becomes intriguing. Conford people her tale with a cast of zany characters who, with their irresistible quirks and quips, manage to make an unbelievable plot seem real. Readers will gradually warm to Paul's integration into this crazy group of friends; by the time the boys are plotting to expose the headmaster, the audience will be completely hooked. A rollicking, surprising finish caps off this riotous tale. Ages 8-12.

NIBBLE, NIBBLE, JENNY ARCHER (1993)

Jana R. Fine

SOURCE: A review of *Nibble, Nibble, Jenny Archer,* in *School Library Journal,* Vol. 39, No. 7, July, 1993, p. 58.

Gr 2-4—During a trip to the mall, Jenny samples a product being tested on the public. After she finds out that her comments about the mysterious pellets will be part of a television commercial, she begins to imagine what her life will be like when she is rich and famous. Then the ad airs, and Jenny is horrified to learn that she has gushed over the delicious taste of gerbil food, and that the producers want to televise the spot nationally. Conford has created another hilarious chapter book about this enthusiastic heroine. Young readers will respond to Jenny's sense of humor and adventure, as well as her emotional ups and downs. While parents and friends are not a major focus, they do provide a loving and stable background for the unfolding of events. This tasty treat will whet children's appetites for more Jenny Archer tales.

Deborah Abbott

SOURCE: A review of *Nibble, Nibble, Jenny Archer,* in *Booklist,* Vol. 90, No. 2, September 15, 1993, pp. 149, 152.

Gr. 2-4. Jenny Archer a TV star? When Jenny samples a new food at the local mall, she learns she has secretly been filmed for a television commercial. The production crew loves her enthusiasm and natural, sparkling manner. The promise of $500 after permission papers are signed launches Jenny into practicing "enthusiasm" and "sparkle," much to the distress of those around her. Jenny finds out when her commercial will be played and urges her friends and classmates to watch it. Her shock and dismay at discovering what she actually ate are compounded immediately by painful teasing. How Jenny feels about what happened to her and what she decides about commercials offer a meaningful lesson. The in-

ventive plot, gentle humor, and apt characterization make this a beginning chapter book that fits the intended audience. However, the ethical implications and legal issues of using a child in this way are somewhat disturbing and offer lots to discuss. The pencil drawings mesh well with the action. A good introduction to Jenny Archer, a likable heroine of many books in the series.

I LOVE YOU, I HATE YOU, GET LOST (1994)

Publishers Weekly

SOURCE: A review of *I Love You, I Hate You, Get Lost,* in *Publishers Weekly,* Vol. 241, No. 3, January 17, 1994, p. 440.

Spoiled romances, aggravating teachers and bothersome siblings are some of the woes humorously depicted in this collection of stories set in contemporary suburbia. Although, for the most part, the characters are cut from the same cloth and their voices are barely distinguishable from one another, their dilemmas are varied enough to carry readers gleefully through muddled affairs and mishaps all the way to the all-too-predictable resolutions. Particularly rib-tickling are the series of minor humiliations experienced by the protagonist of **"Liverwurst and Roses"** as he tries to express his growing infatuation with longtime friend Bonnie and the major embarrassment suffered by the heroine of the title story when forced to take her younger brother along on a date. The universality of the characters' day-to-day conflicts, the intensity of their emotions and their zest are sure to win more fans for the author of ***Dear Lovey Hart, I Am Desperate*** and ***If This Is Love, I'll Take Spaghetti***. Ages 12-up.

Kirkus Reviews

SOURCE: A review of *I Love You, I Hate You, Get Lost,* in *Kirkus Reviews,* Vol. 62, February 15, 1994, p. 224.

Seven entertaining, mostly funny stories with themes that include first love, troublesome siblings, aggravating parents, and horoscopes. Most are in a female first-person voice; one exception recounts a first-day-of-school confrontation between a disillusioned teacher and a student whose brother's reputation has preceded him. A particularly clever vignette, **"Body**

Wave," is a one-sided conversation between a girl and her hairdresser, climaxing in a disastrous—but well-deserved—perm. The prolific author knows her young-teen audience; she keeps the tone light, barely suggesting a serious problem when two reluctant about-to-be stepsisters must spend a day and night together (**"Don't Let the Bedbugs Bite"**). Only one story (**"Arnold Bing, the Carpet King"**) suffers from silliness. Otherwise, thoroughly enjoyable.

Susan DeRonne

SOURCE: A review of *I Love You, I Hate You, Get Lost,* in *Booklist,* Vol. 90, No. 13, March 1, 1994, p. 1245.

Gr. 7-10. As the title of the collection suggests, these stories are light, humorous tales dealing with emotions that YAs experience. In one story, Howie wants to tell best friend Bonnie that he's falling for her in a romantic way, but fear of rejection keeps him from using the direct approach. In the title story, Dana is forced to take her seven-year-old brother on an anniversary dinner cruise with her boyfriend. Little brother plays hide-and-seek, only to fall asleep in the life preserver compartment, scaring Dana and everyone else aboard the ship when he can't be found for hours. In another tale, as an obnoxious, self-centered teen unwittingly reveals her true nature to her hairdresser on the day of a big school dance, the hairdresser knowingly ruins the teen's hair. Each of these entertaining, quick-reading stories sheds humor on a different common problem: trouble with parents, a sibling, a step-sibling, a boyfriend, a girlfriend, or a teacher.

Nancy P. Reeder

SOURCE: A review of *I Love You, I Hate You, Get Lost,* in *School Library Journal,* Vol. 40, No. 4, April, 1994, p. 152.

Gr 7-10—Conford takes a humorous look at some typical teenage situations—the kind that are funny if they happen to somebody else—in this collection of seven short stories. The title story concerns a romantic evening gone awry due to a bratty younger brother. **"Body Wave"** is told by a self-centered, boyfriend-stealing girl while she's getting her hair done on the day of "a really, really major dance"; the stylist "takes care" of her by talking her into a new do. In **"Teacher from the Prehistoric Planet,"** a

student writes a biography of his history teacher, imagining him to be one of the last survivors of the planet Crapton, where all of the young people had died of boredom. The other stories continue in the same vein. The selections are short enough to be read in one sitting, but long enough for the characters and plots to be well developed. The pages are nicely formatted with generous white space and clear type. Light reading that is sure to be popular with younger teens and those searching for high-interest, low-vocabulary titles.

Diana Mitchell

SOURCE: A review of *I Love You, I Hate You, Get Lost,* in *The ALAN Review,* Vol. 22, No. 1, Fall, 1994.

This collection of seven short stories focuses on some of the sticky situations and tough questions that adolescents face. Can a teen relationship survive a romantic evening cruise with one bratty little brother in tow? Can best friends become more than best friends and, if so, who admits their feelings first? Does falling for a good-looking person, even one who has none of the same interests, mean the relationship is doomed? How does one begin to get along with a future stepsister? Are there ways to cope with a teacher who seems to hate you? These fast-paced, mostly humorous stories will delight middle-schoolers who are in the throes of the agony of growing up. Although some characters do seem a little too perfect to be believable, they do help create the acceptance that the characters seek. Through this collection, middle-schoolers can see that teens actually survive embarrassing, humiliating, and uncomfortable experiences and that in retrospect there is often something funny involved in these painful times.

GET THE PICTURE, JENNY ARCHER? (1994)

Joyce Richards

SOURCE: A review of *Get the Picture, Jenny Archer?,* in *School Library Journal,* Vol. 40, No. 12, December, 1994, pp. 72-3.

Gr 2-4—When Jenny Archer's grandparents give her their old camera, she begins to look at things in a new light. She decides to enter a photo contest, but has trouble coming up with an appropriate, exciting subject. When she does, her attempts at candid shots cause her to misinterpret her subjects' actions and remarks, creating complications and strife throughout the neighborhood. The black-and-white drawings add to the overall simplicity of the plot in this easy-to-read, beginning chapter book. As in other titles about Jenny, her naiveté and vivid imagination get her into predictable scrapes, and she is dependent on her irrepressible charm to pull her through.

Hazel Rochman

SOURCE: A review of *Get the Picture, Jenny Archer?*, in *Booklist,* Vol. 91, No. 7, December 1, 1994, p. 680.

Gr. 2-4. In Conford's latest light chapter book about Jenny Archer, Jenny gets a camera. In search of "candid" photographs for a magazine contest, she uncovers what she thinks are deep, dark secrets. She imagines that one neighbor is trying to kill a dog, that another neighbor has stolen a car. In fact, the circumstances turn out to be far more mundane. The book ends abruptly—clearly more episodes are on the way—but there's a welcome realism in that the beginner photographer creates not a masterpiece, but a mess.

Kirkus Reviews

SOURCE: A review of *Get the Picture, Jenny Archer?* in *Kirkus Reviews,* Vol. 63, December 15, 1994, p. 1560.

Jenny Archer (***Can Do, Jenny Archer***, 1991, etc.) is disappointed when her grandfather's ballyhooed surprise for her turns out to be nothing but a used camera. When she sees an ad for a photography contest in *Kid Talk* magazine, however, she decides to give the camera a try. Her first roll is a disaster, but she reads the instruction booklet and tries again, looking for the perfect "candid" shot for the contest. She takes a picture of what she thinks is a neighbor, Mrs. Katz, strangling her dog, Kiss-Kiss, and almost takes one of a plastic-covered car in neighbor Mr. Munch's driveway. Imagining that Kiss-Kiss is in danger and Mr. Munch is a car thief, Jenny writes anonymous letters of warning. The neighbors storm Jenny's house in a rage: Mrs. Katz accuses her of libel and demands the incriminating picture—which actually

shows, not Mrs. Katz strangling Kiss-Kiss, but a large tear in the seat of Mrs. Katz's pants. Mr. Munch tells how Jenny spoiled his surprise birthday present for Mrs. Munch. Jenny apologizes, her parents give her a lecture on jumping to conclusions—she had also thought her mother was having a baby because of a baby-naming book she saw in the garbage—and there the story thankfully ends. Convoluted and dull.

A NIGHT TO REMEMBER (1995)

Publishers Weekly

SOURCE: A review of *A Night to Remember,* in *Publishers Weekly,* Vol. 242, No. 22, May 29, 1995, p. 86.

There's nothing quite like a high school prom—at least if the authors of the four short stories here are to be believed. In Ellen Conford's slapstick **"Social Studies."** two brainy guys set out to win prom dates by studying the methods of the most popular guy in school. Jane McFann's "Three Strikes and a Foul Ball" chronicles the romantic misadventures of a baseball-crazy tomboy whose mother and best friend corral her into seeking a date for the dreaded dance event. A school gossip columnist in "Frankenstein" by Ellen Leroe "imaginates" a dashing guy named Lance Lindsey—only to be saved from the embarrassment of full exposure by the 11th-hour appearance of a Lance impersonator. These three entries are more or less shaggy dog tales; Jean Thesman's "Something Better," however, more than lives up to the romantic promise of the book's dreamy peachy-pink embossed cover. Thanks to a cast of sweetly appealing characters and perceptive writing, the well-worn plot (a girl's gradual realization that the pesky boy-next-door is more than just a loyal pal) seems fresh and new. Despite its flaws, the collection's slick packaging (free rose tattoos are included with every volume) and popular subject matter are likely to please its intended audience. Ages 12-up.

MY SISTER THE WITCH (1996)

Gale W. Sherman

SOURCE: A review of *My Sister the Witch,* in *School Library Journal,* Vol. 42, No. 6, June, 1996, p. 120.

Gr 3-5—Convinced that his older sister is practicing witchcraft, fourth-grade Norman is sure he's doomed. In the end it turns out that Elaine was really just learning the witches' scene from *Macbeth* for an audition. Conford's zippy story, with plenty of action and tension, has great potential if readers aren't initially turned off by the book's layout. The short sentences and large type are suitable for reluctant readers, but are negatively countered by the tiny margins and cramped text. The cover art will surely attract "Goosebumps" (Scholastic) fans, but the interior pencil drawings are mediocre and static. This is the second title in the series, and readers who get past the format will eagerly await the next entry.

THE FROG PRINCESS OF PELHAM (1997)

Ilene Cooper

SOURCE: A review of *The Frog Princess of Pelham,* in *Booklist,* Vol. 93, No. 14, March 15, 1997, p. 1241.

Gr. 5-7. "The Frog Prince" is a fairy tale that has been fractured more than once. This time Conford gives it a go for middle-grade audiences. Chandler, a wealthy orphan, lives with her cousin. He doesn't care about her, and her friends may just like her for her swimming pool. Her cousin goes off to Europe believing Chandler will be at survival camp, but there's a change in plan after Danny, the school's prince of popularity, kisses her on a bet and turns her into a frog. Most of the fun comes from Conford's signature witty dialogue and the nod to pop culture as Chandler tries to solve her problem by going on a TV talk show. But the story gets silly at the end (enter the government) and also lacks internal logic. There is no real justification for Chandler's turning into a frog, and certainly no reason for why or when she changes back. Best not look at this too closely; just enjoy the funnier moments.

Publishers Weekly

SOURCE: A review of *The Frog Princess of Pelham,* in *Publishers Weekly,* Vol. 244, No. 12, March 24, 1997, p. 84.

The conflicts Chandler endures with her compassionless guardian are small compared to the problems that she is about to face: kissed on a bet by Danny Malone, the wealthy but lonely orphan turns into a frog. Kept in an aquarium by Danny, who is more than a little unnerved by the incident, Chandler adapts to amphibian life while her "keeper" tries to think up

a scheme to turn her back into a 15-year-old girl. Conford's (the "Jenny Archer" series) modernized twist on the frog prince's tale offers some interesting and playful observations from a frog's-eye point of view, but the author's intent remains muddy. There seems to be no rhyme or reason for Chandler's metamorphosis. Her return to a "normal" state occurs spontaneously when she instinctively sheds her skin, not through any special discovery; although the experience spurs some positive changes (including being awarded a new guardian), it is questionable how much insight the heroine has gained. Her renewed trust in friends who were worried about her disappearance feels contrived, and readers are left to wonder if her relationship with Danny ever blossoms into romance. While some readers will enjoy the fanciful elements of the story, others, disturbed by inconsistencies, may wish Conford had gone a little further with her premise. Ages 10-up.

CRUSH (1998)

Publishers Weekly

SOURCE: A review of *Crush,* in *Publishers Weekly,* Vol. 244, No. 49, December 1, 1997, p. 54.

In this collection of featherweight but pleasurable romances, Conford (*I Love You, I Hate You, Get Lost*) composes 10 variations on a common theme: getting a date for the Valentine dance, dubbed the "Sweetheart Stomp" by the "social big-wigs" at Cutter's Forge High. Story one, a type of overture, introduces the main players: B. J. Green thinks she has no hope of snagging a beau; Linda Sherman, a budding con artist, thinks she has bamboozled nice Will Moffet ("He dropped forty IQ points whenever she was around," thinks a disgusted B. J.); heart-throb Diane Callahan "uses up boys like Kleenex"; Alexei Grigorov, the Russian exchange student, conveniently forgets his English when misinterpretation proves advantageous. As in her previous works, Conford shows vitality and a keen wit. Tangled situations end up neatly tied into love knots; arrangements that seem all sewn up, however, can just as easily unravel. The more commendable characters win enviable rewards, while the connivers (namely, Linda and "Princess Di" Callahan) receive gratifying comeuppances. Affectionately wrought and cunningly overlapped, these selections are as inviting a choice for Valentine's Day as a candy sampler. Ages 12-up.

Alison Follos

SOURCE: A review of *Crush,* in *School Library Journal,* Vol. 44, No. 1, January, 1998, p. 111.

Gr 5-8—A cast of high school friends links together these 10 mini-romances. The stories follow separate couples as they prepare for and fret over the upcoming Valentine's Day dance. The scene at the "Sweetheart Stomp" is the final story. The stories strive to capture genuine teen voices but come off sounding strained and artificial. The characters are one-dimensional, and their nicknames, such as "Lady Di," "Bugbear," and "Batso," make them appear ludicrous. A few stories have creative touches, but most of them are just too silly. **"The Gifts of the Mangy"** is a take-off on O'Henry's "Gift of the Magi." Amy has spent years getting over her nail-biting habit. Finally, she has grown glorious long, painted, and manicured nails. They are her pride and joy, but her boyfriend, "Batso," hates them. She dislikes his long hair. Meeting before the Valentine's dance, they present each other with six-month anniversary gifts: a manicure set for her, a hair dryer for him. They've compromised, they've sacrificed, yet this story remains a pallid rendition of the original tale. Managing to hit a decent stride, **"Lucky Break"** tells the story of two nonconformists who are attracted to one another because of their differences. It has a plot, interesting characters, and a romantic conclusion. All in all, though, these mini-stories are not worth the money, reading time, or shelf space.

Shelle Rosenfeld

SOURCE: A review of *Crush,* in *Booklist,* Vol. 94, Nos. 9-10, January 1, 1998, p. 794.

Gr 7-12. In a timely collection of interrelated stories about teenagers and love, Conford focuses on a group of high-school students as a big Valentine's Day dance approaches. Addressing such issues as peer pressure, self-esteem, respect, alienation, greed, and heartbreak, the clever stories, which center on several different characters, show how much self-image can differ from outward appearance and reputation. From **"Call Waiting,"** a slapstick view of the result of putting people off by putting them "on hold," to the fairy tale-like **"Lucky Break,"** in which a student's accident leads to potential love, the stories are told with Conford's signature compassion and wit. Teens will find them pleasant, easy reading, as well as a clear demonstration that people aren't always what they seem.

Mary M. Burns

SOURCE: A review of *Crush,* in *The Horn Book Magazine,* Vol. 74, No. 2, March/April, 1998, p. 220.

Ten short stories—eight if the first and last are considered prologue and epilogue—focus on the trials and triumphs of selected students in Room 202 as they hope to celebrate Valentine's Day at the "Sweetheart Stomp." Some, like happy couple Amy and Batso, are assured of dates; others, like B. J. and Doug, can only hope. And then there is Laurel Barker, whose evening is ruined by a freak accident—or is it? Some protagonists tell their own tales; other stories are presented from the perspective of a sympathetic onlooker; all are short, easy on the mind and eye. Variants of familiar scenarios—O. Henry's "Gift of the Magi" recycled as **"The Gifts of the Mangy,"** for instance—are comfortable allusions given an updated twist. Frothy, light entertainment. How about a malt?

Kristin Ramsdell

SOURCE: A review of *Crush,* in *Library Journal,* Vol. 124, No. 3, February 15, 1999, p. 139.

Reprinted and newly packaged for Valentine's Day, Conford's delightful collection of stories linked by a high school Valentine's Day dance is just the thing to set young girls dreaming of all the Valentine's Days to come—or to remind the rest of us of what those high school dances—and romances—were really like! Light, romantic, and filled with Conford's classic wit and humor. Also a popular YA author, Conford lives in Great Neck, NY.

ANNABEL THE ACTRESS STARRING IN GORILLA MY DREAMS (1999)

Publishers Weekly

SOURCE: A review of *Annabel the Actress Starring in Gorilla My Dreams,* in *Publishers Weekly,* Vol. 246, No. 25, June 21, 1999, p. 68.

Conford's (the "Jenny Archer" series) fast-paced and funny first installment of a chapter-book series introduces an appealing thespian, Annabel, whose first paid job requires her to play a gorilla for a children's birthday party. In addition to Annabel, who wants "to be a movie star someday. Or at least a soap opera star," the boisterous cast includes Maggie, Annabel's resourceful friend and budding costume designer, and Lowell, Annabel's arch enemy who nearly closes her run as a gorilla before her debut. Andriani's (*Really, Really Bad School Jokes*) well-chosen comic scenes show Annabel getting into character by pretending to pick fleas out of her father's "fur" while he works on his computer and desperately trying to avoid dropping the birthday cake while being assaulted by her adoring five-year old "fans." In Annabel, Conford has created a persistent heroine smart and capable enough to overcome her small size and makeshift costume. This rising star will likely be a crowd pleaser for this and future performances. Ages 7-9.

Helen Rosenberg

SOURCE: A review of *Annabel the Actress Starring in Gorilla My Dreams*, in *Booklist*, Vol. 95, No. 21, July, 1999, p. 1945.

Gr. 1-3. The creator of Jenny Archer introduces another lovable character, Annabel, an aspiring actress. After placing an ad in the paper ("No part too big or small"), Annabel gets a request to play a gorilla at a child's birthday party. Figuring the job will be good practice, she accepts, and pieces together a costume from an old raincoat lining. On the day of the party, however, her costume falls apart and her neighbor steals her mask, leaving Annabel to rely solely on her acting talent to pull off the show. Annabel's ingenuity and spunk will delight young chapter-book readers, and Renee Andriani's humorous black-and-white drawings are a nice bonus. Perfect for children ready to go beyond the Amelia Bedelia stories.

📖 *DIARY OF A MONSTER'S SON* (1999)

Susan Dove Lempke

SOURCE: A review of *Diary of a Monster's Son*, in *Booklist*, Vol. 95, No. 21, July, 1999, p. 1946.

Gr. 2-4. Kids sometimes have the feeling that their dad is a monster, but Bradley's really is. In diary entries, Bradley describes his outings with his dad—for example, a shopping trip for new school clothing during which the sales clerks are very accommodating. He always writes with admiration and innocence. When he describes his friend Amanda's meeting his dad, he concludes, "She is probably surprised that he is so tall" when her eyes get big. The constant blend of the mundane with the monstrous makes for a fun story, especially when it's infused with tenderness between the father and son. The narrative is highly episodic, lacking a beginning, middle, and end, but children reading early chapter books will be accustomed to this style from their easy readers. Tom Newsom contributes an appealing jacket painting, and the excellent pencil drawings that illustrate the story display his gift for capturing a range of facial expressions. Children are sure to beg for a sequel.

📖 *ANNABEL THE ACTRESS STARRING IN JUST A LITTLE EXTRA* (2000)

Catherine Andronik

SOURCE: A review of *Annabel the Actress Starring in Just a Little Extra*, in *Booklist*, Vol. 97, No. 2, September 15, 2000, p. 239.

Gr. 2-4. The wanna-be actress introduced in **Annabel the Actress Starring in Gorilla My Dreams** (1999) is back with a real chance at stardom. A scary television movie is being shot in Westfield, and a convincing fainting spell on the set lands Annabel a part as a screaming extra in a crowd scene. Although she's disappointed by her performance, she's thrilled to see what a talented director did with her "failure" when the film airs. Chapter book readers will enjoy the fast pace, self-contained chapters (called "scenes"), moviemaking references, and funny dialogue. They'll also like audacious Annabel herself. Line drawings by Renee W. Andriani reflect the humor of the story, focusing on its irrepressible star. Conford captures the daydream of every child with acting aspirations.

Additional coverage of Conford's life and career is contained in the following sources published by the Gale Group: *Authors and Artists for Young Adults,* Vol. 10; *Contemporary Authors,* Vols. 33-36R; *Contemporary Authors New Revision Series,* Vols. 13, 29, 54; *Junior DISCovering Authors; Major Authors and Illustrators for Children and Young Adults; The St. James Guide to Young Adult Writers;* **and** *Something about the Author,* Vols. 6, 68, 110.

Kady MacDonald Denton
1942-

Canadian illustrator and author.

Major works include *Granny Is a Darling* (1988), *The Story of Little Quack* (1990), *The Travelling Musicians of Bremen* (1991), *Jenny and Bob* (1991), *The Umbrella Party* (1998).

INTRODUCTION

Kady MacDonald Denton—dubbed a "watercolorist extraordinaire" by *Emergency Librarian* magazine—creates striking visual images that help project the wonders of a small child's world. Through her own books and her illustrations for others' works, Denton is known for capturing the many moods of preschoolers. At the same time, her books address the realities—some pleasant, some not—faced by a growing child: sibling rivalry, night fears, and even the discovery of death, which is delicately handled in the picture book *Jenny and Bob*.

BIOGRAPHICAL INFORMATION

Canada's Kady MacDonald Denton was born in the big city of Winnipeg in 1942 but has made her home in the prairies of Brandon, Manitoba, for many years. The daughter of a military commander and his wife, Denton once said she developed a "lifelong habit" of drawing and painting as a child. She became an award-winning illustrator, although Denton insists that while growing up her brother and sister were "very talented [and] a lot better than me." Nevertheless, Denton developed her talent, graduating in 1963 from the University of Toronto with a Bachelor's in Fine Arts. As she held doubts about an actual career in art, however, Denton enrolled in the University's architecture program, which granted her a graduate degree in city planning. "I really enjoyed the theoretical side of town planning," she noted, and worked in the field for ten years. By 1977, married and starting her own family, Denton moved back to Manitoba. She dabbled in art while sampling a variety of other careers; a sabbatical to England in 1983 became the turning point. While taking an illustration course at London's Chelsea School of Art, Denton met Pam

Zinnemann-Hope, another mother of a preschooler. Examining the books available for the under-five set, Denton and Zinnemann-Hope agreed that "we could do this. They can't be that hard. Let's have a go at it." Back home in Canada a few months later, Denton got a letter from Pam describing a publisher's enthusiastic response to a sample book the two had put together. Thus the "Ned" series was created, with Zinnemann-Hope doing the writing and Denton painting the pictures. Denton's development from illustrator to author-illustrator came at the urging of her publisher, Walker Books, and her agent. "I was quite innocent about the whole thing," Denton recalled. "It quickly dawned on me that [writing] was a very difficult field to work in, but, by this time, I was in it and having so much fun I thought, 'What does it matter? I'll have a good time. I'll do the best I can,' and so it's continued." When not writing and illustrating books, Denton teaches art in the community schools of southwestern Manitoba.

MAJOR WORKS

Denton is a busy illustrator for other authors as well as a writer. One of her most notable entries is her illustrations of P. K. Page's adaptation of *The Travelling Musicians of Bremen,* published in 1991, which retells the story of rejected farm animals who dream of a new life in music. According to *CM Magazine,* Page and Denton made a compelling team: "Seldom do you find an author and illustrator so perfectly attuned to each other's artistic intent." David Millward provided the words in *Jenny and Bob,* in which two small children confront everyday occurrences, from Jenny's temper tantrum to Bob's discovery of a dead bird. The latter story, *CM* noted, "is handled well with the children first denying that the bird is dead, followed by tears and then the burial of the bird with a final tea party."

In *Realms of Gold,* author Ann Pilling draws on numerous cultures to tell folktales in a volume "copiously—and deftly—illustrated by Denton, whose spot art and larger illustrations display an intriguing amalgam of styles," said *Publishers Weekly.* For prereaders, *Toes Are to Tickle,* text by Shen Roddie, presents a little girl and her baby brother who categorize everything they see: "Morning is for waking up . . . boxes are to see what's in them . . . a purse is to empty . . . a cat is to love." Combining the silly with the heartfelt, Roddie and Denton, said *Booklist,* "evoke the toddler's world in all its tumbling, laughter, hugs and messy comfort." In 1998 Denton illustrated *The Umbrella Party* by Janet Lund. This read-to-me story centers on little Christie, whose birthday party is nearing. She wants but one kind of gift—umbrellas—which are her passion. Her bemused friends oblige with umbrellas of all colors and sizes, which save the day when an unexpected rainstorm threatens the festivities.

Denton wrote and illustrated *The Story of Little Quack,* a much-loved pet of lonely farm boy Jackie. When the duck disappears one day, Jackie grieves. A reunion takes place some weeks later, when Little Quack—now grown up—returns to the farm with her brood of ten baby "quacklings," introducing Jackie to the circle of life. *Granny Is a Darling* serves as a bedtime tale to ease the common fear of nighttime monsters. All the family looks forward to Granny's visit, especially little Billy, who confides to her his fear of the dark. With Granny bunking down in his room, Billy learns one way to confront his fear: by imitating her intimidating, monster-scaring "snnnoooorrr."

Denton explored another childhood phenomenon in *Would They Love A Lion?* This 1995 work finds preschooler Anna awakening from a dream of being a bird. Dreamtime extends into playtime as Anna considers the pros and cons of turning into different animals. The story's subtext revolves around a new baby in the house, which is monopolizing the attention of Anna's mother and older sister. To the child's mind, becoming an animal may draw their attentions back toward her. But what creature will get the best response? "No one notices a bear," she states. "You can't cuddle a dinosaur." Finally, she decides, "Yes, they'd all love a lion." "It is up to the reader to draw the connection between Anna's game and the presence of a newborn," commented *Publishers Weekly,* "but those who miss the point are left with a fully satisfying story nonetheless."

AWARDS

Denton has received three significant awards: the Amelia Frances Howard-Gibbon Illustration Award, 1990, for *'Till All the Stars Have Fallen*; Mr. Christie Book Award, 1991, for *The Story of Little Quack*; and the Governor General's Award for Illustration, 1998, for *A Child's Treasury of Nursery Rhymes.*

GENERAL COMMENTARY

Dave Jenkinson

SOURCE: "Portraits: Kady MacDonald Denton—Watercolorist Extraordinaire," in *Emergency Librarian,* Vol. 21, No. 5, May-June, 1994, pp. 61-64.

While Brandon, Manitoba—a very small city in the Canadian Prairies—is the home of author-illustrator Kady MacDonald Denton, her work is published not just in English in North America, but in many different languages around the world. Kady's route to publication was most serendipitous. A war baby, Kady was born in Manitoba's capital city on July 22, 1942. "At the time, my dad was commander of the military base at Shilo and was training his men to go overseas with the Royal Canadian Engineers. My mother was the only woman in 10,000 men, and she found it a bit awkward. Anyway, she moved from the base to Winnipeg, where I was born. Then, when I was a couple of months old, my dad went overseas, and we moved to Toronto.

"Everyone in the family drew and painted all the time. Both my sister and brother are very talented, though neither makes a living using their art, but they're both very good, a lot better than me. I always liked drawing and drew all the time when I was very young. I remember when, as a child, I visited other people's homes, it struck me as odd that they didn't have art supplies, papier-mâché, little pots of paint, just a general sea of muck and things around. Drawing and painting every day was just something that I did, and it's become a lifelong habit."

Quite naturally, Kady pursued her art interests in university, graduating in 1963 with a Bachelor of Fine Arts from the University of Toronto. "The program's focus was the history of art, which meant some archaeology, general histories and some understanding of Italian and German as well as research into the art of each particular period. At the time, there was just a single studio course each year, related to historical technique. It was a very demanding four years but enormous fun."

With the degree completed, Kady faced career questions. "It had honestly never dawned on me that I would have to earn a living or do something with my life. I had done quite a lot of theater design work while I was at university, summer stock and work around the campus and some Toronto theater work. I thought it would be a lovely career, but not one I could maintain easily. For one thing, it was grueling work, and it paid next to nothing. I was also a little tired of being in basements or filthy cold warehouses. I thought I'd take a short break and do something else and then perhaps go back to the theater or my artwork." Kady's choice was to go "into the graduate program at the U. of T.'s School of Architecture, which led to a professional degree in city and regional planning. I really enjoyed the theoretical side of town planning and the engineering aspects. I worked as a planner for about 10 years."

Kady returned to Manitoba in 1977, when her husband, Trevor, became chair of the Department of Anthropology at the University of Brandon. "When we moved, it was going to be for two years, and we're still here. The universities stopped hiring people, and that glorious golden time of shifting around ended. I'm not sorry at all, except that we picked a tiny house and then we had another child. Bit by bit, I've taken over the whole house for my work. Art wasn't something I made money from until about 10 years ago. I did paint, and I did have a few art exhibits in Toronto, but there wasn't a plan to it at all. It was something I enjoyed doing.

"I've had a variety of careers which have been fascinating and intriguing, but there definitely was again another turn when we were on sabbatical in England in 1983. I took an illustration course at London's Chelsea School of Art. I met Pam Zinnemann-Hope in the class, and we both had daughters who were beginning to read. They teach them at about four in England."

Looking at the books available for this age group, the two mothers thought, "We could do this. They can't be that hard. Let's have a go at it." And it was great fun that year to work out the concept of the Ned books in class and then at each other's homes.

"I returned to Canada, and a couple of months later I got a lovely letter from Pam, written in green ink, that said, 'I chatted to Walker Books, and they think they're wonderful,' and the letter had all these stars and exclamation marks. I didn't really know that meant publication. I phoned her and told her, 'Find us an agent.' She found one, and the four Ned books were published. At the time, I was not working full-time, and the illustrating fitted in well. It was work I

could do at home, and it was 'transportable' work. Because I had stopped jobs at different times as we moved, I thought, 'I've licked it now. I've got work I can take with me anywhere.' Of course, I've never moved since!"

The transition from illustrator to author-illustrator came about because "Walker Books asked if I had any ideas of my own. It didn't occur to me that I couldn't write a children's book. 'Yes, of course,' I said. 'I'd be delighted to.' And then I had to do it. It's like beginning anything new. You assume it's quite possible. Others have done it. It can't be immensely difficult. At least I always assume that, and then to my horror find out halfway through that it's not the case and it's not easy to make a speech or to prepare this body of information or whatever it is I have to do. But I never enter thinking it is that way. Our agent was very helpful in encouraging me to continue working. She just would say, 'Kady, you send me your ideas, and I'll see what I can do for you.' And so I did. I was quite innocent about the whole thing. It quickly dawned on me that it was a very difficult field to work in, but, by this time, I was in it and having so much fun I thought, 'What does it matter? I'll have a good time. I'll do the best I can,' and so it's continued." Kady explains that her story ideas "would not usually come out of family events, but would spring first from a general idea that I'm thinking about, something very current and perhaps not related to children's books at all. It will be a more general idea that I'm puzzling over, and something that doesn't have particular form, even. For example, the story I'm working on now, *Would you love a lion?,* took a long time to write. I was intrigued by how sometimes people seem very different in different settings. I was puzzling over that idea, but I didn't have words and I didn't have pictures. It was just almost a scent in the air. And then it occurred to me that we all have characteristics that shift as we vary our environment, and that it happens quite literally with the young. I remembered how my own children and other children will stick a hat on their heads and tear through a room, screaming, 'I'm an elephant!' And they are. But to chase down words and pictures to go with that idea took me a ludicrously long period of time.

So, often a book begins as a scent of an idea, and then the pictures and words may leap easily to the front, or I will have to work and chase them. Most often, for me, the idea blooms first into one or several key pictures which become illustrations. I'm continually being reminded by my editors that a strong story depends on a rich strong text, and they're quite right, so I will work on that before turning back to develop the pictures. With a young children's book, it's a question of just 40 or 100 words. I can't think what would happen if I had to handle several hundred or thousand words."

The characters in *Janet's Ponies,* a delightful story about a little girl who plays in the house with two "ponies," are rooted in Kady's natal family. "This story was based on something that happened to me when I was a child, and seeing it happening in contemporary homes jogged my memory. My older sister was terrified when I said, 'Janet, I'm writing a story about those things you used to make us do.' She was on tenterhooks until the book was published, and it was quite delicious tormenting her for a year. My brother was the other horse."

Until *Til All the Stars Have Fallen: Canadian poems for children,* all the books that Kady had illustrated were short, simple stories. With *Stars,* she was confronted with a text consisting of more than six dozen poems. "I worried that *Stars* might not hang together, and I restricted the materials that I was using to just a few: watercolor, collage and stencil work with watercolor and acrylic and lots of ink work. It would have been easy to have spread across the illustration spectrum a little more. Each of these poems is so unique, and the poets are so different. My response was quite different in each case, but I think I reined it in pretty well. The stencil work is holding some sort of continuity in the book." The quality of the book's illustrations was recognized with Kady's being awarded the 1990 Amelia Frances Howard-Gibbon Illustrator's Award by the Canadian Association of Children's Librarians.

"In *Stars,* the relationship of text to illustration was my decision. I love it when a manuscript comes in a raw state and I get to set up the pacing of the book. I made tiny dummies of the groups of poems with pencils and watercolor pencils. I took the little dummies with me to Toronto for a general discussion, and things didn't shift much from that. Michael Solomon, the designer, and I met then for the first time. His design instincts are fantastic, and it was fun to bounce ideas back and forth with him. To me, some poems seemed to go together naturally and others didn't. Some seemed to need a whole page. They didn't seem to want to fit with anything else. So that was my placement and my arrangement."

The next year, 1991, Kady received the Mr. Christie's Book Award for the illustrations in *The Story of Little Quack.* The watercolors in this book are particularly bright and alive. Kady explains, "A good watercolor can be intensely vivid and very, very dark. I'm trying to get my own watercolors darker still. It's difficult because you can spoil a watercolor so quickly and easily that the temptation is to stop when it's alright; however, what's beautiful is to continue and go darker and darker and richer and richer. But it's such a difficult medium and so much can be lost so easily. That's why watercolor work tends to be a little light and pale. It's safer."

After *Stars* and among other work, Kady illustrated three additional long books: *Before I Go to Sleep,* a collection of Bible stories, poems and prayers for children; *Realms of Gold,* 14 myths and legends from around the world; and *The Kingfisher Children's Bible,* a retelling of 62 Old Testament and 32 New Testament stories. "Those long books took a lot out of me, each of them. I wouldn't have missed doing any of them. I loved doing them, but I'm glad I'm doing some shorter ones now because it's hard to work with top concentration and under pressure for a relatively long period of time. After a while, the energy thins a little, and that's not good for the book.

"On a normal workday, I start early in the morning because I'm fresh and the light is good. I don't work in the early afternoon. I find that's a time when I make mistakes, and so I will do other things that need to get done. Late afternoon and evening are good work times for me, too. And if I'm getting close to a deadline, or, even if I'm not, but I'm thick into a book, I will tend to work quite late at night and begin early and ride the book through, catching up on everything else days or weeks later. Even if I could, I don't usually finish an illustration in the evening. I'll leave it and check it for consistency in the morning light. Work that doesn't look so good at night sometimes looks fabulous in the morning and vice versa. I don't know why that is. I never send work off as soon as it's done. It always sits around for a little while, and I'll take another look at it."

The Kingfisher Children's Bible contains some 300 illustrations, which range in size from small decorative introductions for stories to illustrations that occupy most of a page. "It was physically demanding, but what a book to work on! It was a challenge." Always the perfectionist, Kady says, "I'm happy with almost all of it. There are about four or five illustrations I would like to have gone back to, but the time ran out.

"With the *Children's Bible,* there was a suggested layout for the illustrations that came for the first few pages, but I changed it and suggested we work with columns, since the script was in columns. The publishers liked that idea. I remember the exhilaration I felt one cold and snowy day when I was alone in the house and I cut, pasted and laid out the whole first section of the text, and realized that my idea of working in columns was going to work."

In illustrating a book, Kady usually adopts a linear approach. "I start at the beginning and work through, but, if the work takes a shift in the process, for example, if the character has suddenly changed and come to life in some way, or, if I've tried a combination of colors that I feel is much better for the book, I'll continue that way and go back and fit the early illustrations into that new decision. I'm not easily satisfied with my work. I get very impatient and try to make it richer and stronger and closer to what I have in my mind."

Because today's publishers are most conscious of foreign sales possibilities, illustrators must keep in mind details that may not be familiar or common to other locales. "Occasionally there will be questions about something I've put in that no one else recognizes. An example of what I mean would be the night light in *Granny Is a Darling.* The French did not know what this was and asked for it to be taken out. I said, 'Look, it's a yellow blob in the middle of the page, and I can't really take it out. It's lying there under layers of washes. Let's just let the kids imagine what this might be,' and so it slipped through. I have to be careful about not making food look North American. No sandwiches. They eat sandwiches elsewhere, I'm sure, but I guess they don't look the same."

While Kady is illustrating more of her own work, she still receives manuscripts that she must decide whether or not to illustrate. The basis for her decision may be as simple as, "I can't do that. I don't feel I'm right for the story, and I'll say 'No.' Sometimes I might not be right for it, but I like it so much I want to have a whack at it anyway, and so I'll say, 'Yes.' Sometimes it's a question of time, but mostly it's simply a feeling that I can't bring something to the story. Nothing flashes into my mind, and there's no visual response in me with the story."

Being an illustrator also requires doing research. "I need to get better at showing all the research I have done. I eliminate so much. Research might mean something as basic as going and looking at a donkey before drawing the donkey for *The Travelling Musicians.* You'd think that I could have just put it

down, but I couldn't. I had to go and sketch a donkey many times and take a few photographs and study the photographs. The impact of research may just come through in the choice of a color. In *Realms of Gold,* the book of myths and legends, I knew that the choice of colors for each story was very important, and so I had to search the context of the story to be able to choose the palette I was working with.

"With *Realms,* I was a bit worried about roaming into areas that are not my own cultural environment, and then I thought, 'I'll dig in, learn the context and then I will respond.' And so I did, and I stopped worrying. I respected the cultures that I was working in and sought to have one or two ideas, lines, ways of working colors that would bring the power of that culture across."

In addition to her careers as writer and illustrator, Kady also does some teaching of art in her community at the Art Gallery of Southwestern Manitoba. "I don't do a lot anymore. It's just the occasional class, and it's only a few hours a week. I've done some introductory classes for adults and all sorts of classes for teens and young children. I like the teaching because it's a very useful way of focusing my own ideas. I'm forced to explain or demonstrate things. For years I had a Saturday children's art class. The same kids came back year after year, and they have all done terribly well. I told the parents it was because they put them into art class early, and I'm convinced that's true. That's why it's important to have artists-in-the-schools programs. I always liked working with the children because they approached the page with no trepidation at all. I loved to see that, and I'd always go home and work more confidently after that.

"I'm working now on *Would they love a lion?,* which will be published next year. Then I go on to something I've never done before, a couple of toddler books for very young children under four. Again I thought, 'Of course I can do it.' Now everyone is telling me something special's involved. I'll have to look into this and see just what they mean. I don't remember seeing things so differently as a little child. When I was young, I was intrigued by very complex pictures, art, paintings and illustration work. I don't remember being given baby things. I'm sure it can't be true, but, to get it right, I'll have to do a little bit of work with some very young children and check out their response to different pages to see if there is a response to brighter colors or thicker lines or simplified pictures.

"The toddler books will keep me going for a while. I have some manuscripts out being looked at and some story ideas in the computer I'm trying to chase down. Happily there seems to be no end of work in this field, and, in these days, that's wonderful. It's a very exciting time for children's books. Think of what is lugged home from the library these days: wonderful books from all over to read in bed or under a tree on a hot summer day! But the time a book has in a book-store or on the market seems shorter than surely it was 20 or 30 years ago. We seem to need so much new. Perhaps part of it comes from the technical advances in the publishing field. The books look so beautiful now, and a publisher wants to have a current, bright contemporary look to a book to make it sell. I mean, I'm cutting off my income here to say it, but I'm happy when I see old classics on the shelves. Lots of old classics, not just the six everyone knows like *Goodnight moon,* which is a joy, but there are others as rich that I would want to see continue. This is why it's important that there be good libraries and children's literature roundtables and book centers and such—that structure—to support the superb publishers we have in Canada and to publicize work, past and present. We need to get the best to children! I guess I'm just saying that there are excellent children's book enterprises in Canada, and I hope, for all of us, this can continue."

TITLE COMMENTARY

📖 THE "NED" SERIES (1987-88)

Diane Roback

SOURCE: A review of *Time for Bed, Ned* and *Let's Go Shopping, Ned,* in *Publishers Weekly,* Vol. 231, January 16, 1987, pp. 72-3.

Parents of toddlers who have outgrown their board books may pounce on this sunny pair of titles. Hope's minimalist dialogue is reminiscent of Dick and Jane but much livelier: "I don't like shopping. I like hopping. Come on, Fred. Hop, hop, hop!" "Ned! Stop!" (This last from a disgruntled father, trying to find a sweater for his boisterous lad.) Ned neatly delays going to bed in one book; in the other he resists a red sweater to the very last, settling on blue for himself and his dog, Fred. Denton's cheeky watercolors give these books a pell-mell pace and turn Ned's mayhem into good-natured mischief. (4-7)

Booklist

SOURCE: A review of *Let's Go Shopping, Ned* and *Time for Bed, Ned,* by Pam Zinnemann-Hope, in *Booklist,* Vol. 83, No. 12, February 15, 1987, p. 906.

Ages 5-7. These two brief picture books have limited vocabularies and a strong sense of fun, making them welcome choices for children just beginning to read. Their protagonist is a little boy who is prone to mischief. In *Let's Go Shopping, Ned* would rather hop than shop for a new sweater. Dad goes anyway with boy and dog Fred in tow. When the trip is over, both Ned and Fred are wearing sweaters and Father is looking quite frazzled. *Time for Bed* has Ned doing his level best to avoid going to bed; his mother prevails, of course, and after a pleasantly splashy bath, Ned is tucked in and kissed good night. Loosely composed, freewheeling watercolors cheerily illustrate both stories.

Nancy Palmer

SOURCE: A review of *Let's Go Shopping, Ned* and *Time for Bed, Ned,* in *School Library Journal,* Vol. 33, May 1987, p. 120.

PreS-Gr 1—A redhead named Ned leads his parents on a merry chase in two small, cheerful titles. In . . . *Shopping,* Ned and his dad try to buy a new sweater. Ned and his dog Fred would rather hop than shop, and Dad is in for a wild afternoon. There's more text, and more careening action in this romp with Ned; kids will laugh out loud at Fred running away with one arm of the sweater while Ned hangs on for dear life to the other end. The same style animates *Time for Bed,* in which Ned repeatedly eludes his mother's grasp as she tries to corral him for bath and bed. Ned cries "No! No! No!" as he gleefully runs away, crawling under the doghouse and diving into the laundry basket, but his closing line is a happy "Good night, Mom." Only 23 different large print words tell the story, and only a few of those appear on each page. Ned's good-natured bolt for freedom is told largely through the bright pencil and watercolor illustrations, which show breezily simple figures full of personality and action. Their style is charmingly out of the ordinary, combining a streamlined economy of line with abstract washes that still manage to convey a wealth of personality. The small, squarish format of these titles marks them for the younger set, although the brief rhymed texts and humor make them ideal for just-beginning readers.

Phillis Wilson

SOURCE: A review of *Find Your Coat, Ned* and *Let's Play Ball, Ned,* in *Booklist,* Vol. 84, No. 21, July, 1988, p. 1843.

Ages 3-6. By the time Ned finds his coat, which is serving as a blanket for his dog, Fred, it has stopped raining, but the search has been half the fun. When Ned and Fred play ball, the peace and quiet are shattered as well as a few other things—until Dad suggests fresh-air fun. In addition to their pleasure as read-alouds, the books' bright watercolors, large type, easy texts, and simple repetitions will have appeal for children just learning to read.

THE PICNIC (1988)

Publishers Weekly

SOURCE: A review of *The Picnic,* in *Publishers Weekly,* Vol. 233, No. 10, March 11, 1988, p. 103.

The illustrator of **Time for Bed, Ned** and **Let's Go Shopping, Ned** returns with a solo effort. Jeremy and Alison want to go for a picnic in the park. But Jeremy's father is too busy, and Alison's mother says "No!" Since the children can't go by themselves, they decide to shrink their parents and take them, too. The four of them have a lovely picnic, and when it's time to go, the children carry their very tired parents home. This is a story children will appreciate for the roles of benevolent power Alison and Jeremy assume over the adults. Denton's pen-and-wash illustrations have an exuberance and delicacy that match the lighthearted tone of the text; in these she carries through the themes of fun and caring. Ages 4-6.

Zena Sutherland

SOURCE: A review of *The Picnic,* in *Bulletin of the Center for Children's Books,* Vol. 41, No. 10, June, 1988, p. 202.

3-5 yrs. Line and wash drawings (clean composition, colors that are both soft and bright, some humor but little grace) illustrate a brief story about two children who, having been told by their respective parents that they can't go on a picnic, solve their problem in a novel way. With a quick shift to fantasy, the parents are washed until they shrink to doll size; a pleasant picnic is enjoyed by all, and after it "Jeremy's father grew tall right away. But Alison's mother decided to

stay small a little while longer." This quirky ending provides the one bit of humor in a simply written but not very substantial story with a concept that may appeal to children.

GRANNY IS A DARLING (1988)

Publishers Weekly

SOURCE: A review of *Granny Is a Darling,* in *Publishers Weekly,* Vol. 234, No. 9, August 26, 1988, p. 87.

A visit from Granny is something Billy eagerly anticipates; she'll sleep in his room. He debates whether or not he should let her know about the dark things that come into his room at night, and decides not to. It's just as well, for when Granny sleeps soundly, she snores, and that's just the noise which makes the scary things back off. Billy even lets out a couple of snores himself, just to finish the job, and his darkened room becomes a safe place. Denton, who illustrated Pam Zinnemann-Hope's Ned books, has a smooth narrative style that complements her softy colored pictures. Swirls of shadow and light delineate the scenes of Billy's fears, and Granny, with her hair net on and padding about in a long flowing gown, truly is a dear. Ages 4-8.

Ilene Cooper

SOURCE: A review of *Granny Is a Darling,* in *Booklist,* Vol. 85, No. 2, September 15, 1988, p. 157.

Ages 3-5. In this charming British import, little Billy is anxiously awaiting his grandmother's visit—everyone says Granny is a darling. But Billy is worried; his grandmother will sleep in his room and she doesn't know that monsters come and go there. Determined to protect her when the wild things arrive, Billy jumps out of his bed, at the ready. Noticing that the monsters seem put off by Granny's snoring, Billy starts making the same noises. Sure enough, the creatures flee in fear, and Billy knows he won't be having monster problems again. The story has a warm, affectionate feel, nicely capturing the devoted relationship between grandmother and grandson. Wispy artwork executed in pale pastels show both style and tenderness.

Patricia Fry

SOURCE: A review of *Granny Is a Darling* in *CM Magazine,* Vol. 17, No. 1, January, 1989.

There are all kinds of ways to overcome night-time fears. In **Granny Is a Darling,** written and illustrated by Kady MacDonald Denton, Granny inadvertently provides her young grandson with a special way to banish spooky creatures from his room.

All members of the family look forward to Granny's visit, but Billy, who shares his bedroom with her, especially looks forward to Granny's visit. It soon becomes obvious that Billy, like many young children, is afraid of the dark. His no-nonsense granny assures him that she'll go right to sleep and that's exactly what she does. Of course, this means that Billy is the only one awake to face the dangers that lurk in the darkness.

Billy's terror mounts as the monsters multiply and he hears a threatening noise that sounds like this: "SSSNNNORRR." As he tiptoes over to protect his sleeping granny, he notices that the sound is coming from her mouth. The monsters notice, too, and immediately they begin to fade away. A snore or two from the now fearless Billy finishes them completely.

The next night, when his grandma has returned home and Billy is alone in his bedroom once more, he uses the snoring trick to take control of his fears. It works. He falls asleep right away!

This book is beautifully illustrated with pastel watercolours on every page. The pictures appear blurred at the edges, giving a soft effect to this gentle story. This book is a short read—less than five minutes to read aloud—and, for that reason, will appeal to parents who are looking for a quick bedtime story.

Bessie Egan

SOURCE: A review of *Granny Is a Darling,* in *School Library Journal* Vol. 35, No. 6, February, 1989, p. 69.

A picture book with a refreshing story line. Billy, who's afraid of the dark, shares his room with his grandmother when she comes to visit and discovers that saving his grandmother from a mysterious sound (which turns out to be his grandmother's snoring) is more important than his personal fears. The text is a combination of dialogue and narrative; full-page watercolor and pen drawings sustain the mood of the story. Children who have shared Billy's fears will find reassurance in this family-oriented picture book, which is reminiscent of Stevenson's *What's Under My Bed* (Greenwillow, 1983).

Sarah Ellis

SOURCE: A review of *Granny Is a Darling,* in *The Horn Book Magazine,* Vol. 67, No. 1, January-February, 1991, p. 109.

Soft, Ardizzone-like watercolors and a pared-down text tell the story of Billy's visiting Granny, who shares Billy's room and whose snores give Billy an idea about how to drive away the lurking nighttime creatures. This original treatment of the familiar night-monster theme succeeds through simplicity. In the muted pictures the monsters, vaguely animal-like, are suggested rather than defined. And the words are straightforward: "Something at the window was very VERY dark. By the door, what was that? In the wardrobe, what was that!" The words and pictures allow the child listener plenty of room for imaginative participation.

The whole book exudes comfort and warmth. The opening pictures are enclosed by delicate frames as Billy is surrounded by his loving, somewhat old-fashioned family, smiles all around. A few understated nursery colors lie cleanly against a white page. As night approaches, with its "scary things," the frames disappear, and shadows, creatures, and darkness impinge on all sides. The background becomes filled with mysterious shapes in gray and blue. The type swirls across the page. But when Billy, brandishing his granny's pink umbrella and imitating her loud snores, drives the monsters away, the frames reappear. The words retreat to their proper place. Smiles creep back, including the barest hint of a smiling moon. The book ends with a beautifully composed, oval-framed portrait of Billy bidding goodbye to his departing granny.

DOROTHY'S DREAM (1989)

Marianne Pilla

SOURCE: A review of *Dorothy's Dream,* in *School Library Journal* Vol. 35, No. 16, December, 1989, pp. 77-8.

PreS—A bedtime picture book with a message that dreams can be so alluring that they can convince any reluctant child to fall asleep. "What will we do with Dorothy?" her parents and siblings wonder when Dorothy won't go to bed. She sings, looks at books, and jumps on her bed, afraid that she'll miss something if she nods off. But one night, her usually "small, pale dreams" are suddenly lightened by one dream which shines. The desire to see more of it lures her to sleep the next night, to the amazement of her family. While the idea is novel, the narration is awkward. The text is choppy, with poor transitions. The light, whimsical watercolors improve the story, but do not redeem it. The cozy, realistic, pastel drawings of the family are offset by the eerie, rust-colored settings of the "cold, sour dreams" which then move into a fanciful full-paged spread. But the magical dreams portrayed cannot make up for this lackluster tale.

'TIL ALL THE STARS HAVE FALLEN: CANADIAN POEMS FOR CHILDREN (1990)

Fran Newman

SOURCE: A review of *'Til All the Stars Have Fallen: Canadian Poems for Children,* in *CM Magazine,* Vol. 18, No. 2, March, 1990.

This truly is a book for all ages. When I went into my local bookstore recently, the owner asked me if I had seen the "beautiful new Canadian poetry book." I hadn't, but as soon as I flipped through the pages, I knew I had to purchase it for my own collection. The review copy in the mail elicited a comment of "Oh, good!"

I have had time to use this book with several classes in the school. Each time I open it, I am excited by the range of poetry found inside and the very lovely full-colour illustrations. The American and British publishers send out this kind of poetry anthology quite often, but Canadian ones have been rare. Kids Can Press is to be commended.

David Booth, who apparently sifted through several thousand poems in order to come up with this selection, is also to be congratulated. I would like to quote from his words in the introduction: "Poets are wordsmiths, spending their lives choosing, bending, shaping, teasing, playing with words. The sounds of language fascinate them so. Poets write words that make your ears sing."

Together, the editors at Kids Can Press, David Booth and Kady MacDonald Denton have produced the vehicle to enable us all to celebrate the poets of our

land. If you buy no other book this year for your library or your home, please find the money to purchase this one.

THE CHRISTMAS BOOT (1990)

School Library Journal

SOURCE: A review of *The Christmas Boot,* in *School Library Journal,* Vol. 36, No. 10, October, 1990, p. 35.

PreS-Gr 1—Just after Christmas, Jeremy and Alison find an adult's black boot in a tree. When presents keep falling from the boot, the two determine that it is a magic one: "'Who do we know with big winter boots and lots of presents?'" Preschoolers are sure to chime in with "SANTA CLAUS!" when this one is read aloud. In a nice piece of child logic, the children know that what comes down must go up so they send it back up the chimney. Watercolor illustrations with thin black line, resembling those of Edward Ardizzone, follow the actions of the children and help the youngest readers keep track of this merry little story.

BEFORE I GO TO SLEEP: BIBLE STORIES, POEMS, AND PRAYERS FOR CHILDREN (1990)

Publishers Weekly

SOURCE: A review of *Before I Go to Sleep: Bible Stories, Poems, and Prayers for Children,* in *Publishers Weekly,* Vol. 237, No. 43, October 26, 1990, p. 66.

In this 96-page collection, 21 familiar stories from the Old and New Testaments are presented in language that is simple without being condescending— Daniel slays Goliath, the infant Moses is rescued from the river, the wise men seek the newborn Jesus. Interspersed among these graceful retellings are poems and prayers by well-known authors both religious (St. Ignatius Loyola, St. Francis of Assisi) and secular (William Blake, Christina Rossetti). In content and style, Denton's soft, spare watercolors are a perfect accompaniment: they manage to be suitably childlike while also conveying a sophisticated flavor that is nicely attuned to each subject. Whether bright and frolicsome for Ruth Sawyer's exuberant yuletide catalogue, "Christmas Morn" or washed with greys for Dietrich Bonhoeffer's "A Prayer for Fellow Prisoners," her paintings bring a warmth and individuality to this attractively packaged book. All ages.

📖 *THE STORY OF LITTLE QUACK* (1991)

Martha Topol

SOURCE: A review of *The Story of Little Quack*, in *School Library Journal*, Vol. 37, No. 5, May, 1991, p. 78.

PreS—There are no cloudy skies in this book, although a young boy almost loses his best friend, Little Quack. But it turns out that Little Quack was just off having some "quacklings" and all ends happily. Lonely Jackie is surrounded by animals—Buck the pony; Buttercup, a clumsy calf; Woof the dog; and others—but they're all too busy to play with him. Thus, his parents give him a pet duck. The two roam the pastures and explore the barn where everyone is having babies—until Little Quack disappears. When Jackie finds his missing friend, he carries her 10 offspring in his floppy hat back to the barn where an old tub is filled with water and the 12 of them splash about, dispelling all thoughts of loneliness. The loose watercolor and ink drawings perfectly complement the story, giving credence to this unusual friendship and adding a dimension of sweet simplicity. The mutual affection between the characters shines through, as does the serenity of Jackie's existence. The young story hour crowd is sure to love this sunny depiction of farm life.

Diane Roback and Richard Donahue

SOURCE: A reveiw of *The Story of Little Quack*, in *Publishers Weekly*, Vol. 238, No. 16, April 5, 1991, p. 145.

In Gibson's first picture book, a lonely boy named Jackie lives on a farm where there are plenty of animals, none of which has any interest in playing with him. When Jackie's mother buys him a pet duck, the two become fast friends, and the boy is very sad when Little Quack disappears. She turns up at a nearby pond, but then takes off again. Many weeks pass before Jackie finds her again—swimming in a brook with her 10 little "quacklings." The duck family returns home with Jackie, who will never be lonely again. This is a pleasant if somewhat prosaic story, competently illustrated with Denton's (*The*

Picnic; *Before I Go to Sleep*) gentle watercolors. Though the book is not particularly distinctive, preschoolers may enjoy identifying the many barnyard animals in Jackie's farm. Ages 4-8.

📖 *JENNY AND BOB* (1991)

Kirkus Reviews

SOURCE: A review of *Jenny and Bob*, in *Kirkus Reviews*, Vol. LIX, No. 17, September 1, 1991, p. 1168.

Three exquisitely simple preschool dramas: **"Angry Jenny"** frightens the cat, breaks her doll, is sent to bed to cry and then makes amends all around; she and friend Bob find a **"Poor Bird"**—not sleeping, they agree, but dead—and honor it with burial and a special guard, including dolls and an interested cat; a **"Rainy Day"** finds the two happily involved in imaginative play in a puddle. Denton's perceptive illustrations are as economical as the text; her small people are unusually gentle and beguiling, yet without sentimentality. Perfect for lap or toddler group. (*Picture book. 2-6*)

Lorrie Ann Clark

SOURCE: A review of *Jenny and Bob*, in *CM Magazine*, Vol. 19, No. 5, October, 1991.

Three separate and distinct stories entitled "Angry Jenny," "Poor Bird" and "Rainy Day" evolve around two main characters, Jenny and Bob, whose names also happen to form the title of this children's book.

The stories of the two small children are about everyday occurrences such as a temper tantrum (Jenny), finding a dead bird (Bob), and the joy of playing in the rain.

Through the simple text and softly coloured pictures, the mood of each story is cleverly sustained. The subject of death is handled well with the children first denying that the bird is dead, followed by tears and then the burial of the bird with a final tea party.

The short stories, simple text and beautiful illustrations would appeal to young children's imaginations as they deal with the reality of a child's world. A cautionary note: the British "macs" is used for raincoats. One should not dismiss the book for this reason, however, as it wonderfully captures the many charms of childhood.

Kay Weisman

SOURCE: A review of *Jenny and Bob*, in *Booklist*, Vol. 88, No. 7, December 1, 1991, p. 705.

Ages 2-5. This trio of tales, presented in picture-book format with scant text, touches upon three experiences of early childhood. **"Angry Jenny"** is mad at the world, but most especially at her cat, her doll, and her mother. After being sent to her room (for kicking the cat and her mother and for breaking her doll), Jenny calms down and is able to apologize to everyone. In **"Poor Bird,"** Jenny and her brother, Bob, find and bury a dead bird. Although adults may suspect otherwise, the children are convinced that Cat will "guard" the bird, now that it has been laid to rest. Finally, the pair don slickers and boots on a **"Rainy Day"** and have a wonderful time splashing in the puddles. Jenny and Bob display a wide range of emotions, and Denton captures them all in her bright watercolor illustrations. The paintings exhibit an appealing warmth and include many interesting details, yet never appear cluttered. A perfect choice for the toddler story hour, this will be welcomed by very young listeners just beginning to sit still for a real story.

THE TRAVELLING MUSICIANS OF BREMEN (1991)

Maryleah Otto

SOURCE: A review of *The Travelling Musicians of Bremen*, in *CM Magazine*, Vol. 19, No. 6, November, 1991.

No more delightful retelling of "The Brementown Musicians" could be imagined than P. K. Page's rollicking version of this ever-popular folk-tale. The text is a combination of prose and poetry and the songs of the four hapless countryside animals who have been condemned by their masters and have teamed up to leave home for what Donkey blithely believes will be a glittering career in the music world of the city. In 1983 the Victoria Symphony asked Page to adapt this story for a performance and thus the idea for a children's book was born.

The familiar tale is now set in the twentieth century. The farmer has no more use for his faithful old donkey because his new red truck is more efficient. Modern vehicles are seen on the highway. Skyscrapers and telephone lines indicate the distant city. The rob-

bers are children in punk rock hairdos, baseball caps, sunglasses and vintage clothes. Their loot includes TVs and VCRs.

Both P. K. Page and Kady MacDonald Denton, the illustrator, are no strangers to prestigious awards. They deserve high praise for their work on this book. Seldom do you find an author and illustrator so perfectly attuned to each other's artistic intent. Page introduces the "rag-taggle cat" with the "hang-dog look" and Denton shows us exactly such a creature. Donkey, fat, dumpy and irresistibly lovable, dances lightly on his hind legs while dreamily playing a make-believe flute on a small leafy twig. He praises Cat's "dulcible voice" and promises her she'll play the glockenspiel if only she'll join the band. Rooster, whose joints are "stiff as an iron weathervane," and Dog, whose "pedigree is impeccable," make up this "great great partnership" jovially singing their way to an unknown fate with an infectious sense of fun. And their song may just go platinum!

> Hee haw Hee haw
> Bow wow wow
> Mee ow Mee ow
> Doodle doodle doo
> Hee Bow How Wow
> Mee Doo Arf Bow Wee
> Mow Eee Dow
> Boodle Moo
> Hee Boo
> Bee Mee Doo

The endpapers, done in light blue and grey on white, are a joy. They show a panoramic view of town and country with the four heroes in the foreground plodding along the road.

Congratulations to Page, Denton and Kids Can Press for bringing an unrivalled treat to the children of the 1990s. The Grimm brothers would have approved.

Publishers Weekly

SOURCE: A review of *The Travelling Musicians of Bremen*, in *Publishers Weekly*, Vol. 239, No. 7, February 3, 1992, pp. 80-1.

In a sometimes meandering, intermittently rhyming narrative, [P. K.] Page retells the Brothers Grimm tale about four animals who set out to make a new life for themselves after their masters reject them. More sophisticated than Hans Wilhelm's interpretation, Page's account introduces a number of words (obsolete, dulcible, despondent) that may prove difficult for many children. Denton's whimsical, somewhat fuzzy drawings also seem better geared to the older reader than are Wilhelm's more traditional pictures. Her setting, for example, is up-to-the-minute contemporary; she depicts the robbers as a stylish group, sporting campy hats and hairstyles. The prose is skillfully crafted, with clever rhythms and deft use of repetition. Despite its shortcomings for the younger set, this rendition presents well-matched text and artwork that aptly deliver the buffoonery of this classic caper. Ages 4-8.

Carolyn Phelan

SOURCE: A review of *The Travelling Musicians of Bremen,* in *Booklist,* Vol. 88, No. 16, April 15, 1992, pp. 1533-34.

Ages 5-8. Page adapts the traditional story to a more modern setting, in which the donkey is obsolete because the farmer has bought a big red truck. Playing with language (Dog states, "My pedigree is impeccable, my past performance perfect") and slipping in and out of rhyme, the colorful text embroiders the tale a bit without violating its sense or spirit. Denton's lively ink drawings with watercolor washes interpret the text with grace and wit.

Susan Scheps

SOURCE: A review of *The Travelling Musicians of Bremen,* in *School Library Journal,* Vol. 38, No. 5, May, 1992, pp. 105-06.

PreS-Gr 4—A modernized retelling that retains the essence of the Grimms' story. Page's use of contemporary conversation filled with colloquialisms, sound effects, and an occasional couplet or quatrain adds to the child appeal; the lightness of style exhibited in the text is mirrored in the whimsical watercolor-and-ink illustrations that flow throughout, taking readers along on the merry escapade. The robbers, who bear a strong resemblance to Burningham characters, appear as school children dressed in outlandish teen costumes (suspenders, oversize shirts, western gear, knee-high boots, punk hairdos) on an illicit outing to a deserted farmhouse. The robber captain is a girl. The loot consists of TV sets, a stereo, gold coins, and costume jewelry; the feast is desserts and fruit. Here is a folktale to be thoroughly enjoyed by readers of all ages. The embellishments of the text make it an engaging read-aloud, and its significant difference from other versions makes it a worthwhile purchase.

REALMS OF GOLD: MYTHS AND LEGENDS FROM AROUND THE WORLD (1993)

Kirkus Reviews

SOURCE: A review of *Realms of Gold: Myths and Legends from around the World,* in *Kirkus Reviews,* Vol. LXI, No. 7, April 1, 1993, p. 462.

An excellent introduction to mythology, with 14 graceful retellings—pourquoi tales like the opener, a West African legend explaining why the Earth Mother's children are so many different colors; stories of love and tragedy (Persephone, the willow pattern story); legendary heroes and fools (Midas, Finn Mac-Cool, Perseus). The brevity of the selections (even Balder's story, with its complex cast of characters, takes just eight pages), large, open type, and profuse illustrations (pen-and-ink with watercolor, marginal vignettes to full-page) make these versions especially suitable for children in the early grades. Many of the colors and design motifs are adapted from the cultures that originated the tales (Greek vase designs, Chinese brush painting, African textiles, Pacific Island carvings). An attractive volume for pleasure reading as well as classroom use.

Publishers Weekly

SOURCE: A review of *Realms of Gold: Myths and Legends from around the World,* in *Publishers Weekly,* Vol. 240, No. 16, April 19, 1993, p. 62.

Pilling draws from the folklore of numerous cultures in this eclectic if ultimately uneven collection. Featuring classic themes of love, greed, jealousy and the battle between good and evil, the 14 entries are of varying length and complexity, making it difficult to pinpoint the appropriate audience. Divided into three categories ("**Earth, Air, Fire, and Water,**" "**Love and Death**" and "**Fools and Heroes**"), the tales range from the succinctly told "**Iyadola's Babies,**" an endearing West African myth that offers an explanation why babies are born with various skin colors; to the labyrinthine "**The Death of Balder,**" a relatively lengthy Norse legend that will be slow-going for most youngsters. Among the volume's best offerings are a lively retelling of the Greek myth "**King Midas**" and "**The Wishing Fish,**" an entertaining Russian story about a magical fish who teaches a lesson to an avaricious woman. The volume is copiously—and deftly—illustrated by Denton, whose spot art and larger illustrations display an intriguing amalgam of styles reflective of the tales' countries of origin. Ages 5-up.

Kathryn Jennings

SOURCE: A review of *Realms of Gold: Myths and Legends from around the World,* in *The Bulletin of the Center for Children's Books,* Vol. 46, No. 11, July-August, 1993, p. 356.

The fourteen stories in this collection are loosely categorized into three sections—**"Earth, Air, Fire and Water," "Love and Death,"** and **"Fools and Heroes."** The tales come from cultures as diverse as West Africa, the Pacific, Norway, and China; also included are three more familiar tales from Greece (**"Persephone," "King Midas,"** and **"How Perseus Killed the Gorgon"**). Although some of the myths typically lack a cohesive plot, the unfamiliar gods and simple style are an appealing combination (". . . and here on Earth we know that Ga-oh the giant is having a happy day"). Occasionally there is an awkward phrase (". . . and he loved Llewellyn's baby son like a mother"). The watercolor and ink illustrations make for lively half-page and borders around a large-print, open text. Although there are no source notes, this is an attractive book with enough variety of content to add to any collection of folktales.

Julie Corsaro

SOURCE: A review of *Realms of Gold: Myths and Legends from around the World,* in *Booklist,* Vol. 89, No. 22, August, 1993, p. 2056.

Gr. 4-6. This wonderful collection includes not only "myths and legends from around the world" but also folktales and fables. Pilling's succinct prose is both eloquent and homey in 14 stories ranging from the humorous west African creation myth **"Iyadola's Babies"** ("I hope you're behaving yourselves, here on earth. I made it you know. I expect you to look after it") to the poignant Welsh legend **"Bedd Gelert."** The appeal is broad, with tales about fools—among them, King Midas and the giant Bennadonner—particularly enchanting for younger children, while older children will best appreciate the heroic adventures of Balder and Perseus. The spacious format has large print set against crisp white space and copious wash-and-line drawings. The illustrations re-

flect a range of cultures with delicate yet sprightly lines, sturdy forms, and a diverse palette. A most welcome offering for storytelling and reading aloud.

WOULD THEY LOVE A LION? (1995)

Publishers Weekly

SOURCE: A review of *Would They Love a Lion?* in *Publishers Weekly,* Vol. 242, No. 17, April 24, 1995, p. 70.

Denton (*Granny Is a Darling, Realms of Gold*) brings an abundance of charm to a familiar scenario, a child pretending to be each in a series of animals. After dreaming of being a bird, Anna decides, "I could be a bird. . . . I could be." So she "flaps her wings," conveyed in the illustration as the girl leaping before the mirror, arms propelling a vast, wing-shaped expanse of bathrobe. She then assumes, in turn, the guises of a bear, elephant, dinosaur and rabbit—effects also achieved by Denton's clever draping of Anna's bathrobe. Throughout, Anna's mother and an older sibling are seen tending an infant; in her final disguise, as a lion, the girl approaches them and lets out a huge roar, which captures everyone's attention. It is up to the reader to draw the connection between Anna's game and the presence of a newborn, but those who miss the point are left with a fully satisfying story nonetheless. And Denton's whimsical pictures—handsomely reproduced on heavy, textured paper afford plenty of child-centered fun. Ages 2-5.

Claudia Cooper

SOURCE: A review of *Would They Love a Lion?,* in *School Library Journal,* Vol. 41, No. 7, July, 1995, pp. 55, 61.

PreS-Gr 1—A reversible plaid bathrobe transforms imaginative Anna into a bird, bear, elephant, dinosaur, rabbit, and finally a lion, wreaking havoc on her family in the process. "Would they love a lion?" Oh, yes . . . especially when it settles down for a nap! Large, full-color cartoons delightfully capture the fanciful preschooler's antics. The terrorized reactions and subsequent mistrust of the family dog and cat are especially charming. The large format is appropriate for group sharing while the simple, sparse text is ideal for beginning readers.

Susan Dove Lempke

SOURCE: A review of *Would They Love a Lion?*, in *Bulletin of the Center for Children's Books,* Vol. 48, No. 11, July-August, 1995, p. 381.

With the aid of her reversible red plaid bathrobe, Anna transforms herself into animals both fierce and mild. Anna, who looks about four, dreams she is a bird, and after waking up, she flaps her bathrobe wings and turns her bed into a nest. When the nest seems too small, she creates a bear cave, but when her mother (holding a small baby) and big brother don't seem to notice at breakfast that they are sitting with a red plaid bear, she goes for something bigger and noisier. Denton's pictures flow from softly realistic to purely impressionistic and everything in between as she captures the spirit of a day of imaginary play, combining watercolors, crayon, and pen-and-ink to accomplish this variety. The climax is a glorious one, as Anna decides "a lion can hide and a lion can roar," sneaks up on her peaceful family, and on the next double-page spread shatters their quiet with an enormous roar, depicted with black-ink sound waves exploding through the room and jagged streaks of color shooting out. Booklovers will especially appreciate the high quality of the book itself, its thick and pebbly paper conveying some of the cozy texture of Anna's wonderful bathrobe.

Stephanie Zvirin

SOURCE: A review of *Would They Love a Lion?*, in *Booklist,* Vol. 91, No. 22, August, 1995, p. 1955.

Ages 3-5. Denton's slight but charming picture book will remind children a bit of Rosemary Wells' stories about lovable, impish Max. Anna's desire to be noticed, to be something special—a rabbit, a bear, a dinosaur, a growly lion—is typically childlike, as are her imaginative, comedic endeavors to use her beloved bathrobe to effect the change. Her goofy antics are delightfully portrayed in the freewheeling, colorful pictures, which capture Anna's undisguised elation at disturbing the status quo.

Judith Saltman

SOURCE: A review of *Would They Love a Lion?* in *Resource Links,* Vol. 1, No. 1, October, 1995.

Kady MacDonald Denton's picture books—such as **Dorothy's Dream**—often touch on the inner imaginative life of the preschooler. In this new work for the preschool audience, she explores the multiple, shifting states of a young child's experience of dream, make-believe, fantasy and awakening. In this, her seventeenth book, Denton matches a simple text with elegant, charming illustrations. Preschooler Anna awakens after a dream of being a bird. What follows is a day-long fantasy as Anna imagines being various animals. But the animal must be just right to be loved by a mother shown in the illustrations to be preoccupied with a baby. So, each animal has limitations: "No one notices a bear," "You can't cuddle a dinosaur," "A rabbit is too quiet," and finally, in a satisfying resolution, "Yes, they'd all love a lion." The illustrations expand on the text, dramatizing Anna's play-acting with her voluminous bathrobe that transforms whimsically into animal shapes. The images quietly address Anna's need to draw her mother's attentions away from the baby. Denton's usual British-style illustrations in her pen-and-ink and wash style are reminiscent of Edward Ardizzone's book art. They are energetic, colourful and spirited, more colourful and tactile than Denton's usual delicate style. Vibrant crayon and pastel tones are given texture by the rich, thick paper. A warm, comforting story that integrates themes of child fantasy life and sibling jealousy with tenderness and joy. Thematic links include: imagination—fiction; babies—fiction.

📖 *TOES ARE TO TICKLE* (1997)

Anne Louise Mahoney

SOURCE: *Quill & Quire* Vol. 63, No. 5, May, 1997, p. 44.

Toes Are to Tickle is a sweet new picture book for babies and toddlers that follows the rhythm of the child's day—from waking up and eating breakfast to saying goodnight. Shen Roddie's text highlights things, animals, and people that have an important place in a young child's world: "a mirror is for making faces," "flowers are to smell," and "boxes are to see what's in them." Each statement is made from the perspective of a little person curious about the world and determined to find out as much as possible about it.

Adding humour, warmth, and pure joy to the text are Kady MacDonald Denton's lovely illustrations, which capture the energy and wonder that young children bring to even the most ordinary activity, such as chasing birds or pushing a stroller. Think of Helen Oxenbury's books for babies, add brighter colours and more detailed backgrounds, and you've got an idea of the look and feel of *Toes Are to Tickle.* The two main characters—a boy about a year old and a girl of about three—are a delight. Their love for life and affection for one another leap off the pages as they chase, play games, and share meals together. Two parents appear on some pages but the children are in the spotlight on every page.

Colourful yet realistic, detailed yet simple, these watercolour illustrations are sure to appeal to a young audience. Kady MacDonald Denton has captured the joy of childhood—even the book's endpapers are fun to look at.

Publishers Weekly

SOURCE: A review of *Toes Are to Tickle,* in *Publishers Weekly,* Vol. 244, No. 21, May 26, 1997, p. 84.

A series of child's definitions for everyday objects and concepts fuels [Shen] Roddie's (*Mrs. Wolf*) often disarming book. Loosely arranged around a day in the life of a girl and her baby brother, it begins with "Morning is for waking up" and ends with "Mommy is for one more cuddle . . . one more story . . . and kissing good night." The examples are all apt, and some are sure to elicit giggles ("A purse is to empty," "Peas are for counting"). Unfortunately, the phrasebook structure doesn't support a start-to-finish read-through—as the number of definitions builds, so does a certain monotony. What revives the reader's interest are Denton's (*Would They Love a Lion?*) watercolors. Dominated by cozy tones of orange, the palette balances the impish spirit of the compositions. The size and framing of the illustrations also vary: a spread usually consists of one full-page drawing facing several smaller renderings, and squared-off tableaux alternate with more energetic scenes that float in white space. It proves to be a savvy visual strategy, giving the book a much-needed texture and drive. Ages 2-5.

Theo Heras

SOURCE: A review of *Toes Are to Tickle,* in *Resource Links,* Vol. 2, No. 5, June, 1997.

The ordinary activities that fill the day of very young children are the focus of this new picture book, *Toes Are to Tickle.* The language is spare and declarative:

"Morning is for waking up!" Thus the book begins and on it goes until bedtime. However, the text would have been stronger and better for reading aloud—which is a must with this book—had poetic language been more consistently employed. The alliterative "Toes are to tickle" has a nice bounce and "A seesaw is for feeling funny in the tummy" a nice ring, but "Ducks are to feed" and "Flowers are to smell" are uninspired. The ordinary becomes extraordinary with Kady MacDonald Denton's jump-for-joy illustrations. The featured youngsters, a preschool sister and baby brother are laughing, exuberant, mischievous little darlings, making the most of every moment. The child's sense of wonder in experiencing the world around him/her is keenly and expressively conveyed in Denton's bright and cheery illustrations. The book's overall design is good for its intended audience: it is a good size for a small lap or to share with one or two; it is of an adequate size for preschool groups. The print is large and clear. The illustrations vary in size from two or three vignettes on a page to one activity on a full page. Particularly successful is "A mirror is for making faces" in which Mommy is applying lipstick, sister is making a silly face and baby is admiring himself. Even the cat gets into the act! *Toes Are to Tickle* is an excellent book for families with very young children and will be a popular "story shelf" book for baby, toddler and preschool library programs.

Hazel Rochman

SOURCE: A review of *Toes Are to Tickle,* in *Booklist,* Vol. 93, Nos. 19-20, June 1, 1997, p. 1721.

Ages 1-4. "Boxes are to see what's in them. A purse is to empty. A cat is to love." Small children (and their caregivers) will recognize the definitions in this exuberant, playful picture book about how a girl and her baby brother view everyday things. Lots of joyful, active line-and-watercolor pictures show the family from early morning and through the day until bedtime. On a walk, "A tree is to hide behind. A seesaw is for feeling funny in the tummy." When they eat, "Jell-O is for wobbling. Milk is to give some to the cat." In the style of Margaret Wild and Julie Vivas' *Our Granny* (1994) and Shirley Hughes' Alfie and Rosie books, there's a physicalness in these words and pictures that evokes the toddler's world in all its tumbling, laughter, hugs, and messy comfort.

Pat Mathews

SOURCE: A review of *Toes Are to Tickle,* in *The Bulletin of the Center for Children's Books,* Vol. 51, No. 1, September, 1997, p. 24.

A day in the life of two toddlers, an older sister and her younger brother, provide the backdrop for this concept book. This is pretty to look at, with a cheerful, sunny-hued palette of watercolor and pen, featuring a cartoonish Oxenburyesque family and their pets in kid-friendly situations as the children get dressed (and undressed), visit the park ("A see-saw is for feeling funny in the tummy"), play ("Blankets are for making tents"), eat ("Jell-O is for wobbling"), and go to bed ("Mommy is for one more cuddle"). Although some of the textual patterns seem a little awkward ("Boxes are to see what's in them"), there is enough visual humor to gently enamor most young lapsitters: the bare little backside of the boy at his bath, the children making faces in the mirror, the boy emptying the contents of Mommy's purse. Roddie and Denton have provided youngsters with a happy concoction of fun and warm childhood scenes. This isn't a bad way for the little loves in your life to end the day.

Amelia Kalin

SOURCE: A review of *Toes Are to Tickle,* in *School Library Journal,* Vol. 43, No. 9, September, 1997, p. 192.

PreS—Children will delight in this simple exploration of a pleasant day as seen through the eyes of a preschooler and her baby brother. The sequential progression from waking up in the morning, going to the park as a family, and saying good night with a loving kiss provides the affirmation of routine that toddlers thrive on. As the siblings encounter common objects during the course of the day, the author describes their function ("A mirror is for making faces") and the illustrator playfully depicts the children's actions in breezy, colorful watercolors (Mom applies lipstick in the mirror as the youngsters stick out their tongues). After the first reading or two by their caregivers, toddlers will eagerly turn the pages to "read" their favorite sections aloud.

A CHILD'S TREASURY OF NURSERY RHYMES (1998)

Publishers Weekly

SOURCE: A review of *A Child's Treasury of Nursery Rhymes,* in *Publishers Weekly,* Vol. 245, No. 35, August 31, 1998, p. 74.

Denton (*Would They Love a Lion?*) rounds up the usual suspects, offers a smattering of mostly well-chosen newcomers, and ends up with a winning collection of more than 100 rhymes. The volume is loosely arranged in four parts: rhymes to accompany the knee-dawdling of babyhood, Mother Goose golden oldies for the toddler years, action rhymes for denizens of the schoolyard, and finally, a potpourri for encouraging participation that ranges from riddles to The Owl and the Pussycat. A few of the selections are misplaced (e.g., the jaunty lyrics of "Baby Face" don't jibe rhythmically with the rest of the poems; Robert Burns's "O, my luve is like a red, red rose . . . " isn't likely to capture the attention of youngsters), but the fresh discoveries far outnumber them. The gently rolling rhythm of a Nantucket lullaby evokes foamy waves and elusive whales; a charmer from Ghana soothes a disquieted little one: "Listen to the tree bear / Crying in the night / Crying for his mammy / In the pale moonlight / What will his mammy do / When she hears him cry? / She'll tuck him in a cocoa pod / And sing a lullaby." Arranging Denton's playful vignettes, spot art and full-spread paintings upon clean white pages, the book's crisp layout ensures that the quantity of material never overwhelms readers. Denton's breezy, often impish watercolors (which owe a debt to Sendak's early work) shake the dust off even the most familiar ditties. Ages 3 mos.-5 yrs.

Quill & Quire

SOURCE: A review of *A Child's Treasury of Nursery Rhymes,* in *Quill & Quire,* Vol. 64, No. 9, September, 1998, p. 64.

Dramas in miniature, scripts for soothing a cranky baby, subversive vehicles of protest, found poems, challenges, invitations to dance and song—nursery rhymes are one of the great gifts of the language. In this country we are rich in illustrated nursery rhyme collections. Barbara Reid's *Sing a Song of Mother Goose* with its funny and good-natured Plasticine illustrations has long been one of my standard new baby gifts. Groundwood's *Mother Goose: A Canadian Sampler* has illustrations from a wide variety of our illustrators and shows the huge range both of our artists and of possible interpretations of these small poems. Sandra Carpenter-Davis's modestly produced *Bounce Me, Tickle Me, Hug Me* includes rhymes from a variety of languages and shows by real-life contemporary examples the power of these rhymes to create connections between parents, children, and communities.

Joining this distinguished company is Kady Mac-Donald Denton's *A Child's Treasury of Nursery Rhymes.* My first reaction on hearing of Kady Mac-Donald Denton and nursery rhymes in the same phrase was "Well, of course." Denton's soft-edged watercolour technique, her gift for portraying the grace and solidity of small children, her mastery of composition and, most of all, the non-cloying warmth and sweetness she brings to moments between adults and children—she seems like a Mother Goose natural.

I wasn't disappointed. This 145-poem collection is indeed a treasury. It is big, good value for the poetry dollar. It is innovatively designed. It is varied. And if you can browse through it, encountering its joyous dancing children, its fat men in the bath, and its bash-ful lovers, without smiling, then you are a certifiable grump.

Denton's choice of rhymes seems to reveal the book's real-life origins. Families end up making their own contribution to the nursery rhyme canon. I know one dad who often soothed his too-tired son by dancing him around the room singing "Wake Up, Little Susie." I myself was a hit in kindergarten because of my ability to recite the description from the back of the Crest toothpaste tube. Looking at Denton's illus-tration to "Skip to My Lou," I was happily reminded of a preschool group I once knew who invented their own verses: "Slime on the stereo, yuck-oh-pooh." Advertising jingles, Beatles songs, original nonsense, it all becomes part of the oral stew. And Denton cre-ates her own very original collection by including poetry by Edward Lear, Rose Fyleman, and Robert Burns. She also includes songs and vaudeville turns: "Ladies and Jellypots, I come before you, not behind you." This collection has the flavour of a set of genu-ine individual family choices.

Nursery rhyme collections also present a challenge in terms of arrangement; the trick is not to be bitty. Denton organizes the collection in four parts that are roughly chronological. Baby-dandling rhymes are followed by toddler-interest material with lots of ani-mals, and then by schoolyard rhymes, and finally by "All Join In," which includes games, riddles, and courtship rhymes. There is a wealth of material to take you all through childhood and, in the case of the adult reader, back again.

The design is lively, achieving unity and variety. The ship and whale illustration for the lullaby "Hush the waves are rolling in" is particularly lovely; single rhymes are illustrated on double spreads, groups of rhymes are arranged thematically about a single illus-tration; some rhymes are in boxes; and some rhymes run across the top of the page with accompanying cartoons.

One of the delights of nursery rhymes lies in their portrait of humankind in all its diversity. Denton cap-tures this range delightfully. The neglected lover in "Oh dear, what can the matter be" looks right royally furious. Denton's interpretation of the "old man clothed all in leather" is of a courtly street person, shy and gallant. The baby in "Jerry Hall, he is so small" is a real scrinched-up newborn. Denton cap-tures whole situations in one gesture. The father in "Hush little baby" is holding a baby who is in one of those rigid-arm arched-back fits. Father hasn't a clue what to do. Thus the desperate offer of a diamond ring. In fact, there are a number of portraits of loving but exhausted parents.

Denton never tries to be too clever but occasionally she brings a whole new slant to the story. Her Wee Willie Winkie is a baby who has escaped from his cot and is running through a town of toys and blocks. Her Jack and Jill are Siamese kittens who are over-confident about their climbing abilities. The old woman in a shoe is a mouse.

Sometimes Denton's interpretations are elaborate. "A Apple Pie" includes a cast of animal characters, one for each letter of the alphabet. More often, and I think, more successfully, her "stories" are very simple. "There once were two cats of Kilkenny, Each thought there was one cat too many; So they fought and they fit, And they scratched and they bit, Till in-stead of two cats there weren't any." Denton chooses to illustrate the aftermath of this episode. A small shy boy dressed in an argyle sweater glances sideways into a corner of the road where there is a heap of fur. We are catching him just at the moment when he re-alizes what he is seeing. The illustration is small, in a limited range of colours (but including Denton's sig-nature use of orange) and simply composed, but it contains a whole plot.

"Girls and boys come out to play, The moon is shin-ing bright as day; Come with a whoop, And come with a call. Come with a good will, Or come not at all." Denton has certainly obeyed the summons to play, with good will and a whoop. The call is contagious.

Hazel Rochman

SOURCE: A review of *A Child's Treasury of Nursery Rhymes,* in *Booklist,* Vol. 95, No. 5, November 1, 1998, p. 496.

Ages 1-5. Canadian illustrator Denton's definition of *nursery rhymes* includes not only Mother Goose but also lots of the best folk rhymes from everywhere and even a few classic poems. The combination works perfectly for very young children. Roughly organized into four sections are chants for bouncing babies, songs that follow a toddler's day, playground rhymes and nonsense about school, and, for older kids, sing-alongs, tongue-twisters, riddles, and limericks. Also included is "My Luve Is like a Red Red Rose" (why not chant it to the baby?) and favorites such as "The Owl and the Pussycat." The selections, mainly British, are good to use with other folklore collections, such as Alvin Schwartz's *And the Green Grass Grew All Around* (1992). There is lots of white space on the oversize pages, and Denton's small, dancing watercolors of people and creatures are light and joyful, wild and funny, expressing the mischief, farce, and tenderness of the verses we all love. Share this with parents and caregivers who want to recite what they remember as they play with their kids.

Isobel Lang

SOURCE: A review of *A Child's Treasury of Nursery Rhymes,* in *Resource Links,* Vol. 4, No. 2, December, 1998, pp. 2-3.

The publishing world does not lack for collections of nursery rhymes for children. But it was with a great deal of pleasure that I read Kady McDonald Denton's venture into the fray. The winner of this year's Governor General's award for illustration has provided us with a well-designed and conceived collection of rhymes, songs, tongue twisters, poems, limericks and chants for children. The book is divided into four sections. "Welcome Little Baby" is for babies and includes well-loved rhymes babies will enjoy. The second section is designed for toddlers and celebrates the ordinary events in a toddler's day with things familiar such as eating, playing, etc. This section has many classical Mother Goose rhymes. The third section is devoted to young school children with chants, poetry and nonsense, and the fourth to older children, with popular poems, limericks, and tongue twisters. The illustrations are colourful, lush and full of charm and humour. The top of each sec-

tion displays an illustrated verse, page by page. The baby section parades the verse "Monday's child is fair of face, Tuesday's child is full of grace. . ." There is the obligatory index of titles and first lines at the back. Many of the verses selected are not as well known as those in standard collections. The book serves a double purpose of being a useful collection for the not so common rhymes, songs and chants for reference collections in school and public libraries but, more importantly, it is a wonderful book for families to own and love as a well worn family treasure that brings back cozy memories of being read to at bedtime. A must for those who can spend the money!

Elizabeth Bush

SOURCE: A review of *A Child's Treasury of Nursery Rhymes,* in *Bulletin of the Center for Children's Books,* Vol. 52, No. 5, January, 1999, pp. 164-65.

Denton hosts a joyous reunion of old timers from Mother Goose's clan, a couple of foreign cousins, and some unexpected visitors. Four sections feature beloved ditties honoring babies, toddlers, school newbies, and anyone who loves fun and games; each is chock full of pictures, rhymes, and songs (sans notation), with some riddles, tongue twisters, and limericks tossed in for good measure. Familiars like Georgie Porgie, Little Boy Blue, and the Duke of York rub shoulders with Little Miss Tuckett (Muffett's peaches-and-cream-eating alter ego) and "two little mice" from Spain who "went tripping down the street, / Pum catta-pum chin chin." Lyrics to "Baby Face" snuggle comfortably along side of the slightly melancholy Nantucket lullaby and a rowdy rendition of "She'll Be Coming Round the Mountain" (asides for shouting graciously supplied). There's no pictorial iconoclasm here—the line and watercolor pictures offer literal interpretations of their subjects—but a more expressive, fun-inducing cast of characters (which seem to pay particular homage to Maurice Sendak's little folk) would be hard to spot. Denton turns the travails of the "three little kittens" into a comical melodrama, leaves "baa, baa, black sheep" standing naked and decidedly startled beside a pair of shears, and transforms "Jack and Jill" into impish kittens scaling the sofa to get at the flower vase. Plenty of white space handily absorbs this abundance of energy and ensures that each entry's illustration can be appreciated (and remembered) on its own merits. This has "classic" written all over it; extra copies are the order of the day. An index of titles and first lines is included.

Dave Jenkinson

SOURCE: A review of *A Child's Treasury of Nursery Rhymes,* in *CM Magazine,* Vol. VI, No. 9, January 7, 2000.

> To be asked to illustrate a collection of nursery rhymes and to make the selection made me feel like a kid in a candy store! I began with rhymes that delighted me as a child and have stayed with me through the years. I added rhymes loved by my children and some classic favourites. I found rhymes that were new to me, from as far afield as China, Africa and India: little gems that made me laugh and reminded me that babies cry, parents soothe and children want to play.

Right from the outset, *A Child's Treasury of Nursery Rhymes* shows itself to be an excellent example of fine bookmaking. Kady MacDonald Denton's two-page "Introduction" clearly explains how she collected and then organized the book's selections. "Thus this collection is split into four sections, designed to appeal to children at different stages in their lives." The first section, "Welcome Little Baby," is, naturally, about babies; the second, "Toddler Time," she says, "follows the pattern of a toddler's day . . ." "In the Schoolyard," the third section "reflects the energy of young schoolchildren with playground chants, verses and nonsense pieces" while "All Join In," the closing portion, "is full of things that older children will enjoy, set within the world of an old-fashioned fair."

MacDonald Denton's watercolours are lively and full of action, expressive of emotions and most colourful. Readers can almost feel the soft chubbiness of her multicultural babies in the opening section. Variety abounds in terms of how MacDonald Denton designs her pages. In most instances, she will have several different selections on each pair of facing pages, but, occasionally, she will interrupt this arrangement with a double page spread that deals with a single verse or rhyme. Frequently, the initial letter of a piece is enlarged and boxed to resemble the face of a child's toy block. An interesting feature, which is continued throughout the book, is a portion of a nursery rhyme that is found in the top corners of each page and which carries over a number of pages. MacDonald Denton also brings a freshness to the familiar, and so Jack and Jill become a pair of mischievous kittens climbing over the hill of a sofa to play in the water found in a vase while Old King Cole's fiddlers three include a "she." "A was an apple" is a remarkable

double page spread which invites its readers/listeners to match each of the letters with a creature that is carrying out the action associated with each letter of the alphabet. For example, "S stole it" sees a spider tugging away a web-enmeshed apple. This superb collection closes with an "Index of Titles and First Lines."

A book to be treasured as a well-read family keepsake and one which needs to be included in all libraries serving young children for its contents include the comfortably familiar along with the delightfully novel.

Highly Recommended.

▥ *THE UMBRELLA PARTY* (1998)

Gwyneth Evans

SOURCE: *Quill & Quire* Vol. 64, No. 3, March, 1998, p. 71.

In *The Umbrella Party,* two notable Canadian artists have created an amusing tale of desire and satisfaction. Christie loves umbrellas and when she invites her school friends to her birthday party, she urges them to give her umbrellas for presents. Plotting to cure her of this boring enthusiasm, the friends all agree to do just what she asks and—sure enough— Christie gets eight umbrellas for her birthday, plus a tiny paper one and a giant beach umbrella from her grandfather. The friends consider this a remarkably boring birthday party until they're taken to the beach for a picnic. Christie takes her umbrellas, too. When a great wind begins to blow and a rainstorm ensues, everyone gathers under Christie's umbrellas, which, her friends agree, have their uses after all. . . .

Umbrellas seem a gift of a subject for an illustrator and Kady MacDonald Denton delights in their mushroom shapes and multifarious hues and patterns. Each of the children mentioned in the text is also given a distinctive identity by the illustrator and can be followed from picture to picture. While *The Umbrella Party* doesn't have quite the sense of surprise and rightness that distinguished Lunn's first picture book, *Amos's Sweater,* it has a similar concern with the assertion of one's individuality, and considerable charm in both pictures and text.

Valerie Nielsen

SOURCE: A review of *The Umbrella Party,* in *CM Magazine,* Vol. V, No. 3, October 2, 1998.

Is there anything that a five-year-old likes better than a party? Today's parents are becoming ever more creative when it comes to birthday parties. Theme parties involving popular characters such as pirates, clowns, medieval princesses and Winnie-the-Pooh are greatly favoured by the four-to-eight-year-old set. Just how much input the child has into the planning and execution of these thematic celebrations is not clear. However, in Janet Lunn's new book for the pre-schooler, ***The Umbrella Party,*** there is no doubt about who is responsible for this amazing and unique birthday party. It is Christie, who loves umbrellas ". . . more than anything in the world." Naturally she asks everyone who is invited to her six-year old birthday party to bring her an umbrella, and sure enough, each one of her nine friends brings her an umbrella. Umbrellas of all colours, shapes and sizes soon cram the living room. Christie is delighted, though her friends are secretly bored and wish for their skateboards and trampolines. When Grandfather arrives with a huge beach umbrella, the party takes an exciting turn, and the children head for the beach with all Christie's new umbrellas piled in the car. An unexpected turn of the weather provides the children with the opportunity for an exciting umbrella rescue. Afterwards, Christie sets up her umbrellas ". . . like a bright flowered tent" to shelter the children from the rain as they eat their birthday cake and sing "Happy Birthday."

Author Janet Lunn, recently named a Member of the Order of Canada, is well-known for her historical novels for young adults. Like her award-winning first picture book, *Amos's Sweater,* ***The Umbrella Party*** is written with gentle humour in language which is wonderfully appropriate for young children. Kady MacDonald Denton's mischievous depictions of a group of five-year-olds—how does she manage to get their expressions so exactly right using so few lines?—and her bright, bouncy water-colours, evoke the mood and setting of the story perfectly.

The book is an excellent read-aloud for the pre-school and kindergarten crowd. Lunn's text is disarmingly simple, plentifully laced with the sort of dialogue overheard in kindergarten classrooms. Complemented by Kady MacDonald Denton's clever illustrations, (observant fives will notice with glee that Christie's

bathing suit and shirt both have umbrellas on them!), the story gives us a quiet little lesson on the power of knowing one's own mind.

The Umbrella Party is a must-have for the picture book collections of early childhood education facilities, elementary schools and public libraries.

Highly recommended.

IF I WERE YOUR FATHER AND IF I WERE YOUR MOTHER (1999)

Dawn Amsberry

SOURCE: A review of *If I Were Your Father* and *If I Were Your Mother,* in *School Library Journal,* Vol. 45, No. 5, May, 1999, p. 86.

PreS-K—Playing on every child's fantasy of being a mommy or daddy, these two books show a parent and child engaged in daily activities while the youngster imagines the glorious things he or she would do with the power of parenthood. The boy in ***Father*** pictures taking his son fishing on a school day and hunting for buried treasure as ideal parenting activities, while the girl in ***Mother*** describes the giant tree house and bathtub full of goldfish she would provide for her daughter. The adults are willing accomplices, each playing along with their child's game and even expanding on it. Both books end with the youngster sitting in the parent's lap, content to return to traditional roles. Although the sentences are short and the vocabulary simple, the author laces the text with the kind of poetry that appeals to young minds, describing the stars as "sprinkles on a chocolate ice cream sky." The watercolor illustrations work well with the stories, using bright colors for the imaginary scenes and a softer palette for the ordinary world. Both books would make good read-alouds for storytime, particularly on Mother's Day and Father's Day, and could also be used in classrooms to inspire discussion about what it would be like to be parent for a day.

Publishers Weekly

SOURCE: A review of *If I Were Your Father* and *If I Were Your Mother,* in *Publishers Weekly,* Vol. 246, No. 21, May 24, 1999, p. 77.

In these affectionate companion books, a girl imagines switching places with her mother, and a boy with his father. The children describe whimsical activities like building a tree house with an elevator and hiding so much buried treasure in their pockets that their pants fall down. But most of the children's ideas hint slyly at what their parents don't let them do: "If I were your mother, I'd let you jump from the sofa to the armchair"; "If I were your father, I wouldn't yell if you stood in front of the TV while I was watching a game." The parent and child banter playfully, building on the scenarios in alternating red and blue text to indicate which line of dialogue belongs to which speaker. Bridges reuses the parent-child call-and-response format of her *Will You Take Care of Me?*, but with greater originality and range. The lightness and warmth of Denton's (*A Child's Treasury of Nursery Rhymes*) watercolors complement the softness of the text. Her impish, wide-faced characters may remind readers of more staid versions of Maurice Sendak's (a few of the girls pose and costumes look borrowed). While the mother and daughter are snugglier than their male counterparts (Dad refers to his boy as "buddy" throughout), the girl is the livelier of the two kids; her dancing, swinging and jumping convey terrific energy. Both books revel in the coziness of a loving relationship. Ages 3-up.

Carolyn Phelan

SOURCE: A review of *If I Were Your Father* and *If I Were Your Mother,* in *Booklist,* Vol. 95, No. 22, August, 1999, p. 2064.

Ages 3-5. These cheerful picture books, written in the form of parent-child conversations, suggest how children would run things if they were the parents. In *Father*, a little boy imagines, "If I were your father, I'd let you shave me with whipped cream in the morning," an idea that leads to many more fantasies from the father as well as the son. The imaginary scenes appear on pages with colored backgrounds facing white pages showing the genial pair talking as they engage in everyday activities, such as getting dressed and fixing breakfast. *Mother* begins with a little girl asking, "Mommy, do you ever wish you were a little girl again?" The daughter imagines herself as the grown-up pampering her mother, now a little girl: offering her a red, silky party dress to wear to school, building a giant treehouse for her, and letting her leap from the sofa to the armchair. In both books, the playful banter highlights the love and trust of the parent-child relationship as well as the imaginative play the characters enjoy. Sometimes recalling

the portrayal of children in early Sendak picture books, Denton's line-and-watercolor-wash illustrations will charm preschoolers and parents alike with their warm colors and their fresh depictions of familiar activities and childlike fantasies. A pleasing pair.

I WISHED FOR A UNICORN (2000)

Gillian Engberg

SOURCE: A review of *I Wished for a Unicorn,* in *Booklist,* Vol. 96, No. 16, April 15, 2000, p. 1545.

Ages 4-8. In this bright, good-natured fantasy, a spunky little girl wishes for a unicorn, which magically appears, bearing a strong resemblance to her white dog. The two set off through a primary-colored "magical wood"; cross a dangerous, beast-infested moat; charge a gleaming castle; "zap" a fierce dragon; hunt for gold; and fall asleep from exhaustion, finally waking up under a peaceful moon in the same backyard where it all began, unicorn once again transformed into dog. The sing-song, rhyming text tells a fairly cliched tale, but the pictures will captivate young readers. Lovely gouache paintings extend the action, adding emotional subtleties, magic, and humor to the story. Young ones will giggle at the dog's obvious transformation from pet to adventurous sidekick and delight in the girl's cheerful moxie as she sticks her tongue out at toothy, spotted monsters and extends a gracious hand to adoring knights. Fun for story time.

Catherine Hoyt

SOURCE: A review of *I Wished for a Unicorn,* in *CM Magazine,* Vol. VIII, No. 4, October 20, 2000.

> I wished for a unicorn.
> I wished so hard
> That I found a unicorn
> In my backyard.

So starts the adventure of a bored child who only has to wish some adventure into her life. When her scruffy unicorn arrives with his bone, they set off for a day of glorious adventure. After they storm a castle and defeat a dragon and an evil wizard, they tire themselves out digging for buried treasure. After a nap, the child awakens to find only her dog asleep on the lawn. But that's ok for tomorrow might be another unicorn day.

Kady MacDonald Denton succeeds again with her charming artwork. These pictures are done in crayon-like gouache which captures this magical world of imagination perfectly. The rhyming text trips off the tongue. Luckily this spirited tale arrived just in time for my preschool storytime on dogs. It was a big hit, resulting in lots of giggles and speculations about this barking unicorn.

Highly recommended.

Sharon McNeil

SOURCE: A review of *I Wished for a Unicorn*, in *School Library Journal*, Vol. 46, No. 8, August, 2000, p. 156.

PreS-Gr 2—A child takes a flight of fancy when the family dog is transformed into a thinly disguised unicorn. The ensuing adventure takes the pair into a world filled with castles, monsters, dragons, and wizards. Exhausted, they fall asleep on the ground and awaken to find themselves home on the lawn. The youngster's imaginary romp is portrayed in clever, full-page pastel illustrations rendered in gouache. The picture of a naked evil wizard running away while the "unicorn" modestly covers its eyes is particularly amusing. The sparse, rhyming text works well as a read-aloud. The theme of this inventive story is reminiscent of Rafe Martin's *Will's Mammoth* (Putnam, 1989).

Additional coverage of Denton's life and career is contained in the following sources published by the Gale Group: *Contemporary Authors*, Vol. 134; and *Something about the Author*, Vols. 66, 110.

Dorothy Canfield Fisher
1879-1958

(Born Dorothea Frances Canfield) American novelist, short story writer, educator, historian, and children's writer.

Major works include *The Squirrel Cage* (1912), *Understood Betsy* (1917), *The Brimming Cup* (1921), *The Deepening Stream* (1930), *Vermont Tradition: The Biography of an Outlook on Life* (1953).

INTRODUCTION

Dorothy Canfield Fisher is numbered among the most influential American women of the twentieth century. Her achievements as a fiction writer include a number of realistic novels and short stories principally focused on the lives of middle-class individuals and frequently set in early twentieth-century Vermont. Among these works, Fisher produced what many critics take to be her greatest contribution to American letters, the 1930 novel *The Deepening Stream*. In addition, Fisher is remembered for her efforts as a civic-minded humanitarian and educator. Fisher was the first woman to serve on the Vermont state board of education, she championed the reforestation movement, worked for twenty-five years as an influential member of the Book-of-the-Month Club selection committee, and wrote several esteemed books for children.

BIOGRAPHICAL INFORMATION

Fisher was born in Lawrence, Kansas, to Flavia Camp Canfield, a painter, and James Hulme Canfield, a university professor. During her childhood, Fisher's family traveled extensively. She divided her time between Paris, France, where her mother's art studio was located, and several cities in the American Midwest. Fisher began her college education at the University of Nebraska, where she began her acquaintance with Willa Cather, and completed her undergraduate degree from Ohio State University in 1899. After a period of study at the Sorbonne, Fisher returned to the United States to complete her Ph.D. studies in Romance languages at Columbia University and to prepare her dissertation *Corneille and Ra-*

cine in England (1904). Fisher then embarked upon an academic career and co-wrote a textbook titled *Elementary Composition* (1906) with George R. Carpenter. She began publishing her short stories in several popular magazines, and produced her first novel, *Gunhild*, in 1907. That year she married John R. Fisher and together the two moved to a farm in Arlington, Vermont, which Fisher had inherited from her late grandfather. For the span of her career, Fisher would divide her time between the Arlington farm and Europe. A trip to Italy culminated in a book on education, *A Montessori Mother* (1912). Fisher's first literary fame arrived with the publication of her second novel, *The Squirrel Cage*, in 1912. Fisher traveled to France and Spain during World War I and served as a volunteer. Fluent in French as well as several other European languages, she assisted in the rehabilitation of wounded French soldiers and cared for sick children. Returning to Vermont after the war, Fisher focused on writing fiction, producing a number of well-received short story collections and popular novels. This period also witnessed many of Fisher's significant civic accomplishments and her continued involvement in education, as well as her twenty-five-year tenure as a member of the Book-of-the-Month Club selection committee. Late in her career, Fisher turned her attention toward children, publishing several works intended for younger audiences. Among her last works are two historical books—*Vermont Tradition: The Biography of an Outlook on Life* (1953) and *Memories of Arlington, Vermont* (1957). Fisher died in Vermont on November 9, 1958.

MAJOR WORKS

While Fisher produced a considerable amount of non-fiction work, including books on education and history, her primary focus was realistic fiction in the genres of the novel and short story. Among her novels, *The Squirrel Cage* is considered her first major work. The book describes the life of Lydia Emery, a well-educated, upper-middle-class woman trapped in a shallow marriage to a man she does not love. Semi-autobiographical in nature, *The Bent Twig* (1915) features the intelligent and willful Sylvia Marshall, who becomes for a time entranced by material wealth and worldly success. Fisher treats a similar theme in *The Brimming Cup* (1921), which introduces Marise and Neale Crittenden, a young couple whose marriage is threatened by the appearance of the materialistic Vincent Marsh. *Rough-Hewn* (1922), the prequel to *The Brimming Cup*, fills in the background of the Crittendens, describing their lives until their wedding. In *The Home-Maker* (1924) Fisher exhibits her belief in equal opportunity. The novel's protagonists, a married couple, happily and successfully exchange roles as wife becomes businesswoman and husband becomes homemaker. *Her Son's Wife* (1926) focuses on Mary Bascomb, who is scandalized by her son's marriage to a crude and uneducated young woman. Partly autobiographical, *The Deepening Stream* is a Bildungsroman that recounts the young life of Matey Gilbert, the daughter of an American university professor. The work features Fisher's liberal sentiments on marriage, education, human rights, and war. *Bonfire* (1933) considers the politics of class relations in early twentieth-century Vermont. The specter of fascism and anti-Semitism in 1930s America figures prominently in Fisher's last novel, *Seasoned Timber* (1939). Fisher's works of short fiction, like her novels, recount stories of ordinary people. Such

is the case in the Vermont sketches of *Hillsboro People* (1915). *The Real Motive* (1916) offers fourteen more tales, with several set in Midwestern university towns or in World War I Europe. *Home Fires in France* (1918) and *The Day of Glory* (1919) contain war stories, while the sketches of *Basque People* (1931) are drawn from the time Fisher spent in the Basque region of the Pyrenees. In 1995 the publication of the collection *The Bedquilt, and Other Stories* brought her work to a new generation of readers. *Understood Betsy,* Canfield's popular tale of a young girl's physical and emotional revitalization, was reissued in 2000.

CRITICAL RECEPTION

During her lifetime Fisher enjoyed a considerable popular reputation. *The Brimming Cup* was hugely successful, as were her novels of the later 1920s and 1930s. Between 1926 and 1951, Fisher greatly influenced a large portion of the American reading public as one of the original and longest-standing judges for the Book-of-the-Month Club Board of Selection. However, despite the popularity of her fiction and the influence of her views, Fisher has generally failed to attract more than superficial critical attention. Her novels have been largely relegated to the category of bestsellers, unworthy of serious criticism. While some commentators have endeavored to correct this situation, the perception of Fisher as a predominately popular writer endures. In the latter portion of the twentieth century, however, a few critics have begun to reconsider the merits of Fisher's fiction and to explore her legacy as an educator and an advocate of liberalism.

GENERAL COMMENTARY

Blanche Colton Williams

SOURCE: "Dorothy Canfield," in *Our Short Story Writers,* Moffat, Yard & Company, 1920, pp. 41-54.

In the twentieth century it is possible for one, before she is forty years of age, to be a doctor of philosophy, master of half a dozen languages, a successful novelist, storywriter, wife, mother, and war worker. Dorothy Canfield is all of these, and in addition, after much travel and living abroad, she is an American of Americans. Her Americanism is the essence of her greatness and her significance for the literature of to-day and to-morrow. It is the foundation on which rise her achievements.

How has she managed to do so much? First, the circumstances of her birth were favorable. Daughter of the late James Hulme Canfield, who was President of the University of Kansas at the time she was born, and his wife Flavia Camp Canfield, artist, Dorothea Frances made her entry dowered with unusual intelligence and æsthetic sensibility. She was born, February 17, 1879, in perhaps the most American region of America, if the land of the free be symbolized by wind-blown skies and boundless plains. The Mid-West setting, however, was balanced by the girl's academic activities at Lawrence and later at the Ohio State University, of which her father was President when she took her A. B. degree in 1899. Thus briefly are indicated the Americanism and the general culture which made possible a Dorothy Canfield. The languages, German, Italian, Spanish, and Danish are explained by her travel; French she acquired in her mother's studio in Paris. When her father accepted the Chair of Librarian at Columbia University, she extended her researches in the graduate school recently opened, and in 1904 took the doctorate degree in Comparative Literature. She combined her knowledge of French and English in her thesis: *Corneille and Racine in England* (1904).

Meantime, in 1902, Miss Canfield while working on her dissertation, served as Secretary of the Horace Mann School, connected with the Teachers College of Columbia University, a position she held for three years. Then out of her association with the late Professor George R. Carpenter, she was urged to further writing. With Professor Carpenter she compiled a text-book, *English Rhetoric and Composition* (1906), and about the same time began to publish stories in magazines. Mr. Grant Overton remarks in *The Women Who Make Our Novels*: "Before *The Squirrel Cage* [published in 1912], Mrs. Fisher was merely the author of a few text-books. After it she was an important figure in American fiction." From the angle of the public, and in a deeply sardonic sense this is more than true. For the reading public would be as indifferent to the scholar who produced a work on the French dramatists as to the technician who contributed to a book on the art and business of writing. It should be stated, however, that many of Mrs. Fisher's stories were published years before they were gathered up into *Hillsboro People* and *The Real Motive*. Some of them appeared as early as 1906: **"The Bedquilt," "The Philanthropist and**

the Peaceful Life"—reprinted, 1915, under the title **"Fortune and the Fifth Card"**—and **"The Great Refusal."** Undoubtedly the success of *The Squirrel Cage* hastened their preservation in book form.

On May 9, 1907, Dorothy Canfield was married to John Redwood Fisher, of New York. Shortly after the event, they went to Arlington, Vermont, where they found far removed from city commerce and pandemonium a house adapted to the art of living and working. No one can read **"At the Foot of Hemlock Mountain,"** the essay that introduces *Hillsboro People* (1915), and fail to be convinced of the real life that Dorothy Canfield Fisher experiences in the town of Arlington. For the essay is reflective of her own village. According to her sentiments, "Like any other of those gifts of life which gratify insatiable cravings of humanity, living in a country village conveys a satisfaction which is incommunicable. . . ." "City dwellers make money, make reputations (good and bad), make museums and subways, make charitable institutions, make with a hysteric rapidity, like excited spiders, more and yet more complications in the mazy labyrinths of their lives, but they never make each others' acquaintances . . . and that is all that is worth doing in the world. . . ."

It is proof of her wisdom and of her fathoming the meaning of the verb *to live* that, after the great cities New York, Paris, and Rome, she turned, a single-hearted American, to the country, not to escape from but to mingle with her fellow beings. All novels, she says, seem badly written, faint and faded, in comparison with the life which palpitates up and down the village street. She commiserates the city dweller who lives through "canned romances, adventures, tragedies, farces," as one who passes blindfold through life.

Yet it is not to be forgotten that Mrs. Fisher is a product of balance, and she continues to maintain that balance. With her husband and children she adventures away from Arlington and seeks what she needs by way of change. In 1911-1912 they spent the winter in Italy. In Rome Mrs. Fisher met Madame Montessori and worked with her at the Children's House at the same time she was translating the works later published under the titles *A Montessori Mother* (1913) and *Mothers and Children* (1914).

Her mounting fame rose with a greater climax, the world war. The years from 1914 to 1919 are crowded with the work of the woman as of the writer. In Paris, she edited a magazine for soldiers; she took care of the refugees; she organized two children's homes at Guethary, in the south of France; she organized at Meudon a home and day nursery for munition workers' children; she ran a camp on the edge of the war zone. Meantime, *Hillsboro People* (1915) and *The Bent Twig* (1915), were followed by *The Real Motive* (1916), *Fellow Captains* (1916) and *Understood Betsy* (1917). *Home Fires in France* (1918) and *The Day of Glory* (1919) placed a gold laurel-leaf crown on the author's work in France. The sketches and stories under these two titles are among the most popular of the many works written during the war and immediately after the armistice.

Although Mrs. Fisher is first of all a novelist she is next a short-story writer. In the future, the literary historian will class her tales, in all probability, as of three periods: before the war, during the war, and after the war. At the moment, the first two divisions are the ones which concern us.

Hillsboro People (1915) and *The Real Motive* (1916) may be discussed as if the titles were merged in one volume; for the stories divided between the two cover the years from 1906 to 1915, with the overflow of 1916 in the latter volume. To read these collections is to feel the invigorating influence of a fresh buoyant optimism, to catch glimpses of a generous sympathy, to come face to face with a democracy which in the best sense is no respecter of persons, whether differentiated by age or social conditions or culture. The stories have their settings in the Middle West, in and near New York, in Paris, and in Hillsboro. (All in the collection of 1915 are connected in one way or other with Hillsboro). The range of time is from the eighteenth century, for example, **"In New New England"** (first published in 1910), to the present, the time of the greatest number. The characters reflect the author's many-sided interests: the librarian is represented in J. M., hero of **"Avunculus"** (1909), and in Miss Martin (**"Hillsboro's Good Luck,"** 1908); the artist is found in Fallères, who painted the college president (**"Portrait of a Philosopher,"** 1911), in **"An April Masque"** (1910), in **"The Deliverer"** (1909), and triumphantly in **"The Artist"** (1911). The college professor figures in **"An Academic Question"** (1910), and **"A Thread without a Knot"** (originally entitled, when first published in 1910, **"An Unframed Picture"**). A baby is the hero of **"Vignettes from a Life of Two Months"** (1915), old men are heroes of **"The Heyday of the Blood"** (1909), and **"As a Bird Out of the Snare"** (1908); an old lady is the humble heroine of **"The Bedquilt"** (1906). Nor does this list exhaust the little world of

her story people; nor is her understanding of any one diminished by her equal understanding of the others. The poor artist in **"An April Masque"** is not unworthy as a companion to the Artist; for life and ideals are greater than art—so exceedingly vaster that the difference between the best art and the worst becomes negligible in the sum of things. So, also, the difference between old and modern education is inconsiderable in the march of the years. **"In New New England,"** Captain Winthrop undertakes the education of Hannah Sherwin, aided thereto by a work entitled "The Universal Preceptor; being a General Grammar of Art, Science, and Useful Knowledge." "Up in our garret we have the very book he used," continues the narrator, "and modern research science have proved that there is scarcely a true word in it. But don't waste any pity on Hannah for having such a mistaken teacher, for it is likely enough, don't you think, that research and science a hundred years from now will have proved that there is scarcely a word of truth in our school-books of to-day? It really doesn't seem to matter much."

Her sympathy for the boy or girl cribbed in by circumstance flashes out repeatedly, as in **"The Bedquilt," "The Deliverer,"** and **"As a Bird."** Aunt Mehetabel aged sixty-eight makes her initial appeal to the reader through the fact that she seems to be regarded a nonentity in the house of her brother. She must ask, even, for scraps to make the quilt. It is no ordinary quilt. Into its perfection go months of work laboriously materializing a design made possible through previous practice and the inspiration of a soul barred from other outlets of expression. When it is finished, her brother declares it must be sent to the fair; later, in an unwonted burst of generosity, he arranges for her to go. When she returns she has nothing to relate, except about the quilt, which has taken the first prize. One sees her sitting there before the glass case, absorbed in rapt contemplation of her own handiwork, marveling that she has done it, deaf to the sounds of the fair, blind to all other sights. **"The Deliverer"** is a story of New England, in 1756, of the days when love of nature was held a sin, when the love of God was not greater than the fear of hell fire. Nathaniel Everett, son to the preacher, believes he is lost: "My heart is all full of carnal pleasures and desires. To look at the sun on the hillside—why I love it so that I forget my soul—hell—God—"His seizures do not avail to cure him. He says to Colonel Hall and M. LeMaury, who were to be his deliverers, "I—I would rather look at a haw-tree in blossom than meditate on the Almighty!" It is a turning point in Nathaniel's life when dying Colonel Hall goes calmly out with the final words to the Rev. Mr. Everett: "*I don't believe in your damned little hell!*" Nathaniel's final deliverance, the story suggests by the dénouement (placed first in the story order), is through LeMaury, whose name the boy took and by whose aid he became a great artist. **"As a Bird Out of the Snare"** shows triumph of spirit; but it is cause for tears to reflect that Jehiel Hawthorn was bound, year after year, to the farm while the pine tree grew high into heaven. He had vowed, "Before it's as tall as the ridge-pole of the house, I'll be on my way."

Not least of Mrs. Fisher's accomplishments is her faithful portrayal of the expressionless New England man and woman. Mehetabel is speechless when she tries to speak of the glories of her quilt; though she longs with her whole soul to convey the splendor of her vision, she falters. She dismisses recollections of hymn-book phraseology as not quite the thing. "Finally, 'I tell you it looked real well!' she assured them." So in **"Petunias"** (1912) Grandma Pritchard comes to the point in her rehearsal where the husband, who she had heard was killed at Gettysburg, returns. "I tell you—I tell you—*I was real glad to see him!*" So in **"Flint and Fire"** (1915) Emma Hulett "stopped short in the middle of the floor, looked at me silently, piteously, and found no word." And so Lem (**"In Memory of L. H. W.,"** entitled when originally published in 1912, **"The Hillsboro Shepherd"**) died, saying, "I'm—I'm real tired."

But such dumb-strickenness is a characteristic not only of New Englanders. In *Home Fires in France,* when Pierre (**"The Permissionaire"**) returns, he and his wife utter scream after scream of joy, "ringing up to the very heavens, frantic, incredulous, magnificent joy." But after the first wild cries had rocketed to the sky, "they had no words, no words at all." When André (**"On the Edge,"** in *The Day of Glory*) returns, Jeanne "knew nothing but that he was there, that she held him in her arms."

More than one critic has declared the stories in *Home Fires in France* to be the finest works of fiction produced by any American in the course of the war. Written, it is reported, while Mrs. Fisher's little daughter was convalescing from illness, they result from her long familiarity with the French people and her "two years intense experience in war work." Her passionate sympathy for the oppressed nation thrills, vibrant, throughout the collection. *The Real Motive* and *Hillsboro People* are but the peaceful expression of a heart aflame in *Home Fires.* Dedicated to General Pershing, whom Dorothy Canfield had known in

Kansas when she was a little girl, the book contains sketches, essays and stories.

Besides **"The Permissionaire,"** already mentioned, there are three other narratives, **"A Little Kansas Leaven,"** **"The First Time After,"** and **"La Pharmacienne."** **"Vignettes from Life at the Rear,"** **"The Refugee,"** and **"Eyes for the Blind"** lack the action that characterizes those named first; but all, alike, are readable, and all are designated as "fiction."

The theme of **"The Permissionaire"** is at once a consolation and a call to carry on. "What was in the ground, alive, they could not kill," and so Pierre reclaimed his asparagus, Paulette her peonies, and the man went back to the front after his furlough and the rebuilding of his destroyed home with a memory of the peas he had planted thrusting their green leaves above the soil. **"A Little Kansas Leaven"** means that a homely, ignorant girl roused by the call from France, spent her small savings to reach Paris and to work there so long as her few hundreds of dollars held out, and that later she returned to Marshallton, Kansas, with a straightforward story that speedily established an ambulance. This leaven worked before America entered the war, and if the dénouement has in this brief summary the suggestion of propaganda, it was needed even when the story first appeared in *The Pictorial Review,* August, 1918. But the struggle of Ellen Boardman is very real, and the absence of love and beauty leaves a stark simplicity which is somehow mightily convincing that it all happened.

"The First Time After" reveals Mrs. Fisher's ability to put herself in another's place, from the stony despair that succeeds blindness to the moment when the heart is stirred by some natural touch to renewed feeling. "He stooped and felt in his fingers the lace-like grace of a fern-stalk. The sensation brought back to him with shocking vividness all his boyhood, sunflooded, gone forever. . . . He flung himself down in the midst of the ferns, the breaking-point come at last, beating his forehead on the ground. . . . Dreadful tears ran down from his blind eyes upon the ferns." Later, he heard a thrush, "trying his voice wistfully." And, later yet, he laughs, the first time since his blindness.

"La Pharmacienne" pictures the sheltered life of Madeleine, wife of the pharmacist; then, in contrast, her heroic struggle to live and to keep her children alive; and, finally, her successful effort to save the pharmacy. Here, as in the other stories, the indomitable spirit of the French race interfuses itself through pages written by an American woman. The self-effacement of the Directrice, in **"Eyes for the Blind,"** who had found in the lists of the dead "two long years before, the name which alone gave meaning to her life"; the self-effacement of Amieux (in **"Vignettes"**), who refused the *croix de guerre* because its possession would indicate to his mother that he had been in danger; the self-effacement of the singing group described in **"The Refugee"**—such effacement means national survival. The Marseillaise has stirred its millions since the time of Rouget de l'Isle, but never has it rung more bravely than when the school children of Cousin Jean sang it, sang the first stanza, the second stanza and the chorus—and the elders joined in. Their singing might have meant death for all; but "There were three hundred voices shouting it out, the tears streaming down our cheeks." Never has it swelled more triumphantly than in *The Day of Glory* (1919) when the throngs of Paris swept to the Place de la Concorde to salute the Statue of Strasbourg. And Dorothy Canfield was there and rushed out into the street and became a part of the spirit of thanksgiving and shared her feelings with us across the sea:

> Allons, enfants de la patrie,
> Le Jour de Gloire est arrivé!

The houses echoed to those words, repeated and repeated by every band of jubilant men and women and children who swept by, waving flags and shouting:

> Come, children of our country,
> The Day of Glory is here!

Of this second and briefer volume, the opening piece, **"On the Edge,"** has been proclaimed the best story its author has written. This tribute is higher praise than it deserves and underestimates Mrs. Fisher's other narratives; but it is admirable in its restrained account of a brave Frenchwoman's struggle to protect and keep alive her family of six, children and foster-children, and for the convincing suggestion of her being 'on the edge,' hovering on the border of insanity. André, she dreamed, had come, home. But there was the watch he had left for his oldest son! And the reader has a sudden revelation of the soldier heart: he had known she was driven almost past the bounds of sanity and that the gold case would remind her his visit had been not a dream but a throbbing reality. Or this is the interpretation that some of us like to make. But if there had not been the watch, there would have risen some other mute evidence of his presence to cheer her and restore her languishing courage.

Without crossing the border-line between sentiment and sentimentality, these stories pull constantly at the emotions. Has any man or woman read either volume without tears?

The struggles Mrs. Fisher finds of moment are between the individual and his environment (**"The Deliverer"**); between the individual and heredity(**"A Good Fight and the Faith Kept,"** first published as **"The Conqueror,"** 1916); between man and false standards of life(**"A Sleep and a Forgetting,"** first published under the title, **"Gifts of Oblivion,"** 1913); between man and eclipsed personality(**"The First Time After"**); the will to survive and the forces that make for destruction—almost all her French stories. The surprise ending has had small influence on her plots. Since she is primarily the novelist, avowedly interested in people, with story mechanics she concerns herself hardly at all. But **"Flint and Fire"** closes on a neat twist, dependent upon a trait of character; **"A Sleep and a Forgetting"** startles by the disclosure that Warren recovered his memory eight years before he admitted the fact.

Vermont and its Green Mountains are the fit setting for a writer whose ideals are so high and whose living is so simple. If the vision of the Ideal Commonwealth ever is realized, perhaps the setting may be Hillsboro.

Dorothea Lawrance Mann

SOURCE: "Dorothy Canfield: The Little Vermonter," in *The Bookman*, New York, Vol. LXV, No. 6, August, 1927, pp. 695-701.

No one has ever questioned seriously the tremendous power in small things. The atom, the electron, even the germ, speak for themselves. They are the Davids and against them the Goliaths of the world have small chance. Consider the unequal contest between a great building and a small stick of dynamite! Little people frequently seem to possess this same driving force, as if their whole being were concentrated will power. Dorothy Canfield once said that if anyone knew what it felt like to live in a small body, in the future he would always choose to be large. There is something quite deceptive about these small people. You would never suspect them of such deadly seriousness. Looking at Dorothy Canfield, it is far easier to believe that she spent much of her youth dancing at West Point than that she has served for several years on the State Board of Education for Vermont. She does not look in the least like the traditional doctor of philosophy, nor as if she learned new languages as a pastime. I believe that Portuguese is the latest of her string of languages, though it may easily be that she has added another in the last few months.

How many people, I wonder, have formulated so definite a philosophy of life as she? Again it is very misleading to think of her as the novelist who lives on the side of a mountain near a little village in Vermont. Perhaps the significant aspect of this circumstance is the fact that her Red Mountain is the mountain pictured on the seal of Vermont! As a matter of fact she is equally at home in France, where she has lived for years at a time. Once she remarked that having an equal number of French and American friends gave one a nice balance in life, for the French women devote themselves too much to their homes and their families, while American women are prone to give themselves too fully to outside interests. Observing the failings as well as the excellencies of both helped one to balance one's own interests.

Variety is what life needs to be well rounded, Dorothy Canfield once told me. You should know country life as well as city life. You should mingle intimately with people of other countries than your own—living among them, not merely traveling through their cities. As an American, it would be well to have at least part of your education in an entirely different section of the country from that in which you live. This last summer she took her own children to a far western ranch, to give them a taste of a life quite unlike either Vermont or France, and the keen joy of a variety of new horses to ride. I recall her comment that every American should live for a little while in the middle west, for without living there easterners in particular can never appreciate the thirst for culture which characterizes these mid-Americans. Unconsciously Dorothy Canfield is apt to give one the impression that their own life has been very narrow and lacking in experience.

She herself to be sure had a good start in this matter of varied experiences. Her father was president of a number of colleges in the middle west—one in Kansas, and Ohio State University—while in his later years he was librarian at Columbia University. Her mother, who by the way set her daughter a good example by taking a trip around the world at eighty-one unaccompanied by any member of her family—dying on the Indian Ocean, she said, would really be no different from dying in one's bed at home—is an artist and author. She also is a little woman with a dynamic quality about her, but her daughter must have

inherited her taste for languages elsewhere, since for all her years abroad Mrs. Canfield has not learned to speak French. She once made a unique trip with one of her daughter's French friends who could not speak English. Though they were quite unable to converse with each other they remained in complete sympathy—proving that after all a great part of our converse is not in words. Part of Dorothy Canfield's childhood was passed in playing about her mother's studio in the Latin Quarter. She once observed that bohemia had no lure if you had known it in childhood! There were other weeks in French convent schools—still another phase of life to add to her collection of experiences. For quite a period in the early days of her marriage she lived in Italy. There was also a year studying in Norway. Since she shared the play as well as the work of her Norwegian friends, she could take a mischievous delight in listening to the comments of visitors from her own land discussing a group of natives, with no knowledge at all that one of the "natives" was an especially clever American.

No one of our novelists has had the charge of writing autobiography laid at her door more frequently than has Dorothy Canfield. It is irritating of course, and yet so completely does she identify herself with her characters that it is not strange. If today she suffers and plans with Mrs. Bascomb of *Her Son's Wife,* even more did she laugh and dream and have moods of terrifying seriousness with Marise of *The Brimming Cup.* Most novelists use material of setting and incident which are familiar to them. In her case there are the deeper spiritual resemblances. She knows at first hand Mrs. Bascomb's passion for children, and very fully does she partake of Marise's articulateness and her need for analysis. She herself longs to think clearly. It is one of her ideals. Many persons say they desire to think clearly, but either their thoughts are gravely bounded or else they know nothing whatever of the true passion for clear thinking—almost for defining the indefinable—which is hers. Yet with it all she is utterly sane. There will come often her hearty laugh, brushing away the cobwebs of abstractions. The practical side of her also finds echo in Marise and her neighborliness. Many authors live at least a portion of their lives in the country, but they remain apart from the community. Dorothy Canfield has always contributed her share—though I am inclined to doubt her statement that her neighbors scarcely know that she writes, since they see her only as a human being. It is clearly a well worn path which leads up the mountain to "Fishers'." She worked with the other women when they made over the schoolhouse to rent as a summer cottage, using the rent money for school equipment. It was almost clear gain, for the energetic Vermonters furnished the cottage from their own homes, and did all the not inconsiderable work of the experiment themselves.

Living in Vermont on the mountain, the Fishers are interested in reforestation. There is a fine tract planted and preserved in memory of Dorothy Canfield's father. The work naturally was interrupted by their four war years in France. It is strange to think of their selling their wood in Vermont that they might live in France and do war work there. To both Mr. and Mrs. Fisher France was the second home, and they could not be happy until they were helping. There has been another year in France since the war, and several summers, for the Fisher children must be at least bilingual and their mother wanted them to learn early what she describes as the French habit of good work. The ideal of good work is something to cling to in life. This in itself is characteristic of her, for though her family came out of New England, there is nothing of the transcendentalist about her. She is tiny in physique, but her feet rest very firmly on the ground. Good work which demands care in its every detail is not bad as an ideal for living. Too many Americans are satisfied with shoddy accomplishment and even with shoddy dreams.

Novelists sometimes say that life is harder for a young writer today than it was during their own apprenticeship. Perhaps—but perhaps too in looking back from the heights of their success they forget some of the doubts and disappointments. Possibly competition was not quite so keen as it has become. Reputations certainly were made promptly and definitely. Dorothy Canfield was one of those who worked on *The American Magazine* in its youthful days. She was also secretary of the Horace Mann School for two or three years. As a matter of fact, *The Squirrel Cage* was not her first book, though it was her first big success. She had taken her Ph.D. in 1904, had married in 1907, and this novel was published in 1912. In a day when most writers seemed to desire the longest and most impressive name possible, she abandoned the "Dorothea Frances" to which she was born for the simpler "Dorothy Canfield."

Her educational books were published later under the name of "Dorothy Canfield Fisher," to the confusion of not a few readers. The educational books have become a thing of the past, but I have an idea that they subtly modified all her work. Her novels are deeply concerned with the training of children. Whatever else her books may contain, the matter of the supreme importance of children always plays its part. Educational ideals were in her blood, since her father was a college president, and from the first she had been hailed as a novelist of ideas. Nevertheless in the early days of her writing career she had spent a winter in Rome, where she became intimate with Madame Montessori, who was having trouble with the translation of her book. The publisher appealed to Mrs. Fisher for help, with the result that after the translation of the book she wrote *A Montessori Mother* for American mothers and children. Her reason for this was that many of the difficulties of Montessori methods in this country arose from the fact that American children advance more rapidly than Italian children. Consequently, large numbers of Americans found Mrs. Fisher's book more helpful than Montessori's own. There was at this time an amusing story of a woman who had enjoyed *The Squirrel Cage* and, seeing a new book by Mrs. Fisher announced, promptly read *A Montessori Mother,* wondering greatly meanwhile at the author's intention! The concentration at this period on educational ideas, combined with the fact that it was the period of the babyhood of her own children, molded Mrs. Fisher's thought perceptibly. The trend was there, however, for we have the teacher who writes novels and the mother who writes novels, without approaching the constructive thinking of Dorothy Canfield.

Ever since their marriage in 1907 in America the Fishers have made their home on Mrs. Fisher's grandfather's farm in Arlington. It was the tenant farmer's house which they took for their own, and Mr. Fisher has done the remodeling himself. Mrs. Fisher can show a series of snapshots revealing the gradual changes made in the bare little New England farmhouse. The postwar generation has set a standard for radicalism hard to match for those who preceded them. Nevertheless it is to be borne in mind that Dorothy Canfield started life as very much a radical. She was an unconventional and strong minded person, who would do nothing simply because it was the customary thing to do. One of her children had a boy for nursemaid. He proved fully as devoted to the baby, and much stronger when it came to lifting him. She might live in New England, but Mrs. Fisher vowed she would never allow herself to be bound, as so many New England housewives were bound, by mere possessions. A home was a necessity, but it should not be so precious that one could not use it or leave it. Life meant more than things! Consequently Dorothy Canfield would have nothing in her house on which she could not easily turn the key when the spirit of wandering came upon her anew. The fine art of living she felt was something more than caring for a house and the dusting of furniture. She must have lived up to her creed, for the little house on the mountain has been closed for a year or more at a time. It was empty several years at the time of the war, and the key must have been left in Vermont, for when the family came home from France they found the house open and a supper awaiting them—though their neighbors had shown the tact to let them enjoy their homecoming unobserved.

All novelists must take their material from the life which they have known, but more than most Dorothy Canfield's work reflects the varied aspects of her life. *The Bent Twig* revealed the life of the university town which she had known in childhood. *The Brimming Cup* was so vivid a picturing of Vermont that all sorts of amusing anecdotes could be told of the persons who believed firmly that she had written her own story. It was certainly a naive touch to believe that a woman who had decided not to leave her husband for a more prosperous lover should confess the fact to the world in a novel! The little American Marise had grown up as a child among French people. Dorothy Canfield herself used to tell of the church on the hilltop which she saw when she first approached France, and the thrill she found in thinking that this was "foreign parts." Never again, she admits, did any portion of the world seem foreign to her. Neale Crittenden—the Neale of *Rough-Hewn*—owes certain aspects of his prosperous, well established youth to memories of Mr. Fisher's boyhood. *Rough-Hewn* stands out to me as an extraordinarily interesting example of the story one is always longing to unravel. So many writers must have yearned to know why it was that their characters, wandering to each other from the far ends of the earth, ever found and loved each other. No other author, so far as I can recall, has ever worked out the problem. I should say that the writing of it must have required two distinct processes. Taking her Marise and Neale of *The Brimming Cup,* those happily married people from their totally different environments, she must first have reasoned back from the Marise and Neale whom she knew to their beginnings. This process was not on paper. The story she tells in *Rough-Hewn* is the story from the beginnings to the night on Rocca di Papa when they discovered their love for each other. This book was not nearly so popular as it should have been, proving no doubt that the public does not care to know too much about the characters of fiction. As in the case of *Raw Material*—where

she presented the incidents from which stories are made instead of the stories made from them—it is quite possible that readers never wholly fathomed the significance of her experiment.

Within recent years Dorothy Canfield, the short story writer, has been almost completely superseded by Dorothy Canfield the novelist. Once, however, it hung in the balance in which medium she would excel. There were two volumes of Vermont stories published before the war. *Home Fires in France* and *The Day of Glory* were volumes of war stories actually written while the author was engaged in war work in France. The last of these books was an especially memorable event in her career. These war stories must have been struck off at white heat. There is no other accounting for them. Today there are secretaries, naturally. In the old days there was always the little one room house in the Vermont field with its desk and stove, near enough to her home so that she could look out of the window at her children at play. In its early days the little house was used alternately by Mr. and Mrs. Fisher, while the one not writing would take over the responsibility of running the home and watching over the children, that the other's writing hours might be uninterrupted. In France everything was hopelessly different. Mr. Fisher was driving an ambulance. He went over in 1915, if I remember rightly, and his family followed him in a few months, despite the protests of grandparents against taking children into the war country. Not only did Mrs. Fisher throw that large energy of hers into various types of war work, but there was seldom a time when her house was not crowded with children in need of care and shelter. When her own little girl had been seriously ill with typhoid fever, her mother took her to the south of France to recuperate, but even under such conditions she could not escape the demands on her sympathy of other children who had suffered in the war. And even in such busy days as these she found opportunity to visit in the hospital another American novelist whom she had not previously known. That apparent leisure is one of her characteristic qualities. She never seems overburdened nor driven for time, like most of the modern world, though her days are extraordinarily full.

Her house in France was always filled, and in spite of it she managed to write some of the finest things she has ever done. Very early I discovered that Mrs. Fisher's characters are real people to her. She talks of them as she talks of her friends. I observed it first when she was talking of Barbara Marshall and her children Sylvia and Judith in *The Bent Twig.* Barbara Marshall remains one of her finest, most balanced characters, while the petty snobbery of the western university town remains a vivid memory. Sturdy little Judy and wilful, luxury loving Sylvia have lost nothing of their reality, though in the last twelve years Mrs. Fisher has written of many other children. One reason why I believe her characters are so vividly realized is the fact that they are always in families, and they have all the human connections which real people possess. As a rule there is an almost equally definite background of community life which seems to plant the characters firmly. They are quite tangible. It would not surprise me to find myself talking with Barbara Marshall or Marise Crittenden, or even the formidable Mrs. Bascomb. Could anything be more definite evidence of this than the volume of protest against Mrs. Bascomb and her high handed treatment of the situation which was menacing the chances in life of her beloved granddaughter? I have seen readers almost speechless with rage over Mrs. Bascomb, which after all is very fine appreciation of Dorothy Canfield's ability at character drawing.

Perhaps the sharpest reason for our present disregard of the radical quality of Dorothy Canfield's ideas is that the radicalism of the postwar generation has centred so largely on sex problems. It would be asking a little too generation—even though they have brought them to knee length dresses and the Charleston!

Dorothy Canfield's sense of humor is keen but she has not wit. Neither does she indulge in the epigram. She has done very effective scenes but she is not a quotable novelist. It comes back, I should say, to the fact that with her the story is the thing. Very earnest people are seldom witty. They have not time to indulge in sideshow. Wit is for those with time to play upon words. Dorothy Canfield is concerned with ideas and with people. She has chapters of passion and beauty, but you must take them as a whole. I personally never lose my delight in that fine love scene on Rocca di Papa. Love scenes may possibly be easy to act, but they are proverbially hard to write. This particular love scene has the added difficulty of opening the book, so that the reader is wholly without emotional reaction with regard to Marise and Neale.

There is neither fear of criticism nor fear of ridicule in Dorothy Canfield. In *The Bent Twig* she tackled that very delicate problem of the little girls with the modicum of colored blood who tried to pass as white children and who disappeared overnight when it was discovered that they were of mixed race. She has a clean literalness in dealing with a situation of this kind—which means that she gives her full meed of sympathy but does not let her sympathy run away with her. One cannot ignore a fact, however much one may sympathize with the victim. Similarly, in *The Home-Maker*—the first of her books to be put on the screen—she refused to ignore that the father was a better home maker and the mother a better business woman. What case has mere convention beside facts? Some trace of Puritanism lingers in Dorothy Canfield. She might, I think, be very lenient if she could discover a human being who had no other human being's claims upon him. The claims of children she places paramount, and with her an adult has no chance at all if he or she is hampering the course of a child's best development. If it is for the best interests of the children, the father should stay at home with them, no matter if the neighbors would laugh at him. If it serves the best interests of Mrs. Bascomb's granddaughter, it is quite justifiable that the mother should spend her days as a nervous invalid. Life sweeps relentlessly on. Because you were scanted in your chance at life is no excuse for scanting a child.

This belief in the supreme right of children has grown on Mrs. Fisher. It has taken the place of her earlier belief in the right of the individual. In *The Brimming Cup* Marise made her choice between her husband and the man who could have given her a renewal of youth and wider opportunities, without excessive emphasis on her children. Vincent Marsh is scarcely reproved when he suggests that Marise is wasting her time doing for her children things which a nursemaid could do as well. Vincent Marsh would doubtless have had a harder time of it with the present Dorothy Canfield!

There are many things which might be said of Dorothy Canfield's work. Her gallery of children is made up of very human little persons, with scarcely a brilliant one in the lot. Some of them are the stolid little Vermonters with their red cheeks and with the fair hair we see in so few sections of the country today. They are real individuals for all that. Her portraits of women are equally noteworthy. It would be hard to find finer, more gracious and lovable women than she has created. There is, I think, an element of the feminist hidden in her which prevents her men from being equally impressive. They are likely to be the weaklings of the story. At least, they serve as backgrounds for their more vital women and children. As a matter of fact, equality between the sexes does not flourish in literature—if it flourishes anywhere. We are born with our inclinations and prejudices.

The later Dorothy Canfield is a trifle breathless and a trifle breathtaking, as though she found life bounded for the promulgation of her ideas. A case of the dynamite again. There is such dynamic force in her. Something has to happen. She will not let you be leisurely and complacent. Life is so short and there is so much to be experienced and enjoyed and accomplished. It is the fundamentals of living and not the fashions and bywords of the moment which concern her. Perhaps too it is because she lives away from cities and refuses to be harried by the unimportant. She is modern and she has been a radical, but life is more than either, and she sticks close to the eternal truths. That is why she can be so completely fearless. That is why she holds out both hands to life.

Grant Overton

SOURCE: "Dorothy Canfield (Dorothy Canfield Fisher)," in *The Women Who Make Our Novels,* Dodd, Mead & Company, 1928, pp. 61-74.

Very fortunately for her work as a novelist, Dorothy Canfield has been able to find direct outlets for a good deal of her passion as an educator. Thus, although her fiction does not escape didactic moods, it remains fiction. Nor is it autobiographical fiction, as some readers of *The Brimming Cup* seem to imagine; while her use of backgrounds and incidents from her own life is easily recognized by all readers familiar with her story.

That story is one of hard work, almost without respites, but the results she can point to depend partly on her scholarly gifts. She has been called "a woman of letters," but the image called up is not easy to associate with so much tireless activity of an unliterary sort. Having spent part of her childhood in France, she felt impelled to help win the war before most Americans were settled in their minds as to which side should win. And having adopted as her home the State of her ancestors, she must become the only woman member of the Vermont Board of Education. Early equipped with French, German and Italian, she insists on adding Spanish, Danish, Portuguese and others until she seems likely to take her place beside Queen Victoria tackling Hindustani at eighty. Her latest book has the title, *Why Stop Learning?*—a query which may reduce some customers to speechlessness.

Her abilities as a novelist are so considerable that readers of novels can only selfishly regret her roundedness as a woman, teacher, publicist and official. No one, not even Dorothy Canfield, can get breath for work like *The Brimming Cup* and *Rough-Hewn* while excelling in other lines of endeavor. Mrs. Fisher would undoubtedly reply that living, in the sense of a rich and fruitful activity, comes first. This is decided, of course, by personal temperament; but it involves the sacrifice of the possibility of the highest place as an artist. For art not only insists on coming first over everything, it frequently tolerates in the race.

II

Dorothy Canfield was born in Lawrence, Kansas, in 1879, the daughter of James Hulme Canfield and Flavia Camp Canfield. The Canfields came to America in 1636, moved to Vermont in 1764, and have owned land there ever since. James Hulme Canfield was an educator, a college professor and president of several State Universities—Ohio State among them. Dorothy Canfield's mother studied painting in Paris and the child learned French about as early as she did English. She was really named Dorothea Frances, but simplified it to Dorothy.

The family was constantly moving about in the Middle West, as Dr. Canfield left one college job for another. From Lawrence, Kansas, where he had been president of the University of Kansas, they went, when Dorothy was about twelve, to Lincoln, Nebraska, Dr. Canfield having become chancellor of the University of Nebraska. At that time an army officer just in his thirties taught Dorothy to ride a horse and introduced her to his hobby, the higher mathematics. This friendship was resumed in France a quarter of a century later, the officer then being General John J. Pershing.

Dr. Canfield went to run Ohio State University. His daughter entered it and emerged a Ph.B. at twenty. These years were an orgy of acquiring knowledge. She saw France, Italy, Vermont. The itinerant educator now became librarian at Columbia University and Dorothy came to New York for a Ph.D. She specialized in the Romance languages, was secretary of the Horace Mann School, took courses at the Sorbonne when in Paris. She also saw the Columbia University football team play. John Redwood Fisher was captain. She was married to him in 1907. They went to live on one of the Canfield farms and Arlington, Vermont, has been their home ever since, except for the duration of the war and for various European excursions.

A year in Norway has got lost somewhere in this reckoning; Norwegian is one of her tongues. As for the mother, Mrs. Canfield, she took a trip around the world at eighty, remarking that dying on the Indian Ocean would be no different from dying in one's bed at home. This assertion remains unverified.

Mrs. Fisher was not long in developing ideas about Vermont; you will find them tucked away in *The Brimming Cup.* Reforestation is one of them and they have set out hosts of baby pine trees on their mountain side while rejuvenating an ancient sawmill to work up the scrub timber.

The two children were born. In a few years the rural schools of Vermont were to have their standards raised in consequence.

As an author of books, Mrs. Fisher had, by this time, three and a half to her credit. The first, a study of Corneille and Racine, was probably her thesis for the doctor's degree. With Professor George R. Carpenter of Columbia she had written an *English Rhetoric and Composition* (1906). *What Shall We Do Now?* (1906) inspires less terror in the young. Her last book had been *Gunhild* (1907).

Now she did a novel, *The Squirrel Cage* (1912), "a singularly uncheerful, grim book showing a fine American girl, too sensitive to be a good fighter, struggling helplessly like a person in a nightmare against the smothering, well-intentioned materialism about her." Her next novel, *The Bent Twig* (1915) was to be a somewhat complementary affair. Its theme is "what happens if too violent a strain is put on human nature to avoid well-intentioned materialism"; it is "what might have happened if the Lydia of *The Squirrel Cage,* to save her daughter from that inner deadness, had brought her up in an athletically bare atmosphere of higher interests alone. Sylvia, the eager, human, selfish, intelligent daughter in *The Bent Twig,* flings impatiently away from the material austerity of her home life, and puts out her competent, energetic hands to grasp ease and luxury.

"In this novel Mrs. Fisher showed what she had shadowed in *The Squirrel Cage,* what she was to paint again in *The Brimming Cup* and in *Rough-Hewn,*— the growth, slow, occasionally groaning and unwilling but sure and triumphant, which carries a finely constituted human being first up to the recognition of spiritual values in life, and then onward to the sense of responsibility which makes him try to shoulder his share of the sacrifice and effort needed to safeguard such values."

Yes, but were they good stories?

They were, reasonably judged. Particularly in *The Squirrel Cage* did Mrs. Fisher succeed in making you feel the intensity of a girl's rebellion and the tightening of the net in which life sometimes catches its creatures. Both novels used the Middle Western background and *The Bent Twig* is a good picture of the university towns of her childhood.

After *The Squirrel Cage* was finished Mrs. Fisher and her husband went to Italy, spending the winter in Rome. Mrs. Fisher became acquainted with Madame Montessori, helped her with the translation of her book about the training of children, and wrote *A Montessori Mother* (1913) to introduce the system to American mothers and teachers. Then, as a sort of general answer to the many letters she got, Mrs. Fisher wrote *Mothers and Children* (1914).

All the while she had been writing short stories. *Hillsboro People* (1916), which deals with Vermonters, and *The Real Motive* (1917) were the first books to collect these. Later the war was to produce *Home Fires in France* (1918) and *The Day of Glory* (1919). *Understood Betsy* (1917) was written after Mr. Fisher had gone into the ambulance service, in the few months before Mrs. Fisher also went abroad. They then or later sold some of their wood in Vermont to get money for relief work in France. The war caught them up. From it they emerged without casualties, although their little girl had typhoid fever and convalesced during most of 1918 in southern France. It was then that *Home Fires in France* and *The Day of Glory* got written. In the spring of 1919 the family returned to Vermont, tired mentally and physically, glad to do some gardening, to plant more baby pines, and to rest. After a good many months Mrs. Fisher was able to begin *The Brimming Cup* (1921).

III

This very long novel is the story of Marise and Neale Crittenden after their marriage. Though written and published later, *Rough-Hewn* (1922) precedes *The Brimming Cup,* and is the story of the pair from childhood until the hour of their discovery that they are in love. Therefore, if one is to read both, he may prefer to begin with *Rough-Hewn.* It is, however, a lesser piece of work.

Springing from totally different environments, there is no doubt that Marise and Neale are destined for each other. When *The Brimming Cup* opens it is with a glimpse of them in their happy hour of confessed love. The scene is Italy, the year 1909.

The scene changes to Vermont in March, 1920. The remainder of the novel covers a period of a year. Marise and Neale have three young children. And the novel proper opens with a moment when Marise is getting these youngsters ready for school. After they go, "she continued gazing at the vacant road. It seemed to her that the children had taken everything with them."

She has ceased to be physically in love with her husband. There comes upon the scene one Vincent Marsh. He is, apparently, a traveled and cultivated individual. Marise and he find much in common and the flame springs up. The rest of the book is taken up with Marise's temptation and resistance. Neale, remaining perfectly quiet, comes nevertheless to know what is going on; indeed, his wife contrives to discuss the situation with him. She must, he tells her, "walk right up" to the thing she is afraid of. Privately, with a great effort and agony, he decides that he must keep his hands off, not constrain her in any way.

With this main story, developed in full and with dramatic intensity, are interwoven other threads. There is Eugenia, who considers Vermont a wilderness of crudity—as does, for that matter, Vincent Marsh—and who would like to capture Neale. There is old Mr. Welles with a story of his own. The life of the Vermont village and countryside are sacked for incident and color. Marise's and Neale's children have parts in the complicated series of tableaux. And all through the book there is a diffusion of ideas of every kind, economic, social, cultural, quasi-religious. Neale's theory of occupation and industry for Vermonters burdens this page, Eugenia's preoccupation with lace work, that one. A passage of the sort following is a fair example of the book's digressions. Eugenia has put on some massage cream and is resting.

> As she lay stretched in the chaise-longue by the window, reading Claudel, or Strindberg, or Remy de Gourmont, she would suddenly find that she was not thinking of what was on the page, that she saw there only Marise's troubled eyes while she and Marsh talked about the inevitable and essential indifference of children to their parents and the healthiness of this instinct; about the foolishness of the parents' notion that they would be formative elements in the children's lives; or on the other hand, if the parents did succeed in forcing themselves into the children's lives, the danger of sexual mother-complexes. Eugenia found that instead of thrilling voluptuously, as she knew she ought, to the precious pain and bewilderment of one of the thwarted characters of James Joyce, she was, with a disconcerting and painful eagerness of her own, bringing up to mind the daunted

silence Marise kept when they mentioned the fact that of course everybody nowadays knew that children are much better off in a big, numerous, robust group than in the nervous, tight isolation of family life; and that a really trained educator could look out for them much better than any mother, because he could let them alone as a mother never could.

We may limit our scrutiny to the three or four principal characters and their interrelationships. The final feeling is then, perhaps, and despite the emotional intensity with which Marise is realized throughout, one of dubiety. Neale is not too good to be true; he is only too good to be truest. He is a type of man most women endure least well since he refrains from aggression when, in their view, it should be spontaneous, an instinctive—almost a reflex—action. All his highly conceived notions about not constraining Marise, though women may agree with them in principle and as intellectual concepts, inspire in the feminine breast an impatience amounting to abhorrence. Even Marise can be heard asking frenziedly at the back of her mind, at the root of her nervous system: "But isn't he going to *do* anything?" Nine hundred and ninety-nine women of a thousand, in Marise's place—or reading the book and so assuming her place—would prefer a husband who in such circumstances did something, did anything, even if he did the wrong thing.

The explanation is simple. The Marises of the world who show her hesitation do so fundamentally—underneath all their surface of scruple—because of a lingering doubt as to whether they may not, after all, still be in love with their Neales. That doubt can only be put at rest by him. He can settle it in his favor only by some affirmative act, some renewal of courtship, some show of possession or some chastisement of the intruder upon his rights or privileges. He cannot put the doubt at rest by mere solicitousness or attitudes of considerateness or by any form of words.

It must be granted that Marise is no average woman. Such a one would never discuss her plight with her husband in the fashion of Marise's talk with Neale. She would scarcely put herself in the position of going to him and saying: "You are in danger of losing me; aren't you going to do anything about it?" Still less, when he seemed to be obtuse and noncommittal would she continue with what is virtually a cry: "Oh, please, please do something about it!" His piercing glance, his kindly sympathetic tone, his high-minded words would perhaps end the natural suspicion that he was a dumb-bell but only by arousing, even confirming, in his wife's mind the more horrible conviction that he didn't really care.

Another thing. Vincent Marsh, as created by Mrs. Fisher, will impress most readers as much too cheap a specimen to arouse such issues in the breast of a woman like Marise. It is entirely possible that she would feel physically attracted to him; but either she would admit this to herself and put it resolutely aside or she would yield to him and satisfy the thing that was too much for her. The last thing, one feels, that she would do would be to confuse this physiological need with the rest of living—magnify it, drag in her husband and weigh her children in its false scale, allow it to threaten the foundations of her whole existence and her thought-out happiness. How little Mrs. Fisher knows about the Vincent Marshes is sometimes painfully apparent. Either they are more subtle, particularly in utterance, than she has made him, or much bolder; and in no case do they depend so extensively on the persuasiveness of words.

When the turn of the book comes, Marise makes her decision in an intellectual vigil. Neale's belief that she was strong and not weak has been her staff.

> Neale being his own master, a free citizen of life, knew what a kingdom he owned, and with a magnanimity unparalleled could not rest till she had entered hers. She . . . had only wished to make the use of his strength which would have weakened her.

She decides that when next she meets Vincent she can look and see what is there. The next day comes the encounter in the course of which he kisses her. She does not respond; stung, he asks her if she is too old for love. Marise reflects. "Yes, I think that is it. I find I am too old."

It is singularly unconvincing; all "written," one feels.

IV

Not so many years ago a woman of seventy was recounting the story of Keable's "Simon Called Peter" to her fifty-year-old daughter.

"And then, Cora," she went on, matter-of-factly, "you know, he had all those feelings."

"Yes, Mamma. Mamma, do you think we had better serve chicken patties?" For Cora was blushing. In the front seat Cora's daughter, convulsed, tried to keep her back uncontorted.

What saves *The Brimming Cup* for most readers is the manifest fact that Marise "had all those feelings." They don't pretend to grasp her ratiocinations; and it may be that there is not a good deal in them to grasp.

After *The Brimming Cup, Rough-Hewn* could hardly avoid a certain anti-climax. Mrs. Fisher's free use of material from her husband's boyhood and youth rekindled the most unjustifiable suspicion that *Rough-Hewn* and its sequel were autobiographical. "It was certainly naïve," observes Dorothea Lawrance Mann, "to believe that a woman who had decided not to leave her husband for a more prosperous lover should confess the fact to the world in a novel."

During 1921 and 1922 Mrs. Fisher worked on the translation from the Italian of Papini's *Life of Christ* (1923) and on *Rough-Hewn.* In the spring of 1923 the family went to Europe and spent the following year in France and Switzerland. *Raw Material* (1923) is a collection of character portraits, the material of stories which Mrs. Fisher exhorts the reader to construct for himself.

The Home-Maker (1924) presents a family where the wife, an immaculate housekeeper, is unfitted for child-rearing and hates her task. The husband is equally unfitted for the jobs the world offers men. When he is crippled by an accident, husband and wife change places, to the relief of each and the great benefit of the children. The dramatic suspense comes over the question of whether the husband can recover. If he can walk about again, public opinion and the laws of the universe will be annulled; both will be made unhappy and the children will suffer. Happily, the doctor, taking in the situation in all its bearings, utters the necessary lie.

Such a synopsis does the story considerable injustice. There is some convincing detail; more plausibility than is managed in *The Brimming Cup.* By the time she wrote *The Home-Maker,* Mrs. Fisher had come to feel that the rights of the children transcend all other human rights. But she was to offer this view in another novel which offers it without so decidedly asserting it; which, in fact, raises great moral problems and compels the reader to decide them while leaving him free in his decision; and which is much the best book she has ever written up to this time.

This novel is *Her Son's Wife* (1926). It contains Mrs. Bascomb, who arouses in some readers a nearly inarticulate fury. An outline of the story must be attempted here.

Mrs. Bascomb, a strong, intelligent, capable woman is not unnaturally disconcerted to find that her son has rushed into a marriage with a no-account girl. The prospect is quite cheerless; for young Bascomb has none of his mother's strength or keenness. Mrs. Bascomb takes them to live with her—a charity, all things considered. But of course it works badly and her son is on his wife's side. Of this Mrs. Bascomb has no complaint to make; but she alone is capable of solutions in that family. She moves away and for some years sees nothing of them.

One day she runs upon her granddaughter. Here is a pretty and intelligent child without care, control or direction—on the road to acquiring all her mother's tastes for the tawdry. The grandmother weighs the situation, decides, and acts on her decision. She invites herself back to live with Lottie and her husband. Lottie, sick of housekeeping, is rather glad to have her, and Mrs. Bascomb's son feels the same way.

Lottie, who has put on much weight, has trouble with her feet. Mrs. Bascomb suggests that she ought to keep off them. "Why don't you go to bed?" Lottie does. The mother-in-law sends for someone to treat her. The man she summons is not averse to creating practice for himself. Lottie, he finds, is really in quite a bad way. Mrs. Bascomb does everything to make invalidism a novel and attractive rôle for Lottie. All the movie magazines. Pillows and delightful negligees. Candy. Delicious and tempting food—too much food. Lottie, who has no pain to speak of, is quite happy. This goes on for years. Meanwhile Mrs. Bascomb at last can take her granddaughter in hand. Her son, a great hand for ball games, finally discovers some skill as a reporter of sport for a newspaper. Mrs. Bascomb sees her granddaughter graduate from high school and begin auspiciously in college. She is a girl with whom Mrs. Bascomb can be entirely satisfied, of whom she may easily live to be proud. . . .

This fresh and powerful novel is of almost startling originality in this respect: It creates a moral problem for a woman that has nothing to do with taking a lover and is yet of paramount importance. Mrs. Bascomb's inspiration comes with Lottie's illness. It is true that she puts Lottie to bed and keeps her there. Mrs. Bascomb, and no one else, is responsible for making Lottie helplessly bedridden. The mother-in-law is not without her moments of stricken remorse, but she never abandons her purpose. Mrs. Fisher understands her completely and puts her on paper with consummate skill. Can it be right to do this thing to the mother for the sake of the child? The issue is

quite as momentous as that which must often be decided in the hour before birth itself—as momentous and to most minds, more real. And far, far oftener to face.

Other issues not less profound are involved. The Nietzschean one, the right of the stronger, raises its head. The rational one, the right of the greater intelligence to rule, is at stake. Christian doctrine moves to condemn Mrs. Bascomb and then falters, remembering that Christ stressed the sacredness of the child. Skepticism challenges Mrs. Bascomb's premise, asking how she can be sure that her training of her granddaughter is Ultimate Good. Theology bids Mrs. Bascomb to weigh her responsibility, tells her that she will be answerable for what she does, and assures her that she will be judged with reference to her appreciation of her acts, her fineness of conscience, her awareness and honesty.

Mrs. Bascomb's struggle has none of the grandiosity of Marise's in *The Brimming Cup.* Yet in its plain, practical everydayness her problem makes Marise's problem seem paltry. Mrs. Bascomb is not a pretentious person and *Her Son's Wife* wears none of the earmarks of an "ambitious" novel. But the character and the book are of a substance few readers will miss, for all the homeliness of the setting and the simplicity of event.

V

She has shown what she can do. Now, if the world will contrive to run itself for a little while, she may have a chance. . . .

Elizabeth Wyckoff

SOURCE: "Dorothy Canfield: A Neglected Best Seller," in *The Bookman,* New York, Vol. LXXIV, No. 1, September, 1931, pp. 40-4.

Dorothy Canfield has been a famous novelist for a good many years now. One has to be in one's forties to remember the excitement with which we followed *The Squirrel Cage* as it came out in *Everybody's Magazine* in 1911. And every year or so since that time, something interesting has appeared over her signature. It might be a long and absorbing novel, such as *The Bent Twig* or *Rough-Hewn.* It might be a juvenile in *Saint Nicholas,* called *Understood Betsy,* so wise and so humorous that sophisticated mothers and spoiled little girls read it with the same pleased shame; it might be a book about the Montessori method, or short stories about Vermont farm people; there was, of course, a book of war stories. When there was a longer time than usual between books, one always wondered what she was doing, what she was thinking about, and hoped, as one hopes of a non-letter-writing friend, that nothing had happened to her.

That she and her thoughts are so much a part of the mental background of most American women is, I dare say, one good reason why as a novelist and literary personage she has not been taken more seriously. She has phrased theories of life (and created life-like exponents of them) which many people cherish as ideals, and many more think they do. It is difficult to separate the literary craftsman in her work from what there is no better word for than the propagandist—a fluent and creative propagandist, to be sure, but always advancing some immensely interesting, adventurous or courageous way to live. Her own life, as a matter of fact, has been as consistent and as courageous as that of any of her heroines. The same thorough-going reliance upon a sound, feminine combination of head and heart—once head and heart have worked out their decisions—has given her life a continuity of motive that few people achieve.

She was born in Kansas, the daughter of a college professor-president and his brilliantly musical wife. The reflection of her life as a child in small college towns of the West, in faculty society and as an undergraduate is vivid in the early parts of *The Bent Twig, The Squirrel Cage,* and *Rough-Hewn.* Her father's subject was the Romance languages, a fact which occasioned many family trips to France and Italy and the consequent love of France and the French that no doubt made so obvious and so necessary to her the years she spent with her entire family in France during the war.

An article by Zephine Humphrey, in the *Woman's Journal,* gives a detailed account of her amazingly active life. After her college degree, she did graduate work at Columbia; at some very early age she had earned her doctor's degree in the Romance languages and had written several scholarly books, one a study of Racine and Corneille, another a text-book with Professor George Carpenter. An academic career seemed indicated, and a brilliant one. But she had had enough of it. In 1907, shortly after she had inherited a farm in Arlington, Vermont, she married John Fisher, a Columbia friend, and, with what is most easily described by the Emersonian cliché of "plain living and high thinking" as a guide, retired

with him to that remote spot to live. Their apparent distaste for the capitalist system, their insistence on the dignity of work, the beauty of primitive human relationships, the desirability of a simple life and only a small *quid pro quo* as a fair reward of effort, all come out at later dates in her books. The theories are lived always by heroines who, no matter how they may be described in the flesh, live and breathe Dorothy Canfield's own philosophies. Here in Arlington a daughter, Sally, was born, and *The Squirrel Cage* (1912) written. In 1914 a son, Jimmy, was born, and in 1915 two books, *Hillsboro People,* short stories of Vermont life, and *The Bent Twig* were published.

In the spring of 1916 her husband went to France as an ambulance driver, and in the autumn Mrs. Fisher, with the two babies, followed him. Her first war work was with the blind; later, after her husband was made head of a training camp for ambulance drivers, she was for some time *Brigadier de l'Ordinaire,* in other words camp housekeeper. A Red Cross home for refugee children at Guéthary also took much of Mrs. Fisher's time, and, I suspect, a large part of the royalties from *Home Fires in France* and *The Day of Glory.* Sally caught typhoid in France, but recovered; fortunately no irreparable catastrophe marred the Fishers' elaborate pilgrimage.

In 1919 they all returned to Vermont, where Mrs. Fisher has carried on ever since what she calls a normal woman's life. This involves a simple and happy family life, housekeeping, with one maid, in the original farmhouse, much work for the Vermont Children's Aid Society, the State Education Board, the Parent-Teachers Association, and much lecturing as well as the writing of several novels. A large brick house in Arlington which recently descended to her was given to the town as a Community House, with a wing reserved for her own guests. Mr. Fisher's service in the state legislature is in line with the public spirit of both. This past year a short book, called *Why Stop Learning?*, of the type which, as Arnold Bennett used to do, Mrs. Fisher throws off between novels, has become the voice and watchword of the national adult education movement. Mrs. Fisher writes in a cabin on a hillside, and her friends tell of seeing her working absorbedly in odds and ends of time that most writers cannot manage to use.

Now the children are growing up, and Mrs. Fisher has been a best seller for years. Her early public is in its forties and fifties and can look at her, if they will, with a detached and middle-aged judgement. With

The Deepening Stream, her latest novel, fresh in our minds, it is not a bad time to look at her work and her place in contemporary letters. Disregarding the friendly affection of her really great public, where would a dispassionate critic place her in any scale of present-day novelists?

A review of her career and a re-reading of the earlier novels is a rather surprising experience. The only novel that really "dates" is ***The Squirrel Cage.*** That book, reread in 1931, seems undeniably brilliant and competent, but also undeniably adolescent. It is like hearing one's own girlish agonies over again to read the heroine's speeches. The plot—how vital it seemed then and how trivial now—hangs on the struggle of an idealistic middle-class young woman to get away from the material things of a small-town society. She was not, you remember, quite strong enough a character to defy her circle successfully; she married the tiresome young business man and not the dimly Christlike and socialistic young hermit whom her family deplored. She was thoroughly miserable and even ill. An accident removes the husband—Mrs. Fisher has never had to finish a novel and a villain in this fortuitous manner since then—and at the end of the book one is sure that happiness and a crust are to be the portion of heroine, hero and the child of the first husband. ***The Squirrel Cage*** was a feminine form (and incidentally a better made book than most of them) of the novels of the type of those by Winston Churchill, Owen Wister and Henry Sydnor Harrison. A woman served as the "hero," romance and idealism were embodied in a shadowy male character, and every girl and woman who read the book identified herself with the sensitive, frustrated and, of course, neurotic heroine. Incidentally, even at this early date and with no blowing of horns, there is much sound modern psychology behind the story. (Perhaps, however, there is only the shrewd innate knowledge of people of the genuine novelist; as a clever scholar, mixing his dates a little, might five hundred years from now demonstrate a great deal of Freud or Jung from the novels of George Eliot.)

The Bent Twig, three years later, was a great advance over ***The Squirrel Cage.*** The theme was the exact converse of that of the first book. The heroine in this case was brought up to plain living and high thinking, and tried to get away from both, but in the end the twig bends as it was inclined and she marries a socialist millionaire who, renouncing his fortune to establish a foundation for the benefit of his employees, retires to a small property in Vermont, where they are to lead a quiet but productive and happy life. ***The Bent Twig*** is an extraordinarily good novel, head and shoulders above most novels of its time. There are some first-class characters, notably the heroine's professor father, her placid but far from stupid mother, her inarticulate extrovert sister. Sylvia herself is at first rather an unsympathetic character as she leads her egotistic young years of shame because her father and mother not only have shabby friends who drink beer and play the cello, but give parties with charades and sandwiches and do not keep up with the faculty society of the western university town where they live. But as she grows older and develops not only in character but in the ability to think clearly, she comes to a full-grown mental and emotional stature that was and is, even on re-reading after fifteen years, a stirring thing to read. The best emotional scenes in the book are described with a sureness and accuracy of detail that Mrs. Fisher apparently had no time for in ***The Squirrel Cage.***

The Brimming Cup and ***Rough-Hewn*** are a pair of novels about the same people. They are quite as good as ***The Bent Twig*** and the heroine is from the start a much nicer person. The hero, too, is Mrs. Fisher's first really successfully delineated hero. The story of Marise and Neale of course has more continuity and scope, as it goes on through years of married life, here again the married life of a pair who are building a beautiful life in an unworldly way in a small Vermont community. Marise weathers the temptation to return with a *tertium quid* to the cosmopolitan life which she had renounced for love and theory, and emerges after one of the most searching and beautiful passages in any of Mrs. Fisher's novels into a completely satisfactory state of mind and heart about her husband. Both books are rather too long, rather lacking in humour. These are captious criticisms, however, for books written and published during and just after the war.

Between these two novels and ***The Deepening Stream,*** in which for the first time Mrs. Fisher has used the war as a factor in a novel, were ***The Home-Maker*** and ***Her Son's Wife***—both books concerned with superficially simple but really difficult and intricate situations. ***The Home-Maker,*** again competent and vivid, and rather ahead of its time, is the story of a family in which the traditional functions of the parents are completely reversed and not shared in varying proportions, as is more usual; the father looks after the house and children and the mother earns the income. ***Her Son's Wife*** contains a remarkable piece of character-creation and development—the middle-aged widowed school teacher, sure of herself, efficient, a little bossy and grim, but happy, whose only son brings home as his bride a girl the exact opposite of everything that Mrs. Bascom has always liked and approved. If an English novelist had written this book or a new American writer who was not already the idol of the 2,600,000 purchasers (and three to five times as many readers) of a woman's magazine, as well as a steady best seller, the critics would have fastened many more laurels upon Mrs. Fisher's brow, I am sure. As it was, she had the usual excellent reviews but caused no excitement. For the first time the heroine is not the author herself, or her ideal. She is a genuine creation, moving in a real plot to a genuine dénouement of the spirit.

Last of all we have her *The Deepening Stream,* written long enough after the war for the author not to be carried away by the emotions of the time. At first one sees merely a familiar pattern; here is again the sensitive, gifted girl, this time unhappy over sex because of the remembered bickerings of her parents, who is delivered from an inhibited life by falling in love with a gentle, rather average, inarticulate young man. There is a pleasant picture of village life in the Hudson River valley, and Quaker family local colour; then the scene changes when Matey and Adrian pick up the children and go to the war, just as the Fishers actually did. The picture of Paris in wartime, the French family of old friends with whom Matey lives and works, is unforgettable. Here Dorothy Canfield shows a power of concrete description, of character suggestion, of dramatic and emotional control of her material that is so fluent and so sure that one never pauses to say "What excellent writing this is!" but only reads on in order to understand the people and find out what happened, whether Ziza's husband was ever found, whether the children in the cellar of the Lycée would escape the air raid, what Matey and Adrian were ever able to work out as a way of life after such thorough experience of so horrible a war. There is at the end, no matter how Matey may try to look ahead in the lives of her children, and in working with her husband in his little village bank, that weariness and questioning that only the generation of men and women who are old enough to have taken little children through the war years can quite understand. If the book had been ended with an adequate answer to Matey's situation in 1920 it would be much less true a book.

It is very probable that Dorothy Canfield is not at all troubled by lack of literary recognition. She undoubtedly takes greater pleasure in the response of her audience than she could get from any criticism however laudatory. And, of course, if she had wanted to lead the literary life, she could have stayed in New York and lived it. But her own detachment is no reason for ignoring or taking her for granted. Indeed, to leave her out of serious discussion of the American novel is becoming more than a little ridiculous.

As a matter of fact Dorothy Canfield belongs in the succession of novelists that begins with George Eliot and continues with Mrs. Humphrey Ward and Mrs. Deland—all of them warm-hearted women (yes, even Mrs. Ward; did she not create Marcella?), all of them full of a motherly understanding and tolerance of human beings, all of them a little omniscient, like most women, and all of them except George Eliot with her minor characters, too interested in life and people to be humorous or even witty in their books. Only a deep female humour could underlie many of their conceptions of character, but there is no surface wit. They never laugh at their characters. If you smile now and then yourself, it is a motherly smile.

Where the next generation may put Dorothy Canfield I do not prophesy. One does not think of her in the same breath with G. B. Stern, Virginia Woolf, or any of the young followers of Proust or Hemingway. In spite of an academic tendency to class her with Sinclair Lewis as a merely journalistic novelist, there is an emotional force in both writers—rather greater in Dorothy Canfield's books, I think, except perhaps for *Arrowsmith*—that it seems to be fashionable deliberately to ignore. In the matter of form, Miss Cather, needless to say, excels Dorothy Canfield. But the big canvas and the perfect etching may both be genuinely enough works of art. On the other hand, Dorothy Canfield never slips into the near-hysteria which keeps both Edna Ferber and Fannie Hurst from finishing their novels as well as they begin.

There is an unself-consciousness and a lavishness about the outpouring of the old-fashioned born novelist of Dorothy Canfield's sort that is unmistakable. No considerations of form or current literary enthusiasms affect a writer of this type who has in early life fashioned a good working style, flexible and ready to hand, who has some people to write about, a story to tell and—they cannot help it—a theory or a thesis to uphold. Wells, Sinclair Lewis, George Eliot, Dickens—the fluent, deeply emotional novelists are a type by themselves and Dorothy Canfield belongs with them. Because she has been popular from the beginning of her career, because her shrewd common sense and understanding of the conditions of everyday life, even more than her emotional power, make her the "favourite author" of enormous numbers of unanalytical women who find in every story some illumination for their own lives, she has never had the recognition which her work deserves. She is journalistic to the extent that she produces constantly. She is unliterary partly because she is completely unselfconscious. If she achieves a beautiful passage it is because the words and sentences express what she has to say, and not because she is interested in beautiful writing except as a tool.

The younger generation may find Mrs. Fisher's taste too refined. Surprisingly enough, even with reservations, someone put *The Deepening Stream* in a list of "pleasant" novels in the *Atlantic Monthly* the other day. And yet one can understand the choice. She can write about almost any horror without being offensive. No doubt the younger generation, too, cannot understand how her thorough-going feminism, which she always takes for granted, can be combined with her simple and emotionally primitive conception of the obligations of marriage and motherhood. The women who live this life cannot ordinarily write about it, and when they are old enough to understand it they are not usually writing book reviews or paying much attention to them. I expect that most of the men who write criticism of fiction think of Mrs. Fisher as a popular woman's magazine novelist, and little more. They should read the last half of *The Deepening Stream.*

Quarreling with prize awards has come to be the favourite American indoor sport—and it is an invidious and odious business, particularly when an award has been given to an honest and witty, interesting and workmanlike novel, written by a woman with a delightfully observing eye and a discriminating mind. Yet when there was no Willa Cather novel last year Dorothy Canfield should have had the credit for being one of the few American novelists of either sex who have, with a competent and restrained technique, that inexhaustible, unwearying and tolerant understanding of human nature which is the distinguishing mark of first-rate novelists and of first-rate novelists alone.

William Lyon Phelps

SOURCE: "Dorothy Canfield Fisher," in *The English Journal,* Vol. XXII, No. 1, January, 1933, pp. 1-8.

One day more than twenty years ago as I was at work in my house in New Haven, I was pleasantly interrupted by the advent of a distinguished-looking elderly gentleman accompanied by an extremely shy and timid young girl. The man was the librarian of Columbia University, formerly president of Ohio State—how fortunate to be able to exchange the terrible job of college president for the agreeable position of librarian!—and the bashful girl was his daughter Dorothy. Dr. Canfield never wasted time or words on preliminaries.

"This is my daughter and she has got to write a thesis in Old French for her Ph.D. at Columbia."

I said fervently, "God help her!"

"No, *you* help her!"

"But I don't know anything whatever about Old French. The only French that interests me is modern French."

"Yes," said he, "but you once wrote a thesis in English and got a Ph.D."

"That is quite true; and I made up my mind then that if the Lord would forgive me I would never write another."

"Well, this thesis has got to be written, and we have come to New Haven to discuss the method of its production with you."

Then we had a delightful conversation. Dr. Canfield was one of the most interesting men I ever knew. Of course I did my best to point out the way in which "original work," if it were to be valuable and important, must be done; what to include, what to emphasize, what to omit. Merely as a matter of record, I will say that Miss Canfield wrote her thesis with the customary bloody sweat, successfully met all the requirements, and has whatever rights and privileges go with the title of "Doctor."

In the summer vacation of the year 1912, as I was sitting in my house in Michigan after the diurnal eighteen holes, the diurnal parcel of new books contained a novel by a woman unknown to fame. The novel was *The Squirrel Cage:* the name of the author, Dorothy Canfield. I did not connect this name in my mind with that of the quondam aspirant to the doctorate; but the title of the book was beguiling, and the first paragraph caught my attention. I read the book from beginning to end with steadily increasing admiration. Somewhere during its perusal I *heard* the timid, almost inaudible voice of that terror-stricken, thesis-haunted girl in New Haven. I wrote a letter to her in care of the publisher asking if it were really she. I received a reply from Mrs. J. R. Fisher in Arlington, Vermont, confessing everything. What a development in four years! The timid girl had become a Ph.D., a wife, and a novelist!

As I considered *The Squirrel Cage,* I thought how strange it was that this author had ever supposed her "vocation" lay in Old French or in anything other than creative work. For although she has since written better novels, this particular specimen has intrinsic value. It is emphatically a good novel. It contained unmistakable evidence that its author was a genuine, realistic writer—realistic without being sensational. Her realism is unlike the gorgeous ironical mimicry of Sinclair Lewis, unlike the unassorted heaps of building-material dumped by Theodore Dreiser, unlike the shock-for-shock's-sake style of Ernest Hemingway. She creates real people who act and speak naturally, in a way recognizable by all who live in civilized communities.

I dare say that the labor in Old French was not fruitless: the painstaking accuracy of that thesis was transferred to a wider and more interesting domain. Her education in France, where precision of language is still thought to be important, was as valuable for her as for her older contemporaries, Anne Sedgwick and Edith Wharton. All three have a thorough knowledge of the French language and literature.

The Squirrel Cage describes a typical American family, with its daily pleasures, worries, tasks, recreations, quarrels, intimacies, and misunderstandings. After twenty years I can remember vividly the telephone orders given by the wife, while the husband listens with increasing dismay.

In her next novel, *The Bent Twig,* Dorothy Canfield produced the best story of undergraduate and faculty life in America that I have read. She describes a co-educational state institution, the kind of thing she knew as a child; for, as I mentioned before, her father had been president of Ohio State University. Indeed it was at his inauguration that one of the pleasantest and best known of presidential tales had its origin. When the ceremonies were over and President Eliot of Harvard was about to leave, he remarked with a smile, "Well, Canfield, now you are a college president and everybody will say you are a liar." "Why, Dr. Eliot, did they ever say *you* were a liar?" "Worse than that, they *proved* it!" If the story is apocryphal, it is truer than fact. I remember years ago asking my old friend Tom Bacon, professor of his-

tory at the University of California, what he thought of President Holden. "He is a very able man, but the truth is not in him." Then I asked Dr. Holden what he thought of Tom Bacon. "Doesn't he look just like a hired assassin? Wouldn't you hate to meet him on a dark night?" These university amenities!

Most college novels seem true only to those who are unfamiliar with the particular college in question. A novel must have some kind of a plot, and college life itself has no plot. Just as a thing must have "news value" in order to reach the first page of a newspaper, so the things that make up the pages of a novel must somehow be made interesting. Now the daily life of students and professors, however interesting the routine may be to them, has as a rule no conceivable sensational interest for the "general reader"; hence the average novelist, spurred by hope of fame or fortune, seeks for exciting details: athletic sports, dissipation, unclean "bull" sessions, and other features.

Thus I have read novels of university life which would give a foreigner the idea that American colleges specialized in iniquity; that the conversation of the students was devoid of intellectual interest; that decency and even sanity were unknown.

The Bent Twig gives a fair and on the whole truthful picture of the immensely varied activities in a modern American university. Study, athletic games, societies, play their proportional rôles; and considerable space is given to a very real evil, faculty politics. I have lived in a college faculty for forty-one years, and I admire my colleagues. They are a fine lot of men and I would rather live with them than with any other group of persons I have ever known. But they are not angelic and college politics are not always clean. Men who devote their lives to learning and to the teaching of youth should at any rate try to set an example of breadth of mind and bigness of view. Unfortunately, magnanimity is almost as rare here as it is elsewhere. The root of all evil seems to be jealousy. Every professor, whether engaged in "special research" or in something else, should rejoice in the success of any one of his colleagues. He should, but—vanity and jealousy are unlovely but common in all inclosed communities like military garrisons, college faculties, and monasteries.

During the war Mrs. Fisher went to France, where her accurate knowledge of the language and of the people made her presence of the highest value. Many women, and some elderly men, feeling that they ought to "do their bit," managed to cross the water, where they were, in innumerable instances, a nuisance. They could not speak or understand the language with facility, they fell sick and had to be taken care of, and when they were well, they had a genius for getting in the way of those who were useful. But Mrs. Fisher knew exactly what she could do, knew how to do it, and did it. She took care of blind soldiers and of their children. This would not be worth mentioning in an estimate of her literary art if it were not for the fact that it aided in producing some of her best writing. The stories she wrote as a *liaison* officer had for their object something other than the production of literature. She wished to help the Americans to understand the French temperament. But the inspiration she received from her years in France during the war-madness tipped her pen with fire; some of her most beautiful compositions resulted. Her story about the small shopkeeper who refused to have his commodity marketed on a large scale is a contribution to international understanding and a work of literary art.

As a short-story writer, indeed, she ranks among our best. Her tales of Vermont and of the Basque country are exceedingly well done. And in these specimens she is free from her worst fault—a tendency to diffuseness. She has the bad habit in some of her books of multiplying words. This is why I have never admired **The Brimming Cup** nearly so much as some of her other works.

She has never recovered from the teacher's point of view. Her interest in education has been shown in some of her treatises. The danger of the teacher when he comes to address a mature audience, is repetition. Long experience at the desk in the classroom has taught him the value—nay, the necessity—of emphasis by repetition. But it is bad for literary composition.

This does not mean that she lost more than she gained by her early academic environment or by her interest in the welfare of others. I myself have learned much by the allusions to education in her novels. I remember in one of her latest books a conversation between a professor and his wife in which they ask each other at what college it was their child had scarlet fever or some distemper. There she points out the weakness of those traveling professors—birds of passage—who are ever moving from one college to another in the hope of more salary or better surroundings, and who lose the influence and the productivity that come from an abiding background.

Sinclair Lewis no doubt performed a service as well as a work of art when he wrote *Main Street*; he gave a devastating picture of the ignorance, the complacency, the conceit, the vulgarity, the affectation, the pettiness of much small-town life. But he gave nothing else. For the sake of tremendous emphasis, which he certainly attained, he omitted the finer qualities and the nobler characters which are also characteristic of every American village. Dorothy Canfield, who has lived in Paris, in rural France, in a Middle West city, and in a Vermont village, has pointed out the fact that every country has its Main Streets. We might imagine that in a small town in France glorified by one of the finest cathedrals of the world the life of the inhabitants would take on some of the culture and some of the aspiration of its chief adornment. Did you ever talk with the residents?

One of our Yale professors, now no longer living, who was born in France, was so impatient with what he thought was the vulgarity and ignorance of America that on a sabbatical year he went over to France thinking he would escape for a time from a distressing environment. I discovered him in a village in Brittany. He was desperately homesick for America. "Why," said he, "I never thought such ignorance, stupidity, and vulgarity could exist as I have found in this French village. And the language of the old women when they speak angrily to each other!" He was unfortunately able to understand everything they said.

Well, we know what Flaubert thought of small-town life in France. And Dostoievski said that in Russian villages the inhabitants spent so much time poking their noses into their neighbors' affairs that one would think they would all be great psychologists. "On the contrary, they are nearly all idiots."

Now Dorothy Canfield believes that a New England village contains an almost complete assortment of the various types of human nature; there one can study them better than in a large city. With her large, tolerant view of human nature, and her womanly sympathy, she gives us not a travesty, but a picture.

Of all her novels I like best **Her Son's Wife.** In the first place, her attention is concentrated on three characters; from multiplicity of characters arises a tendency to diffuseness. This book deals with a fight between two women for the possession of one man. When two men fight for a woman, the spectacle is not particularly interesting, both because it is so common and because there is a pact known as a gentleman's agreement—who ever heard of a lady's agreement? When two women fight for a man, the struggle is interesting because there are no rules. In this particular novel a mother, accustomed for many years to domination over her son, finds that he has married without previously consulting her; and has married the most detestable female in the world.

The mother is a school-teacher. On arriving home from her professional duties one afternoon she sees in the hall a woman's hat. Now just as a zoölogist can from the sight of one bone reconstruct the entire animal, so a woman from the sight of one hat can visualize the entire form and character of its wearer. This hat is not reassuring; in fact, her worst fears are confirmed.

Mother, wife, and son begin the disastrous experiment of living together. Mother is not only the bread-winner (teacher's salary) but has to do all the housework. She has always been a dust-hunter, the terror of servants. She has a place for everything, with everything in its place. As a school-teacher, she has taught an excellent diction, pronunciation, enunciation; she abhors vulgarities of tongue. Her son's wife is like a movie actress without salary; she talks slang dialect; she leaves everything around the house as if there were ten servants to clean up after her; her cooking would not appeal even to those who were starving. Every word she utters, every movement she makes, is torture to the correct, orderly, well-disciplined school-teacher; and she is her son's wife!

Although the mother teaches morning and afternoon at the public school, she has herself to do all the housecleaning, dish-washing, and bed-making at home; her short hours in bed are made wakeful by her hatred for the besom that has turned domestic peace into a cyclone. Why then does she not break down?

The answer is interesting to all teachers. We are familiar with the story of the clown, stricken with mortal illness, who nevertheless had to amuse audiences every night. This is called a tragedy; but, as a matter of fact, the clown was fortunate in having his professional work, which took his mind off his own horror. We often say that pupils enter the schoolroom thinking of everything except their lessons; that it is therefore the first duty of the teacher to divert their minds from their various interests, and attract them to the matter in hand. A teacher, we say, is like a court lawyer; unless he interests the jury, he loses his case.

But what is true of the pupil is true of the teacher. The average teacher comes from worry at home to confront a roomful of turbulent youth, who have everything except nerves. He must forget his own troubles in order to carry on his professional work.

Now some have read Dorothy Canfield's story and have wondered how this protagonist could have done her teaching when the hours before and after were filled with nerve-shattering misery. I say that it was her professional work that saved her life and her soul. For the daily round of teaching is like the work of a military captain in action. There are certain kinds of toil that can be done mechanically; the work goes on while the mind is otherwise employed. But the blessed thing about teaching is that it demands unrestricted attention. When the teacher is alone in the classroom with her pupils, no other person can help her, and she cannot for a single moment think of anything else. Many teachers are doing brilliant and successful work in the classroom while suffering from ill health, financial worry, and the anxiety that comes from a cloud of difficulties at home. Work is the chief of human blessings, for we are unhappy only while we are thinking about ourselves. That is why the loss of income is only one of the tragedies of unemployment.

In this novel Dorothy Canfield reached her highest point. The conclusion of the struggle is profoundly affecting, and touches the deepest things in the human heart.

Her faults as a writer usually arise from a superfluous elaboration of mere language, from a concentration on ideas so intense that the manner of presentation suffers, and from an invincible desire to leave the world better than she found it. In other words, she is a woman first and an artist second. But her very devotion to her daily duties as wife and mother, her sympathy for all sorts and conditions of men and women and children, make her realistic novels more truthful. And she does know how to write.

I regard her novels as a contribution to American literature. She has won a place in the first rank of America's woman novelists, and there she stands with her peers—Edith Wharton, Willa Cather, Anne Sedgwick, Edna Ferber, Zona Gale, Ellen Glasgow. . . .

Percy H. Boynton

SOURCE: "Two New England Regionalists," in *College English,* Vol. 1, No. 4, January, 1940, pp. 291-99.

Dorothy Canfield Fisher, invincible Vermonter, has had a drought to record . . . Vermont crumbles but is not wrecked. In all her stories Vermont character is asserting itself more or less vainly to oppose irresistible forces. The success of the resistance is never included in the stories, but it is usually implied at the end as the obvious theme of an unwritten sequel. Slow crumbling is too vague to submit to chronicle treatment; it needs reinforcement by plot structure, and Mrs. Fisher has her constant factors for this plot: a native Vermonter who has strayed from home and has been distracted by wealth and dazzled by European sophistication preserves his integrity by taking refuge in the old ways of self-fulfilment as a hill villager. In *Rough-Hewn* the Boy, after showing promise as a New York business bandit, takes a year off to find himself in travel, and finding the Girl astray in Europe, the daughter of American expatriates, returns with her to take up life at the old family sawmill. In *The Brimming Cup* the Vermont story has a precedent European background. In *The Bent Twig* the Girl of the right stock rejects a rich young tomcat and is bewildered by a wealthy aunt who almost estranges her from the family and by an art broker who almost alienates her from the elect Native Son. He, in turn, has inherited Colorado mines, which he gives back to the workers, and the lovers retire to his home acres and a reforestation project.

Better than these, most effective of Mrs. Fisher's output, is *Bonfire.* The formula persists, but it is overwhelmed by the human elements in the tale. The central factor this time is not an individual but the composite personality of the village. This is taciturn toward strangers, loquacious when left to itself, capable of the most extreme group reactions under excitement and of every sort of personal eccentricity in times of peace. Mrs. Fisher describes its behavior when the village doctor scandalizes it by marrying a girl of dubious character from "the Shelf," an upland hillside slum:

> The first reaction of Clifford people to Doctor Anson's marriage and all that went with it was a reflex group response such as follows an earthquake or a flood—something that happens to all as much as to one. No matter what their individual temperaments, they all cried out the same things when they talked, held their tongues by instinct on the same occasions. For, of course, even the children knew enough to shut their mouths during the few days when detectives, newspaper reporters and other prying outsiders were around, vainly looking for clews. . . . No other silence about Doctor Craft's marriage was kept in Clifford than the little oasis of it about his sister. . . . It was felt that self-control need go no further. In fact talk and plenty of it was called for. To exclaim and condemn was right and proper. . . . As

> it was, the fire of disapproval . . . presently began to burn itself out. The stronger souls . . . emerging a little from collective mob feeling, began out of sheer boredom . . . occasionally to turn the conversation to something else. . . . People went back to their own naturally different ways of looking at life.

These different ways are the theme of the book's opening pages, in which thumbnail sketches of the dramatis personae are given: Sherwin Dewey, nature-lover and homely philosopher, and Sherwin Dewey's dog; Mr. Lawrence Stewart, keeper of a museum, his own perfect ancestral home, and Lawrence Stewart's cat; Father Kirby, the ascetic rector; the elderly Kemp sisters, inseparable in their difference; the Deans, the Merrills, the Nyes; the elect, who lived on The Street; the lower middle class, though never so described, who lived at Clifford's Four Corners; the folks beyond the pale on Searles Shelf. All these were to react to Doctor Craft, gifted and restless young physician, and to Miss Anna, his sister, who had just returned from a year in Paris to her visiting nurse's round in the township. And all were to be affected by the subtly seductive presence of Lixlee Burdick, the Searles Shelf girl, who could take on the ways of politer society, who was too lovely of skin and hair and contour, and who was the perennial type of amoral carnality which found its perfect hunting ground in a tidy New England village. In the end she changed life for almost everyone she passed. She turned the heads of all the men, she estranged the women, and by the forces she set in motion she united the doctor's sister and the rector in holy wedlock, captured old Mr. Stewart in the bonds of unholy matrimony, drove Isabel Foote into effective professional life, handed a rich and eligible husband to Olivia Merrill, even by indirection founded a co-operative home for the poor upland children who were impossibly far from school.

In all this there is none of the play of economic forces that are so devastating to Maine and its people. The only machine in the novel is the locomotive which annually brings and takes away the alien city dwellers, who do not care to know and are not permitted to see the inner life of the village. The story goes back of the machine to the vulnerable nature of man. Lixlee is the serpent in the Garden of Eden, and she is Eve after her talk with the serpent. She is original sin in a Calvinistic hamlet, playing upon the natural depravity of the townsfolk. Life is unfertilized there, or unfortified, by the contact of the seamen with the outer world. A few who have fared forth save their souls, but the many are nearer to the native instinct of Sherwin Dewey's dog, which belongs in the wilds, and of Lawrence Stewart's cat, which has disreputable relations with a rover from the woods. It is a real distinction between Mrs. Fisher's characters and Miss Chase's; and it is a distinction which accounts for disintegration rather than noble defeat.

Bonfire seems the truest of the Vermont stories because it is not complicated by Mrs. Fisher's loyalty to Vermont. For once she does not conclude with the implication that the leading characters are finally on the verge of living happily ever after. This tale ends with Anna Craft's observation that life teaches one a good deal and with her confession, when queried, that she can't quite make up her mind what the lesson is.

In *Seasoned Timber,* however, Mrs. Fisher has been carried along by the tide of events. The change is from absorption in Vermont character as a product of the past to vindication of Vermont character as a bulwark against the present. And it is also, explicitly, a change from instinctive allusion to Henry James, recurrent in the earlier works, to inevitable allusion to Sinclair Lewis. For in this latest novel Mrs. Fisher declares with a sober face what Lewis has declared with his tongue in his cheek—that fascist materialism, leading to Yahoo, Black Legion savagery, "can't happen here" in Vermont. She acknowledges at last that Vermont, like Maine, is losing its basic resources. Sheep have gone; granite and marble are giving way to synthetic materials; woodenware, to metal; woolen, to the pressure of southern wage scales. Vermont has one final defense, its native backbone. Henry James cannot help her in this crisis; but she is so conscious of her new ally that in the midst of a caricature of George Clarence Wheaton, a magnified Babbitt, she interpolates, "Really Sinclair Lewis is a phonograph record! When you read him you think he's laying it on too thick. Not at all. He doesn't exaggerate a hair." Mrs. Fisher, too, lays it on thick in the anti-fascist propaganda which dominates the latter part of the novel, but in the long approach to this she continues in the more nearly Jamesian fashion of her more nearly Americo-European novels. The resultant product is a hybrid, but an interesting one, with its appeals to popular response from various types of reader: the people who love Vermont, the people who love any kind of localism, the people who love nature, the people who love a love story, the people who love noble sentiments, the people who hate bigotry of any sort and anti-Semitism in particular. It is effective argument, though as art it suffers by comparison with *Bonfire.*

Joseph P. Lovering

SOURCE: "The Friendship of Willa Cather and Dorothy Canfield," in *Vermont History: The Proceedings of the Vermont Historical Society,* Vol. 48, No. 3, Summer, 1980, pp. 144-54.

Most readers know of the many friends that Willa Cather had and treasured and who in turn seemed to appreciate her great gifts—the Menuhins, Edith Lewis, the McClungs, and the Hambourgs, Elizabeth Sergeant, Sarah Orne Jewett, Mrs. Fields, the D. H. Lawrences and many more. Yet the students of Willa Cather's life know that she remained an essentially private person, an artist who valued her privacy intensely and guarded it with great care. In this respect she resembled Henry James whom she early admired. Both knew the nature of their artistic gifts; the sacred flame had to be tended. But even the writer of the greatest talents needs to share problems both of a personal and of an artistic nature with others.

The considerable number of books which treat the life of Willa Cather almost always contain brief recognition of the friendship between the famous novelist and her lifetime friend Dorothy Canfield Fisher, herself a novelist whose years spanned approximately those of Miss Cather. Their friendship deserves greater stress. It lasted over a period of some fifty-eight years and was an important friendship for both of these writers whom the American reading public and the world have long regarded with high esteem, especially, of course, Willa Cather. Without overstating the case, Willa Cather had a special regard for Dorothy Canfield which derived from a special trust and admiration for her as a person. Their mutual friendship might have become an even more important friendship had the exigencies and circumstances of their lives been somewhat different.

Dorothy Canfield's father, James Hulm Canfield, served as Chancellor of the University of Nebraska from 1891 to 1895, precisely the years Willa Cather spent at the University. Dorothy was still in the Latin School of Lincoln, Nebraska, in 1894 when she and her friend Willa Cather won a first prize for their jointly-authored short story **"The Fear That Walks by Noonday."** A two-part narrative, the story tells of the highly bizarre influence that a recently dead football player has on the outcome of a college game in the Northwest. Though tolerably well written, the story was not work that Willa Cather would later desire to receive much notice. The ghostly power of a deceased player dominates the game, causes icy winds to throw a deadly chill over the opponents' efforts, and even carries his weird spell into the postgame party of the losers. The story builds upon a kind of athletic hubris. The local heroes become a little too proud of their attainments and learn a lesson by the intervention of the dead. Dorothy Canfield was fourteen years old, in her first or second preparatory year at the Latin School, and Willa Cather a twenty-one-year-old college junior when the story appeared. The writing certainly has enough sophistication in fictional technique alone to make it appear to be the writing of the older student.

Willa Cather's Campus Years (1950) carries twenty-two letters of recollection and impression solicited from classmates of Willa Cather at the University of Nebraska. Approximately half of these letters testify to the early friendship of the two writers, and several of these letters stress the special nature of the friendship of the two.

Dorothy Canfield earned her bachelor's degree from Ohio State University where her father had been called to the presidency after leaving the University of Nebraska. Dorothy went abroad to study at the College de France, working under the advisement of the Modern Language Department of Columbia University. When she returned to America, she spent four years on doctoral study at Columbia, where her father then held an appointment as Head Librarian. Willa Cather came to admire Dorothy's expertise in French literature. Dorothy Canfield worked from 1902 to 1905 as a secretary at the Horace Mann School in New York, where she met her husband John Redwood Fisher in 1903. They married in 1907 in Pleasantville, New York, and came in that same year to live in a very old farmhouse in Arlington, Vermont, just north of the village and a little way up Red Mountain. It was their wedding present from Mr. Canfield. In this beautiful section of Vermont along the winding Battenkill the Fishers made no effort to farm, but instead they labored at the reforestation of the mountainside. When World War I came, husband, wife and the two young children went to France for three years, there Dorothy edited a soldiers' magazine, organized reading rooms and day nurseries for workers' children, helped to run a refugee camp, and started a braille service for blinded soldiers. Her husband served in the ambulance corp as a volunteer. Afterwards, she lived with her husband in Arlington until her death in 1957.

Dorothy Canfield wrote ten novels published over a period of about thirty-two years from 1907 to 1939. Although her work received a large popular acclaim during these years, scholars pay little critical attention to her work. Her years of novel writing nearly paralleled those of Willa Cather. Dorothy Canfield's first novel *Gunhild* appeared in 1907; her second *The Squirrel Cage* (1912) came in the same year as Cather's *Alexander's Bridge*. Her precedence into novel publishing may have had some bearing on the nature of their developing friendship.

Dorothy Canfield wrote three novels prior to the American entry into World War I: *Gunhild, The Squirrel Cage* and *The Bent Twig* (1915). The latter two novels reveal her serious interest in the relation of the individual to American community life. Her stories resemble Cather's at least in their rejection of a growing materialism which placed a premium on commercial success and social prominence gained at the expense of human values. In *The Bent Twig* Canfield pictures successfully the academic community of one of the growing midwestern universities. In having the hero of the novel voluntarily choose a life dedicated to community welfare and service and give up a large inheritance, she reflects her own sense of values.

Returning from France after the war she resumed writing and further developed her powers as a realistic novelist. Her three novels, *The Brimming Cup* (1921), *Rough-Hewn* (1922), and *The Home-Maker* (1924), stress the individual's adjustment to the life of the family and also to the small New England community. In the twenties she wrote two novels which stand among her best achievements in fiction: *The Deepening Stream* (1930) and *Her Son's Wife* (1926).

The Deepening Stream, considered Canfield's best work, presents the growth of her heroine from childhood through adolescence to full maturity when Matey Gilbert finally discovered the underlying significance of the pattern of events which have shaped her life. In handling World War I, Canfield makes an honest attempt to evaluate the dramatic changes which affected American life. She urges a positive acceptance of the human frailties of people involved in that catastrophe, and she points towards the making of a better world.

In the thirties Canfield published her final two novels, *Bonfire* (1933) and *Seasoned Timber* (1939). In her rejection of fascism as a way of life for Vermonters in *Seasoned Timber,* in a strong reaction to Sinclair Lewis' novel, *It Can't Happen Here* (1936), she shows herself a champion of individual freedom.

Her novels reveal a writer with a natural gift for narrative, even though the novels frequently have shortcomings in their structural unity. Her interest centers largely on the feminine character; her central characters are always women, although she pioneered in the realistic portrayal of small children. Most admirers of Willa Cather sense the deep spiritual and moral significances underlying her novels; a close examination of the writings of Dorothy Canfield reveals a similar commitment to spiritual values, and that at a time when such values were undergoing severe scepticism and even denial.

In 1947 Dorothy Canfield wrote a reminiscence on her friendship with Willa Cather, which concentrated primarily on the years in which Willa Cather taught and worked as a journalist in Pittsburgh before taking the post of editor of *McClure's* in New York. "As we grew on into the twenties and thirties," she remembered, "this difference in years dwindled to nothing at all, as such differences do to adults, so far as any barrier to our close comradeship went. But my lifelong admiring affection for Willa was, at first, strongly tinctured with the respectful deference due from a young person to a successful member of the older generation." In this statement Canfield made an honest attempt to evaluate her attitude towards Willa Cather which contains some irony in that Canfield seemed to implicitly use her friend as a norm for her own career.

The Vermont novelist records how she would frequently stop over in Pittsburgh on her travels from Arlington to Ohio State University in order to keep up her friendship with Willa Cather. On one occasion she spent the entire Christmas holidays with her friend. She rejoiced in Cather's early literary success and shared in the friendships that her older companion had already made in Pittsburgh with the McClungs, the Andersons, and the Seibels.

Leon Edel gives Dorothy Canfield Fisher singular praise for her assistance with his writing of the Pittsburgh chapter in *Willa Cather: A Critical Biography,* citing her complete and careful answers to his detailed questions. And Mildred Bennett records how the manuscript of a book that Willa Cather worked on about 1903 and which never got published ended up in the Fishers' Arlington attic. Clearly the Cather-Canfield relationship continued to grow beyond the college years.

One episode in the lives of these two American novelists continues to survive as a favorite anecdote of biographers and commentators. During Cather's tour of Europe in 1902, along with Isabelle McClung, a visit was made to the English poet A. E. Housman. Isabelle McClung and Willa Cather had prearranged to meet Dorothy Canfield, already living that year in Paris where her mother, Flavia, an artist, had a studio. Isabelle and Willa, before meeting Dorothy in London, journeyed to the Shropshire country, toured Ludlow castle and returned to a not-so-fine apartment in suburban London where Housman, teaching at Cambridge, lived. Housman did not expect the visit, and the rapport left much to be desired. Most accounts of the visit carry the overtone that Willa Cather (her *April Twilights and Other Poems* [1923] certainly shows her awareness of Housman's art) was the most anxious of the three to meet Housman, but as the visit progressed, she realized that things were not going smoothly. The accounts generally credit Dorothy Canfield with saving the day, as Housman found in her conversation a common bond of interest—classical philology, which she worked at through her studies in Romance languages at the École des Hautes Études in Paris. Housman began to ask questions and found common scholarly interests with the young language student from America. Evidently these common interests averted the embarrassment which otherwise might have resulted from the unscheduled visit to the scholar-poet.

This visit to Housman later became the chief subject of an exchange of letters between Dorothy Canfield and Willa Cather immediately before the latter's death in 1947. Willa Cather wrote a letter to Dorothy Canfield on April 17th of that year asking that her friend supply her with a detailed and accurate account of the Housman visit in order to satisfy some editor's request. In this letter Cather writes disdainfully of the harassment by young scholars who forwarded their critiques of Housman to the aging and tired novelist and expected her commentaries on them. (Shades of Horace must have risen in Willa Cather's mind on those occasions. *Odi profanum vulgus!*) This letter, the last one that Willa Cather ever wrote, with Cather's remembrance of the Housman visit, fully substantiates the standard description of Dorothy Canfield's part.

Canfield replied immediately with an extended latter regarding the celebrated visit. She quickly received a note from Sarah Bloom, a faithful secretary of twenty years, affirming that Willa Cather had received the letter before she died. Dorothy Canfield's careful recollection does not change the basic description of the event. She does add these closing remarks in her letter:

But I really felt very uneasy, about what seemed bad manners on my part, and after we had gone, and were sitting on top of the bus, going back to our lodgings, and I saw you were weeping, my heart was simply broken because I thought I had spoiled the whole occasion for you. But generously, warmheartedly, you relieved me by assuring me that your feeling had nothing to do with anything I had done during the visit. I thought it then (and still think it) characteristically greathearted of you not to have minded.

With all my love, dear old comrade, your devoted

Dorothy

The Canfield papers at the University of Vermont contain two files of letters and brief notes written by Willa Cather to Dorothy Canfield, the earliest dated from Pittsburgh in 1897, a social note enquiring after Dorothy's mother, Flavia. The last letter, already alluded to, was the last one Willa Cather wrote to anyone. In between the collection contains over seventy pieces of correspondence, mostly handwritten letters of six to eight pages. These lively and friendly exchanges discuss their literary endeavors, their mutual friends, and their personal hopes and expectations. The largest gap in the continuity of the letters is between late summer of 1904 or 1905 and the spring of 1916 when Dorothy Canfield received a two-page letter of consolation at the time of her father's death. The letters which follow the resumption of the correspondence make it clear that the two friends had a falling out. A letter written in the late summer of either 1904 or 1905, addressed not to Dorothy Canfield but to her mother, laments that Willa had caused the breach in the friendship with Dorothy. That it was not merely of a passing nature seems indicated by the cautiousness of Willa Cather's approach and the tone of the letters when the correspondence resumes more than a decade later. Cather's letters have a carefully stated apologetic and conciliatory tone indicating that too much time has separated a very fast friendship dating back to their school days in Lincoln. Willa Cather never mentions the specific cause of this breakup. Did the break follow some sort of social slight, which the older woman, more successfully launched on her writing career, gave to her young friend? One can only conjecture in the absence of a *specific* mention of the cause.

When they reestablished the friendship (which has more significance than the separation), there continued a sympathetic and lasting bond between the two women until Cather's death in 1947. Whenever the name of Willa Cather came into my conversations with Dorothy Canfield, she clearly manifested a loyalty to her memory and sometimes added an admonition about her desire to support Willa Cather's sense of privacy and the restrictions she made in regard to her papers.

As the correspondence between the two resumed in 1916, they mentioned, for example, their current output of novels, *The Bent Twig* and *The Song of the Lark* (1915). Sometimes Cather comments that Canfield can well speak more knowingly about the Cather novels because she had known the struggle behind the novelist's climb to success.

In a letter to Dorothy Canfield dated April 8, 1921, Cather urges that they meet. She confides that she always saved the criticisms of her books in letters from her friends, and she implies their friendship means more because they have known something of the past together. This letter also reveals that Willa Cather had some serious concern about the writing of the last part of her current work, *One of Ours* (1922). If any one thing was instrumental in bringing the two women back together again, it appears from these letters of Willa Cather to be the psychological support she derived from Dorothy Canfield's critical support for *One of Ours* at a time when Cather was undergoing more uncertainty about the worth of her creation, apparently, than she had with any of her other novels. Willa Cather had, as many know, a very deep critical sense of her own books, even as she wrote them. The tone of her letters to Dorothy Canfield indicates that Cather was experiencing more than ordinary difficulties over the satisfactory completion of this novel.

When Willa Cather finished her work on *One of Ours* in February, 1922, she asked Dorothy Canfield to read the page proofs of the novel and to note any discrepancies in factual matters or other false notes. In another letter, about a month later, Cather confided to Dorothy Canfield what she had told to only very few, if any, others (not even Alfred Knopf) that she drew from her real life cousin, Grosvenor P. Cather, Jr., for her hero of *One of Ours,* Claude Wheeler. Grosvenor was killed at Cantigny, France, on May 27, 1918. Willa Cather had known the young man quite well, since he grew up on a farm adjacent to her father's in Nebraska where she had helped to take care of him. The real life Grosvenor, Cather implies, had much in common with the fictional Claude Wheeler in that he had a difficult time in finding himself in his growth to manhood and then had his life ended abruptly through the ultimate irony of the Great War.

Apparently Dorothy Canfield reacted critically in reading the page proofs of the segment of the novel in which David Gerhardt, an accomplished violinist and Claude's primary friend overseas, brings Claude with him to visit David's friends and relatives. At their visit to Mlle. Claire's, David, who had gone to war as a humane act, is prevailed upon to play the Saint-Saen violin concerto with Mlle. Claire as accompanist. In the novel Cather writes of Claude, "The music was a part of his own confused emotions. He was torn between generous admiration, and bitter, bitter envy. What would it mean to be able to do anything as well as that, to have a hand capable of delicacy and precision and power?"

In her reply to Dorothy Canfield's comments, Willa Cather expressed amusement and said that she really had not drawn that sequence from talks with AEF (American Expeditionary Forces) soldiers (as she had gotten certain other background materials for this novel). Rather, she said that Claude's reactions to the music were the feelings that she had actually experienced at a time the two women novelists were in France together (and, presumably, at a time when Dorothy Canfield had played the violin at some social occasion). Cather affirmed that Dorothy Canfield was not aware of those feelings at that time, but she thought that the way she felt must have been the way many soldiers felt. Several more letters during April, May and June of 1922 continued this vein of sympathetic exchange about *One of Ours* and especially about Claude Wheeler.

In a letter in May, 1922, Cather may have revealed the key to the earlier, troubled relationship. She commented on the differences in the cultural background and social status between herself and her Vermont friend. She pointed out the fact that Dorothy's father and mother were intellectually inclined and that Dorothy had grown up in a college atmosphere. Willa Cather once again linked her own past with that of Claude Wheeler and stated how her friend Dorothy Canfield can understand how she, the author of *One of Ours,* had had such a struggle for her place in the sun. In 1921 Cather recognized that she could look with greater tolerance on any misunderstanding they had in the past.

Willa Cather probably did not have a large concern about her friend's critical remarks about the novel, and more than likely she did not change anything in her text because of Dorothy Canfield's responses. Importantly, however, at a point in her career that many critics signal as the most crucial, Cather turned to an old friend and continued her efforts at maintaining the friendship, and she found genuine comfort from the support she received in return. Great and critically sensitive artist that Cather was, she must have sensed that the war episodes in *One of Ours* were not quite right and that even the moral support from Dorothy Canfield represented more the benevolence of a friend than an adroit critical assessment.

In an extended letter to Dorothy Canfield during this same period Cather wrote that she seldom dreamed, but that when she did, Dorothy Canfield commonly appeared as the subject. Cather, in her fifties, spoke of herself entering that period of her life when reflection had become a pattern or habit, though she had never really practiced it before in her life. Especially, she remarked, she would look back upon admired, familiar figures of her youth and see them in much clearer perspective. Such cherished friends were always several years older than herself, and Dorothy Canfield was the exception to this rule. Willa Cather in unequivocal terms stated that her friend was the only one of the younger set with whom she had very strong ties, even though Dorothy Canfield used to vex her somewhat in those earlier years by pursuing so many interests that Cather regarded as ephemeral. (Along with music, writing, and other interests Dorothy Canfield also practiced fencing.)

The pattern which emerges from the letters shows the older novelist as genuinely attracted to the personal charm of Dorothy Canfield and, more important, beneath the charm a sincerely gracious human being whose life rested on solid values. Dorothy Canfield probably quit her successful career writing fiction simply because she saw many other things that she might do which she found more important. The promotion of the Book-of-the-Month Club was just one of many projects that Dorothy Canfield undertook and pursued steadily until her eyesight prevented further effective participation. As a charter member of its board of judges, she hoped to upgrade and influence the reading habits of a very large group of Americans. Dorothy Canfield simply felt quite strongly that life could be better served in social action rather than by continuing to write fiction. Her good friend Willa Cather would never come to a similar decision about her own career as a novelist. Cather cherished the work of the writer and was at work on her Carcasonne story at the time of her death.

The letters of Willa Cather to Dorothy C. Fisher continued for the next two decades without any large intermission, and their tone does not change significantly. The two old friends exchanged brief comments on the books that each wrote and they commented on mutual friends such as Robert Frost whom Dorothy Canfield knew very well from Bread Loaf and other occasions. Frost, a fellow Vermont writer, may have been first introduced to Willa Cather by Dorothy Canfield. They also wrote of plans for an occasional visit with each other. Willa Cather, who is buried in the Monadnoc Region of New Hampshire, and who used to frequent the MacDowell artists' colony in Peterborough at an earlier period, saw a resemblance between Housman's Shropshire country and southern New England. Dorothy Canfield's Arlington, Vermont, was not very far away, and the letters indicate Willa Cather and Dorothy Canfield exchanged occasional visits.

Dorothy Canfield wrote an article about Willa Cather in 1933 which she entitled **"Daughter of the Frontier"** and in which she made a serious effort to interpret the spirit and the Willa Cather she saw in and behind the fiction. She found Cather's fiction the most significant of any American author writing about the life of the hundreds of thousands of immigrants who came into Nebraska and neighboring states between 1880 and 1900 and assumed the responsibility of making a new life and new communities. She viewed Cather's family from Virginia as part of that immigration. Young Willa Cather herself was caught up in the frontier effort, and just when it seemed that the frontiersmen were succeeding in their great venture, in a single decade there came severe crop failures from a series of droughts. These same years coincided with the Cather years at the University of Nebraska. In Canfield's estimate Willa Cather's spirit largely was shaped in those years. The great effort she expanded towards gaining first a position for herself in the world of journalism and then recognition among many other fine writers, Canfield saw as best understood as deriving from her life on the frontier. "She intended to live not to brood over a communal heartbreak she could not help. She put out a strong hand and began to take what she wanted. Why not? What she wanted was hers by right. She took it away from no man." Yet what Cather took, she gave back in another way in her creations of pioneer men and women. Her career commands our respect, rewards our reading interests and, in a true sense, nourishes our spirits long afterwards.

Dorothy Canfield also grew up in the plains region during those difficult years. But her father, a very successful humanities scholar and later a college administrator, provided his daughter with more of the amenities of life than the Cathers could give to their daughter. Under these circumstances it becomes easier to understand how the younger "daughter of the frontier" became a role model for her older friend. And perhaps it is even understandable how there might have been a straining of their relationship as the two young women began to make their way separately in the world. But their friendship proved to be very strong.

Like Antonia Chimerda and Jim Burden these two had shared the Optima Dies which, even if they are the first to flee from us, also have power to bind as well. Cather and Canfield "possessed together the precious, the incommunicable past."

Mark J. Madigan

SOURCE: "Willa Cather's Commentary on Three Novels by Dorothy Canfield Fisher," in *ANQ: A Quarterly Journal of Short Articles, Notes and Reviews,* Vol. 3, No. 1, January, 1990, pp. 13-5.

In her 1922 essay "The Novel Demeublé," which was first published in the *New Republic* and later collected in *Not Under Forty,* Willa Cather claimed that the novel had been, for a long while, "overfurnished" (43). She argued in that essay for a clearing away of unnecessary novelistic "furniture," for an uncluttered prose style: "Whatever is felt upon the page without being specifically named there—that, one might say, is created. It is the inexplicable presence of the thing not named, of the overtone divined by the ear but not heard by it, the verbal mood, the emotional aura of the fact or the thing or the deed, that gives high quality to the novel or the drama, as well as to poetry itself" (50). Cather, who had little patience for what she considered to be the excesses of certain realists, went so far as to say that "the importance of material objects and their vivid presentation have been so stressed, that we take it for granted whoever can observe, and can write the English language, can write a novel" (43). Considering that Cather seldom wrote book reviews after becoming a successful author, four letters to her long-time friend, novelist Dorothy Canfield Fisher, provide interesting evidence of her literary theories in practice.

In an October 1922 letter (which, like all Cather's letters, may not be quoted due to a restriction in her will), Cather complimented Fisher on her novel published that year, **Rough-Hewn**. Cather's reaction to the book—which tells the story of Neale Crittenden and Marise Allen, two young Americans who fall in love in Rome and eventually make a life together in Vermont—echoed the principles set forth in "The Novel Demeublé." Neale's father, Daniel Crittenden, and Marise were especially vivid characters to Cather. She told Fisher this was because they were portrayed more suggestively than literally. Fisher's economical rendering of character allowed Cather more imaginative freedom as a reader.

Fisher was not as successful with Neale Crittenden, whose character seemed unfocused to Cather because too much was told about him. She said Neale would have been more clear if he had been presented in far less detail. The section on Neale's college life, "An Education in the Humanities," could have been reduced by half, according to Cather, who compared this over-characterization to the way a brother and sister can become so familiar with each other that they lose all sense of their individuality. In life and in fiction, Cather told Fisher, characters may be better perceived from a distance.

Cather responded similarly to Fisher's 1930 novel, *The Deepening Stream.* In December of that year she wrote to Fisher expressing her satisfaction with two characters, Morris and Jessica Gilbert, the father and mother in Fisher's autobiographical novel of her youth. The elder Gilberts seemed real to Cather, but that quality was lost in the portrayal of the Gilberts' daughter Matey because her character was brought too close to the reader. Matey could be seen best, according to Cather, in relation to her family and surroundings, rather than through direct description.

Cather admitted to Fisher that she once made the same mistake of telling too much about a character when writing of Thea Kronborg in *The Song of the Lark.* In a March 15, 1916 letter, Cather explained that she should not have followed Thea's later years in such close detail, since the development of an artist's life moves from the personal to the impersonal. She later made her statement public, writing in the preface to the revised edition of *The Song of the Lark* in 1932, "Success is never so interesting as struggle—not even to the successful, not even to the most mercenary forms of ambition" (v). Cather edited the latter sections of the original edition to reflect that belief.

Continuing in the 1930 letter on the subject of *The Deepening Stream,* Cather named Marcel Proust as a writer who used minute detail. Cather said Proust's method should only be used in the first person, however, and she quoted his *Cities of the Plain* to make her point. If one grew tired of Proust's extended description of Albertine, Cather said, one could simply stop reading and fault the author directly. She concluded by saying that most writers used the third person too intimately, as though it were first person narration.

In 1939 Cather read Fisher's *Seasoned Timber*—the tale of a middle-aged high school principal who falls in love with a young teacher—and in a letter dated November 8, she lauded the author for her accomplishment with Miss Peck, an innkeeper in the novel. Cather's response was consistent with her statement in "The Novel Demeublé" and her 1920 essay "On the Art of Fiction," in which she wrote: "Art, it seems to me, should simplify. That, indeed, is very nearly the whole of the higher artistic process; finding what conventions of form and what detail one can do without and yet preserve the spirit of the whole—so that all that one has suppressed and cut away is there to the reader's consciousness as much as if it were in type on the page" (*On Writing,* 102). Once again, Cather said Fisher was successful with Miss Peck because she selectively used detail. In Cather's view, Fisher achieved her most vivid characterization when she suppressed her inclination toward direct description in *Seasoned Timber.* Fisher's characters were then brought to life by the quality which marks the best of Cather's own fiction: a quality "felt upon the page without being specifically named there."

TITLE COMMENTARY

📖 *THE DEEPENING STREAM* (1930)

Joseph J. Firebaugh

SOURCE: "Dorothy Canfield and the Moral Bent," in *The Educational Forum,* Vol. XV, No. 3, March, 1951, pp. 283-94.

Two or three years ago I shocked an elder colleague in a Department of English by saying that I always taught introductory courses somewhat in the manner of a moralist. Because he had been trained by a severe linguistic doctorate, he evidently believed that I was introducing a dangerous subjectivism into literary study; that I was failing in my duty of teaching the weak student to read comprehendingly, and the good student to know something of linguistic and literary history. For my part, I was shocked to discover that anyone could consider those very desirable aims to be at all adequate.

If there is one quality which human beings have always had, it is the moral bent. Early literature was usually a codifying of moral law, or an exemplification of the lapses from or the conformity to such law. Dr. Samuel Johnson, by no means least in the hierarchy of those dear to departments of English, would moralize upon any excuse, or indeed upon no excuse. Nor has the literature of the last century altered this fundamental emphasis. Oscar Wilde, aesthete though he was, was a thorough-going moralist. T. S. Eliot, the literary symbol of our own day, has never ceased to be a moralist.

At the same time that literature was busy responding to or developing new systems of morality, a sort of scholarship became dominant in the academic world which lost itself in the worship of the fact. This method paralleled roughly the development of naturalism in the literary world and the development of objective methodology in the biological and physical sciences. Even these methods constitute a kind of morality, a judgment, that the fact has at least the good of being undeniable and irrevocable; the implication being that nothing is good which is deniable and revocable. Since critical and moral judgments are often both deniable and revocable, they are to be shunned, and scholarship succeeded for about fifty years in shunning them. That they were not altogether evaded in the classroom was due to the fact that many teachers were not, in the accepted sense of the day, scholars; that fact is, I believe, all that saved American literary education from pseudoscientific irresponsibility.

Every teacher of literature is accustomed to hearing the questions, concerning some fictional or poetic statement of a moral proposition, "Is that good?" or "Is that true?" The questions are less naïve than their expression. Most of us have been guilty on occasion of shameless amusement when such questions have arisen. Yet such questions press daily upon all of us and cannot be evaded. We cannot be expected to answer them finally; but we can be expected to show our students, so that even the most unsophisticated of them can understand, why we cannot answer such questions, why our lives are only a search for such answers as we can tentatively approve, and why their search for truth is not likely to be very different from ours.

I

In attempting to satisfy the moral urge which every student has in common with every teacher, some of my colleagues and I have found Dorothy Canfield's *The Deepening Stream* (1930) to be a highly valuable book. In using it we have inevitably met the adverse criticism of those of our colleagues who believe that works for undergraduate instruction must be drawn from some canon of great books. Clearly the novel belongs in no such canon; as a genial colleague of the opposition once put it, the novel technically is "Marcel Proust written up for the *Ladies' Home Journal*." (This remark does not seem to me as scathing as it was intended to be; if some of the technical methods of the great French modern can be made familiar through a minor work, no irremediable loss would seem to have occurred.)

The Deepening Stream, a semi-autobiographical novel, tells the story of Matey Gilbert, the daughter of a brilliant, arrogant American professor of French. Her childhood is one of emotional insecurity and repression, but various circumstances prevent her from becoming the sterile, maidenly adult that her elder sister, Priscilla, becomes. Matey marries happily, has children, with her husband throws herself and her small fortune into French war relief during the first World War, and returns to America with her husband after the war, ready to live a quiet mediocre life, helping her husband in his father's small savings bank, and resting content in the deep enrichment that life's experiences have brought her. It is a novel concerning domestic tranquillity; a novel about a woman, by a woman; a novel filled, in its later chapters, with the joy of maternity and wifehood. A student of mine, not realizing the amusing blend-word he had made, called it a "soap-box opera." The fact that it has something of the soap-box about it, only recommends it to the teacher who will admit his own moral bent and that of his students. And the fact that it shares with the soap-opera a domestic and matriarchal emphasis, will not perturb him either, if he is willing to admit that the American woman seems incurably both; that Dorothy Canfield does avoid the domineering qualities of a real matriarch; and that none of the sticky sentimentalism, violent jealousy, or blatant materialism of the true soap-opera disfigures her work.

The moral values which Miss Canfield accepts and advocates may be examined under the following headings: (1) Marriage and the Family; (2) Education; (3) Success; (4) Adjustment to the Environment;

(5) Religion; (6) War. When we have examined the novel under these six categories, we will perceive that Miss Canfield has expressed an attitude towards life which is highly characteristic of certain American thinking during the first half of our century. If it is within the scope—as I happen to believe that it is—of undergraduate literary study, to bring the student into a frame of mind in which he can examine critically some of the underlying concepts of his own times, *The Deepening Stream* will assist in the process. Let us see specifically how it is able to offer this assistance.

II

In their own family relationships, Matey Gilbert's brilliant parents are constantly jockeying for position, each seeking an advantage over the other. Professor Morris Gilbert has a sarcastic tongue and a ready wit; hence he usually wins the verbal tilts. When his wife busies herself with amateur theatricals—an activity for which Professor Gilbert has no talent—he ridicules from a distant vantage, never making the mistake of exposing his own lack of dramatic talent. He seldom fails to win; one such instance occurs when a friend of his wife, Mrs. Whitlock, challenges successfully his dominance at table-talk. Even then, Mrs. Gilbert's triumph is short; having failed to defeat Mrs. Whitlock, he joins her, thus spoiling his wife's advantage. Matey as a child and young girl sees instance after instance of this sort: once, in a Paris department store, while Mrs. Gilbert flounders in a strange tongue, Professor Gilbert observes silently, and then interposes with especially "diamond-faceted" French.

The two girls, Matey and Priscilla, are caught in this family fusillade. They receive little affection and no sex-instruction. Priscilla grows up sensitive and repressed, consumes her adolescent energies in tennis, rejects proposals of marriage, and becomes a crisp, efficient teacher of French in a fashionable school for girls. Her marriage, ultimately, to a widower, is a marriage of convenience only; she never overcomes her adolescent horror of the sex relationship. Her parents' lack of demonstrative affection for each other and for the children, assures that the children will have difficulty in expressing themselves emotionally.

Matey almost falls into the same sort of repression that seizes Priscilla. That she does not do so, is caused by two facts: a small dog, Sumter, which she is permitted to own, and which receives her adolescent affection; and the fact that, at her father's deathbed, she suddenly sees that the parents' bickering was a superficial thing which concealed from their children the genuine affection which was at the basis of their marriage. Only Francis, the son, an unsubtle person who is much like his father but not brilliant, escapes repression.

Matey escapes narrowly, and enters a marriage which is richly gratifying. Her husband, Adrian Fort, Jr., is a gentle quiet man, lacking either the ambition or the brilliance which had made Professor Gilbert charming, remarkable, and disagreeable. Here something of the matriarchal nature of American marriage becomes apparent; but Miss Canfield is fully aware of it; when Matey and Adrian go to France for their wedding-journey, Matey finds to her amazement that her French friends say, "I hope you will make your husband happy," instead of the skeptical "I hope he will make you happy," which is what she was accustomed to hearing in America. Their marriage is in all ways coöperative; it lacks utterly the competitiveness of her parents' marriage. Yet the matriarchal urge is fully present when, at the close of the novel, Matey joins her husband at his bank, helping him in this way to conquer the depression which the years of war have left with him. By working at his side Matey is going to be mother and wife, protector and companion, all in one; and at the same time she is emancipating herself (though nothing is said on this subject) from the kitchen. Unlike many of her generation, however, Miss Canfield does not talk of woman's independence. Matey is essentially domestic: marriage without subservience: dependence without subordination: that would seem to be her programme. The name of John Dewey springs at once to mind; and, if the teacher is so inclined, Dewey's beliefs can be discussed in this connection.

III

In one sense the novel is about nothing but education. The title, *The Deepening Stream,* stands for the continual enrichment by experience of the individual human life. But Miss Canfield is quite specifically interested in educational matters. Her attitude towards family life and towards education are often merged—as they are, indeed, in her treatment of the separation which exists between different generations. Although this theme is considered at several points in the novel, the following instance will suffice: As a child in a small Middle Western university town, Matey becomes aware of the division existing between adult and child. Childhood was seen largely as a time of carefree play, free of responsibility; adulthood as a time of work, of responsibility, of care. The adults slumped down on their front porches after the evening meal was ended, too tired from the day's work to do more than seek rest. The children, in the meantime, spent their energies in the physical exuberance of play. In the popular mores, the adults envied the children's freedom; the children saw adulthood as a time of stolid joyless endurance. This separation of life into years of freedom and years of responsibility is precisely the separation which Dewey protests in his educational writings; men ought not, he thinks, divide life into a time of dependence and a time of independence, a time of irresponsibility followed by a time of responsibility, a time of preparation and a time of achievement, a time of education and a time of fixed attainment. Freedom fills all of life, and so does education. Dependence is not to be shunned by the adult, nor is independence to be sought as the highest goal of maturity. Like John Dewey, Miss Canfield believes that education and freedom and responsibility are co-existent with life itself; education, like life, is growth.

Dewey's idea of education as shared experience is developed in that portion of the book which contrasts an American family—the Gilberts—with a French family—the Vinets. During one of Professor Gilbert's sabbatical leaves, Matey, still a hoydenish child, lives *en famille* with the Vinets, who are Parisian *petit bourgeoisie*. M. Vinet teaches in a *lycée*; Madame Vinet gives music lessons. Matey learns piano from Madame Vinet, and other subjects from the tutor of the French children.

Matey is impressed by the enthusiasm with which the family enters into its activities. Music they take very seriously. They all share its pleasure. Their studies are more demanding than any that Matey has yet been subjected to. She responds uncertainly to theme subjects which demand that she use her mind on a philosophical problem. The sense of family solidarity which is apparent in the Vinet household at this period, is contrasted with the atomistic family life of the Gilberts. Culture, which the Vinets possess in great measure, despite their lack of money, is almost the catalyzing agent: the family solidarity is the result of a family purpose—the pursuit of culture and the sharing of experience. Matey's own family, certainly highly cultivated in the American sense, and much better off in the world, appears, by contrast, selfishly individualistic, its members seeking what they seek only for self-aggrandizement.

Yet all is not well with the Vinets. Henri, the son, intends to become a teacher in a *lycée,* as his father has

done. The sense that the examinations are rigorous, and that failure is possible, is not a remote feeling. Matey sees that it is a fundamental motivation, yet she does not believe that the motivation is entirely evil. Deweyite that Miss Canfield is, she recognizes the values which result from a questionable system of competitive motivation. Certain "pleasures and interests—music, reading, the theatre, study, art, thinking—could not be enjoyed or even approached by people who had not been rigorously fitted for them. . . . They were not open to money, but only to those who had the right keys. With all the haste and effort, one's childhood was hardly enough to learn how to handle the keys which opened the doors to the world."

The Vinets are rather shocked, when they go for walks, by Matey's tomboyish behavior. The freedom of her Middle-western childhood has never been known by these Parisians, reared in apartment houses, taking their exercise in decorous strolls through parks or streets. Without didacticism, Miss Canfield thus brings into sharp juxtaposition American liberty from restraints, and European standards of deportment. Nor does she make any effort to decide between them. Rather, she sees the advantages of both.

We perceive here that the physical freedom of the young Americans, which makes them appear like little savages to the French, has by no means kept them free of psychical inhibition. The repressions produced by their "free" but atomistic lives are severe ones, both in Matey and Priscilla. One would hesitate to say that they are freer of conflicts than their Parisian friends, even after seeing, later in the book, that severe conflicts have raged in their breasts, too.

No solution is offered, then, of the problems of repression and neurosis. No solution, that is, unless tolerance might be considered one. And tolerance is the most consistent attitude of Miss Canfield and of the characters whom she admires.

IV

Miss Canfield is not, however, particularly tolerant of successful people or of the standards of success which they represent. Professor Morris Gilbert is an eminently successful and brilliant man. He is interested in the world's approval, and he is skillful in gaining it. Matey, when she first takes a course from her father, feels surprise that he is so very good a teacher. Yet at the same time she sees that he is only her father with his clever company manners on; and these company manners have caused her most profound anguish; "for an instant she stared bleakly at something from which it was her life-work to avert her eyes;" and as she sees the small self-congratulatory smile form on her father's lips, she reflects that she would like to be able to bring her little dog to class.

Professor Gilbert's standard of success is not, of course, the usual American materialistic one. When the University of Corinth offers him an identical salary to the one he has made at Hamilton, he accepts, chiefly because of the opportunity to teach more graduate students. In his new position, moreover, "he became very popular with his classes, and was so elated with the chance to use his old effects on a new audience that for more than a year he radiated good humor." One feels rather sorry for Professor Gilbert: so eager for the world's applause that he failed to secure the applause of his own daughter; that he secured, instead, her entire disapproval, her fixed resentment because he was more interested in external, public appearances than he was in the internal, domestic realities.

Later in her life, Matey learns even more about her father's selfishness. By sheer coincidence, she meets in Paris, during the war years, a girl whose great-aunt, Priscilla, had been jilted by Professor Gilbert, and had died a spinster, specifying in her will that she be buried in Rustdorf, the old family seat of the Gilberts. This new awareness of her father's ability to perform an act of selfishness, only reinforces Matey's opinions concerning him.

One feels that Matey is rather unfair. Her own life has been easy for her. Her own love life has been extraordinarily uncomplicated. Passion she hardly knows. Right shows itself too easily to her. Domesticity and righteousness come with incredible ease. She suspects little of the complex human motivation which her father must have known. Life is too simple for her. She is an excessively passive character to whom life brings much because she had asked so little of it. At one point she remarks: "I should say that the matter with me is that there is *nothing* I want very much to do." Her passivity diminishes as she grows older, as the stream of life deepens, but there is little passion that might not be found in any orderly domesticity and maternity. Intensity of desire and ambition—she is cut off from these as sharply as if she had never heard of them, as completely as if she had not had a very ambitious father, and a successful brother.

Matey's brother Francis is successful in a much more crass sense of the word than Professor Gilbert had been, and Miss Canfield offers him as a kind of antithesis to the man Matey marries, Adrian Fort, Jr. After he leaves college Francis goes to the industrial center of Pittsburgh. We next see him when he visits Rustdorf on the occasion of Matey's engagement. "The aroma of power scented any room where he sat." Francis, like his father, has deserted the first girl he was engaged to; and there is no doubt in Matey's mind as to why; her grandmother's money had been left, not to the granddaughter, but to the Presbyterian church; his new love is the daughter of the senior partner of Francis' law firm. And his marriage, like his father's, turns out unfortunately; Miss Canfield punishes him, as she does Professor Gilbert, for breaking his promises.

Matey's husband, Adrian, is (in the usual sense of the word) a failure already when he enters the story; he has failed to become a painter and he is adjusting himself to a humble life as clerk in his father's bank. Francis characterizes him as no better than a settlement worker, and promises Matey, that if she will not marry Adrian, he will introduce her to the inner circles of Pittsburgh society, where she may find a wealthy husband. It is precisely Adrian's unworldliness that appeals to her. She has had too much of a successful father. Indeed when, later in the book, she sees President Wilson accepting the plaudits of the Parisian crowds, she finds herself deeply suspecting his self-satisfied smile, his long bony college-professor's face. Her dislike of her father becomes one of the most profound motivating forces of her life. The new awareness of Freudian psychology during the first third of the present century is of course apparent here and elsewhere throughout the novel.

Miss Canfield again presents the world of power in unflattering terms when, later in the book, her brother Francis, having come to Paris with the Peace Commission, gives a dinner in Matey's honor. Matey sees the power which he and his guests display, and she finds it contemptible. She does what she can to spoil the picture which Francis is giving to his powerful friends—a picture of a noble little woman who has sacrificed her fortune for French war relief. In the presence of men who are on familiar terms with generals and colonels, she flaunts the fact that her husband has been only a lieutenant in the Ambulance Corps. If it can be said of Matey that she is smug—and I think that it can—she is aware anyway of her smugness, in this scene at least, and she feels rather guilty concerning it. But one of the most unsatisfactory aspects of the novel is that Matey too often sees herself as the calm well-balanced wife and mother, bandaging the wounds of those near to her, if not of the world itself; her justification, and that of her husband is, in her own eyes, just that they are not successful.

Indeed with Walt Whitman, Dorothy Canfield may be seen as saying, "The Commonplace I Sing." There are at least three basic symbols which express this idea—symbols which, incidentally, are simple enough to provide the beginning student with an elementary notion of the literary use of symbols. There are Aunt Connie's tulips, and the "incredible" fact that such beauty can spring from the unprepossessing soil of a very ordinary flower-bed; there are the flowers of the broom, each very tiny, growing on an ugly, rough plant, but each contributing to the beauty of the whole hillsides of broom; the owl-feather, which suggests that even the infinitely small can be infinitely perfect, and which has the function of telling Matey that the work of war-relief, which she and Adrian are considering, can have infinite value; and, finally, there are the ants, millions of anonymous obscure lives, contributing their mite to the infinite perfection of the whole.

Matey's attitude towards money is that of her father-in-law. On the occasion of her first visit to his bank, Matey hears a young woman depositor apologize to Adrian Fort, Sr., for withdrawing money from the bank for a new hat. The old man assures her that money is saved in order to be spent. His attitude towards money is purely pragmatic. He sees his little savings-bank as not an opportunity to amass money but as an opportunity to be of use to his community. (I would avoid the word "service" in this context because it has become so badly debased, but service, not profit, is certainly Adrian Fort's ideal.) Francis Gilbert can see this banking method as only impractical and idealistic; for his part, money should be put where it reproduces itself most rapidly; money for the sake of money, not for use merely—this would be Miss Canfield's conception of his belief. To her, his attitude is that of the typical business man, intoxicated with visions of wealth and power.

One may see, in this admiration for coöperation rather than competition, for service rather than exploitation, for use rather than profit, the ideological background of the New Deal. Published in 1930, shortly after the Great Depression had begun, *The Deepening Stream* must have summarized for many their deep discontent with the direction American economic and social

life had taken. It summarized the period of pre-war, war and post-war, the hope and cynicism and despair, the inescapable pragmatic individualistic democracy of the first third of the century. That is why, though it is little qualified to be called great literature, it is an extraordinarily useful book to anyone who would introduce the student to the America of the early twentieth century.

The complacency of the American undergraduate, his callow uncritical acceptance of things as they are, of the success ideal of modern American folklore, can be attacked frontally through the use of *The Deepening Stream.* Professor Gilbert's arrogance, Francis Gilbert's brass, are certainly the obverse side of the coin of success. To let the American student accept that coin as true, before he has seen its other side, is to do him a thorough disservice. If there are attitudes that need to be cultivated in the young, one of them certainly is that of a healthy criticism of the American mores; the popular press and the radio are busily emphasizing one side; Miss Canfield's volume provides a point of departure for a more critical attitude.

V

Darwinian theory has turned the attention of our civilization to survival by adaptation; modern psychology has emphasized adjustment to the surroundings. What has often been neglected is the fact that some environments, some ways of living, are more suitable to human beings than other ways. Our quality is changed, our humanity altered, by adaptation to certain physical or social phenomena. Are, or are there not, certain ways of life that are more completely human than other ways?

Matey's father has moved his family from place to place as his work has directed him. By the time Matey has reached late adolescence, the family has made four major moves; each time her roots have been torn from the soil in which they have tentatively grown. It is not particularly surprising that she is an extraordinarily passive young woman when first she goes to Rustdorf, more likely to be acted on by the environment than to act upon it, feeling that nothing can matter much. Nor can it, for a person who next year may be elsewhere. Small wonder that she remains for the rest of her life a relatively passive person.

Rustdorf, an old Dutch settlement on the Hudson, has a placid permanence. Few come and few go. It has none of the hurly-burly of arrival and departure which afflicts every academic town in the United

States. Here one may put down roots and live, secure in the knowledge that old friends and the elders of the family are always at hand.

Here, moreover, there is no height of aspiration, no need to startle others with brilliance either intellectual or social. Here there are no severe conflicts; no depths of passion are either felt or sought. Contentment is of more value than achievement, satisfaction worth more than range of experience.

As a student Matey had not understood the passion of love as treated in the French novel. Nor, despite her growing sexual awareness, does she ever. Rustdorf, like Adrian, Jr., represents to her a retreat from conflict and from passion; her retreat is less complete than Priscilla's retreat; but it is no less real.

Even a retreat involves a judgment of values; one retreats *to* as well as *from*. Matey moves to a different world. It is her judgment of values that it is a better world than the one she has left. In the fact that the Rustdorf world was largely nonexistent in Matey's day, and that it is even more so now, rests the particular value of the book. Contentment is a much underprized virtue in the twentieth century.

Contentment seems not to be merely adjustment to the environment. Adaptation to certain ways of life seems, paradoxically, to bring perpetual maladjustment as one of its prices. Some ways of life are more fitted to humanity than other ways. Matey's judgment is that the Rustdorf life is such a life; and that there are ways of living, socially or environmentally produced, to which adjustment can be seen only as loss.

The Deepening Stream, then, is a defense both of mediocrity and contentment, of domestic virtue rather than public achievement. Thus it is out of the main stream both of current fiction and of current journalism. The merit of some books, for public as well as for student, consists just in that they are out of the main stream. The book has the weaknesses of all literature of self-justification (whether there is any other kind I do not propose to decide here): it justifies not only the author but also the sympathetic reader, thus inducing a kind of complacent pride. Those who see in the book only a complacent praise of the ordinary are, however, judging in favor of a value which Miss Canfield simply would not accept; to judge the book by another standard than its author's is of course a legitimate critical procedure, but

it carries with it the risk of ignoring merits which are peculiar to the range of values the author has chosen to set forth. Those values have their reality. A fundamentally aggressive generation needs to have quietistic values interpreted with sympathetic comprehension.

VI

The religious faith which Miss Canfield finds most attractive is the Quaker religion of Adrian Fort and his family. Her heroine's religious upbringing had been largely ignored: religious observance, that is to say, had been a matter of occasional external conformity. It was one fragment of the fragmentary life which the Gilberts led. And that is why, when Matey marries into the Rustdorf community, she finds the complete integration of the religion of the Friends so attractive to her. In it she finds no separation of life and religion.

The Vinet family are anti-clerical and skeptical, and they rear their children in that tradition. One feels that their irreligion is more religious than the Gilbert's placid neglect. For the Vinets speak respectfully of all the great religious teachers, and object chiefly, in the Voltairean manner, to hypocrisy. Years later, however, their daughter Mimi, having married and left home, embraces Catholicism, and becomes so ardent that she will not allow her mother unsupervised access to the grandchildren, for fear that their faith will be spoiled. Mimi is experiencing the same need for something to depend upon, that Matey experienced before she visited Rustdorf. Matey is tolerant of Mimi's conversion, as of Madame Vinet's skepticism, but is grieved to find that the remarkable family unity, which had once appeared so admirable, has by no means been without flaw.

"There is no big or little in infinity," remarks Adrian on the occasion when a tiny owl's feather flutters down in the night. The Spinozist unity thus suggested is one of the important articles of Matey's faith—and of the faith of her father-in-law. Tolerance of other people and their ways (though Matey is not always able to practice it) is a part of this belief in unity. The belief in the Inner Voice, one of the qualities of the admired Quaker faith, is not without its relation to Spinozist pantheism. Her real faith, and that of Adrian, Sr., who is her spiritual spokesman, is in mankind, good, bad, or indifferent. Miss Canfield does not carry sentimentalism about the Common Man to the depths it was later to reach. But she will not condemn humanity.

VII

Hence arises a conflict about war. Opposing war, as in their faith they must, leads Matey and her husband to the years of war work—Matey among her friends in Paris, and Adrian as an ambulance driver at the front. When those years are ended, they are physically exhausted. And Adrian returns deeply troubled in spirit; for, in spite of his beliefs, he has enjoyed his wartime experiences. He has rejoiced at the news of victorious battles, although he knows that this news means the death of men. So with the human race: it somehow enjoys war.

In a crucial conversation towards the end of the novel, Adrian Fort, Sr., offers, not an answer to this problem, but an invitation to reflection. Just as it has been foolish for the French to look upon Woodrow Wilson as a savior of mankind, so it is foolish for Matey and Adrian to look to Adrian, Sr., for an answer to this most difficult of problems. And to Matey, his answer seems at first a defense of war. For he remarks that man cannot live without a sense of purpose; war provides man with such a purpose: a "poor, false, imitation purpose," to be sure, but a purpose none the less. And finally, he assures Matey that he is not defending war—only men.

One thinks immediately of William James's essay, "The Moral Equivalent of War," and its suggestion of ways by which men may be given a purpose, in battling, not other men, but the forces of nature which—except man himself—are his chief enemies. The integrated course can proceed at once to a consideration of that essay and of the problems it presents. And the teacher of literature who does not believe that he must confine himself to the work under discussion, who believes that it is his duty to step from literature to life, will not hesitate to discuss the problems involved: the problems of bringing to all men a sense of purpose and an opportunity to express that purpose. For they are after all the problems of our generation; or rather, they are problems which in the Roosevelt era our generation took the first faltering steps towards solving, and which, we may hope, the generations we are now preparing will deal with more tellingly, more on an international scale, than we have heretofore been able or willing to do.

VIII

One cannot be impressed with the notion that in treating literature in this way one is transgressing upon ground sacred to sociology or philosophy. To permit the educational reactionaries who talk in such terms to have their way, would be to strengthen the departmental induration which colleges and universities are now beginning to abandon. It is a point of view which is fatal, not only to the integrated courses which are being newly developed, but also to the courses in literature, philosophy, sociology, and so on, which the reactionaries are endeavoring to defend. Whatever teachers in the past have thought about learning for learning's sake, students have never believed in it; they have taken courses in literature, philosophy, sociology, or what-not, for "what they could get out of them"; there seems little reason to make it more difficult than necessary to "get something out of them." The new integrated courses, in the institutions where they are being inaugurated, may help direct the conventional courses towards an acceptance of the reality of a world beyond books. Where the conventional courses are still the accepted ones, their advocates can yet save them from the attacks to which they have been so justly subjected.

A few months ago I called on a former teacher of mine, now retired, whose international fame as a scholar and teacher is now bringing him the kind of invitations which must make his emeritus status one of the most rewarding periods of his life. He and I talked of the new integrated courses in which I am so deeply interested, and specifically of the Humanities program with which I was then associated. He disapproves of the new integrated courses in the Humanities. "I'm writing an article against 'em now," he said. "I'll send you a reprint. But I have to admit that we've brought it on ourselves."

Not all conservatives are as enlightened as my former teacher, who never taught literature in a vacuum; nor did he as a policy employ the kind of men who would do so; hence he cannot be said to be one of those who "brought it on themselves." Those who are guilty, are now in the vanguard of those who regard the new integrated courses as a fate worse than death to specialized departments; not realizing that such courses can point the way to renewed life for departments which are willing to recognize the unity of all knowledge—a unity within which the specialized departments acquire the only meaning which they can have.

As a novel which serves as a starting-point for such a unity of view, *The Deepening Stream* recommends itself to the teacher who is more interested in education than in acquiring a property, barricading himself therein, living the life of the hermit crab, and moving—when he moves—backwards.

📖 *VERMONT TRADITION: THE BIOGRAPHY OF AN OUTLOOK ON LIFE* (1953)

Helen MacAfee

SOURCE: "Good Neighbors," in *The Yale Review,* Vol. XLIII, No. 3, March, 1954, pp. 464-66.

It is not always easy for the reader of this book, [*Vermont Tradition: The Biography of an Outlook on Life*] to see just where Mrs. Fisher leaves off and Vermont begins. Nor is it always clear whether she is telling time by her own or her grandfathers' clocks. This, I think, is as she would have it. So would I, for one of the pleasures in following her text lies in the interweaving it discloses of dates, places, and people. To the people the times are all Modern Times, and however they may range, their foundations stand within the borders of the Green Mountain State.

Among its earliest colonial settlers were the author's family, the Canfields, who went to Arlington, Vermont, by way of New Milford, Connecticut, taking with them habits of reading and writing, thrift and hard work, and qualities of decency, independence, and neighborliness, which some of us like to associate with Connecticut though we know they are far older. These have been literally the saving graces throughout the ages, and must continue to be if human dignity is to survive on this small planet.

Mrs. Fisher finds that her northern climate and the people have, on the whole, agreed with each other as she looks out on both from Arlington—still her home after two hundred years. Vermont's lack of great natural resources has put a premium on the laborer's industry, skill, adaptability, and careful husbandry, as the sparseness of the population has promoted coöperation, true sociability. She shows that there is less tribal or occupational snobbishness here than in most parts of the country, and a marked respect for schooling and independence of mind.

With those who regard her neighbors as parochial, dour, or hidebound, and equally with those who picture the State as an idyllic if static community, she takes sharp issue. Abundant evidence from oral tradition as well as written record is offered in support of the views presented. That the tilling and clearing of Green Mountain acres has been a backbreaking task even outsiders should have known. But few realize the variety of the local industries or the number of major economic changes the State has had to make as the demand for its lumber, potash, Merino sheep, and Morgan horses, rose and fell in the world beyond its borders. Through economic pressure Vermonters have learned to develop a good deal of ingenuity along with persistence, hardihood, and thrift. If, as Mrs. Fisher keeps reminding us, many of them had ever been the ultraconservative introverts of folklore, their past could not have come down to the present day.

On the political side this book selects for emphasis the Vermonters' strong taste for self-government and their readiness from the beginning to help liberate others, not merely as an expression of loyalty to a cherished ideal but from a practical sense that only by so doing can their own liberties be secured. For one example, Mrs. Fisher relates in detail incidents of their long "cold war" during the middle of the eighteenth century against the rich Hudson Valley estate-owners, in which the Vermonters aided the rebellious tenants because they sympathized with the tenants and because the Duanes and the Van Rensselaers threatened their mountain freeholds. Doubtless this was, as she believes, a formative experience, leading directly to the part taken by Ethan Allen's men in the American Revolution and forestalling a trend to isolationism in their descendants. Here again, what she has heard lends vividness to what she has read.

This and other chapters of the book are further enlivened by Mrs. Fisher's personal observations, her questions about the meaning of the past, her musings about the future. It can be no surprise that with a head start of several generations she comes out at the end on the side of Vermont or that Vermont comes out on the side of the angels. That is to say, in its plain terms, on the side of free men making the most of their minds, their bodies, and their land for their own satisfaction and the welfare of their neighbors. Mrs. Fisher has long been a pioneer in the extension of good neighbor policies. Readers of *Vermont Tradition* will be pleased to find themselves among her many beneficiaries.

📖 *KEEPING FIRES NIGHT AND DAY: SELECTED LETTERS OF DOROTHY CANFIELD FISHER* (1993)

Mark J. Madigan

SOURCE: An introduction to *Keeping Fires Night and Day: Selected Letters of Dorothy Canfield Fisher,* edited by Mark J. Madigan, University of Missouri Press, 1993, pp. 1-22.

I

In 1948 Dorothy Canfield Fisher (1879-1958) wrote to literary critic Albert L. Guerard about the University of Vermont's proposal to establish a collection of her papers at their Burlington campus:

> Their idea is not a bad one I think, not to wait until an author has been dead twenty or thirty years, and his children and grandchildren have lost most of his papers—for who nowadays with families moving around all the time could possibly keep a mass of papers together?—but to collect them while the author is still alive. Most of them will not be of any interest to anybody, perhaps none of them will be. But no harm is done in placing them in a fire-proof building instead of in a truck under the eaves in the attic. (Letter 154)

These remarks reveal much about Fisher: her interest in public education, her foresight, her modesty, and her common sense. They also raise an important question: Of what interest and significance could Fisher's letters possibly be? The letters themselves present the best argument for their publication: set against the American historical and cultural landscape from 1900 to 1958, they are the firsthand account of a singularly gifted, intelligent, and spirited woman who, among many other accomplishments, became one of America's most popular novelists.

Named after the heroine of *Middlemarch,* Dorothea Francis Canfield was born on February 17, 1879, in Lawrence, Kansas. She and her older brother, James, were the children of James Hulme Canfield, a university professor, and Flavia Camp Canfield, an artist. Dorothy grew up in a cultured home and traveled widely while still a child. She moved from Lincoln, Nebraska, to Columbus, Ohio, and then to New York City as her father relocated for academic appointments, and she paid frequent visits to the Arlington, Vermont, home of her father's relatives, and to Paris, where her mother kept a studio. Her early homelife was loving and supportive, but it was not without difficulty. Biographer Ida H. Washington notes that young Dorothy was sensitive to a strain of incompatibility between her parents—a conflict Fisher described in a fictional guise in *The Deepening Stream.* About the relationship of James, an idealistic, ambitious teacher and school administrator, and Flavia, an equally fervent devotee of the arts, Washington writes, "Her quickness of speech and action were, however, to make problems for him as great as those his sense of social responsibility created for her. The differences in temperament created a home in which a sensitive little daughter grew into a deeply perceptive novelist."

Fisher received her bachelor's degree from Ohio State University, where she had concentrated on languages and literature, particularly French. She pursued her scholarly interests at the graduate level, and her academic career culminated in 1904 when she received the Ph.D. in French from Columbia University with a dissertation on Corneille and Racine. Although her training qualified her for a university teaching career, Fisher turned down an offer of a professorship at Case Western Reserve University for family reasons and became secretary at the Horace Mann School in New York. In 1907 she married John Redwood Fisher. A fellow graduate of Columbia, he had been captain of the football team and roommate of Alfred Harcourt, who would later become Dorothy's publisher. They soon moved to Arlington, where she had inherited her great-grandfather's farm. From that Vermont home base she pursued one of the most productive careers in all of American literature.

In all, Fisher published twenty-two works of fiction (for business purposes under her maiden name, Dorothy Canfield) and eighteen works of nonfiction covering a remarkably wide range of subjects. She introduced the child-rearing methods of Dr. Maria Montessori to the United States in *A Montessori Mother* (1912), was a pioneering advocate of adult education in *Why Stop Learning?* (1927), translated Giovanni Papini's *Life of Christ* (1923) and Adriano Tilgher's *Work: What It Has Meant to Men through the Ages* (1931) from the Italian, chronicled the history of Vermont (her adopted home state and the setting for much of her fiction) in *Vermont Tradition* (1953), and wrote several highly regarded books for children (now commemorated by the children's book award that bears her name).

A woman of manifold talents, Fisher's achievements were hardly limited to the literary world. She spoke five languages, founded a Braille press and a children's hospital in France during World War I, organized the Children's Crusade for Children during World War II, was the first president of the Adult Education Association, and was the first woman to serve on the Vermont State Board of Education. Shortly before Fisher's death, Eleanor Roosevelt referred to her as one of the ten most influential women in America.

The variety of her activities notwithstanding, it was primarily as a fiction writer that Fisher was best known and as which she wanted to be remembered. She said in 1944 that writing fiction was "like falling in love" (Letter 134) and worried a year before her death that a biography in progress was "saying too much about actual material actions and activities of mine, and giving too little space to the novels and short stories" (Letter 185). To Fisher, writing was the chief means for making a decisive difference in the world, for educating her fellow citizens, for promulgating moral principles, for initiating social change. Her novels *The Brimming Cup* and *The Home-Maker,* for instance, critique the evils of racism, sexism, and materialism while promoting the virtues of equal access to education and employment.

Yet she did not view her fiction as merely ideological. She was an accomplished critic and was ever-conscious of the flaws in her own work. A tireless reviser, she often felt a sense of artistic inadequacy upon finishing a story or novel. In 1925, she wrote to the author of a soon-to-be-published rhetoric: "I can dimly remember a happy time when I could look at a page of mine and think 'Well, I don't see what more I can do to that.' Never any more! Any page of mine, taken at random, throws me into an acute fever of remorse for the mistakes in it, and an ardent desire to sit down and wrestle with it. This does not increase the joy of authorship, of course, but I hope it increases the quality of the product" (Letter 64).

What emerges clearly from the correspondence is that Fisher lived her life as one piece, drawing together many interests and concerns, so that it is virtually impossible to separate the literary from the biographical, the private from the public. Indeed, to understand the primacy of writing to Fisher is to appreciate its interrelation with the other elements of her life.

II

Fisher's literary career began, like that of many American authors of the early twentieth century, by way of publication in popular magazines—especially women's magazines—such as the *American, Everybody's,* and *Harper's Bazaar.* She had little trouble placing her work and was publishing a steady flow of stories and articles within a few years. Her first novel, **Gunhild,** was published by Holt in 1907, sold only six hundred copies, and received little critical attention. *The Squirrel Cage* appeared five years later to far more favorable reviews. For example, a notice in the *San Francisco Call* read, "We do not quarrel any more about 'The' great American novel, but no reader will deny that this is 'A' great American novel," while the reviewer for the *Progressive Woman* unabashedly stated, "*The Squirrel Cage* deserves to rank as one of the best American novels yet written."

As a result of the novel's reception and the burgeoning market for her magazine work, Fisher attracted the attention of Paul Reynolds, the first literary agent in America. Although reluctant to employ an agent at first (Letter 11), Fisher prospered from her association with him. Through his connections in the publishing world, Reynolds brought Fisher's name to a wider readership, and she soon expressed surprise at the prices he was able to secure for her stories.

Such business considerations were vital to her since she supported a husband and two young children (a daughter, Sally, was born in 1909 and a son, James, in 1913). When Dorothy and John married, they planned to support themselves as professional writers. However, when Dorothy's literary career blossomed and outgrew his own, John assumed the role of secretary and editor of her work. Since they were rarely separated, John Fisher remains a background figure in the letters. (One exception is Letter 8 to Céline Sibut, in which DCF writes at length about her impending marriage.) All indications are that he was deeply loved by Dorothy and that he provided her with invaluable support. Biographer Ida H. Washington has called their home life "harmonious but unconventional." Washington writes, "Dorothy was the chief breadwinner, and John assumed an editorial, consultative relationship to her work. Dorothy thus played the major role in the outside world; at home, however, her respect and affection for her husband were constant, and she sought his judgment on matters practical and literary and submitted to his direction in the details of everyday life." John also tended to the demanding physical chores of rural Vermont life and became involved in local and state politics, serving on the Vermont State Board of Education for many years.

Fisher's popular reputation continued to grow with publication of **The Bent Twig** (1915), a novel, and **Home Fires in France** (1918) and **The Day of Glory** (1919), collected stories based on her experiences in France during World War I. But she could hardly have imagined the success **The Brimming Cup** would encounter upon publication in 1921. Characterized by William Allen White as an "antidote" to the negative portrayal of small-town life in *Main Street*, **The Brimming Cup** finished the year just behind Lewis's novel, as the second most purchased novel in the country. The work brought Fisher to her highest prominence so far; with that attention came the various honors and distractions attendant upon fame: requests for interviews and speeches; invitations to dinner receptions and university commencements; appeals to join committees, support worthy causes, and read the manuscripts of fledgling writers; and a flood of mail from readers across the country.

Nor did Fisher's reputation diminish. Her translation of Papini's *Life of Christ* was second on the best-seller list for nonfiction in 1923, and **The Home-Maker** was among the ten best-selling novels of 1924. **Her Son's Wife** (1926) also sold well and received considerable critical acclaim. William Lyon Phelps wrote to publisher Alfred Harcourt: "**Her Son's Wife** is Dorothy Canfield's masterpiece and it is also *a* masterpiece. It is a profound, subtle analysis of human character and human life and a very remarkable book. I predict that it will win the Pulitzer Prize for 1926. It deserves it" (August 25, 1926). Not surprisingly, the comment was featured in the novel's advertising. Although Sinclair Lewis won (and declined) the Pulitzer for *Arrowsmith* that year, Fisher remained one of America's best-known writers for decades.

The thirties brought three more popular novels, **The Deepening Stream** (1930), **Bonfire** (1933), and **Seasoned Timber** (1939), and two collections of stories, **Basque People** (1931) and **Fables for Parents** (1937). A Dorothy Canfield Club was established in 1934, but there is perhaps no more impressive testament to Fisher's popularity than the fact that the serial rights to **Bonfire** were under contract for thirty thousand dollars at the lowest ebb of the Depression. The end of the decade was marked by the publication of Fisher's last novel, **Seasoned Timber** (1939). **"The Knot-Hole"** was published in the *Yale Review* in 1944 and won second prize among the stories in the O. Henry volume that year. Fisher revised earlier stories for **Four-Square** (1949), oversaw the publication of an anthology, **A Harvest of Stories** (1956), and

continued to write children's books and magazine articles until near the time of her death in 1958. A letter to Mary C. Jane reveals that Fisher was at work on a history book for children in 1957, which was published posthumously (1959) as **And Long Remember** (Letter 187).

Yet even if she had published none of these works, Fisher would be a notable figure in American letters for her role as a Book-of-the-Month Club (BOMC) judge. She was one of the members on the Board of Selection from its inception in 1926 until 1951 (serving on the original Board with Henry Seidel Canby, William Allen White, Heywood Broun, and Christopher Morley, and later with Clifton Fadiman and John P. Marquand). The board chose the "book-of-the-month," which was regularly bought by more than half of the club's subscribers, and Fisher has been called one of the two "most influential" members of the board and its "most conscientious reader." In fact, she read to the point of near-blindness, averaging fifteen books a month over her twenty-five-year tenure. Since by 1950 a million Americans belonged to the club and read the selections, it would be modest, but not incorrect, to say that she helped determine popular literary taste in America for nearly three decades. She did more: she shaped authors' careers. Pearl Buck, Isak Dinesen (Karen Blixen), and Richard Wright were among the many writers Fisher introduced to the American public through the BOMC.

During her lifetime, Fisher was awarded the honorary degrees and prizes reserved for famous writers, and her works were anthologized and translated into several foreign languages. Yet lasting recognition has eluded Fisher. Her fiction was popular with the reading public, but not subsequently favored by those modernist critics who instead championed Faulkner, Fitzgerald, and Hemingway from the same period. Fisher's authentic narratives of everyday American life were deemed unfashionable, her narrative technique was considered too conventional, and she was relegated to a marginal position in the literary pantheon. She was not entirely ignored, though. In 1952, Edward Wagenknecht offered a dissenting estimation in *The Cavalcade of the American Novel*:

> She is often regarded as a merely "popular" writer, and criticism has done little with her work. Yet few novelists have had a richer intellectual background or enjoyed wider or more fructifying contacts with life. It is her great virtue that she has refused to shut her eyes to the horror and terror of human experience, at the same time declin-

ing to close her mind against the conviction that life is shot through with spiritual significance.

But the damning appraisal of F. Scott Fitzgerald held sway: "Dorothy Canfield as a novelist is certainly of no possible significance." The first doctoral dissertation on Fisher, Joseph P. Lovering's *The Contribution of Dorothy Canfield Fisher to the Development of Realism in the American Novel,* appeared in 1956, and Elizabeth Yates's biography, *Pebble in a Pool,* was published in 1958, but without a solid base of critical support for the subject, a long period of silence followed.

However, interest in Fisher was revived again in the eighties, due in part to a re-evaluation of neglected women writers. Ida H. Washington's biography was published in 1982, scholarship on the BOMC grew, Fisher's friendship with Willa Cather received increased attention, paperback editions of *The Brimming Cup, The Home-Maker,* and *Her Son's Wife* were reissued, and Fisher's name began to appear once more in the *MLA Bibliography.* Given the current reappraisal of the American literary canon in terms of race, class, and gender, the time for a re-evaluation of Fisher's work is clearly at hand. Although her *ouevre* is uneven, she did write much that is of enduring value and interest. Fisher's stories based on her World War I experiences in Europe, for instance, provide a valuable and well-crafted counterpoint to the handling of similar subject matter by such male contemporaries as Hemingway. *The Brimming Cup,* too, is as rich in material detail as Sinclair Lewis's fiction, yet written from the woman's perspective, which Lewis's work lacks. *The Home-Maker,* finally, is a story of role-reversal in a marriage and has contemporary relevance to issues of child-rearing and women's rights. Fisher's letters collected here thus document the life of one of the twentieth century's most remarkable women in a way that no biography nor even the most autobiographical of her own works can. Here, in her own words, is the story of her life and literary career as told in correspondence spanning nearly six decades.

III

Dorothy Canfield Fisher was a prolific letter-writer. Her former secretary, Helen Congdon, recalls that she wrote several letters in her study nearly every day, usually in the afternoon or evening after finishing her professional writing. She wrote to friends, relatives, fellow authors, politicians, publishers, and

readers. During a period in the mid-twenties, the quantity of Fisher's mail necessitated the use of a card that explained that she was unable to answer all of her letters. But she did respond to many of them, with letters to readers whom she had never met often running several pages. In 1943 her housekeeper, Elizabeth Cullinan, said, "Characteristically, she answers letters promptly, handles her own correspondence. It's enormous." Soon after Fisher's death, Bradford Smith also noted the volume of correspondence: "Into the house, as Dorothy's audience widened, poured a great tide of correspondence. Her writing made readers think of her as a friend. The mail literally came by the basketful. After it had come in, the small study often looked as if a whirlwind had struck it, with letters piled here and there according to the way they were to be handled.. . ." The list of recipients in even a selected edition such as this bears evidence of the diversity of Fisher's correspondents. The eye may light on the famous names, but some of the most interesting letters are to common folk. There are also the names of the once famous, but now lesser-known, much like Fisher herself: Cleghorn, Suckow, Webster, and Yezierska. Lamentably, there are few extant letters to Fisher's immediate family— John, James, and Sally—as she was rarely apart from them.

Fisher's letters were usually typed on letterhead stationery, although occasionally she wrote by hand, during short trips away from Arlington, Vermont. Her typing could be erratic, but Fisher was generally attentive to details of spelling and grammar. Even though her eyesight began to fail in the mid-forties, Helen Congdon reports, Fisher continued to correspond by dictating her letters into a tape recorder. She registered her dissatisfaction with "the remoteness of that way of answering letters" in 1955, but found no better alternative (Letter 181). Fisher once told Paul Reynolds that the process of writing a novel "usually ends by carrying me off my feet so that I can't think of anything else" (Letter 60), and she was absorbed by her letter writing in similar fashion. The enthusiasm she felt for crafting the language, for communicating her thoughts, feelings, and ideas is evident in both the quantity and quality of her correspondence. In many cases, what were intended to be polite notes turned into full-length epistles. Nearing the end of such letters would often come a sheepish apology like that offered to William Lyon Phelps—"I oughtn't to bother you with such a long rambling letter. I didn't mean, when I began, to do more than to thank you" (Letter 44)—or some wry acknowledgment of the letter's generous length, such as her closing line to Harry and Bernardine Scherman, "Hastily—though you'd hardly believe it!" (Letter 101).

There is an immediacy to these letters, as though Fisher is conversing with her correspondent in person. They are peppered with colorful expressions of speech: "get-up-and-git" (Letter 29), "honest in-jun" (Letter 39), "a durn sight worse" (Letter 41), "wrestling like Jacob" (Letter 63), "a calorific meal" (Letter 104), and "a real Jenny-welcome" (Letter 174). Fisher's opening sentence to Pearl Buck, "How you and I always feel the impulse to put our heads together, to clasp hands closely, to share what is in our hearts, in grave moments of crisis!" (Letter 126), and poignant closing paragraph to Christopher Morley, "There, that's my news bulletin—of what's going on within. Little, really nothing—to report of what is visible physically—a quiet old country woman, deaf, with dimmed eyes, partially paralyzed, going slowly along the paths where she used to outrace her own children" (Letter 179), are but two examples of the intimacy she shared with her correspondents.

IV

The letters say a good deal about Fisher on a personal level. The complexity of the individual they reveal is commensurate with Fisher's wide interests, learning, and activities. What becomes immediately apparent is that Fisher lived in two worlds, one literary, one domestic. As a woman, wife, and mother of two children, she was expected to fulfill several roles. From the birth of Fisher's first child, Sally (who would also become a children's book author), in 1909 through her child-rearing years, Fisher's letters bear witness to the competing forces of art and domesticity in her daily life.

According to her mother, Fisher used to hold her son, Jimmy, to her breast with one hand and write with the other. In 1912, she told Paul Reynolds that her daughter was growing older and needed "more time and attention" and that her literary output was "very limited" because she had "a great deal to do besides being an author" (Letter 11). Subsequent letters refer to the increased demands, which now included her elderly mother. She wrote to Alfred Harcourt in 1920: "We have been having a real siege here, with John in bed with a badly infected knee and a high temperature and us in quarantine with both children whoop-

ing it up with chicken-pox, and the thermometer at twenty below and me keeping fires night and day and tending to my sick-a-beds," (Letter 39). After spending a summer abroad to concentrate on the writing of **Rough-Hewn,** Fisher told Julia Collier Harris of the conditions under which she normally worked: "As a rule I work in the midst of a very stirring family and neighborhood life, with a thousand interruptions of all sorts. This is the first time I've been separated from the children for more than a day, since they were born, and the first time I've not kept house, the regular three-meals-a-day-routine, since I was a young girl. It seemed so strange to get up in the morning with nothing to do *except write!*" (Letter 49). Virginia Woolf's *A Room of One's Own* comes to mind when reading of how often the silence of Fisher's study was broken by her children, neighbors, and other visitors. The challenge Fisher faced was the same she articulated for women readers of **Mothers and Children**: to be a good wife and mother *and* to maintain interests outside of the home. As she told Henry Kitchell Webster, she did not believe that giving her children "orange-juice at the right hour" should be the sole concern of any woman (Letter 21). Fisher sought to define herself not only in relation to the needs of her family—which were paramount—but also as a writer. Her record of publication testifies to her success at finding time to write, but her letters show that the work was not produced without great effort and many distractions.

The same strong will that enabled Fisher to write amidst divergent responsibilities evinces itself elsewhere in the letters. In fact, Fisher was willing to risk her life for her beliefs, as illustrated by her participation in the World War I relief effort. In 1916, she made a perilous trip across the Atlantic with her two children to join her husband, who was working for the American Ambulance Corps in France. Before the war's end, she had founded a Braille press for blinded soldiers and a hospital for refugee children. Her readiness to volunteer is discussed in a letter to Sally Cleghorn:

> As you say, *now* is the time to stick to our principles . . . and it has made me sick to hear such crowds and crowds of Americans all writing vociferously to the papers that the Allies are fighting the cause of civilization for us, while we stand off in safety and profit by their blood and suffering . . . and yet nobody has done anything! Even John and I who have felt so keenly that France was standing between our world and all that threatened its permanence, have done nothing but send money, we haven't been willing to sacrifice our comfort and convenience . . . for that is practi-

cally all we are thinking of sacrificing now. There will be some danger of course, but not more than there always is in doing something worth doing. . . . (Letter 18)

Further evidence of this fiery side of Fisher's character is displayed in her description of a debate about modern literature with critic John Aldridge in 1949: "So by and by, I took an axe in one hand, a hatchet in the other and a knife between my teeth and sailed in. No courtesy is needed between an old woman and a young man, and my foot was on my native heath, and I wasn't under obligation to anybody—quite the contrary—for having invited me to Vermont" (Letter 162). The *Burlington Free Press* called the discussion, which was part of a literary symposium sponsored by the University of Vermont, a "slugfest." And Fisher was not one to couch her opinions in euphemisms. Commenting on Henry James's satire of Boston reform women and his charge that they were destroying "the sentiment of sex," she wrote: "Is *that* a joke! As if anything could! And this fear lest the 'sentiment of sex' be diminished, from a man who, as far as the eye can see, never had a bit of it. Something like the Pope telling the world in all the modern languages about what the relations between husband and wife should be" (Letter 173).

Although she was at various times a social crusader, a campaigner for moral improvement, and a famous author, Fisher had a modest sense of self-importance and did not lack a sense of humor. A small woman, she often expressed her self-consciousness about her size through humor. In a 1916 letter to Louise Pound, she enclosed a photograph of herself standing next to a donkey and joked, "Now if you know how big a donkey is, you can see how tall I am" (see Letter 19 and photograph). In the same letter, she referred to a published photograph of herself with an upraised hand as being "ridiculously like the hand of a bishop, bestowing the episcopal blessing." Later, she wrote to Pound about publicity photographs in general, "The less people know how I look, the more they'll think of me" (Letter 22). This despite the fact that Fisher was, by all accounts, an attractive woman.

The letters also portray a woman of great generosity. That Fisher gave of her time and money to numerous worthy causes is a matter of public record. But the letters show her magnanimity in other ways. There is praise and support for her friends' work, as exemplified in the letters to Pearl Buck and Ruth Suckow. There are the offers to lend her name to the publicity of worthy books, such as James Weldon Johnson's *God's Trombones* (Letter 69). There are the efforts to

get good books published, as in the case of Isak Dinesen's *Seven Gothic Tales*; and the careful readings of works-in-progress, as in the case of Anzia Yezierska's *All I Could Never Be*. There are also the more modest kindnesses, such as Fisher's response to an invitation to read: she suggested to the club woman that she also invite Sarah Cleghorn and pay her the honorarium in full (Letter 106).

One of the most intriguing episodes in the letters in regard to Fisher's character involves Willa Cather. The story of the Fisher-Cather friendship is chronicled in the 104 letters (all but five from Cather to Fisher), written during the years 1899 to 1947, that constitute the Cather file of the Fisher papers at the University of Vermont. Included in this collection are twenty-five letters (twenty by Cather, three by Fisher, one by Cather's mother, and one by Cather's friend Isabelle McClung) that had remained unread by anyone save the correspondents themselves until July 1987, when they were found in a barn on the Fisher homestead in Arlington. Along with assorted manuscripts and related material, they had been inadvertently left behind when Fisher's letters were donated to the university. These letters, like all of Cather's, may be neither published nor directly quoted, as specified by provisions in the author's will. Cather drew up these restrictions to protect her privacy and professional reputation; for the same reason she destroyed nearly all the letters she received.

Cather and Fisher were first drawn to each other by their mutual interests in French literature, painting, and music. Their friendship began in 1891 when Dorothy's father became chancellor of the University of Nebraska, where Cather was a student. Cather was then publishing stories and reviews in local and campus papers; Fisher was her younger admirer and protégée. Fisher felt most honored at the time to collaborate with Cather on a short story, **"The Fear That Walks by Noonday,"** which appeared in the university's literary magazine (and was reprinted in 1931, see Letters 84 and 88). Soon after Cather's death in 1947, Fisher remarked upon the regard in which she held her older friend: "Later on, of course, as we both grew into the twenties and the thirties, this difference in years [six] dwindled to nothing at all, as differences do to adults, so far as any barrier to our close comradeship went. But my lifelong admiring affection for Willa was, at first, tinctured with the respectful deference due from a younger person to a successful member of the older generation."

Cather and Fisher stayed in touch after leaving Nebraska, as they would for most of their lives. Yet long gaps in the correspondence from 1905 to 1921 remained a mystery to Cather and Fisher scholars and occasioned a good deal of conjecture; it is only recently, with information from the newly-found Cather-Fisher letters, that the rift may be understood. The dispute had its basis in Cather's first trip to Europe in 1902, when she met Evelyn Osborne, a friend and fellow graduate student of Fisher's. Although only passing reference is made to Osborne—a young woman with a prominent facial scar and a taste for extravagant clothes—in Cather's letters at the time of the trip, it was she who would later stand at the center of the disagreement over "The Profile"—significantly, the story of a young woman with a grotesque facial scar and an interest in extravagant clothes.

More specifically, "The Profile" is set in Paris, where portraitist Aaron Dunlap is commissioned to paint Virginia Gilbert, whose face bears a jagged scar on one side. Throughout their ensuing courtship the scar is never mentioned between the two, although Dunlap desperately wants to share the burden of Virginia's disfigurement. Even after their marriage and the birth of a daughter, Virginia's vanity prevents her from discussing the scar with Dunlap, which creates a gap between the husband and wife. When Dunlap becomes attracted to Virginia's cousin Eleanor, who is their houseguest, his wife leaves him. On the night of her departure, she arranges for a dressing table lamp to explode in Eleanor's face, so that she, too, is permanently disfigured. The story closes as Dunlap, mercifully divorced from Virginia, marries Eleanor.

Fisher first expressed concern about the story, which was to be included in *The Troll Garden,* Cather's first collection of short fiction, in a telegram sent a few days before Christmas 1904. Writing from Arlington to Cather in Pittsburgh, Fisher said she had just heard of "The Profile" and that she would "suspend judgment" until hearing from Cather, whom she implored to reply immediately. Cather did so, claiming that the story was not really cause for concern since, in her opinion, Virginia Gilbert did not resemble Osborne except for the scar on her face. She pointed out that the protagonist was married, unlike Osborne; that Osborne's taste in clothes was not nearly so bad; and that the story focused on the character's domestic infelicities, which could not possibly be traced to Fisher's friend. Scars were not so uncommon, Cather said, that one would link the character to Osborne specifically.

Fisher next asked Cather for a copy of the story, which reached Arlington on December 30. She wrote to Cather just two days later, pleading that it not be published for fear of the damage it would do to Osborne's delicate psyche: "I am quite sure you don't realize how exact and faithful a portrait you have drawn of her—her beautiful hair, her pretty hands, her fondness of dress and pathetic lapses of taste in wearing what other girls may, her unconsciousness—oh Willa don't do this thing. . . . I don't believe she would ever recover from the blow of your description of her affliction" (Letter 3; ellipsis mine).

Fisher's letter was answered promptly, not by Cather but by Isabelle McClung, to whom Cather had turned for advice. McClung firmly supported Cather's right to publish the story. Cather followed up McClung's letter with one of her own in which she said that the page proofs of *The Troll Garden* had already been returned to the press and that to omit "The Profile" would make an already slim volume too small to publish. She asked for Fisher's understanding and hoped that their friendship would remain intact.

Fisher, though, persisted in her efforts to protect Osborne. She told Cather that she had consulted with her parents about the affair and that they had recommended the matter be referred to *The Troll Garden*'s publisher, S. S. McClure, if Cather did not withdraw the story herself. When Cather failed to respond, Fisher wrote her final, uncharacteristically terse, letter on the matter, threatening "further action" (Letter 5). In "Autobiography in the Shape of a Book Review," the poet Witter Bynner, once Cather's editorial colleague, mentions a dispute over "The Profile" that took place at McClure's office. He describes the meeting between the two parties as "tense" and claims that Cather insisted on publication, even though it was suggested that Osborne might commit suicide if she read the story (253). Bynner did not name those who objected, but we can now be sure Fisher was among them. Finally, neither side could claim victory, for although the story did not appear in the 1905 edition of *The Troll Garden*—which was dedicated to Isabelle McClung—it was published two years later (June 1907) in *McClure's*. There is no evidence of whether Osborne ever read the work and no further mention of her in the Cather-Fisher correspondence.

The rift between the two authors was not bridged until nearly fifteen years later, when Cather enlisted Fisher's help in authenticating the details of the French setting of her Pulitzer Prize-winning novel, *One of Ours* (1922). They maintained a faithful correspondence thereafter, with Fisher paying Cather occasional visits at her New York apartment. Fisher's letter to Cather recollecting their 1902 visit to A. E. Housman was among the last Cather read before her death in 1947 (Letter 148).

The disagreement over "The Profile" is instructive for what it says about Fisher as an artist and person. While she was at the time of the dispute a published writer who had devoted a major part of her life to the formal study of literature, Fisher valued Osborne's feelings over Cather's story. She was also willing to risk Cather's longtime friendship for what she believed to be an issue of personal privacy and moral decency. As to the propriety of Fisher's actions, there is much to be said on both sides, but what is indisputable is her passion and resolve in defending Osborne. Some years later, Fisher took issue with Anzia Yezierska over modeling fictional characters after real people. In 1932, she objected to Yezierska's use of Arlington citizens as the basis for characters in her novel *All I Could Never Be* (Letter 91) and voiced her concern to the book's publisher, G. P. Putnam (Letter 89). Other letters document the care Fisher took to mask the identities of real people represented in her own work, including *The Deepening Stream* (Letter 81), *Seasoned Timber* (Letter 107), and **"The Bedquilt"** (Letter 138).

V

Readers will find these letters to be filled with information on American literature in general and Fisher's writing in particular. They deepen our knowledge of Fisher's sources and influences, her method of composition, and her authorial intentions. They offer the perspective of an author who was otherwise reluctant to "explain" her own works. They portray a serious artist who was concerned with the formal qualities of her writing, one who would not produce stories and novels carelessly for the high prices they commanded. At the same time, even as she wrote for traditional women's magazines, she could be experimental. A 1920 letter to William Lyon Phelps, for example, speaks about Fisher's use of point of view in *The Brimming Cup*:

> I have tried to make a glass door through which the reader looks into the heart and mind of one and another of the men, women, or children in the story, so that, once and for all, he knows what sort of human being is there. From that time on, it has been my intention to leave the reader to interpret for himself the meaning of the actions of that character, without the traditional explanations and re-iterated indications from the author. (Letter 44)

Among the broad patterns we observe in the letters is the growth and maturation of Fisher as a writer. Her progression from literary neophyte to self-assured professional manifests itself in several ways, one of which is a shift in tone in her correspondence with her agent and publishers. The earliest letter in this collection, to Louis Wiley of the *New York Times,* and a later one to Curtis Hidden Page are strikingly deferential in their phrasing. The nascent author informs Wiley that she would be willing to write an article on Spain "wholly subject" to his specifications and approval (Letter 1), and tells Page that "I handle my pen as I do my tongue and that is alas, quite without art" (Letter 3).

By 1924, however, Fisher's voice had grown more sure and authoritative. When pressed by her agent Reynolds to begin work on **Her Son's Wife** that year, she spoke her mind in no uncertain terms: "I do protest against being lumped in with the loafing authors who don't work unless they're hurried into it. No sir, by gracious, that is not me. Nobody *can* hurry me" (Letter 60). As she became a more experienced author, her letters to people in publishing took on a brisk and executive air. As far as the actual writing was concerned, though, she never lost the excitement and anxiety felt by a beginner. After almost fifty years as a professional author, Fisher told Bennett Cerf that she still never began work on a book "without butterflies in the stomach, like a singer going out on the platform for a solo" (Letter 163).

Fisher was assertive as far as the artistic integrity of her works was concerned. By all evidence, her business relationships were amicable—as long as the business people did not interfere with her creative talent. For instance, she refused to alter a story line dealing with anti-Semitism in **Seasoned Timber** that drew criticism from an editor considering the book for serialization. She wrote to Paul Reynolds:

> The story would lose its point if that strong element were left out. . . . I think race prejudice is creeping in insidiously to American life (for instance I bet you a nickel that the Country Club of your own town of Scarsdale is closed to Jews—without regard to their individual refinement or desirability). I'm ashamed of it, and I think most decent Americans would be ashamed of it, if they stopped to think about it. (Letter 105, ellipsis mine)

While nonfiction articles and serialized versions of novels were primarily a source of income, Fisher saw her books as her contribution to the world of letters. From romantic, often sentimental, magazine stories, she turned to novel-length examinations of human relationships and sought to portray them with depth and skill. As she once told William Lyon Phelps, "the richness and endless variety of human relationships . . . that's what authors, even the finest and greatest, only succeed in hinting at. It's a hopeless business, like trying to dip up the ocean with a tea-spoon" (Letter 44). Even in the case of serials, she could be reticent to compromise.

After a meeting with a magazine editor concerning the possible serialization of *The Brimming Cup,* she objected to the suggestion that each installment end with a "big crisis": "I said earnestly that I wouldn't guarantee her that, nor even that I would in any degree try for that, and I wanted her to understand that fully, before she thought any more about the matter. In fact that I wouldn't guarantee her *any*thing in the way of style or 'action' etc." (Letter 41). And in the case of *Bonfire,* Fisher wrote two versions: a streamlined one, which was less risque in certain details of setting and plot for serialization, and another, "doing it as I want to do it" for book publication (Letter 87). While she habitually expressed doubt about the finished product, her commitment to the craft of writing is clear.

Fisher's letters also add a wealth of new information and insight to what we know of her literary taste and aesthetics. The breadth of her reading is immediately apparent. Trained as a scholar of French literature and foreign languages, her reading interests were far-ranging. She knew the classics and read widely in contemporary literature for the BOMC. The letters make plain her affection for Shakespeare, for the great Russian novelists, especially Tolstoy, and for the French, including Balzac and the fabulist LaFontaine. More modern preferences are also indicated for Buck, Cather, Dinesen, Frost, and Wright. In addition, she wrote to Julia Collier Harris in admiration of Harry Stillwell Edwards's and Joel Chandler Harris's stories featuring African-Americans (Letter 70), and a 1948 letter notes an early appreciation of Eudora Welty (Letter 152).

Fisher freely acknowledged the distinguished efforts of her peers in her published reviews, but restricted most negative criticism to her letters. In them we find some of her most lively, engaging literary commentary. She clearly had little taste for works containing rough language, explicit sex, or graphic violence. (John O'Hara, whose *Appointment in Samarra* Fisher criticized for an overabundance of those very elements, once referred to her as "Dorothy, I can field—no great pleasure, Mrs. Fisher"). Nor was she enamored of what she perceived to be a preoccu-pation with alienation, corruption, and meaninglessness in modern literature. Yet she did not care for escapist fiction either, as she explained to a Book-of-the-Month Club subscriber, who complained that the judges' choices were unsuitable for young people:

> No good is ever done, I think, by pretending that anything is different from what it really is, either in our explicit statement, or by implication. The prettifying of human relations in conventional old-fashioned, mid-nineteenth-century fiction, was responsible for some ghastly shocks when the readers of those pleasant books came up, in real life, against something which the novels they had read had led them to assume did not exist. (Letter 141)

At a time when moral values and meaning and even human communication were considered outmoded, Fisher held fast to her belief that the true artist wrote with a desire to express, in a helpful way, some new understanding about human life. She summarized her view in a 1945 letter: "The impulse of the writing person is to share this new understanding with the rest of humanity. He feels its importance as a help to understanding what takes place around us, and can hardly wait until he has put it into some form in which, he hopes, others may see the significance of events in human life which they have been taking perhaps callously, perhaps just with dull or slow lack of understanding" (Letter 138). Thus, Fisher did not reject modern literature per se, but bristled at many of its salient tendencies. In the modern tradition, she believed that literature should reflect the reality of the human condition. In her judgment of fiction for the BOMC, she was said to exercise "exacting standards" and to focus on "the accuracy of image, the unity of plot, the depth of characterization." Her optimistic world view and belief in moral values, though, set her apart from the literary mainstream.

The correspondence also affords an opportunity to observe the application of Fisher's literary principles to specific works. An admirer of the tales of Hans Christian Andersen (see Letter 6), she did not hesitate to suggest that highly praised books of both past and present wore no finery. Such was the case with James Boswell's *Life of Samuel Johnson, LL.D.* Prior to a 1950 BOMC meeting in which *Boswell's London Journal, 1762-1763* was to be considered as a selection, she wrote to Harry Scherman to vent her dislike of Boswell and eighteenth-century literature as a whole. Her purpose in writing to Scherman in advance of the meeting was to avoid offending her colleague and friend Christopher Morley, who had written an adulatory "Introduction" to the newly discovered journal. "I have felt all my life, that Boswell's *Life of Johnson* is enormously overestimated by professors of English Literature, and really is a bore to most people (as it certainly was to me)," she wrote (Letter 167). Fisher found the *Life* overly long and saw no need for the further elaboration in the London journal. She held nothing back in her letter to Scherman: "To add to that, *more* Boswell saying tiresomelessly over and over what has already been told to us in other books, about a period of no importance anyhow, and about a shallow-natured, trivial-minded man—." The journal was, finally, not chosen as a book-of-the-month but sent to subscribers as a dividend.

A striking example of Fisher's disdain for a more contemporary work is found in her letter concerning the Detroit ban against the sale and library circulation of Ernest Hemingway's *To Have and Have Not* (Letter 109). In reaction to complaints by the Detroit Council of Catholic Organizations, the novel was ruled to be obscene by city authorities in 1938. The League of American Writers protested the censorship, and Archibald MacLeish drafted a letter of protest, which was signed by Van Wyck Brooks and Thornton Wilder and published in the *Nation*. The letter charged that the real reason for the censure of the book was that the Catholic Church objected to Hemingway's involvement in the war in Spain. "Only a prurient mind could possibly find the book offensive," MacLeish wrote. When Fisher, an otherwise ardent supporter of public libraries and free speech, was asked to add her signature to the letter, she replied, "I don't feel like signing it myself." She argued that MacLeish's reasoning was weak, but she also let it be known that she and several of her peers found the book to be "offensive."

Other notable figures who are subject to pointed criticism in the letters include George Santayana (a "heartless" man, Letter 122), John Steinbeck (*The Wayward Bus* was "false to human probability," Letter 146), Norman Mailer (*The Naked and the Dead* was vulgar, Letter 153), Sinclair Lewis (Fisher picked up his books "as with the tongs," Letter 156), John Dos Passos (the characters in *The Grand Design* were "nothing but names on the page, floating in and out of the interminable cocktail drinking, gossiping *talk* which fills the book," Letter 157), Arthur Miller (*Death of a Salesman* evinced an "odd lack of connection with reality," Letter 160), and D. H. Lawrence (whose works presented Indians as "demi-gods," not real people, Letter 165). The list goes on, but even this brief catalogue illustrates Fisher's distaste for

some of the most eminent American writers. Her reading for the BOMC kept her in touch with the current of modern literature, but she obviously felt little affection for much of what now constitutes the canon of the period.

Fisher's correspondence also sheds new light on her activities and influence as a member of the BOMC Board of Selection. Created by advertising executive Harry Scherman and publisher Robert Haas in 1926, the BOMC claimed more than sixty thousand subscribers within a year. The operating principles were straightforward: members agreed to buy a newly published book chosen monthly by the five-member Board. They paid full price with an option to exchange the book, upon inspection, for an "alternate" choice. Soon after, readers were asked to buy only four books a year and allowed to substitute the alternate selection before shipping. Fisher at first hesitated joining the group, but after observing the emptiness of Brentano's bookstore in New York in contrast to other stores, she decided there must be a better method of "getting books into the hands of American readers."

Although Fisher de-emphasized the significance of her position with the BOMC, remarking in a 1941 letter that she was "surprised and somewhat daunted" by the influence one subscriber attributed to the monthly choice (Letter 115), she did play a key role in the careers of at least three well-known authors: Pearl Buck, Isak Dinesen (Karen Blixen), and Richard Wright. Fisher nominated Buck's *The Good Earth* for special consideration by the board after a first reader's report underestimated it, and then recommended the eventual Pulitzer Prize-winner strongly at the judges' monthly meeting. The result was that *The Good Earth* was the book-of-the-month for March 1931, the first of six works by Buck selected during Fisher's time on the board.

Dinesen owed no less than her first American book publication to Fisher, who was sent the manuscript of *Seven Gothic Tales* by the author's brother. As her letters from 1932 to 1933 indicate, Fisher put the book in the hands of its eventual publisher, and she wrote a "Preface" introducing Dinesen to the American public. *Seven Gothic Tales* was a book-of-the-month (April 1934), as were four subsequent titles by Dinesen.

Wright's association with the BOMC was important to his early success as well. His *Native Son* and *Black Boy*, now ranked among American classics, were distributed by the BOMC as monthly choices, and Fisher not only wrote reviews and introductions, but also suggested important revisions for both. Fisher's role in the textual history of *Black Boy*—documented in her correspondence here—is discussed by Janice Thaddeus in her 1985 essay "The Metamorphosis of Richard Wright's *Black Boy*," while Arnold Rampersad's notes to his Library of America edition of Wright's works explicate the *Native Son* connection.

VI

Ancillary to the explicitly personal and literary letters are those dealing with the social concerns that underpin much of Fisher's fiction. Three subjects are most prominent: the importance of education, women's rights, and the African-American struggle for racial equality.

Fisher's interest in education can be traced back to her upbringing as the daughter of an academic: her father was (in chronological order) a professor at the University of Kansas, chancellor of the University of Nebraska, president of Ohio State University, and librarian of Columbia University. In a letter to the president of Middlebury College in support of coeducation there, Fisher noted that she knew both sides of the issue because she had been "brought up on the discussion of it all my life" (Letter 52). She viewed education as the means by which American citizens could best develop their individual potential and contribute to society, and she made two major contributions to the field. First, she introduced the Montessori method of childhood education to America. Her explication of the system appears in *A Montessori Mother* (1912), published after her visit to Maria Montessori's Casa dei Bambini in Rome, *A Montessori Manual* (1913), and *Mothers and Children* (1914). Montessori principles are also present in the novel *The Bent Twig* (1915) and her well-known children's book *Understood Betsy* (1917), the story of a pampered city girl who learns the value of hard work and responsibility when she moves to a Vermont farm. The book highlights, in a fictional framework, Fisher's conviction that both boys *and* girls should be raised to be independent and self-reliant. Secondly, Fisher helped establish the Adult Education Association, the first organization of its kind in the U.S. Her belief that education is a lifelong enterprise is expressed in *Why Stop Learning?* (1927). The enduring significance of the book to Fisher is evident in a later letter (1929) to Alfred Harcourt in which she wrote, "I'd like not to have people forget that book. I've said some things in it I'm glad to have said" (Letter 75).

Closely related to Fisher's commitment to education was her active support of women's rights. Surprisingly, Fisher once wrote that she "was never a feminist." She explained, "It was my older generation, my father and mother, who were. I was rather (as it often goes in generations) in reaction from their extreme zeal for 'women's rights'" (DCF to Helen K. Taylor, no date). Her devotion to the cause of equal opportunity for women, though, is unmistakable. Both Fisher's fiction (most notably *The Home-Maker,* in which the protagonist, Evangeline Knapp, is a wife, mother, and the family breadwinner) and her letters speak to her strong belief that women should not be limited in their access to education and job training, nor should they be bound by societal conventions. Characteristically, in a 1946 letter to Margaret Mead, she lamented "the social pressure, invisible and tyrannical, which the United States puts upon its women and girls" (Letter 142). The restriction of women's roles—and men's too: in *The Home-Maker,* the husband, Lester Knapp, draws great satisfaction from staying at home and caring for his children—seemed, quite simply, impractical to Fisher. She reasoned that since everyone is born with unique abilities, limitations, and temperaments, one's place should not be determined by gender. It was only when each person was in a role he or she was suited for that society could function productively, and Fisher lectured and wrote in support of that principle. As she remarked to Julia Collier Harris:

> So large a majority of fathers of our girls are heart-and-soul business men, it stands to reason that the girls themselves might do better if they were not automatically shoved off into being cultured teachers . . . although goodness knows our country needs cultured teachers enough sight more than business-people. Still, folks have to do what they are best fit for, and every opportunity for women means one less chance of a square peg living miserably in a round hole all its life. (Letter 68)

Nearly thirty years later, Fisher still worried over the obstacles women faced:

> I'm very much struck by the fact that although America offers us a life astonishingly safe from most physical dangers, it plunges us into another danger which is devilishly insidious because it falls so imperceptibly about us as we live—and that is the danger of becoming held and mastered by triviality. The little things of life, of no real importance, but which have to be "seen to" by American home makers, is like a blanket smothering out the fine and great potential qualities in every one of us. (Letter 181)

Lastly, a deep vein of concern for the problem of racial prejudice against African-Americans runs throughout Fisher's letters. The issue certainly was not foreign to her forebears. In a letter to Pearl Buck, Fisher proudly explained that her great-grandmother kept the bell of her Vermont village church tolling "from dawn to dark" on the day of John Brown's execution, that her grandfather had accompanied Henry Ward Beecher on his trip to England to influence British public opinion in favor of the abolitionists, and that her father, when he was president of Ohio State University, had created considerable controversy by inviting Booker T. Washington to lunch at their home. Fisher herself carried on the family tradition: she lectured against racial prejudice and wrote for the *Crisis*; she befriended African-American writers such as James Weldon Johnson and Richard Wright; and she was a trustee of Howard University (1945-1951). Fisher, who counted African-Americans among her childhood friends (see Letter 47), also voiced her opposition to racism in her stories **"An American Citizen"** and **"Fairfax Hunter"** and in her novel ***The Brimming Cup,*** the first bestseller to contain such opinions. In that book, Ormsby Welles, a retired business executive, forsakes his comfortable life in Vermont to aid in the struggle against racial oppression in the South. In a letter to W. E. B. Du Bois, Fisher explained her reason for including the subplot in her popular novel about the married life of a Vermont couple:

> I wish never to lose a chance to remind Americans of what their relations to the Negro race are, and might be, and so into this story of Northern life and white people, I have managed to weave a strand of remembrance of the dark question. It is a sort of indirect, side-approach, a backing-up of your campaign from someone not vitally concerned in it personally, except as every American must be, which I hope may be of use exactly because it is not a straight-on attack, but one of a slightly different manner. (Letter 45)

The very idea of racism was antithetical to Fisher's democratic principles and she minced no words when discussing the subject. To Paul Reynolds she wrote:

> After seeing what idiots the Germans made of themselves for two long generations over that fantastic and so far, entirely unproved idea of Count Gobineau's, and what a well-deserved punishment they got for it, it does seem as though Americans might leave it alone. . . . The Ku Klux Klan (which of course has nothing but this Gobineau idea of inherent racial superiority at the bottom of its imbecilities) may make it odious enough to shorten its stay with us. (Letter 56, ellipsis mine)

Given her efforts on behalf of racial equality, it is appropriate that the last letter in this collection, written less than two months before Fisher's death, is an inquiry about the opportunities available to African-Americans at the U.S. Naval Academy (Letter 189).

VII

Fruits of further investigation will belong to the readers of these letters, who will develop further what is revealed so explicitly and, at times, so wittily or so poignantly. Fisher's personal trials—the wars in Europe, the loss of her son, who died while serving as a doctor in World War II, her later physical disabilities—are revealed here, often with startling and painful clarity. Her personal enthusiasms and interests—including classical music, art, history, sports, and current events—help fill in the biographical record and suggest new approaches to her writing. The range of historical and cultural subjects discussed—the "New Woman" and the suffrage movement, racial discrimination and the emergence of the NAACP, the development of the national education system, both world wars, the Depression, book clubs, and the literary marketplace among them—should encourage not only literary approaches to the use and interpretation of her work and her correspondence, but interdisciplinary ones as well.

Dorothy Canfield Fisher was well born—into a distinguished and cultivated family that gave her a fine education and a sense of self-worth. Her strong principles underpin her beliefs and writing; that she was to extend these concerns to independent women, to new forms of education, and to issues of racial oppression and respect for individual merit was the core of her achievement. Her letters amply display her own recognition of these facts, of this achievement.

THE BEDQUILT, AND OTHER STORIES (1995)

Publishers Weekly

SOURCE: A review of *The Bedquilt, and Other Stories*, in *Publishers Weekly*, Vol. 242, No. 45, November 6, 1995, p. 84.

War, greed, love, women's rights, marital discord and race relations are prominent themes in the unaffectedly realist stories of Fisher (1879-1958), once a best-selling novelist (***The Brimming Cup***, etc.). The

11 stories and two essays reprinted here (all but one from a long out-of-print 1956 anthology) resonate with contemporary relevance. In the title story, an elderly New England spinster, invisible in her brother's home, finally receives recognition for her housework by exhibiting at a county fair the magnificent quilt she spent five years making. In **"Through Pity and Terror . . . "** Fisher, who founded a hospital for refugee children in France during WW I, draws on firsthand experience to describe a young mother's struggle to survive as German soldiers ransack her home and her husband's pharmacy. Abhorrence of war also permeates **"The Knot-Hole,"** a powerful WW II tale evoking the ordeal of Allied POWs confined for months in a German boxcar. Stories of rural residents of Vermont (the Kansas-born writer's adopted state) probe the depths of feeling beneath their sardonic, laconic exteriors; the same fierce independence animates the Basque folk of the stories based on Fisher's years spent living in Southwestern France. In **"An American Citizen"** (1920), an African American elevator operator finds dignity and equal treatment only by moving to France. Though at times sentimental and didactic, Fisher's stories are nevertheless engaging and still timely.

Brad Hooper

SOURCE: A review of *The Bedquilt, and Other Stories*, in *Booklist*, Vol. 92, No. 7, December 1, 1995, p. 609.

A forgotten author who is well worth remembering, Fisher (1879-1958) was a highly regarded and pro-lific novelist and short story writer in her heyday, the 1920s through the early 1940s. This selection of 11 of her best stories seeks to restore her name. The placid surfaces of Fisher's stories, achieved by a consummately limpid style, do not blunt their effectiveness as honest explorations of emotional provinces. Racial and social questions are treated with compassion and with a clear-sighted view of the less-than-noble traits in humanity. Fisher's settings are not restricted; she writes as comfortably about war-torn France (World War I, that is) as she does about small-town America. Two autobiographical essays contribute to our understanding of the muse of this excellent story writer of whom lovers of the form should no longer be ignorant.

UNDERSTOOD BETSY (REPRINT, 2000)

The Horn Book Magazine

SOURCE: A review of *Understood Betsy*, in *The Horn Book Magazine*, Vol. 76, No. 1, January, 2000, p. 60.

A distinctive new edition of an old favorite, in which a neurotic, sickly little girl grows healthy and happy with the help of Vermont farm living, no-nonsense child-rearing techniques, and Montessori-based schooling. Root's pencil sketches add intimacy and life, and the book design is generous and appropriately old-fashioned. With an introduction to the novel and an afterword on Dorothy Canfield Fisher by Eden Ross Lipson.

Additional coverage of Fisher's life and career is contained in the following sources published by the Gale Group: *Contemporary Authors*, Vols. 114, 136; *Contemporary Authors New Revision Series*, Vol. 80; *Dictionary of Literary Biography*, Vols. 9, 102; *Major Authors and Illustrators for Children and Young Adults*; *The St. James Guide to Children's Writers*; *Twentieth-Century Literary Criticism*, Vol. 87; and *Yesterday's Authors of Books for Children*, Vol. 1.

Russell Freedman
1929-

(Full name Russell Bruce Freedman) American biographer and author of nonfiction.

Major works include *Children of the Wild West* (1983), *Lincoln: A Photobiography* (1987), *Franklin Delano Roosevelt* (1990), *The Wright Brothers: How They Invented the Airplane* (1991), *Eleanor Roosevelt: A Life of Discovery* (1993), *The Life and Death of Crazy Horse* (1996).

For further information on Freedman's life and works, see *CLR,* Volume 22.

INTRODUCTION

Armed with the belief that a work of nonfiction can be written as engagingly as fiction, Russell Freedman has written dozens of nonfiction books for young readers on subjects including animal behavior, the pioneering days of the American West, and the lives of American presidents. For many of his books, Freedman heightens the interest of his subject by offering expressive photographs to accompany the text. Through painstaking research, Freedman endeavors to find the most appropriate images available to lend a sense of immediacy to his words. While highly praised for his thorough and engaging studies of animals, Freedman is most appreciated for his historical works. Critics have commended him for a consistently evenhanded, objective approach to subjects that are often distorted and romanticized, and generations of readers have been drawn in by Freedman's compelling and dynamic style.

BIOGRAPHICAL INFORMATION

Born and raised in San Francisco, California, Freedman knew from early on that he wanted to be a writer when he grew up. His father, a sales representative for the publishing company Macmillan, and his mother, who worked in a bookstore for a time, loved books and encouraged their son to read. The Freedman family frequently hosted authors in their home, including such luminaries as John Steinbeck and William Saroyan. Freedman has written, "I had the good

luck to grow up in a house filled with books and with the lively conversations of visiting authors." As a child, some of his favorite books were fascinating works of nonfiction; a lasting impression made by these books was that nonfiction did not have to be dry and boring. If told well, Freedman reasoned, a true story could be every bit as gripping as one created from an author's imagination.

Freedman attended San Jose State College and the University of California, Berkeley; he earned a Bachelor of Arts degree from the latter in 1951. After graduating, Freedman was drafted into the Army and spent two years in Korea, splitting his time between combat duty and U.S. counterintelligence. Upon his return to the United States, Freedman began working as a reporter and editor for the Associated Press in San Francisco, a job that honed his writing skills. He later moved to New York for a job as a publicity writer for various television shows, but this work did not satisfy him. His career changed direction after he happened to read a newspaper article about a sixteen-year-old blind boy who had invented a Braille typewriter. He then learned that the Braille system itself had been invented by another sixteen-year-old, Louis Braille. His curiosity piqued, Freedman began doing some research that not only led to his first book, *Teenagers Who Made History,* but also began a distinguished career as a nonfiction writer.

MAJOR WORKS

Many of Freedman's early works focus on the animal kingdom. He began by writing comprehensive scientific explorations of animal behavior. Critics admired his thoroughness and his ability to explain technical subjects in a clear, interesting way. Freedman, however, longed to write books that would be read from start to finish instead of used for occasional reference. He decided to try a different approach, concentrating on a small group of animals or a particular type of animal behavior rather than writing a definitive volume on a larger topic. He also realized that the use of vivid photographs to illustrate the subject would help the book come alive for young readers. The fruit of these realizations was *Hanging On: How Animals Carry Their Young,* a book highlighting a variety of animal babies, from exotic creatures to the house cat, that need to hang on to their mothers to survive. Freedman went on to write several more books about animals, including *Animal Superstars: Biggest, Strongest, Fastest, Smartest* (1981), and *Sharks* (1985).

In addition to books on animal behavior, Freedman has written numerous nonfiction works about the pioneering days of the American West. To prepare for these books, he traveled throughout the Western states, visiting historical societies and libraries. His research led to *Children of the Wild West,* a book that highlights the experiences of young people and their families as they journeyed to Western settlements during the nineteenth century. Critics have praised Freedman's straightforward account of everyday life on the frontier, noting that the book's powerful photographs help bring the text to life. Freedman's next book in that vein, *Cowboys of the Wild West* (1985), explores life on the cattle range in the 1800s. Reviewers have admired Freedman's frank assessment of the cowboy era in American history, commending his ability to uncover the myths about this romanticized group while still capturing the fascinating elements of their lifestyle. While both of these books contain some information on the lives of Native

Americans, Freedman subsequently devoted several books to the Indian experience. With high-quality archival photographs enlivening the text, *Indian Chiefs* (1987) examines the lives of six tribal chiefs, including Sitting Bull and Red Cloud. Described by critics as moving and tragic, *Indian Chiefs* is also noted for its author's careful research and objectivity. Several years later Freedman devoted an entire book to a biographical study of an Indian leader. *The Life and Death of Crazy Horse* (1996) tells the life story of the great Lakota Sioux chief in what critics describe as Freedman's characteristically honest and engaging style. He further explored the world of nineteenth-century Native Americans in *Buffalo Hunt* (1988) and *An Indian Winter* (1992).

While he has received praise for numerous works, Freedman has perhaps been most lauded for his biographies of important figures in American history. For his first full-length biography, Freedman chose the difficult subject of Abraham Lincoln, about whom more books have been written than almost any other American. Fascinated by descriptions of Lincoln's complex and melancholy character, Freedman decided to delve into the research about Lincoln's life and try to present what he learned in a way that would grab the attention of young readers. According to reviewers, Freedman succeeded in his goal with *Lincoln: A Photobiography.* Winner of the Newbery medal in 1988, *Lincoln* is described as a realistic, compelling portrait of a fascinating yet little-understood figure. Freedman's next subject for a biographical work was another iconic American president: Franklin Roosevelt. In choosing Roosevelt for his subject, Freedman was once again attempting to shed new light on a figure whose life had inspired numerous scholarly works. His detailed research and straightforward approach in *Franklin Delano Roosevelt* again brought favorable reviews from critics. Though Freedman aroused controversy by candidly writing of Roosevelt's marital infidelities in this book and in his biography of Eleanor Roosevelt, many critics agreed with the author's assertion that the Roosevelts' stories could not be told honestly and completely without addressing that subject. Describing *Eleanor Roosevelt: A Life of Discovery,* a *Publishers Weekly* reviewer wrote: "This impeccably researched, highly readable study of one of the country's greatest First Ladies is nonfiction at its best."

Extending his reach beyond presidential figures, Freedman has written biographies on a wide range of subjects. Combining an interest in significant inventions with a skill for relating life stories, Freedman explores the beginnings of air travel in *The Wright Brothers: How They Invented the Airplane.* Critics have commended his use of such primary sources as letters and diaries, as well as photographs taken by the Wright Brothers themselves, to bring a fresh perspective to history. In 1997 Freedman returned to one of the subjects that first inspired him to write nonfiction for young people: Louis Braille. *Out of Darkness: The Story of Louis Braille* (1997) relates the story of the sixteen-year-old inventor of the Braille alphabet, a system enabling the blind to read by touch. Reviewers praised Freedman's evenhanded yet inspiring treatment of Braille's life, and Martha V. Parravano wrote in *Horn Book* that the book "brings the central figure to life as vividly as only Freedman can." Freedman's more recent biographies have covered a diverse range of celebrated Americans, including *Martha Graham: A Dancer's Life* (1998), which relates the story of the influential dancer, instructor, and choreographer of modern dance. Freedman has also written a biography of one of the greatest American athletes of the twentieth century, *Babe Didrikson Zaharias* (1999). Freedman's latest work, a departure from his numerous biographies of late, returns to the early days of the American republic. *Give Me Liberty: The Story of the Declaration of Independence* (2000) provides background and context for one of the most important documents in American history.

AWARDS

Several of Freedman's books have received honors, awards, and citations. The National Cowboy Hall of Fame awarded *Children of the Wild West* the Western Heritage Award in 1984; the same book was named *Boston Globe-Horn Book* Honor Book for Nonfiction in 1984 and winner of the Jefferson Cup Award in 1986. *Lincoln: A Photobiography* won a Golden Kite Award Honor Book citation in 1987 and the Newbery Medal and Jefferson Cup Award in 1988. Another Golden Kite Award Honor Book citation was given to *The Wright Brothers: How They Invented the Airplane* in 1990; *The Wright Brothers* also received the Orbus Pictus Award and the Jefferson Cup Award in 1991, and another Jefferson Cup Award and a Newbery Honor Book citation in 1992. For *Eleanor Roosevelt: A Life of Discovery,* Freedman won the Golden Kite Award in 1993 as well as the *Boston Globe-Horn Book* Award and a Newbery Honor Book citation in 1994. Freedman received the American Library Association's Laura Ingalls Wilder Medal for his body of work in 1998.

AUTHOR COMMENTARY

Publishers Weekly

SOURCE: "Coming Attractions: A Variety of Authors and Artists Discuss Their Projects for the Fall Season," in *Publishers Weekly,* Vol. 237, No. 30, July 27, 1990, pp. 128-31.

"Franklin Delano Roosevelt was the president of my childhood," says author Russell Freedman. "My earliest memory of politics is sitting by the radio and listening to a fireside chat, and hearing that serene and confident voice saying, 'My friends . . .'"

Franklin Delano Roosevelt, Freedman's latest biography, will be published in October by Clarion. His last book, ***Lincoln: A Photobiography,*** garnered him the 1988 Newbery Medal.

As a subject, Freedman says, Roosevelt was a natural successor to Lincoln. "According to a recent survey of historians, FDR is ranked as the second most important president after Lincoln," he points out. Roosevelt was also a highly controversial president, something that left an indelible impression on Freedman as a child. He recalls the day in junior high school it was announced that the president had died. "When our homeroom teacher dismissed us, her voice hardened and she said, 'Thank God that awful man is dead.' And then when we went out into the hallway, I saw other teachers weeping. So I left the school with those two images in mind."

Freedman has been writing children's nonfiction for 30 years, and he says he's pleased by the changes that have occurred in his field—changes both in terms of production values and editorial tone.

"I think there's a more critical approach to the subject today," he notes. "In the past, a lot of children's nonfiction, especially history and biography, tended to be somewhat sanitized, idealizing the subject. Today, children's books can be more honest about the world and there are fewer taboos."

His own new book is a perfect example of this. In it, he writes frankly of FDR's relationship with Lucy Mercer, an affair that caused a rift in his marriage to Eleanor. This would have been unheard of 30 or 40 years ago, Freedman says—even in books for adults.

Freedman says the Roosevelt biography took much longer to write than did the one on Lincoln—mostly because of a small distraction called the Newbery

Award. "I was already working on Roosevelt when they made the Newbery announcement," he says with a chuckle, "but then that was wonderfully disruptive. I had to stop and write my acceptance speech, which took almost as much time as the book!" Between the speech and subsequent speaking engagements, it took Freedman two years to complete the book on FDR, as opposed to just eight months for the Lincoln biography.

And what does he have up his sleeve for the future? First up: a book about the Wright brothers. He read an article about a collection of photographs that the brothers—both avid amateur photographers—had kept, chronicling their experiments. Freedman immediately detected a possible book subject. "They took photographs of every stage of the development of the airplane," he explains. His book will include many of these little-known photographs.

As soon as he's finished with the Wright brothers, Freedman adds, he plans to start work on a biography of Eleanor Roosevelt. "I've already done a lot of the research, of course, because of my work on FDR. I want to know more about this woman." With characteristic enthusiasm, he adds, "I can't wait to get into it."

Russell Freedman and Stephanie Zvirin

SOURCE: "The *Booklist* Interview," in *Booklist,* Vol. 88, No. 10, January 15, 1992, pp. 926-27.

It's no surprise to Russell Freedman that kids like nonfiction. After all, he has been writing it for 30 years and has come away with top honors from both children and grown-ups. In 1988, he was awarded the Newbery Medal for his photo-biography of Lincoln; last year, *Franklin Delano Roosevelt* earned him the Orbis Pictus Award from the National Council of Teachers of English; and now, *The Wright Brothers* has been awarded *Booklist*'s first annual Top of the List Award for children's and young adult nonfiction. He brings facts to life in a way few other writers manage to do.

BKL: You were a journalist for the Associated Press at one point. What made you decide to make the jump from reporting to writing children's books?

FREEDMAN: Like so many other things in life, it happened accidentally. I came across a newspaper article that suggested an idea that lent itself to being a children's book. It was an article about the 16-year-old blind boy who invented a braille typewriter. That

got me thinking and doing more research, and in 1961, I came up with a book called *Teenagers Who Made History.* I discovered, then, that I was a writer of nonfiction books for kids and that I liked doing it very much.

BKL: Do you write mainly about things that really interest you?

FREEDMAN: Not mainly—*only.* I wouldn't dream of writing about a subject that didn't interest me. It's hard to write a book. It takes time, part of your life. If you don't have a compelling interest in the subject, if you don't want to live with that subject for months, you're not going to have the energy that's necessary to carry you through the writing process.

BKL: After you've gotten an idea, how do you go about researching and writing? Do you go to the library?

FREEDMAN: I start out at the library. I usually start with the most recent books on the subject and go through their bibliographies, working my way backward. I try to familiarize myself not only with current literature on the subject, but also with literature that goes back as far as I want to go. Whenever possible, I do field research. For *Lincoln,* I made two trips. I followed the Lincoln Trail, and I tried to visit every place that Lincoln had lived, starting with his log-cabin birthplace in Kentucky. It isn't that I pick up that much new information in the field—I just think the more you can see with your own eyes, the stronger your feeling for the subject and the more authentic the writing is going to be.

BKL: There's certainly a tremendous amount of material to go through when you're doing a biography of someone like Lincoln. How do you decide what you're going to put in and what you're going to leave out?

FREEDMAN: Well, the first thing I decide is what I'm going to read. It's impossible to read even a fraction of what's been written about Lincoln. Luckily, a friend in Chicago, a librarian who knew I was about to embark on a Lincoln biography, sent me an article from the *Chicago Tribune* about a place called the Abraham Lincoln Book Shop. So I hopped on a plane and went to Chicago. I walked into the shop unannounced, asked to see the manager, and told him what I was about to do. He told me to sit down and be calm. Then he spent half a day with me. By the time I walked out, I had a very good idea which books I should read and reread carefully, which I should skim, and which I could ignore. I don't know what would have happened if my friend hadn't sent the article—I'd probably still be doing research.

Then, of course, there's the other part of your question: How do I decide what to include and what to leave out? That's the toughest thing in writing any kind of book. That's where you try to exercise your art. Writing for children is a very special type of writing; in some ways, it's almost like writing a sonnet because you have certain restrictions. Though you never entirely solve the problem of what to include and what to leave out, the restrictions force you to come so close to your subject that you can reduce it.

BKL: Is there always something you wished you'd put in?

FREEDMAN: Always. I'm now working on a biography of Eleanor Roosevelt. I had a biography of FDR published in 1990, and I've come across several things that I wished I had included in it. I've also reassessed *Lincoln.* In my next life, I'm going to rewrite that.

BKL: The photographs in your books are just wonderful. Where do you find them? What do you look for when you select them?

FREEDMAN: I do all the photo research myself because my concept of the book involves the photographs. I select all the photos myself, too. I choose them with the text in mind, and every photo is keyed to a specific paragraph in the manuscript. While I do research for the text, I make notes on photo sources. By the time I'm ready to look for photos, I have a comprehensive list of places that might have the type I want. I do the photo research before I do my last draft.

BKL: Then you may have to travel across the country to find the pictures you need.

FREEDMAN: Yes. For *Lincoln,* I spent a week at the Illinois State Historical Library in Springfield, Illinois, and several days in Washington at the Library of Congress and the National Archives. For *Children of the Wild West,* I spent a week in the Western-history department of the Denver Public Library.

BKL: What about **The Wright Brothers?**

FREEDMAN: That was easy. There were only three sources—the Smithsonian Aeronautics and Space Museum, the Library of Congress, which owns all of the original glass-plate negatives, and Wright State University in Dayton, Ohio, which has all of the prints that the Wright brothers made themselves. If there are just two or three photographs from a source, I do things by mail. It's a lot of fun to do photo research. It's part of the puzzle of what to include and what to leave out.

I get photocopies to start with. It's too expensive to get the prints before I've made my final selection. I may have 200 or 300 photocopies. I spread them out on the floor of my study looking for various ways to arrange them in each chapter. When artists do picture books, they're thinking of pacing and variety. They don't want the same kind of picture on every page. A nonfiction book illustrated with photographs needs the same type of variety. It has to surprise the reader. And I want the photographs not only to illustrate the subject at each stage of life, but also to tell something about the individual's world.

BKL: Why did you decide to do the photos yourself?

FREEDMAN: I felt that I wanted more control over the books. It wasn't that I wasn't satisfied with them or anything like that. It just suddenly occurred to me while I was looking at a magazine that I could go out and find photographs and design my own book. I could do a dummy. I could experiment with the format and design of the book myself. The first book I did that was based on photographs was called *Hanging On.*

BKL: Not everyone has a publisher that will agree to that.

FREEDMAN: That's true. But I think that if an author supplies a whole package, then maybe the publisher will. Anyway, Holiday House let me do it. I was having such a good time designing books.

BKL: How do you think children's nonfiction, particularly biography, has changed since you first began writing?

FREEDMAN: It's changed in a great many ways. One of the most important is in the look of the books. They're more sensitively and intelligently designed, and they have all variety of visual aids. I think television has had a big influence on that. Books now have to appeal to a generation of young readers who expect some visual impact.

Nonfiction today is addressed to a different type of reader, a more sophisticated child. The books are more honest, not nearly as sanitized. Thirty years ago, most biographies for kids were fictionalized, and writers invented dialogue and manufactured scenes, the theory being that fact had to be dramatized in order to hold reader interest. Well, a writer can make reading interesting without inventing things. There are personal letters: people say things on documented record. Writers simply can't get away with inventing things now, and it's surprising they ever could.

Also, a great many subjects that were taboo in children's books at one time are now fair to write about. I think a very telling example is the Caldecott Medal picture-book biography of Lincoln by the D'Aulaires, published during the 1930s. It's a tremendously charming, very artful book, but it reflects the attitudes toward children's literature of that time. In the book, Lincoln is not assassinated. Instead, the Civil War ends, and he sits down in his rocking chair for a well-deserved rest. There's no indication that anything happened after that. Kids won't put up with that sort of thing today.

BKL: Why don't you include footnotes in your books?

FREEDMAN: The footnote question comes up a lot, and I find it very difficult to answer. A scholarly book is based on original research, on historical documents, letters, that sort of thing. A children's book is usually based mainly on secondary sources. If I spent months at the Franklin Delano Roosevelt Library looking at a lot of original correspondence, I would have to use footnotes in a book about Eleanor. But that's not what I'm doing. I'm writing a book based on Eleanor's autobiography, which was published in three volumes, a book by Joseph P. Lash, and group of other published books. I'm also speaking to a group of people who knew her, but none of that seems like the type of full-scale scholarly enterprise that justifies footnotes.

BKL: You're not selling yourself short, are you?

FREEDMAN: I don't know. What do you think?

BKL: Well, I suppose some people would say that footnotes indicate the extent of work that's gone into a book.

FREEDMAN: I don't think you prove that with footnotes. You prove the effort by the writing, and you give an honest bibliography or a bibliographic essay. I feel that footnotes are intimidating; the worst thing that can happen is that the reader doesn't keep reading. I want to tell a compelling story, not simply write books that are used for reports. That's boring. I

want my books to be read with a sense of joy and discovery. I also think adding footnotes would change the way I write. I think they can begin to direct what you include and what you leave out. It's a very troublesome question.

BKL: Has what you've discovered about the various people you've written about over the years affected you in any way?

FREEDMAN: You cannot possibly be engaged with a subject—I mean in the sense of grappling with the subject, sleeping and waking up with it—without being changed. Any book I write changes my ideas in some way. Writing about Roosevelt changed my political ideas. Despite the fact that he was devious and all that, he was a president who cared very deeply about social justice and about governmental responsibility. He had a strong vision of the role of government in ensuring a fair and civilized society. Writing about him sharpened my sense of political outrage, and I think that today's younger generation should know about him. They should know about a president with a strong sense of social justice and a real vision. After all, they're going to be voters in a couple of years.

BKL: You were awarded the Newbery Medal for Lincoln *in 1988. It's unusual for the committee to recognize nonfiction for this award, isn't it?*

FREEDMAN: Well, they have recognized it, you know. I think there have been six nonfiction Newbery winners, although there was a long dry spell. The one before **Lincoln** was in 1956. At one time, there were no awards of any kind for nonfiction. Then Milton Meltzer wrote a watershed article in the *Horn Book*. I think he was one of the first people to bring the problem out into the open. Nonfiction, when it's successful, has just as much right to be considered literature as fiction does. I'm sorry it's called "nonfiction," though.

BKL: What would you have it be called?

FREEDMAN: Faction.

BKL: That removes the negative connotation. And, after all, a lot of children read nonfiction for pleasure.

FREEDMAN: And why should that be so surprising? A lot of adults read nonfiction for pleasure, and if they look back to their childhoods and recapture themselves in the third or fourth grade, they'll probably remember liking nonfiction then, too.

BKL: When you read for pleasure what do you read?

FREEDMAN: I try to read fiction.

BKL: Do you read children's fiction?

FREEDMAN: Yes. Recently I've been reading Katherine Patterson. I was on a panel with her at IBBY, and that motivated me to get some of her books. I especially enjoyed *Bridge to Terabithia.* In the last few months, I've also been reading some Jean Fritz.

BKL: More history?

FREEDMAN: Yes, but I read *Homesick* and *China Homecoming* because I was interested in Fritz's own story. As for adult books, I've been trying to read things I missed in high school and college. If I don't get around to these books at this stage of my life, I'm never going to read them. But probably 70 to 80 percent of my reading time is focused on the project I'm writing about. It has to be. I'm reading books about Eleanor now, and strangely enough, I haven't gotten tired of her yet. She's the most interesting subject that I've ever dealt with, one of the most mysterious in some ways and also one of the most inspiring. I plan to have that book finished by the beginning of the year. It should be published by the beginning of 1993.

BKL: You have a book coming out in March, don't you?

FREEDMAN: Yes. It's called **An Indian Winter.** It's about Swiss artist Karl Bodmer and his patron Prince Alexander Philipp Maximilian, a German prince and pioneering anthropologist. They traveled up the Missouri River in 1833 and spent the winter with the Mandan Indians in what is now North Dakota. During the course of the trip, Bodmer painted about 300 watercolors and did a lot of sketches while Maximilian kept a journal. I based my text on the journal, and the book will be illustrated with reproductions of Bodmer's watercolors, which are gorgeous. Bodmer is considered to be probably the most ethnographically accurate painter of native American peoples whose cultures were still intact. He did wonderful portraits of people, landscapes, and scenes of everyday life. And virtually his entire body of work is at the Jocelyn Museum in Omaha, Nebraska. I was able to go there and see all of the originals.

BKL: Your books are just as fascinating for adults as they are for children.

FREEDMAN: I think that has to be true of any good children's book. If an 88-year-old can't read a book that an 8-year-old can enjoy, then there's something wrong with it. I think that a good children's book can't have an upper age limit. If it doesn't appeal to the grandparents, it's cheating the kid in some way.

Russell Freedman

SOURCE: "Why I Voted for Lincoln and Roosevelt," in *The Horn Book Magazine,* Vol. 68, No. 6, November-December, 1992, pp. 688-93.

Recently, I was discussing presidential politics with a naturalized citizen who came to this country from Malaysia as a scholarship student in 1969. When she left home, her parents took her to the airport in Kuala Lumpur, where she would set out on her long journey to a different culture and a new life.

Before she boarded the plane, her father gave her an assignment. He told her that America was a great country—not because it had helped liberate their own country from the Japanese, or because it had just put a man on the moon, but because it took care of its weakest citizens. "I want you to go over there and find out how they do it," her father said.

I was struck by the irony of that story. It expresses a vision of American society that is held as a matter of faith by people all over the world, and that we here at home are still struggling to achieve. I wondered what my friend's father would say today, two decades later, after the go-go '80s when the number of American children living in poverty grew by more than a million. Currently, according to the Children's Defense Fund, one in six American children lives below the official poverty level.

The vision of a nation that values and defends its weaker citizens was shared by the two American presidents I've chosen to write about—Abraham Lincoln and Franklin Delano Roosevelt. Both are recognized as strong chief executives who left a powerful impression on the office of the presidency. In a recent survey of historians, Roosevelt moved past George Washington to be ranked as the second greatest president in our history. He is excelled in the eyes of the historians only by Lincoln—a distinction that certainly would have rankled some of FDR's contemporaries.

While I was working on my biography of FDR, I discovered that he was a great admirer of Lincoln. In fact, one of his speechwriters was the playwright Robert E. Sherwood, whose *Abe Lincoln in Illinois* won the Pulitzer Prize in 1939. Before the movie version of the play opened across the country in 1940, a special White House screening was arranged for Roosevelt. The star, Raymond Massey, sat between the president and Sherwood. As the lights came on at the end of the film, after Lincoln's funeral train chuffed slowly out of Springfield past his weeping fellow citizens, FDR shook his head and muttered, ". . . and he wrote all those speeches *himself*!"

Of course, Lincoln and Roosevelt were two very different men in different situations. Lincoln grew up as a poor backwoods boy whose family lived in a one-room log cabin with a dirt floor. Roosevelt, a pampered Hudson River patrician, spent his boyhood in a sixteen-room mansion staffed by an English butler and French maids. Lincoln was self-taught. Roosevelt had the best education money could buy. Lincoln was brooding and melancholy, enveloped by a tragic sense of life. Roosevelt breezed through life with an air of confident and incurable optimism. Lincoln didn't drink, or use tobacco, or bet, or swear. Roosevelt mixed a mean martini. He was famous for his cigarette holders (and probably died from the effects of smoking); he played poker regularly; and he sometimes used language that was not fit to print in a family newspaper.

They were different, yet they shared some fascinating parallels and similarities. Both were men of mysterious and impenetrable reserve who concealed their innermost thoughts and feelings behind a screen of jocular humor and good fellowship. Both had deep moral convictions about freedom and human rights. Both were skilled politicians; when necessary, they could be ruthless. And both provoked cries of tyranny and dictatorship when they did what they thought they had to do to save the republic.

Lincoln was feared and hated by many of his contemporaries because he challenged the established slavery-based social order. He was an enemy of entrenched privilege. Even before he took office—in the interim between the 1860 election and his inauguration the following March—hate mail threatening his life began to arrive. No chief executive had ever received such malignant correspondence. And later, during the most dispiriting days of the Civil War, as demoralization spread across the North, Lincoln and his war and his racial policies became the target of massive opposition. From all over the North came cries that the president was a tyrant, an abolitionist dictator, an incompetent charlatan unfit for office. The most unpopular president the nation had ever known, he was called a "black-hearted radical," a "mobocrat," a "dangerous lunatic."

Roosevelt inspired abiding hatred for similar reasons. Much of his New Deal legislation seemed directed against the privileged and the wealthy. It was said that the first hundred days of the Roosevelt administration comforted the afflicted, while the second hundred days afflicted the comforted. Roosevelt raised taxes and regulated business practices. He brought the disenfranchised—women, blacks, Jews, and Catholics—into the federal government for the first time. No wonder he was called "a traitor to his class." No president since Lincoln had aroused such intensely personal attacks. At a country club in Connecticut, the mere mention of FDR's name was forbidden as a health measure against apoplexy.

If this seems excessive today, it is well to remember that a relatively modest New Deal reform like Social Security was the target of enraged opposition and was attacked as "socialistic," as undermining traditional American values of thrift and self-reliance. Originally, the Social Security Act included a rudimentary form of national health insurance, but in order to get the act through a resisting Congress, FDR was forced to compromise. He had to drop the health insurance provision. A half-century later, the United States remains the only industrial nation in the world, except for South Africa, without a national health plan.

From my personal point of view, the biggest difference between Lincoln and Roosevelt is that I can remember Roosevelt. He was the president of my childhood—"that man in the White House," as he was called by those who could not bear to say his name. Like most Americans of my generation, my earliest memory of politics is sitting by the radio and hearing that voice, so serene and confident, saying, "My friends." I remember the Movietone newsreels at Saturday matinees, sandwiched among the double feature, the latest chapter of the Flash Gordon serial, the Bugs Bunny cartoon, the short subject, the previews of coming attractions—the newsreels, showing President Roosevelt greeting the king and queen of England, or touring some European battlefield in a jeep, or splashing about in the pool at Warm Springs.

I remember as a boy being bewildered at the extreme emotional reactions to Roosevelt that I noticed around me. People seemed to love him or hate him, even in my own family. The dinner-table debates, the raised voices, the looks of pained exasperation! I couldn't understand it. I remember the day Roosevelt died. His death was announced at school, and we were let out early. When my homeroom teacher at Presidio Jr. High School in San Francisco dismissed us, her face hardened and so did her voice, and she said: "Thank God that awful man is dead!" I was shocked. Yet as I left the school, other teachers were standing in the hallways weeping, sobbing.

I knew, of course, that Franklin Roosevelt was a victim of polio. And I've searched my memory, trying to recall if I actually realized back then that the president of the United States could not stand on his own feet. On the arm of a son or an aide, he appeared always erect. He was so active, he projected such a dynamic personality, that he gave the impression he had no disability. People tended to forget that Roosevelt couldn't walk, or even stand up, without help. Some visitors to the White House were ready to swear that as they were being ushered into the Oval Office, the president rose from his desk and strode forward to greet them.

That's one reason why Roosevelt is such a terrific subject for a biography. On the personal level his life is the dramatic story of his struggle to overcome a crippling handicap. That struggle helped forge his character, just as Lincoln's struggle to overcome his log-cabin origins helped form his character.

Lincoln's first great act in life was to escape from his father's world, from a life of unrelenting physical toil. He had to fight his way up and out of the grinding poverty into which he had been born. As a respected attorney—and a wealthy man—he believed passionately in the words of the Declaration of Independence, which states that "all men are created equal" and that all are entitled to "life, liberty, and the pursuit of happiness." Lincoln took this declaration to heart. He took it personally. To him it meant that every poor man's son deserved the opportunities for advancement that he had enjoyed. He believed that the Declaration of Independence, the charter of American liberty, meant just what it said—*all* men, black as well as white, were entitled to the rights it spelled out.

"I am not ashamed to confess that twenty-five years ago I was a hired laborer, mauling rails, at work on a flatboat—just what might happen to any poor man's son," said Lincoln. "I want every man to have a chance—and I believe a black man is entitled to it—in which he can better his condition."

Roosevelt's life changed abruptly when he was thirty-nine years old, a handsome, cocksure individual admired for his boundless energy and charm. Overnight he found himself paralyzed and in agonizing pain. It was probably the first time in his life that he was afraid. Before his illness, most things had come easily to him. Now he knew what it was like to be helpless, to be weak, to be dependent on others. It would have been easy for him to retire to the comfortable privacy of Hyde Park, as his mother begged him to do, and to lead the pampered life of a wealthy invalid. Instead, he struggled to conquer his handicap and lead an active life. Those who knew him well believed that he emerged from that battle a bigger man. His friend Frances Perkins felt that he had experienced a "spiritual transformation." "Having been to the depths of trouble," she wrote, "he understood the problems of people in trouble."

Roosevelt and Lincoln both came to the presidency during critical moments in history, when the American system had to redefine itself. The Civil War has been called a test of American ideals. The Great Depression and Hitler's rise to power were also, each in a different way, tests of American ideals.

One lasting effect of the Civil War was to transform and expand the concept of liberty in America. The war gave "liberty" a new meaning. Until then, liberty had always meant freedom from government power—the notion that the individual must be protected against state coercion. The Civil War made it mean freedom of opportunity, which only government power could guarantee. The federal government became the agent of freedom, rather than its enemy. Lincoln saw that if all men truly are created equal, then freedom from government intrusion must yield to freedom enforced by government power. The Civil War, he said, was "a struggle for maintaining in the world that form and substance of government whose leading object is to elevate the condition of men—lift artificial weights from all shoulders . . . to afford all an unfettered start, and a fair chance, in the race of life."

During the Great Depression of the 1930s, Roosevelt acted in this tradition by using the state to expand the choices available to the poor and the powerless.

"We have come to a clear realization of the fact that true individual freedom cannot exist without economic security and independence," he said. "'Necessitous men are not free men.' People who are hungry and out of a job are the stuff of which dictatorships are made."

Roosevelt had learned the hard way that the stern doctrine of self-reliance had limitations. He had to depend on helping hands for such simple tasks as getting dressed or getting out of a car. A man who could not stand up without help knew that self-reliance can carry one only so far. And so, like Lincoln, Roosevelt wanted to use the power of the federal government to guarantee certain rights. During FDR's administration, the federal government, for the first time, made itself responsible for the welfare of those Americans who had been victimized by economic forces beyond their control. In his annual message to Congress in 1938, Roosevelt expressed his philosophy about the duty of the state: "Government has a final responsibility for the well-being of its citizens. If private cooperative endeavor fails to provide work for willing hands and relief for the unfortunate, those suffering hardship from no fault of their own have a right to call upon the Government for aid; and a government worthy of the name must make a fitting response."

Both Roosevelt and Lincoln changed the fundamental relationship between ordinary citizens and their government. And they shared another quality: both were motivated by an illuminating moral vision of the America they wanted to see. They shared the belief that a society must be judged by the way it treats its weakest citizens. That is why their stories—their lives and accomplishments—have an enduring meaning as each new generation of Americans embraces the privileges and responsibilities of citizenship.

Russell Freedman and Shannon Maughan

SOURCE: "Russell Freedman: The Newbery Medalist Delivers Another Revealing Biography for Young People," in *Publishers Weekly,* Vol. 240, No. 29, July 19, 1993, pp. 228-29.

"I went to bed with Eleanor Roosevelt every night and I woke up with Eleanor Roosevelt every morning," says Russell Freedman about the subject of his latest biography for young readers, *Eleanor Roosevelt: A Life of Discovery,* due next month from Clarion. His thoughtful examination of the esteemed First Lady is a memorable portrait, and further proof

that Freedman is a master of what he calls "the art and craft" of writing biographies: "trying to decide what to leave out and what to include." *Eleanor* marks Freedman's 39th work of nonfiction for children, a field in which he is noted for his careful research, candid writing style and the ability to bring historical figures to life for a contemporary audience. Freedman's 1988 title, *Lincoln: A Photobiography* (Clarion) won that year's Newbery Medal awarded by the American Library Association for the most distinguished contribution to American literature for children, and is one of very few nonfiction books to be so honored.

Freedman elaborates on the focus of his books when he says, "I am trying to capture the essence of a subject for my audience. I'm not writing a definitive biography, but rather an introduction that will hopefully lead the reader to other books on the same subject. You have to boil it down and make decisions about what is most important about this person's life, career and personality."

In an area of children's publishing that was once—and not so long ago—dominated by dry textbook-type materials, Freedman makes the encapsulation of a subject lively and immediate for young readers. He combines a wealth of factual information, eloquent writing and dramatic photographs to form often stirring portraits of famous Americans, such as Sitting Bull and F. D. R., or to illuminate such topics as the buffalo-hunting skills of the Plains Indians.

PW meets Freedman in his airy Manhattan apartment one recent summer morning. A tall and unassuming man with graying curly hair and a thick mustache, the author wears his working outfit of khaki pants and a shirt unbuttoned at the neck. He speaks softly but often lets loose a hearty laugh when sharing his anecdotes. His very large cat offers a vociferous greeting, then settles her smoky brown body under a nearby coffee table where she observes the conversation.

Although a number of factors are involved in choosing the subject of a book, Freedman has one major rule: "It has to be something that I'm personally interested in. One of the big advantages to writing nonfiction is that there are always more things that you're genuinely interested in than you could possibly write about.

"I also take into account whether I think it's a subject that kids can respond to. I don't want to be just blowing in the wind; I want an audience for the books. If you want to reach kids and speak to them, you have to find the right door."

Walking through that door means making deliberate decisions about which elements of a subject's life to present to a readership primarily—though, Freedman insists, not solely—made up of 10- to 17-year-olds. (Freedman says he does not write for young adults, but for "anyone capable of reading a book at that level," which ranges from "fourth grade to senility.") Several of Freedman's books—namely *Eleanor* and his preceding biography, *Franklin Delano Roosevelt*—profile somewhat controversial figures. "I think I'm attracted to subjects who had a strong sense of injustice and felt in a very deep personal sense that there were things that are wrong that have to be fixed. And because of that they're controversial; they're stepping on toes and threatening the status quo."

In the case of the Roosevelts, controversy included such things as marital infidelity, which Freedman discusses frankly in both books. "If you're writing a biography for kids in the 1990s," he states, "you have to be honest. Kids don't have to be protected in the same way they did a generation or two ago. After all, when Roosevelt was beginning his political career, divorce was shameful, it was scandalous. This is a different world, and you can't write an honest book about either Franklin Roosevelt or Eleanor Roosevelt without mentioning Franklin's affair with Lucy Mercer, because that changed his life, and it changed Eleanor's life even more. It helped her liberate herself. It gave her permission to assert herself. It isn't fair to kids to conceal that."

Freedman did not, however, see a need to discuss any extramarital romantic relationships—lesbian or otherwise—that Eleanor may have engaged in, in contrast to Blanche Wiesen Cook's recent biography for adults, *Eleanor Roosevelt 1884-1933: A Life: Mysteries of the Heart, Vol. 1* (Viking). "I tried to include everything about Eleanor's life, including her emotional life and her erotic life, that can be substantiated," he says. "Anything beyond the facts that I presented is merely speculation." Yet Freedman also feels that it's healthy for controversial topics to be aired, "to give people something to think about."

The controversies notwithstanding, nothing could shake Freedman's conviction that Eleanor Roosevelt is an inspiring figure. "If there ever was such a thing as a role model for both girls and boys, I think she is one. She's an example of somebody who took control of her own life," he says firmly.

Freedman is also confident that despite frequent jeremiads about children's reluctance or inability to read, there will continue to be a core group of young people looking for books about role models. "I think some kids are naturally drawn to nonfiction," he says. "It may be that the standards have risen, or that there is more available to kids and the approach to nonfiction is more authentic, and more inviting than it has been, but kids have always read nonfiction. Fiction and nonfiction are just two different roads leading to the same destination, to an enlarged understanding of the world around you, and feeling part of the human family—that's what reading's all about."

Though he has been writing for most of his adult life, Freedman cites sheer serendipity for the breakthrough that led to his career. Born in 1929 and raised in San Francisco, he graduated from the University of California-Berkeley with a major in English, then was drafted and served in Korea for two years. Upon his return to the States, Freedman began graduate school in English at Berkeley and shortly thereafter landed a job with the Associated Press. In 1958, he headed for New York City and went to work for the J. Walter Thompson advertising agency, where he wrote television publicity for such programs as "Father Knows Best." "It was good training for writing," he says. "I really learned some things about capturing a reader's interest."

Although Freedman had vague yearnings to write a book, he says he had no self-confidence about his ability and no burning idea to communicate. One morning he saw an article in the *New York Times* about a 16-year-old blind boy who had invented a Braille typewriter. Freedman subsequently discovered that Louis Braille was also 16 when he invented the Braille system. Here was a book waiting to be written, Freedman realized; he did so, and called it *Teenagers Who Made History.* The next part was almost too easy: Freedman's father knew George Scheer, a sales rep who sold for Holiday House, and told him about his son's manuscript. The result was a lunch with Holiday House publisher and founder Vernon Ives, who published the book in 1961. "*Teenagers* did very well," Freedman notes, "and before I knew it I was off and running. I've never looked back and I've been having fun ever since."

Freedman still publishes with Holiday House, where Margery Cuyler is his editor. But since he was quite prolific in his early career (he wrote in a white heat, completing more than two books a year), Cuyler suggested he take some of his work to Dutton, where he formed a strong relationship with editor Ann Troy. When Troy moved to Clarion Books, Freedman came with her. Troy died in 1989, and Freedman's editor at Clarion is now publisher Dorothy Briley.

Typically Freedman invests months of intense research before he embarks on a new writing project. "I have to soak myself in the subject," he says. He begins by reading all available material starting with the most current sources, whose bibliographies lead him to earlier works. Then he investigates original, contemporaneous materials such as newspapers of the time, or memoirs by people who knew the subject. What Freedman calls the "eyewitness" portion of the research journey involves visits to the various places the person lived and interviews with his or her relatives or friends, which provide "a feeling about the texture, the flavor, the mood, something. It's indefinable, but you get it," he says.

A beguiling feature of his book-lined study is a simple wooden toy airplane suspended from the ceiling like a mobile. Freedman bought the plane in Paris, and he claims it was instrumental in his research for *The Wright Brothers* (Holiday House, 1991). The same work area contains a fax machine, but no word processor resides here—Freedman writes longhand on legal pads and uses what he terms a "Humphrey Bogart" Underwood typewriter. He writes at least four drafts and then does several polishing drafts as well. (He typed the manuscript for *Eleanor* five times from beginning to end.) He also does his own photo research, which he won't trust to anyone else, "since I know the text so well."

The completion time for a book project varies, and is of course subject to change. As exciting as it was, winning the Newbery Medal had several unsettling ramifications, not the least of which was that Freedman had to write an acceptance speech. Freedman concedes that the speech took nearly as long to write as did *Lincoln* itself.

"That changes everything," says Freedman of the Newbery. "It makes it extremely difficult to write the next book. And then after you finally relax a little, I think it gives you a lot more freedom to pick subjects and to spend as much time as you want on a book." Another indefinable factor, he says, is the "undeniable feeling of pride. It's wonderful to be acknowledged for writing a good book," he says quietly.

Freedman's schedule has become tighter and more structured since he won the Newbery. Meeting his publishing deadlines has forced him to scale back his numerous school visits. Asked if he enjoys such appearances, Freedman answers, "Yes and no. It's exhausting. Nothing is harder than a school visit, but nothing is more stimulating, because you're eyeball to eyeball—you're not in an ivory tower. It's rejuvenating in a sense." Freedman also makes sure that every letter he receives from a child is answered, most of them personally. "You've got an audience where the books really mean something and you're making an impression," he says.

Looking pensive, Freedman fondly recalls the passion he had for books—especially nonfiction—as a child. A desire to provide books with integrity for today's young readers is surely an inspiration for his writing in this field. The honest and informed reaction from fans obviously gives Freedman a sense of satisfaction as well.

Next up for this busy author: a biography of photographer Lewis Hine, famous for his photographs of Ellis Island immigrants, tenement poverty and child laborers during the early 1900s. The book is due in fall '94 from Clarion. Freedman says it's the story of "how a man used a camera as a tool for social change." He is working closely with the National Child Labor Committee for his research, and already anticipates the difficulty of culling 50 photographs from a trove of over 6000 in the committee's archives.

No matter how daunting the task, Freedman says he follows a simple credo: "One of the greatest pleasures in life is a job well done." So far his meticulous attention to his work has provided volumes of insightful and inviting information, and earned him a coveted and revered position in the world of children's books. Readers will be glad to know that his drive shows no signs of slowing.

Russell Freedman

SOURCE: "Bring 'Em Back Alive: Writing History and Biography for Young People," in *School Library Journal,* Vol. 40, No. 3, March, 1994, pp. 138-41.

Grownups sometimes seem surprised when a youngster picks up a nonfiction book and reads it willingly and with pleasure, not just to satisfy a school assignment or write a report. But why should it be surprising? Like the rest of us, children want and need all kinds of books. They are drawn to nonfiction by their curiosity about the world around them.

From a kid's point of view, classifications like fiction and nonfiction are irrelevant. A book is either absorbing and fun to read, or it's stuffy and boring. As

Peggy Lee once said, speaking about her early days as a singer, "I didn't think of it as swing or jazz, it was just good music."

A good book about American history, or natural history, or any other subject, can be just as compelling as any adventure story. The word *history,* remember, is made up mostly of the word *story.* Historians traditionally have been storytellers. Going all the way back to Homer and beyond, historians have been people who were telling, singing, reciting epic poems about the past. They were storytellers sitting around the fire inside the cave, holding their audience spellbound on a winter's night.

First, a Storyteller

When I begin a new book, that's the tradition I like to remember. I think of myself first of all as a storyteller, and I do my best to give dramatic shape to my subject, whatever it may be. I always feel that I have a story to tell that is worth telling, and I want to tell it as clearly, as simply, and as forcefully as I can.

By storytelling, I do not mean making things up, of course. I don't mean invented scenes, or manufactured dialogue, or imaginary characters. As a writer of nonfiction, I have a pact with the reader to stick to the facts, to be as factually accurate as human frailty will allow. What I write is based on research, on the documented historical record. And yet, there are certain storytelling techniques that I can use without straying from the straight and narrow path of factual accuracy.

When I speak of storytelling, I'm using the word "story" in the sense of igniting the reader's imagination, evoking pictures and scenes in the reader's mind. Storytelling means creating vivid word pictures of people, places, and events—creating a convincing, meaningful, and memorable world. It means pulling the reader into that world. And it means using a narrative framework, a storytelling voice, that will keep the reader turning the pages with a mounting sense of anticipation and discovery.

Nonfiction can and does make use of traditional storytelling techniques. One of the most effective storytelling techniques, for example, is to create a vivid, detailed scene that the reader can visualize—like a scene from a movie, if you will. In my book ***Children of the Wild West*** (Clarion, 1983), I use that device to help establish the setting and the mood, and to pull the reader into the story:

It was a typical wagon train of the 1840s. The swaying wagons, plodding animals, and walking people stretched out along the trail for almost a mile.

Near the end of the train, a boy holding a hickory stick moved slowly through the dust. He used the stick to poke and prod the cows that trudged beside him, mooing and complaining.

"Get along!" he shouted. "Hey! Hey! Get along!"

Dust floated in the air. It clogged the boy's nose, parched his throat, and coated his face. His cheeks were smeared where he had brushed away the big mosquitoes that buzzed about everywhere.

Up ahead, his family's wagon bounced down the trail. He could hear the *crack of his father's whip* above the heads of the oxen that pulled the wagon. The animals coughed and snorted. The chains on their yokes rattled with every step they took.

Now, that is nonfiction. The scene is dramatized in order to make it visual, and in order to convey the texture and flavor of the event and the time. But it is entirely factual. And it introduces the storyline—the narrative framework—of the book. ***Children of the Wild West*** is the story of children who accompanied their parents on the great westward journey and the story of what happened to them after they arrived.

Developing Character

Another familiar storytelling device is to develop character, to create convincing word pictures of people. One way to do that is to point out the small but telling personal details that help characterize a person. There are plenty of small personal details that provide glimpses of Abraham Lincoln's life in the White House, for example. He said "Howdy" to visitors and invited them to "stay a spell." He greeted diplomats while wearing carpet slippers, called his wife "Mother" at receptions, and told bawdy jokes at cabinet meetings. He mended his gold-rimmed spectacles with a piece of string.

One passage in ***Lincoln: A Photobiography*** (Clarion, 1987) that people often seem to remember and comment on is the simple inventory of the president's pockets after he was assassinated: spectacles folded in a silver case, a small velvet eyeglass cleaner, a large linen handkerchief with "A. Lincoln" stitched in red, an ivory pocketknife trimmed with silver, a brown leather wallet lined with purple silk, and inside that wallet, a Confederate $5 bill and eight newspaper clippings praising the President, clippings that Lincoln himself had cut out and saved.

It's important for the reader to picture people and events, but it's also important to hear those people talking. In real life, the way we get to know people is by observing them, and also by *listening* to what they say. In a nonfiction book, quotations from diaries, journals, letters, and memoirs can take the place of dialogue in a fictional story. Quotations help give a book a sense of immediacy, or reality.

One of my favorite quotes about Lincoln, and one of the more revealing, comes from his law partner, William Herndon. Lincoln adored his sons, denied them nothing, and seemed incapable of disciplining them. He liked to take Willie and Tad to the office when he worked on Sundays, and their wild behavior just about drove his partner mad. Herndon complained:

> The boys were absolutely unrestrained in their amusement. If they pulled down all the books from the shelves, bent the points of all the pens, overturned the spittoon, it never disturbed the serenity of their father's good nature. I have felt many and many a time that I wanted to wring the necks of those little brats and pitch them out of the windows.

As far as Lincoln was concerned, his boys could do no wrong. His wife Mary remarked:

> Mr. Lincoln was very exceedingly indulgent to his children. He always said: "It is my pleasure that my children are free, happy, and unrestrained by parental tyranny. Love is the chain whereby to bind a child to its parents."

THE APPEAL OF ANECDOTES

Another essential storytelling device is the use of anecdote. My desk dictionary gives two definitions of anecdote: 1) a short account of some interesting or humorous incident, and 2) secret or hitherto undivulged particulars of history or biography. The word comes from the Greek word *anekdota,* meaning "things unpublished," which gives us some idea of why anecdotes are so appealing—because they're so closely related to gossip. A good anecdote can do wonders to reveal character and bring a subject to life.

Here's an anecdote from my latest book, ***Eleanor Roosevelt: A Life of Discovery*** (Clarion, 1993). It tells us something about Eleanor's character and personality, and about her relationship with Franklin:

> Although FDR listened to his wife, he was keenly attuned to what he believed was politically possible. If he felt that Eleanor threatened to stir up more public controversy than he was willing to tolerate, he would ask her to pull back. She understood that as First Lady, there were limits to what she could say or do. "While I often speak strongly on various subjects, Franklin frequently refrained from supporting causes he believed in because of political realities," she wrote.

One of their sharpest disagreements concerned America's participation in the World Court, which had been set up after World War I to help settle disputes among nations. Eleanor had worked hard and long to promote American entry into the court. Opponents of the court argued that the United States should not be involved in international organizations. The issue was so controversial that Franklin tried to avoid it during his campaign for president in 1932. Refusing to take sides, he withdrew his earlier support for both the World Court and the League of Nations.

Eleanor was furious. When Franklin saw how upset she was, he invited her good friend Agnes Leach, head of the League of Women Voters, to lunch. "Eleanor is very fond of you," he explained, "and you can make peace between us. She hasn't spoken to me in three days."

But Agnes Leach, like Eleanor, was a dedicated internationalist and peace advocate. She turned down Franklin's invitation. "That was a shabby statement [about the World Court]," she told him. "I just don't feel like having lunch with you today."

Afterward, Eleanor phoned her friend and said, "Agnes, you are a darling, darling girl. I hear you upset Franklin very much. I didn't know you had it in you."

While I was working on this book, I discovered that Eleanor Roosevelt served on the editorial board of the Junior Literary Guild (now the Junior Library Guild) from the time of its founding in 1929 until her death in 1962. And she wasn't just a figurehead. As with every project she undertook, she involved herself completely and worked diligently. She read books that were being considered as Guild choices and offered her opinion.

Guild Director Marjorie Jones sent me some of Mrs. Roosevelt's reader's reports. One is dated June 22, 1962—about four and a half months before she died. It's a prepublication report of Madeleine L'Engle's *A Wrinkle in Time,* which would win the 1963 Newbery Medal:

Dear Miss Doumenjou:

I have read *A Wrinkle in Time* and I think Miss L'Engle has used modern situations in space to create a fantasy which will appeal to the young people of the present day. It is pure fantasy but no more astonishing than many facts. The way she had presented it teaches some of the really important values which have always existed and which we do try to get across to the young people. I have a feeling that this book may not only be interesting for your people but may also have a good deal of real value for this age group.

RESEARCH & SERENDIPITY

When I'm working on a book, I'm a great believer in serendipity—making fortunate and unexpected discoveries by accident. For instance, I had one such experience when I visited Dayton, Ohio, hometown of Orville and Wilbur Wright. Their 1905 Flyer, one of their early experimental airplanes, is on display in Dayton at Carillon Park, and naturally, I wanted to see the plane. Carillon Park was not yet open for the season, but even so, Mary Matthews, the park's director, took me over there and showed me around.

The Wright brothers' great discovery—their breakthrough insight—was the realization that they could control an aircraft in flight by changing the air pressure above each wing. They accomplished that by twisting the wingtips in one direction or another. Now when I started work on *The Wright Brothers: How They Invented the Airplane* (Holiday, 1991), my own knowledge of aeronautics was limited to my ability to fasten a seatbelt. And at first, I found it maddeningly difficult to understand just how their wing-twisting actually worked.

I mentioned my problem to Mary Matthews as we were standing beside the 1905 Flyer, which occupies its own building at Carillon Park. "It's difficult to visualize the wing-twisting," I said.

"Well," she replied, "why don't you try it yourself?"

She summoned the mechanic who is the custodian of that historic aircraft, and the next thing I knew, I was lying face-down on the lower wing in the pilot's position, actually working the wing-twisting control myself. That unexpected hands-on experience was quite a thrill, and it proved to be an invaluable part of my research. It helped me understand, and explain to my readers, just how the pilot navigated that early airplane.

Serendipity played a big role in writing *Franklin Delano Roosevelt* (Clarion, 1990). When I visited my doctor for my annual physical, he asked, "What are you working on now?"

"A biography of Franklin Roosevelt," I replied.

He looked thoughtful and then said, "Is it possible that Roosevelt's doctor is still alive? A colleague of mine has a patient, a man in his eighties, who claims he was FDR's physician . . ."

That man turned out to be Dr. Howard Bruenn. In 1944, as a young U.S. Navy medical officer and heart specialist, Dr. Bruenn was detailed to the White House to keep a close watch on the president's health. He was with Roosevelt at Warm Springs, Georgia, when the president suffered his fatal stroke on April 12, 1945. He was kind enough to share some of his memories with me.

Another example of serendipity occurred shortly after I began the book, when I made a routine visit to my attorney's office. "What are you working on these days?" he asked.

"A biography of Franklin Roosevelt."

"FDR?" he said. "How interesting. His grandson is one of my clients. Would you like me to arrange a meeting?"

So the three of us got together for lunch—me, my attorney, and Curtis Dall Roosevelt, the son of Franklin and Eleanor's only daughter, Anna. It so happens that Curtis and his sister—known within the family as "Buzzie" and "Sistie"—virtually grew up in the White House, living there for about seven years. Their mother traveled a great deal, leaving them in the care of their grandparents, Franklin and Eleanor. Curtis provided some valuable insights into daily life in the White House, and into the personalities of his famous grandparents.

He told me a story that may be apocryphal, but which nevertheless reveals something important and true about both his grandparents. In 1928, seven years after he was stricken with polio, Roosevelt was asked to return to public life and run for governor of New York. At first, he did not want to run. "It's not that I'm afraid to try," he told Eleanor. "It's that I'm afraid to try and fail."

"Then don't," Eleanor replied.

"Don't try?"

"No, don't fail!"

Capturing that kind of spirit can bring nonfiction books to life for readers of any age.

Russell Freedman

SOURCE: "Eleanor Roosevelt: A Life of Discovery," in *The Horn Book Magazine,* Vol. 71, No. 1, January-February, 1995, pp. 33-6.

Eleanor Roosevelt would have enjoyed this gathering very much indeed. She would have felt right at home here today among her fellow writers, and among her colleagues in the field of children's literature.

She was a prolific writer, the author of numerous books on a wide range of subjects, including a couple of children's books. I love to point out that her earnings from writing and lecturing usually topped the salary earned by her husband, the president. Her three-volume autobiography was an essential source for my own book. Her words add an immediacy, an authenticity, a flavor, that could not be achieved in any other way. So in a very real sense, Eleanor Roosevelt the writer shares in this award.

Along with her books and magazine articles, she was a popular newspaper columnist. Her syndicated column, "My Day," appeared in dozens of American newspapers, including, I am happy to report, the Boston *Globe.*

Eleanor was deeply involved with children's books. In 1929, when Franklin was governor of New York State, Eleanor joined the editorial board of the newly founded Junior Literary Guild. And when Franklin became president in 1933, she insisted on continuing her work as a Guild editor. As a happy result, children's books filled the White House library.

She wasn't just a figurehead at the Guild. She didn't simply show up for photo opportunities and pose with a bunch of smiling kids and a book. As with every task she undertook, she involved herself completely. An active member of the Guild's editorial board for more than thirty years, Mrs. Roosevelt reviewed hundreds of books that were being considered as Guild choices. One of her last reader's reports—dated June 22, 1962—was a rave review of Madeleine L'Engle's *A Wrinkle in Time* (Farrar), which went on to win the 1963 Newbery Medal.

Collaborating with Helen Ferris, the Guild's editor-in-chief, Mrs. Roosevelt co-authored two popular books for young people—*Partners: The United Na-*

tions and Youth and *Your Teens and Mine* (both Doubleday). And while she was still first lady of New York, she was instrumental in helping her friend Augusta Baker get her first job as a children's librarian, which led to Baker's later appointment as Coordinator of Children's Services in the New York Public Library.

While I was growing up during the Great Depression, Eleanor Roosevelt was the most famous woman in America. She was as well known as any movie star—even as famous as my personal favorite, Maureen O'Sullivan, who played Tarzan's wife, Jane. But while everyone knew Eleanor, not everyone approved of her. One of my earliest memories of politics is sitting at the dinner table and listening to the grown-ups argue about President Roosevelt and that wife of his. I remember the raised voices, the table-pounding, the looks of pained exasperation. As a boy, I was bewildered by the emotional fireworks of those heated dinner-table debates. People seemed to love the Roosevelts or hate them—even within my own family circle.

A few years ago, I decided I wanted to write a biography of FDR. Such a project would give me a chance to revisit memories from my own past and to explore some of the forces and personalities that have shaped the world we live in today. And wouldn't you know it: a funny thing happened while I was working on my book about Franklin Roosevelt. I fell in love with his wife. I knew from the beginning that Eleanor was a major presence on the American scene during the Roosevelt administration, but as I immersed myself in Franklin's life and career, Eleanor came into focus as a compelling figure in her own right. By the time I had finished my book about Franklin, I was eager to write a separate book about Eleanor.

Her story is a biographer's dream. What a life! A poor little rich girl, an "ugly duckling" as she called herself, timid and fearful, afraid of almost everything, yet she finds the courage to defy convention, to take charge of her own life, and she becomes the most influential woman of her time. This is a story so filled with drama and conflict and striving, it almost tells itself.

Beyond the story, I was drawn to Eleanor Roosevelt because of the quality of her heart; because she had the capacity to recognize and fight for people without power; because she was outraged by injustice. Many of the issues she faced fifty years ago are still with us. As early as 1936, she used her influence to muster support for a program of national health insurance. Her efforts helped lead to the proposed Wagner Health Act of 1939, but the American Medical Association raised the cry of "socialized medicine," and the bill never came out of committee.

Early this year, a neighbor of mine named Walter stopped me on the street and congratulated me for receiving a Newbery Honor for my Eleanor Roosevelt biography. He paused, looked at me through his rimless spectacles, then announced: "She saved my life, you know."

"Saved your life?" I asked.

Walter explained. As a teenager after World War II, he found himself barely surviving in a displaced persons' camp in Germany. His camp was one of those visited by Eleanor Roosevelt, who, alone among the American delegates to the United Nations, had taken a special interest in the plight of Europe's displaced persons. Walter was one of the refugees at his camp who met Mrs. Roosevelt and presented her with a petition. Later he was released and allowed to emigrate to the United States. And he gives Eleanor Roosevelt the credit.

"I remember the day she died," he said. "It was 1962, November 7th to be exact. When we heard the news, this fellow at work blurted out, 'It's about time that old Commie finally croaked.' I glared at him," continued Walter, whom I have always known as a shy, soft-spoken man, a consummate gentleman. "I glared at him. Then I stepped back, hauled off, and knocked him down!"

Telling me this, he stepped back once again and still seemed surprised at his impulsive act some thirty years ago—surprised but pleased. Then he smiled and confessed, "That's not like me, you know."

While I was writing my book, I had a chance to meet many people who had encountered Eleanor Roosevelt at some point in their lives. As I traveled around the country, speaking at conferences and conventions and before local groups, I'd mention that I was working on an Eleanor Roosevelt biography. And without fail, people in the audience would come up after my talk and tell me about the time they met Mrs. Roosevelt at a function, or heard her speak, or saw her passing in a crowd. They never forgot the experience, so powerful was the impression that Eleanor Roosevelt made. "She gave off light," said one of her friends. "I cannot explain it better." It is that light that I hoped to capture in my book.

I am very proud to receive this award. I thank the judges for honoring my book, and I thank all of you for your enduring commitment to the cause of good reading for children.

Russell Freedman

SOURCE: "Waxing Creative: Noted Authors and Illustrators Muse on the Inspiration for Their Work," in *Publishers Weekly,* Vol. 242, No. 29, July 17, 1995, p. 141.

I hadn't expected to become a writer of nonfiction books for children. I had wandered into the field by chance and immediately felt right at home. I couldn't wait to get started on my next book. It was as if I had found myself—even though I hadn't really known that I had been lost.

The term *nonfiction* has always seemed unfortunate to me, because it is so negative. Fiction implies art, imagination, creativity. We take it for granted that good fiction will be a pleasure to read. Nonfiction is supposed to be utilitarian. It's expected to do its duty—to inform, instruct, enlighten. And yet a hardworking, nose-to-the-grindstone nonfiction book should be just as absorbing as any imaginary story, because it is, in fact, a story, too.

Writers of nonfiction have traditionally been storytellers. The word *history,* remember, is made up mostly of the word *story,* it derives from the Greek *historein,* "to inquire"; a *histōr* was a learned man. Going all the way back to Homer and beyond, historians have been storytellers sitting around the fire inside the cave, holding their audience spellbound on a winter's night.

When I begin a new book, that's the tradition I like to remember. I think of myself first of all as a storyteller, and I do my best to give dramatic shape to my subject, whatever it is.

Russell Freedman

SOURCE: "1998 Laura Ingalls Wilder Medal Acceptance Speech," in *Journal of Youth Services in Libraries,* Vol. 11, No. 4, Summer, 1998, pp. 353-56.

I am happy to be here this evening. As you can well imagine, there's no place I would rather be! I want to thank the American Library Association for celebrating children's books in this manner, as it has been doing since the inception of the Newbery Medal seventy-six years ago. And I especially want to thank the members of the Laura Ingalls Wilder Committee for recognizing my books; it's an extraordinary honor, and I accept it gratefully. I don't mind telling you that this is one of the very, very great moments of my life.

Most of you are familiar with the time-honored rituals that go along with these awards—the committees meeting secretly through the night behind closed doors, the mounting suspense, and, finally, the early morning phone calls to the winners, followed by the public announcements and lots of excitement. As you know, the deliberations of the Newbery and Caldecott committees are often accompanied by rumors, by conjectures and speculation, even by straw polls, and the winners, when announced, are not always unexpected. That's not the case with the Laura Ingalls Wilder Committee, which meets not just behind closed doors, but apparently with the lights dimmed. When it comes to closely guarded secrecy, the Wilder Committee should be giving lessons to the Central Intelligence Agency. So when I tell you that this award came out of the blue, as a stunning surprise, please believe me.

I was not thinking about the award or about the ALA Midwinter Meeting when my phone rang on the morning of January twelfth. I was trying to write my next sentence, and I looked at that ringing phone with some annoyance. Now, when you pick up the receiver, and then, after a pause, hear an unfamiliar voice asking for you by your full name, what do you expect? I assumed, as anyone would, that this was a solicitation call. And at nine-thirty in the morning! Thank heavens I didn't say, "Please take my name off your calling list!" Before I could say anything, the caller identified herself as Kathy East, chair of the 1998 Wilder Committee. So yes, this award came as a complete surprise, as one of those wonderful moments when your heart leaps joyfully into your mouth and leaves you speechless.

But alas, there's no such thing as unalloyed joy. When I hung up after stuttering my thanks, I realized I would have to write a speech, a daunting prospect when you've been speaking about your work and yourself for years and feel certain that you have nothing left to say, that by now they've heard it all. When you are honored for a particular book, you can talk about that one book when you give thanks—about its inspiration, its challenges, and so on. It's quite a different matter when you're told that you're being honored for "a body of work." What an expression! A body of work! It sounds as though you are ready to be embalmed!

My body of work goes back thirty-seven years to the publication of my first book by Holiday House in 1961. Since then, I've been lucky enough to spend my working life exploring subjects that interest me and that I hope and believe will interest my readers. Recently I've enjoyed writing about men and women I admire for some reason, people whose lives have something to tell us, perhaps, about leading our own lives. If you want to know who my heroes are, take a look at my books. I was drawn to Eleanor Roosevelt because of the quality of her heart; to Crazy Horse because of his courage and his uncompromising integrity; to Abraham Lincoln because of his spirit of forgiveness (and, not the least, because he wrote his own speeches).

I've always been a history buff. I believe that a book of history or biography can carry within its pages a certain magical power; it can convey all the life and immediacy of great fiction while retaining the authenticity, the additional power, of truth. Biographies, in particular, have always commanded a wide audience among readers of all ages. They appeal to us because we have an insatiable hunger for stories about other people, whether it be the latest gossip or the life of Samuel Johnson. And those biographical subjects who have had to struggle the hardest are the ones who engage our imaginations most deeply.

For children, especially, a book of history or biography offers the satisfaction of knowing that the people and events portrayed are "really real." Writing for that audience of impressionable young readers imposes a special responsibility. You must keep in mind that your book may be the first they have ever read on that particular subject. They will come to it with great expectations. And if you do a good job as author, your book may still be alive in their memories fifty years from now. A quiet children's book can have an impact on the future in ways that few bestsellers can. All of us here know that.

To a child, anything that happened before he or she was born is history—ancient history. What kid hasn't asked, "Tell me about the olden days, Mom"? Children have a basic human need to know how their world came into being. In every culture, you find children listening avidly to stories about the past. A knowledge of the past is part of every child's birthright. One reason for the enduring appeal of

Little House on the Prairie and other books by Laura Ingalls Wilder is that they combine vivid history with a compelling story.

Someone once asked Dr. Seuss, Theodor Geisel, why he chose to write for children, and he replied, "I'd rather write for kids. They're more appreciative. Adults are obsolete children, and I say to hell with them."

It's certainly true that kids are the most appreciative and responsive audience any author could hope for. Who else but a writer of children's books would receive a letter like this: "Dear Mr. Freedman, I read *Cowboys of the Wild West* and I want to know where you get such good ideas. Did you get all your information from older cowboys? Or are you a cowboy yourself?"

If I can convince that reader that I am a cowboy, then I must have written a very persuasive book.

My favorite question from a reader—and forgive me if you've heard this, but with this audience, I can't resist—came from a fifth-grader in Indiana who wrote, "Dear Mr. Freedman, I read your biography of Abraham Lincoln and liked it very much. Did you take the photographs yourself?"

That boy came away from my book with the feeling that Abraham Lincoln was a real person who must have lived the day before yesterday. He was someone whom I might have known. That's always my objective: to make the past seem real, to breathe life and meaning into people and events that are dead and gone.

Nonfiction books for children have changed dramatically, in both content and form, since I've been working in the field. Today they have to be better than ever. They have to compete for the reader's affections with technological wonders like cable television, video games, and personal computers. They have to win over youngsters who are in mortal danger of succumbing to stimulus stupefaction and to uncontrollable attention drift. The antidote is reading—the quiet, contemplative, warmly satisfying act of reading.

When I published my first books in the early 1960s, children were still being shielded from the real world to a far greater extent than they are today. Today we have the freedom, and the responsibility, to write about a great deal more. We can recognize life's complexities and ambiguities. We can encourage children

to ask questions. *The Story of Mankind* by Hendrik Willem Van Loon, winner of the first Newbery Medal in 1922, would be a very different book if it were written today. Telling that story, the story of humankind, honestly in the light of today's values and understanding, is a challenge for anyone who cherishes children, who wants to encourage their idealism and shield them from cynicism, and yet still give them forthright history.

When I received the Newbery Medal in 1988, I expressed my thanks to a long list of people whose support and friendship over the years have meant so much to me. It is a measure of the enduring sense of community in the children's book field that I can stand here this evening and thank those very same people again, those who are still with us, because the passage of ten years has only strengthened the bonds of friendship and affection that I feel toward every one of them. To my Newbery thank-you list of ten years ago, I now want to add Dorothy Briley, my wise and wonderful editor at Clarion Books, and Regina Griffin, my stimulating new editor at Holiday House.

One of my favorite quotations comes from Orville Wright. It refers to the Wright brothers' 1901 wind-tunnel experiments, which provided the scientific data they needed to build their first successful airplane. For many weeks they were absorbed in painstaking and systematic lab work—testing, measuring, calculating. The work was tedious. It was repetitious. But they were exploring unknown territory, and they would look back on those weeks as a time of great excitement, when each new day promised discoveries waiting to be made. "Wilbur and I could hardly wait for morning to come," Orville recalled, "to get at something that interested us. That's happiness," he said.

After nearly four decades of writing for children, I can hardly wait for morning to come to get on with my latest book. That's happiness, too. And I thank all of you so very much for making that possible.

Russell Freedman

SOURCE: "Russell Freedman Accepting the Golden Kite for Nonfiction for *Martha Graham: A Dancer's Life*," *http://www.scbwi.org/goldkitespeech98.htm*, August 8, 1999.

One of my chief considerations when I pick a subject for a new book is that I want to learn more about that subject myself. That was certainly the case with

Martha Graham. I've been going to dance performances of various kinds for years, and while I have usually enjoyed them, I haven't always understood what was going on up there on the stage. It was like watching a baseball game without knowing the rules.

So, I figured if I took the time to research and write a book about Martha Graham and the invention of modern dance, I would greatly enhance my own life. I'd be better able to understand and appreciate what was happening in a dance performance—and that's exactly what happened. While I was working on the book, I attended more than one hundred dance performances of every imaginable kind, from the New York City Ballet to experimental dances at La Mama in the East Village. And the best thing about it was that it was all tax deductible, all part of my research.

Martha Graham came from a proper Victorian family that frowned on dancing as a career. It just wasn't considered respectable. But she was a headstrong girl, her family knew it, and they gave her some leeway. Most future dance performers start serious study by the time they are nine or ten years old. Martha was twenty-two before she started. She was considered too old, too short, too heavy, and too homely to be taken seriously. "She's hopeless," her first teacher said.

But she became the greatest modern dancer of her time, and she created a new art form. In my book, I wanted to tell why she did it, how she did it, and what she had to sacrifice—which was plenty.

I'm thrilled to receive this Golden Kite, and I want to thank everyone concerned. I feel like dancing—but don't worry, I won't.

Russell Freedman and Leonard S. Marcus

SOURCE: "Talking with Authors," in *Publishers Weekly,* Vol. 247, No. 7, February 14, 2000, p. 98.

Q. What kind of boy were you?

A. I was a baseball fan. I loved books and history. And I always wanted to be a writer.

My father worked in the West Coast office of a major publishing company, Macmillan, and would invite the authors he met home for dinner. John Steinbeck; England's poet laureate, John Masefield; and Margaret Mitchell, the author of *Gone with the Wind,* all had dinner at our house. As a boy, I would sit at the table and watch and listen to those colorful, larger-than-life men and women. I wanted to be like them.

Q. How do you choose the subjects of your biographies?

A. First of all, I choose a person I admire. I don't know if I would ever want to write about someone I didn't admire. Writing a biography takes a year of my life. It means in a sense that I live with that person for a year. I go to bed at night thinking about that person and I wake up in the morning thinking about him or her.

I also choose subjects whose lives have something to tell us about leading our own lives. I think of a biographical subject as a kind of teacher—for me and for my readers. A third consideration is that I don't like to get stuck in a rut. Crazy Horse, a mystic and a warrior, was an Oglala Sioux. Martha Graham, who invented an entirely new form of dance, spent her whole life living in Manhattan. No two people could be more different than Martha Graham and Crazy Horse. That was one of their appeals for me; another was that I admired them both.

Q. What's the best part about being a writer?

A. Being a nonfiction writer means that I can explore any subject that interests me. Being a writer means that I can explore myself: It's impossible to write well about any subject without examining your own deepest feelings about it. Also, writing, like carpentry, is a craft. It's very satisfying to make a beautiful object with your mind and hands. To write a good sentence that makes the reader see a picture vividly or feel an emotion strongly or dream a dream is a wonderful experience. To write a good book is a thrill.

GENERAL COMMENTARY

James Cross Giblin

SOURCE: "Russell Freedman," in *The Horn Book Magazine,* Vol. 74, No. 4, July-August, 1998, pp. 455-58.

Russell Freedman might well have had a successful career in broadcast journalism, following in the footsteps of reporters like Edward R. Murrow. His deep, rather solemn voice, lightened by frequent touches of humor, makes him a compelling speaker. One attendee at a recent Clarion sales conference, hearing Russell present his latest book, a biography of the great modern dancer Martha Graham, said: "He reminds me of one of my favorite college professors. I could sit and listen to him for hours."

Fortunately for young readers, Russell decided to pursue a different profession. Since 1961, he has written more than forty nonfiction books for children and been honored with just about every major award a writer can receive: the John Newbery Medal for *Lincoln: A Photobiography* (1987); two Newbery Honors, for *The Wright Brothers: How They Invented the Airplane* (1991) and *Eleanor Roosevelt: A Life of Discovery* (1993); the *Washington Post* Children's Book Guild Nonfiction Award; the Regina Medal of the Catholic Library Association; and now, capping the others, the Laura Ingalls Wilder Award for his body of work.

All of these honors have not gone to Russell's head. As he said recently, "I'm grateful for the awards I've won, but you don't write with awards in mind. You write because you have something you want to say. If there's a secret to writing, that must be it. The most satisfying award is a letter from some kid who has been touched by one of your books."

Although he appreciates fine food and well-cut clothes, Russell Freedman is basically a man of modest tastes. He has lived for more than thirty years in a roomy and comfortable, but completely unpretentious, apartment on New York City's Upper West Side.

If I had to choose a single word to characterize Russell, it would be loyal. He is loyal to his friends, keeping in close touch, for example, with his five best college friends from the University of California, Berkeley. Whenever any of them comes to New York, he knows he'll be welcome to stay at Russell's apartment. He is loyal to his publishers (a decided rarity these days). Holiday House brought out his first book, *Teenagers Who Made History,* in 1961, and Russell has been a regular on that list ever since. He has also published steadily with Clarion Books since the early 1980s. Above all, Russell has remained loyal to himself—to his interests, his talent, his integrity as a writer and as a human being.

One of Russell's Berkeley friends, the late Frank J. Dempsey, wrote a witty and insightful profile of Russell that appeared in this journal along with Russell's

Newbery acceptance for *Lincoln* (July/August 1988 *Horn Book*). I won't repeat here the information about his family background, college years, and army experiences that Dempsey covered so well. Instead, I'll pick up the story in the fall of 1960 when a mutual friend introduced Russell and me. At that time, he was in the midst of writing *Teenagers Who Made History* and looking for part-time work to pay the rent (his five-hundred-dollar advance on the book having been exhausted). I was a beginning editor of children's books at Criterion Books, a long-vanished imprint, and had some freelance copyediting jobs to give out. Thus began what Russell recently reminded me is his "oldest publishing friendship."

Our paths diverged somewhat in the next few years. Russell published one book after another with Holiday House and began the series of animal books— *Animal Architects, How Birds Fly, Animal Fathers,* etc.—that would occupy him for most of the 1970s. I went from assistant editor at Criterion to associate editor at Lothrop, Lee & Shepard to editor-in-chief of children's books at The Seabury Press—the list that eventually became Clarion Books. I didn't forget Russell, though, and when I arrived at Seabury I approached him about writing a book for the list. We had several meetings to discuss the idea, but he ultimately decided he was too busy with his Holiday House projects and a new list of books he was developing with Ann Troy, senior editor at E. P. Dutton.

Then, in 1980, Ann joined Clarion as senior editor and said she'd like to bring Russell to the list; and of course I was delighted. By then, Russell had turned away from animal books and begun to focus on American historical subjects, starting with *Immigrant Kids* (Dutton, 1980). His first book for Clarion, *Children of the Wild West* (1983), was in this vein, and Russell followed it with a well-received companion volume, *Cowboys of the Wild West* (1985). And after that, in 1987, came *Lincoln*—the last of his books to be edited by Ann Troy, who died in 1989.

Russell sees a definite link between his animal behavior titles and his subsequent historical explorations and biographies. "When I was writing the animal books, I learned how to do photo research, and how to lay out a book so that the photos and text are synchronized, forming a kind of counterpoint with each other," he says.

A photographic exhibit inspired *Immigrant Kids*. As Russell tells it, "In 1978, I went to an exhibit at the New York Historical Society commemorating the

125th anniversary of the Children's Aid Society. The walls of the exhibit rooms were lined with big, blown-up photos dating back to the mid-nineteenth century showing children playing, working, going to school, in tenement apartments, and just hanging out on the New York City streets of that era."

"I was impressed by the magnetic power of those old photographs," he continues, "by the way they seemed to defy the passage of time. Far from being faded and musty shadows of the past, they made the past come alive, and I realized as I lingered at the exhibit that archival photos can evoke the past in a way that nothing else can."

Archival photos played a crucial role in the success of such later titles as *Children of the Wild West* and *Kids at Work: Lewis Hine and the Crusade Against Child Labor* (1994). And when Russell started to write biographies, unusual and revealing photographs of the subjects figured significantly in the way the books were conceived.

Russell's switch in the 1980s to a more visual approach couldn't have been better timed. His books, with a striking photograph or work of art on almost every other page, appealed greatly to a generation that was accustomed to getting much of its information from television. Vivid illustrations also helped Russell to sharpen and focus his writing even more succinctly, and to achieve effects that came close to poetry in such titles as *Buffalo Hunt* (Holiday, 1988) and *An Indian Winter* (Holiday, 1992).

When he finishes writing a book and assembling the illustrations for it, Russell tries to take a long trip before starting the next one. "Traveling to some distant place helps clear my mind and offers a fresh point of view," he says. "Seeing people and places for the first time gives you a chance to look at the world with the eyes of a child, to recapture some of that childish curiosity."

Accompanied by his friend Evans Chan, a Chinese-American filmmaker, Russell has traveled in recent years to Indonesia, Australia, China, Europe, and Mexico. "A couple of years ago I was in the ancient Chinese city of Lijiang, in the foothills of the Himalayas," he says. "There I met a blind masseur, a young man who was learning to read Braille as adapted to Chinese ideograms. This encounter was especially meaningful to me because I had just finished writing a biography of Louis Braille."

Russell bristles when he's asked, as he often is, if he wouldn't prefer to write for adults. "A writer of books for children has an impact on readers' minds and imaginations that very few writers for adults can match. But beyond that, writing nonfiction for children gives me, or any writer, tremendous artistic freedom. I can write about almost any subject that interests me and that I believe will interest children. I can be a generalist rather than a specialist."

As he warms to his subject, Russell's voice becomes even more intense. "It's a much greater challenge to convey the spirit and essence of a life in a hundred pages than to write a 600- or 800-page 'definitive' tome that includes every known detail about that life," he says. "A nonfiction children's book requires concision, selection, judgment, lucidity, unwavering focus, and the most artful use of language and story-telling techniques. I regard such books as a specialized and demanding art form."

If they'd won as many awards as Russell has, some writers might be tempted to take things easier, to rest on their laurels. But not Russell. "When I begin a book, I have an ideal image in mind of the way that book is going to turn out. It never does. Every book falls short in some way. But," he goes on, "there's always the next one. When people ask which of my books is my favorite, I always answer, quite honestly, 'The one I'm working on now. That's the one that's really going to be good!'"

TITLE COMMENTARY

📖 *BUFFALO HUNT* (1988)

Publishers Weekly

SOURCE: A review of *Buffalo Hunt,* in *Publishers Weekly,* Vol. 234, No. 11, September 9, 1988, p. 134.

By supplying food and raw materials closely linked with survival, the buffalo (American bison) was the most essential animal to the Indians of the Great Plains of North America. The migration of the buffalo ruled the rhythm of the Indians' daily lives, and the spirit of this sacred beast was incorporated into sacred rituals and tribal lore. A successful hunter became a man of influence and importance. Freedman, author of the Newbery Medal-winner *Lincoln: A Photobiography,* has written a gripping account of the sacred relationship between the Great Plains Indian and the buffalo, whose slaughter by whites assured the destruction of the Indian way of life. Illustrated throughout with reproductions of paintings and drawings by 19th century artist-adventurers, this book tells a poignant tale about a once-indomitable animal and the independent people who were its hunters. Ages 8-12.

Sylvia Marantz

SOURCE: A review of *Buffalo Hunt,* in *The Five Owls,* Vol. 3, September/October, 1988, p. 9.

The image of the American Indian that galloped across the plains of our childhood imagination still intrigues the child of today. Separating the myth from the reality without destroying the fascination is the kind of difficult task that Russell Freedman does so well. In his Newbery Award acceptance speech last July, Freedman noted that, in contrast to the fictionalizing of older nonfiction, "today's youngsters seem to prefer the facts." And as he has done in his previous books, he gives them the facts, carefully researched, finding quotations and the appropriate art and photographs to support them. Using simple language with an almost legendary cadence, he fills in the necessary background information and then takes the reader on a buffalo hunt, from organization and choice of weapons through the heat of the chase to the distribution of the kill and the offerings of thanks to the gods. Be prepared for the reality of devouring "raw liver, still warm and smoking" and "mouthfuls of raw brains," and for questions from readers on the use of buffalo dung. Finally, Freedman gives us the sad facts about the disappearance of what seemed endless herds, with the resulting end of the whole way of life for the tribes. It then becomes painfully clear to any reader why the native Americans began their ferocious attacks on the wagon trains and settlers. The format of *Buffalo Hunt* is that of a picture book, but it obviously provides information and excitement for all ages. The illustrations which Freedman has located have been carefully chosen and placed on the pages to not only illustrate what is discussed there but to fulfill the design. The paintings, most by immigrants or visitors but a few by native Americans, are well-reproduced and, with a few black-and-white drawings, engravings and a photograph, add an immediacy to the narrative that pictures done today would lack. Used as a factual companion to the legends of the Olaf Baker/Stephen Gammell *Where the Buffalos Begin* (Warne, 1981) or of Paul Goble (*Buffalo Woman,* Bradbury, 1984, for

example) *Buffalo Hunt* can add a new dimension for young dreamers.

George Gleason

SOURCE: A review of *Buffalo Hunt,* in *School Library Journal,* Vol. 35, No. 2, October, 1988, p. 167.

Gr 6 Up—Freedman's book has two levels of appeal: that of the wonderfully conceived and vividly executed paintings (full-color reproductions of stunning paintings by such they-were-there artists as George Catlin, Karl Bodmer, Albert Bierstadt, uncluttered by inclusion of photographic every-detail), and that of an informative, accessible text. The title may by itself mislead some, as Freedman presents not a story or description of one hunt but descriptions of the many ways that buffalo hunts were made—by Indians, and later by the whites whose ferocious, firearm slaughter of the "shaggies"—as they were called—brought the species to near extinction. This is superior to two recent picture books on the general subject of buffalo: Dorothy Hinshaw Patent's *Buffalo: the American Bison Today* (Clarion, 1986) and Cary B. Ziter's *The Moon of Falling Leaves* (Watts, 1988). A thundering success.

Betsy Hearne

SOURCE: A review of *Buffalo Hunt,* in *Bulletin of the Center for Children's Books,* Vol. 42, No. 2, October, 1988, p. 34.

Gr. 5-8. After an introduction to the role of the buffalo in Native American lore and life-style, the author describes preparations for a Plains Indian hunt, techniques for approaching and attacking a herd, and the women's work of using everything "from the brains to the tail." Finally, he discusses the appearance of repeating rifles, bounty hunting, and railroad sports shooting as death knells. "The days of the buffalo hunters had faded like a dream," to be kept alive in legend alone. Freedman has hit his stride in terms of selection, style, and illustration: the color reproductions of historical art work form a stunning complement to the carefully researched, graceful presentation of information. The paintings of George Catlin, Charles Russell, Karl Bodmer, and others, including a robe by a Crow artist, speak in moving visual terms of a lost culture and the environment upon which it was based. A book brilliantly designed in all aspects.

📖 *FRANKLIN DELANO ROOSEVELT* (1990)

Kirkus Reviews

SOURCE: A review of *Franklin Delano Roosevelt,* in *Kirkus Reviews,* Vol. 58, September 15, 1990, p. 1324.

The author of a splendid, Newbery Award-winning **Lincoln** (1987) uses a similar approach to smother monumental figure. The result is a carefully researched biography, extended by a wealth (125) of well-chosen b&w photos and presented with clarity and precision. Roosevelt is a substantially more difficult subject than Lincoln: his most significant years spanned two historical cataclysms (the Depression and WW II); he is still (as Freedman makes clear) quite controversial; his complex, ambivalent personality was even more enigmatic than Lincoln's; and the abundance of material available about him presents a formidable challenge to any biographer. Perhaps as a result, Roosevelt's story here seems less compelling, his personality less vividly realized than Lincoln's. Still, this is a valuable achievement, easily the best biography of its subject available at this level.

Daniel Dailey

SOURCE: A review of *Franklin Delano Roosevelt,* in *The Five Owls,* Vol. 5, September/October, 1990, p. 13.

My favorite good-luck piece is a "Rebuild with Roosevelt" coin from FDR's 1932 election for the presidency. I was lucky indeed to have had an opportunity to review Russell Freedman's new biography of FDR, a worthwhile and handsome book. Whether the reader is coming to this piece of history for the first time or returning as an oldtime familiar, Freedman's lively text provides a satisfying and at times spellbinding portrayal of a great man who reshaped his calamitous times. From the end of the nineteenth century to World War I, the Great Depression, and World War II, the sweeping succession of world events that were the focus of FDR's energy and genius is presented in lucid and enlightening detail. The photographs that Freedman has selected to illustrate his narrative are a delightful mix of the familiar and the unusual. The photo captions are nuggets of interesting and surprising facts that provide a flavor of just how gifted and complex Franklin D. Roosevelt was. If there is one small disappointment in this book, it is that Freedman gives in to the temptation to

speculate about what might have been . . . if only Roosevelt had sooner recognized the true dimensions of the Holocaust and allowed more Jewish immigrants to enter the United States . . . if only FDR had not turned a blind eye to the imprisonment and civil rights abuses of Japanese-Americans. When one considers that FDR was born into a world that accepted minstrel shows and "manifest destiny" as acceptable and normal, and when one considers the upheaval, confusion, and change that were FDR's wartime world, one can appreciate, with Freedman's help, that Roosevelt was one of the truly great innovators of his age. Freedman seems to forget that FDR was making things up as he went along. His path was unexplored and perilous. Errors and lapses of judgment had to occur. But do these particular lapses expose a fundamental failure of character? Having raised the question, Freedman leaves it to us to decide. FDR was one of the most controversial men who ever lived. On the whole, Freedman's presentation of FDR's story is well-balanced, fair, and a joy to read. It is to be recommended for every American and world history library collection.

Diane Roback and Richard Donahue

SOURCE: A review of *Franklin Delano Roosevelt,* in *Publishers Weekly,* Vol. 237, No. 41, October 12, 1990, p. 66.

Newbery Medalist Freedman (**Lincoln: A Photobiography**) breathes new life into the subject of our 32nd president. FDR (1882-1945) emerges in all his complexity: Freedman succinctly presents the privileged student "content to squeak by" on a "gentleman's C"; the suitor defying his mother; the polio victim whose suffering taught him compassion for the common man; and, of course, the statesman and leader who shepherded the U.S. through the Depression and WW II. Liberal use of judicious quotations vivifies every discussion. The 125 photographs and prints are equally well-chosen—requisite images of the FDR era are included along with the more unusual, and nearly all are stirring. Fortunately, this fine biography does not apologize for FDR's failings. He is specifically castigated for his failure to save European Jews from Hitler; his "romance" with Lucy Mercer is also mentioned, as well as its profound effect on Eleanor (who is admiringly captured throughout). Young readers will need help interpreting some of the terminology here ("trickle-down" economics, for example), but Freedman's heartening pace and equable tone will stimulate the reader to seek that help. Ages 9-up.

School Library Journal

SOURCE: A review of *Franklin Delano Roosevelt,* in *School Library Journal,* Vol. 36, No. 12, December, 1990, p. 22.

The life and times of the dynamic and controversial president are presented in a cogent, evenhanded manner. Against a backdrop of the Great Depression and World War II, FDR's public stances and his private convictions are compared and discussed, giving readers a frame of reference to formulate their own judgments. Numerous vintage photographs add dimension and depth to this topnotch portrait.

Hanna B. Zeiger

SOURCE: A review of *Franklin Delano Roosevelt,* in *The Horn Book Magazine,* Vol. 67, No. 2, March-April, 1991, pp. 213-14.

Illustrated with black-and-white photographs. In a finely crafted and well-researched book, Freedman traces the personal and public events in a life that led to the formation of one of the most influential and magnetic leaders of the twentieth century. Using photographs and text, the author presents the young Franklin Delano Roosevelt as an active, athletic young man from a wealthy and privileged background attending Groton and Harvard. After his marriage to Eleanor and appointment to a law firm, Roosevelt ran for the New York State Senate and had his first taste of political campaigning. Woodrow Wilson's offer of a position as assistant secretary of the navy allowed him to throw his vast energies into that post, which he held through World War I. Stricken with polio in 1921, he fought his way back to active life in spite of his paralysis, and at the 1924 Democratic convention placed Alfred Smith's name in nomination for the presidency in a dramatic speech that was an important step to his own election to the presidency in 1932. Assuming the office when the country was in the midst of the Great Depression, Roosevelt made the government responsible for the welfare of Americans suffering hardship. "'They have a right to call upon the government for aid,' he said, 'and a government worthy of the name must make a fitting response.'" With the help of his "brain trust" of advisers and of his wife, Eleanor, a social reformer in her own right, whom he called his "'eyes and ears,'" he continued to lead the country through World War II, serving as president for an unprecedented twelve years. His fourth term in office was ended by his death on April 12, 1945. In this definitive biography,

Freedman captures the impact of Roosevelt with a quote by Frances Perkins, his secretary of labor and an old friend, who called him "'a man who . . . will be loved as a symbol of hope and social justice long after his generation and his works have passed away.'" Bibliography and index.

THE WRIGHT BROTHERS: HOW THEY INVENTED THE AIRPLANE (1991)

Diane Roback and Richard Donahue

SOURCE: A review of *The Wright Brothers: How They Invented the Airplane,* in *Publishers Weekly,* Vol. 238, No. 20, May 3, 1991, p. 73.

Newbery winner Freedman (*Lincoln: A Photobiography*) has again produced a vivid, superior biography. This time focusing on a well-known pair of brothers, he effectively transforms our perception of the subjects as distant cultural icons into tireless, flesh-and-blood heroes. In understated, involving prose—skillfully laced with pertinent excerpts from journals, letters and contemporary accounts—Freedman lays out a clear and compelling history of the early aviation experiments that culminated in the legendary flight at Kitty Hawk. As with Lincoln, photographs are integral to Freedman's exposition and he makes ample, effective use of the many astonishing photos taken by the brothers in order to better document their experiments. Youngsters cannot fail to come away with a heightened understanding of the Wrights' dedication to manned flight and to the painstakingly slow process of invention. Ages 10-up.

Kirkus Reviews

SOURCE: A review of *The Wright Brothers: How They Invented the Airplane,* in *Kirkus Reviews,* Vol. 59, June 15, 1991, p. 788.

Using illuminating facts and incidents to place the story of this monumental achievement in the history of aeronautics and in the brothers' personal lives, Freedman focuses on the events that led to the first successful flight and on the Wrights' subsequent improvements on their invention. Diagrams and lucid explanations of the principles of flying make the years of tinkering, experimenting, reasoning, and problem-solving even more fascinating. Though Freedman doesn't characterize Wilbur and Orville in depth, he does provide telling glimpses of the two unmarried brothers devoting themselves to working enthusiastically and amiably together ("They tinkered and fussed and muttered to themselves from dawn to dusk," reported one observer. ". . . At no time did I ever hear either of them render a hasty or ill-considered answer . . ."). In Freedman's deceptively relaxed narrative, the facts themselves are disarming: e.g., the local postmaster helped to haul the planes back uphill, and the fire brigade came regularly to stand by. The brothers' own excellent photos, reproduced in a generous size, make an outstanding contribution to both format and authenticity; they're well supplemented with appropriate additional photos. Like *Lincoln* (Newbery Medal, 1988), this is familiar but retold in a manner so fresh and immediate that reading it is like discovering the material for the first time.

John Peters

SOURCE: A review of *The Wright Brothers: How They Invented the Airplane,* in *School Library Journal,* Vol. 37, No. 6, June, 1991, p. 116.

Gr 4-8—What unusual people the Wright brothers were! Despite a four-year difference in age, the two grew up to be as close as twins, a patient bachelor pair who methodically set out to prove the possibility of powered, controlled human flight. Just as methodically, they promoted their new flying machine, made lots of money, and overcame the U.S. government's stubborn lack of interest. In his own inimitable way, Freedman takes readers back to that exciting time, using not only the Wrights' written descriptions and the accounts of awed observers, but also a large selection of the careful photographs that Wilbur and Orville took to document their experiments. After an opening chapter to set the stage, the author creates a detailed family portrait. He closes with discussions of the photographs, sites to visit, and sources of further information about the Wright brothers. Freedman's achievement is as splendid as those of his subjects.

Zena Sutherland

SOURCE: A review of *The Wright Brothers: How They Invented the Airplane,* in *The Bulletin of the Center for Children's Books,* Vol. 44, No. 10, June, 1991, p. 236.

Gr. 6-10. Profusely illustrated with well-placed photographs of the craft and flights of the first airplanes (those of the Wright brothers primarily, but also those of other early aviation pioneers), this is an account that, for all its attention to technical details, remains lively and forceful. The photographs, many by the Wrights themselves, will interest camera buffs as well as flight fans. Freedman's research is, as usual, impressive, and his organization of material excellent; the focus is on the experiments and improvements made by the inventors, as indicated in the subtitle. An appended note describes the photographic work of the Wright brothers and is followed by a list of places to visit, a bibliography, and an index.

Margaret A. Bush

SOURCE: A review of *The Wright Brothers: How They Invented the Airplane,* in *The Horn Book Magazine,* Vol. 67, No. 4, July-August, 1991, pp. 475-76.

"'I cannot but believe that we stand at the beginning of a new era, the Age of Flight.'" Orville Wright's 1909 prophecy provides a pivotal theme of this beautifully rendered examination of the accomplishments of the legendary inventors Orville and Wilbur Wright; their deep commitment to the idea of a flying machine and their contribution to aviation history are the book's focus. Russell Freedman's mastery in winnowing materials and shaping his narrative seems to become more finely honed with every new work; in this completely engrossing volume Freedman draws deeply on letters, diaries, and other well-documented sources, while many fine photographs provide absorbing, striking views of the early gliders and planes and of the people involved as flyers, assistants, and audience. The book begins with a brief scene featuring the 1904 eyewitness account of beekeeper Amos Root, who was on hand to witness the Wrights' first successful controlled flight—the circling of a cow pasture in Dayton, Ohio, lasting one minute and thirty-six seconds. Freedman then moves back in time to the brothers' childhood and early adult years as printers and bicycle mechanics, showing how their complementary skills and personalities— Wilbur was "fascinated with the big picture"; Orville with its individual parts—and their close relationship contributed to their success. A chapter on "The Art of Flying" describes the previous aeronautic efforts and theories that sparked the Wrights' interest. Their remarkable progress—from 1899, when they first became seriously devoted to the idea of flying, to 1909, when they opened an airplane factory—is examined in a superb synthesis of people, places, mechanical problems and solutions, key events, and mounting excitement and competition. In a stunning conclusion

Freedman reminds us that Orville Wright lived to see many more developments in flight; and just twenty-one years after his death the historic *Apollo II* mission carried to the moon "a piece of the original cotton wing covering from the Wright Flyer that gave birth to the Age of Flight on that windy December morning in 1903." This fresh, illuminating look at an old story concludes with information on turn-of-the-century photography, a list of places to visit, and suggestions for further reading.

📖 *AN INDIAN WINTER* (1992)

Kirkus Reviews

SOURCE: A review of *An Indian Winter*, in *Kirkus Reviews*, Vol. 60, April 1, 1992, p. 464.

In 1833, a German prince, Maximilian of Wied (1782-1867), hired the young Swiss artist Karl Bodmer (1809-93) and set out with him to study Native Americans. They wintered with the Mandans in what is now North Dakota; Maximilian spent the next four years editing his extensive journals, producing a book illustrated with engravings that Bodmer made from his own paintings (which were then sent to Wied, where they stayed until 1962; they're now in a museum in Omaha). Quoting extensively from Maximilian's account, Freedman describes the journey and, especially, the Mandans and Hidatsas as Maximilian found them: their customs, artifacts, social structure, and the individuals who became their close friends. Bodmer's paintings and sketches—landscapes, portraits, and active scenes—appear on almost every double spread, occasionally varied with his engravings or other illustrations, e.g., self-portraits by Mandan friends who were interested in Bodmer's technique. The book closes with the Indians' later history (these tribes were devastated by smallpox in 1837) and five "Places to Visit." As he has clone so often, most recently in *The Wright Brothers* (1992 Newbery Honor), Freedman combines a lucid, gracefully written, impeccably authentic text with beautifully chosen historical illustrations in a handsome and fascinating book; the result here is especially compelling because the material will be new to most readers. Another splendid achievement. Starred Review.

Publishers Weekly

SOURCE: A review of *An Indian Winter*, in *Publishers Weekly*, Vol. 239, No. 21, May 4, 1992, p. 58.

The Newbery Medalist returns to the subject matter of *Indian Chiefs* and *Buffalo Hunt*—though with a narrower scope—in this recounting of the 1833-1834 expedition of Prince Maximilian of Germany and the artist Karl Bodmer up the Missouri River. While Maximilian's own journal provides details of a difficult trek, the book's primary focus is the winter spent by Bodmer and the Prince with the Mandan and Hidatsa tribes—details of their daily lives, customs, modes of dress and beliefs. The book is generously if unevenly illustrated, chiefly with works by Bodmer, whose watercolors of individuals are direct and immediate. However, engravings later produced in Europe seem stereotyped, and several large oil paintings are not well reproduced. Background information and sites to visit today fill out the volume. Readers of Freedman's other titles on Native American topics will find much of interest here, though some may question the reliability of two European dilettantes concerning a culture they visited only briefly. Ages 10-up.

Patricia Dooley

SOURCE: A review of *An Indian Winter*, in *School Library Journal*, Vol. 38, No. 6, June, 1992 p. 132.

Gr 4 Up—In 1833-34, Maximilian, a German prince, and Karl Bodmer, a Swiss artist, travelled by river to what is today North Dakota. There they wintered with the Mandan and Hidatsa, fascinating and flourishing peoples who would be all but exterminated in the 1837 smallpox epidemic. Drawing expertly on his own knowledge and on Maximilian's own detailed account, Freedman tells the story of the Europeans' adventure against the background of the Indians' culture. In a simple but assured style, he conveys copious information effortlessly in the course of a compelling narrative. His ability to bring the Mandan and Hidatsa vividly to life is rendered especially poignant by his final description of their passing. The superb, limpid prose alone would make this book a winner, but the outstanding illustrations guarantee its irresistibility. Bodmer was a competent draughtsman but a master of figure studies. The Mandan were stylish dressers, and Bodmer delighted in depicting them in ceremonial regalia. Unforgettable, bright watercolor portraits punctuate genre scenes of domestic life and landscapes delineating the villages, river, fort, etc. It is hard to imagine a more appealing tribute to the best of two cultures: Native American integrity and European intrepidity.

Karen Hutt

SOURCE: A review of *An Indian Winter*, in *Booklist*, Vol. 88, No. 19, June 1, 1992, p. 1760.

Gr. 6-9. In 1832, Alexander Maximilian, a German prince, naturalist, and explorer, traveled to America to pursue his interest in the Plains Indians. With a servant and a young Swiss artist named Karl Bodmer, he spent several months at Fort Clark, an American Fur Company post (in present-day North Dakota), located near the Mandan village, Mih-Tutta-Hang-Kush. Though Maximilian and Bodmer never lived with the Mandan, they were invited to observe tribal life and acquired information from Mandans who visited the fort to share stories and have their portraits painted. In words and pictures, the artist and the prince recorded their observations of the Mandan and the Hidatsa, a neighboring tribe. Their account, which was published in several languages, provides a glimpse of traditional Mandan life before a smallpox epidemic killed most of the tribe. Drawing on translations of Maximilian's work and incorporating Bodmer's detailed sketches and watercolor paintings, Freedman makes the unique record available to young readers, doing an excellent job of preserving a sense of the original material. As he notes in his introduction, the visually appealing and beautifully written work is a view of "Native American life and culture through the eyes of European strangers." Today, the Mandan, Hidatsa, and Arikara, known as the Three Affiliated Tribes, share the Fort Berthold Reservation in North Dakota. A list of places to visit, a list of illustrations, and a bibliography are appended.

Elizabeth S. Watson

SOURCE: A review of *An Indian Winter,* in *The Horn Book Magazine,* Vol. 68, No. 4, July-August, 1992, pp. 466-67.

In a work based on the journal written by German prince Maximilian in the early nineteenth century, Freedman has woven selected passages from the journal together with his own clearly written and accessible text. The bulk of the text describes the winter of 1833-34, which the prince and his party spent with the Hidatsa and Mandan peoples in what is now North Dakota. The importance of the information is underscored by the fact that only three years later a disastrous smallpox epidemic killed about a quarter of the Hidatsas and all but 130 Mandans—in effect destroying the scenes described by Maximilian. Freedman has chosen illustrations from the sketches and paintings executed by the Swiss artist who accompanied the prince on his journey. The pictures are particularly effective in presenting rich details of village life, clothing, ceremonies, and customs. Both the book's specific information about native peoples and its use of primary-source material make it a valuable creation. Bibliography and index.

☐ *ELEANOR ROOSEVELT: A LIFE OF DISCOVERY* (1993)

Publishers Weekly

SOURCE: A review of *Eleanor Roosevelt: A Life of Discovery,* in *Publishers Weekly,* Vol. 240, No. 25, June 21, 1993, p. 105.

A natural follow-up to Freedman's biography of FDR, this impeccably researched, highly readable study of one of this country's greatest First Ladies is nonfiction at its best. As a role model for girls and an inspiration to both genders, Eleanor Roosevelt remains unsurpassed. Freedman relates how she transcended both an unhappy childhood (her parents separated when she was six; her mother died when Eleanor was eight, and her father, an alcoholic, died two years later) and a timid nature to become one of the most outspoken, vigorous, highly regarded women in history. The vast range of her interests and activities—journalism, politics and social activism—becomes even more remarkable as the author deftly considers Eleanor Roosevelt's times and her social milieu. Approximately 140 well-chosen black-and-white photos amplify the text. Freedman writes both authoritatively and compellingly, and the Eleanor that emerges is a complex, flesh-and-blood individual, not a dull heroine of textbook history. He also deals plainly with some of the more sordid aspects of the Roosevelts' married life (namely FDR's infidelity), but he never sensationalizes, and his honesty and candor signal his respect for his subject and for his readers. This biography cannot be recommended highly enough. Ages 9-up.

Hazel Rochman

SOURCE: A review of *Eleanor Roosevelt: A Life of Discovery,* in *Booklist,* Vol. 89, No. 21, July, 1993, p. 1962.

Gr. 5-9. "Eleanor Roosevelt never wanted to be a president's wife." but she never told her husband. From the first page, the style of this admiring photobiography is as direct and unpretentious as its subject, capturing her splendid public role and also her personal sadness. With a wealth of compelling photographs, Freedman draws heavily on her memoirs, allowing her simple intimate words to speak to all of us. With a new strong First Lady under attack now, it would have been interesting to know more of what Eleanor Roosevelt's opponents said about her, especially since Freedman provides a fine bibliographic essay but no notes and no references to criticism. What humanizes this portrait is the sense of her vulnerability, the strain of melancholy that underlies her shining intelligence and passionate sympathy. The chapters on her childhood make a poignant story: words and photographs show the shy, awkward outsider ("You have no looks, so see to it that you have manners." her beautiful mother told her). Then there's the drama of the ugly duckling's transformation: first when a great teacher "shocked" her into thinking; then later, when she changed from dutiful spouse, docile daughter-in-law, and society hostess to outspoken partner with her own radical political agenda. Her discovery of her husband's love affair is not sensationalized, but the drama is there: we feel her lifelong sense of betrayal. While Freedman does not go into the recent speculations about her passionate relationships, he talks about her long, close bonds of friendship and mutual affection with both men and women. Like his biography *Franklin Delano Roosevelt* (1990), this is a book to read across generations. The plain words and photographs evoke the cataclysmic times and the person, her celebrated political career and her private grief.

Kirkus Reviews

SOURCE: A review of *Eleanor Roosevelt: A Life of Discovery,* in *Kirkus Reviews,* Vol. 61, July 1, 1993, pp. 858-59.

A timid child from a dysfunctional family, Eleanor Roosevelt became a courageous woman whose career was propelled by a series of devastating events: FDR's polio, his relationship with Lucy Mercer, his election to offices that doomed his wife to supportive roles, his death; each time, with energy, determination, and an eye for the essential, Eleanor found new outlets and broke new ground with her accomplishments. Giving up her Democratic Party office when FDR was elected governor, she became his eyes and ears—a role she expanded as First Lady, touring the country and the world to observe and ask questions, winning over critics, reporting, advising, and acting as bellwether for forward-looking ideas on social policy and women's rights. After FDR's death, she chaired the UN commission that drafted the Universal Declaration of Human Rights. And always, she wrote—articles, books, a daily column; presided over a large family with its share of troubles; and kept in touch with an ever-growing circle of close friends. In this generously full history (longer than his *Franklin Delano Roosevelt,* 1990, and with more numerous,

equally fine b&w photos), Freedman focuses, properly, on the public life more than the personal one, as Mrs. Roosevelt herself did. Even so, synthesizing a wealth of resources (ably surveyed in a descriptive bibliography), he brings her wonderfully to life as a rare blend of honesty, intelligence, deep concern for humanity, and ability to inspire loyalty and convey her ideas. Freedman at his best: a splendid achievement. Starred review.

Ruth K. MacDonald

SOURCE: A review of *Eleanor Roosevelt: A Life of Discovery,* in *School Library Journal,* Vol. 39, No. 8, August, 1993, p. 196.

Gr 6-12—Roosevelt has long been considered an appropriate topic for children's biography. A public figure who lived both a traditional woman's role in her support of her husband and family, she achieved celebrity in her own right and championed causes around the world. However, it is only in those books written after she left public life that the painful details of her private life have been revealed. Freedman avoids inventing incident or dialogue, relying on the copious documentation that the Roosevelts left behind from their long careers of public service. He covers new ground in the frankness with which Roosevelt is permitted to speak, about her early childhood, her adolescence, and her marriage. The compensations as well as the self-denial she practiced so faithfully throughout her life are detailed, as well as examined and explained. Nothing is so poignant as her admission of a lack of love for her husband after his affair with Lucy Mercer, and yet her own words are not permitted to stand as the only interpretation of events; her continued commitment to the marriage is duly noted as mute testimony to her devotion. The sensitivity and frankness of this volume, as well as the extensive, supporting black-and-white photographs, mark this as a wide-ranging, honest appraisal of this admirable, courageous woman.

Elizabeth S. Watson

SOURCE: A review of *Eleanor Roosevelt: A Life of Discovery,* in *The Horn Book Magazine,* Vol. 70, No. 1, January-February, 1994, pp. 87-8.

At last, children have a biography of Eleanor Roosevelt equal to its subject! The author has created a sensitive portrayal—certainly sympathetic, but not overly adulatory; it captures the spirit of the woman.

Freedman describes the sad life of a serious, lonely child barely tolerated by her vivacious, socialite mother and neglected by her alcoholic father; her late teen years when she found happiness at school; and her growing maturity as a person and statesperson to the end of her life at age 78. The beautifully crafted text flows smoothly, compelling the reader to follow. Eleanor emerges as a seriously committed humanitarian who created her own identity with very little help from her parents or her husband. Her way was a simple way, and Freedman's text unfolds simply as well. While he describes her near and dear friendships, some of the more complicated relationships in her life are not examined in detail. In discussing the more unfortunate aspects of the Roosevelts' personal life, Freedman has wisely chosen a restrained approach appropriate for the audience: "their relationship had changed forever. It became more a partnership than a marriage—a very close and affectionate partnership based on mutual interests and a shared past, but without the intimacy of marriage." The text is accompanied by an excellent selection of over one hundred photographs portraying Eleanor at every age and with dignitaries and ordinary people all over the world. A person of prodigious energy and strength of will, Eleanor worked unceasingly on her projects; wrote, spoke, and influenced for over forty years. Yet with the characteristic modesty that she exhibited all her life, she summed up her immense contributions plainly: "'As for accomplishments, I just did what I had to do as things came along.'" What adults should do is make sure that this book reaches young readers, particularly young adolescent girls, who will find inspiration, hope, and guidance in the life of this outstanding woman. Bibliography and index.

Kay Parks Bushman

SOURCE: A review of *Eleanor Roosevelt: A Life of Discovery,* in *The ALAN Review,* Vol. 21, No. 2, Winter, 1994.

Freedman has created a high-interest, easily readable, inspirational work on this former first lady, focusing on her tragic and lonely childhood; her secret courtship by Franklin; their changing relationship over the years; her domination by her mother-in-law; and her maturation into a confident, self-reliant, committed, and serving American woman. The text is filled with excerpts from Eleanor's journals as well as numerous photographs throughout her years, which should provide not only a personal connection between Eleanor and the young adult readers but also a motivation

through her accomplishments for today's young people to gain strength to overcome some obstacles of their own.

Claire Rosser

SOURCE: A review of *Eleanor Roosevelt: A Life of Discovery,* in *KLIATT,* Vol. 31, No. 3, May, 1997, p. 21.

A Newbery Honor Book and ALA Best Book for YAs, this is an ideal biography for the junior high school reader, but it could be enjoyed by high school readers, as well. It does have the look of a children's book, but there is nothing childish about the text, which should interest many YA readers. The main theme of the book is that Eleanor Roosevelt was an unhappy child, painfully shy, who overcame her handicaps to be an important political leader in her own right. Freedman does mention how FDR's infidelity crushed Eleanor and changed their relationship forever. He stresses Eleanor's "life of discovery," how she learned and changed and met new challenges throughout her life. A good introduction, with plenty of photos as illustration, to an impressive 20th century woman.

KIDS AT WORK: LEWIS HINE AND THE CRUSADE AGAINST CHILD LABOR (1994)

Publishers Weekly

SOURCE: A review of *Kids at Work: Lewis Hine and the Crusade against Child Labor,* in *Publishers Weekly,* Vol. 241, No. 26, June 27, 1994, p. 79.

A schoolteacher-turned-investigative reporter, Lewis Hine (1874-1940) traveled the United States from 1908 to 1918, photographing some of the millions of underprivileged children who labored as a regular part of the work force. He emerged with an array of shocking pictures and stories—of a five-year-old shrimp picker in Mississippi; a four-year-old oyster shucker in Louisiana; boys and girls working in often dangerous conditions and for pitiful wages in mills, mines, sweatshops, fields and factories in every corner of the land. Exhausted, ragged, often filthy, their faces peek out from the 61 photos reproduced here, their testimony certain to move the reader. As always, Freedman (*Eleanor Roosevelt*) does an outstanding job of integrating historical photographs with meticulously researched and highly readable prose, this time combining biographical information about Hine with a history of the campaign to end child labor in America. The result is thoroughly absorbing, and even those who normally shy away from nonfiction will find themselves caught up in this seamless account. Ages 12-up.

Kirkus Reviews

SOURCE: A review of *Kids at Work: Lewis Hine and the Crusade against Child Labor,* in *Kirkus Reviews,* Vol. 62, July 15, 1994, p. 984.

Another fine photo-essay by the author of **Lincoln** (1987, Newbery Award). Hine (1874-1940) took up photography while teaching at NYC's Ethical Culture School and was soon photographing immigrants at Ellis Island as a teaching tool. He followed his subjects into their city tenements and photographed their children, often hard at work in sweatshop conditions. He's especially remembered as an investigative reporter (1908-18) for the National Child Labor Committee, touting the US to record children as young as three years old working, for long hours and often under very dangerous conditions, in factories, mines, and fields. Freedman offers the salient facts of Hine's life but focuses, with characteristic thoughtfulness, on this phase of his work and the message it so powerfully conveyed, beautifully summed up in the NCLC's 1913 "Declaration of Dependence" on behalf of children, which proclaimed children's right "to play and to dream," as well as to get "normal sleep" and an education, and called for "the abolition of child labor." But as Freedman points out, legislation—thwarted until the Fair Labor Standards Act of 1938—was ultimately the result of economic pressure (adults' need for jobs) rather than humanitarian motives. Sixty-one of Hine's poignantly telling, beautifully composed b&w photos are an integral part of the story. An excellent complement to *Cheap Raw Material*; like Meltzer, Freedman concludes by emphasizing that child labor is a continuing problem.

Stephanie Zvirin

SOURCE: A review of *Kids at Work: Lewis Hine and the Crusade against Child Labor,* in *Booklist,* Vol. 90, No. 22, August, 1994, pp. 2035-36.

Gr. 5-9. The selection of photographs in Freedman's works (he generally picks the photos himself) is usually as impressive as the text. That's certainly true of this book, which uses pictures to chronicle the state of child labor in early-twentieth-century America while profiling the life of reformer-photographer Lewis Hine. In his characteristically direct, unpretentious fashion, Freedman explains what Hine discovered as an investigative photographer for the National Child Labor Committee (a "militant" group that crusaded for such things as compulsory education), illustrating the revelations with haunting black-and-white pictures—many secured without the permission of factory owners—that bear witness to deplorable working conditions. Anecdotes and Hine's own words will pique interest in both the situations encountered and in Hine himself. The history and biography are not as smoothly entwined or as well detailed here as they have been in some of Freedman's other books (there's not quite enough about the socioeconomic underpinnings to satisfy report writers, and Hine's later life gets short shrift), but there's still a great deal to arouse and to inform, and the visual impact is unforgettable. Freedman's bibliography can guide readers toward more information, while materials like Meltzer's recent *Cheap Raw Material* can flesh out the necessary background. A book that makes history relevant to young people by putting them in the center of it.

Susan Knorr

SOURCE: A review of *Kids at Work: Lewis Hine and the Crusade against Child Labor,* in *School Library Journal,* Vol. 40, No. 9, September, 1994, p. 227.

Gr 5 Up—Using the photographer's work throughout, Freedman provides a documentary account of child labor in America during the early 1900s and the role Lewis Hine played in the crusade against it. He offers a look at the man behind the camera, his involvement with the National Child Labor Committee, and the dangers he faced trying to document unjust labor conditions. Solemn-faced children, some as young as three years old, are shown tending looms in cotton mills or coated with coal dust in the arresting photos that accompany the explanations of the economics and industries of the time. Both Freedman's words and quotes from Hine add impact to the photos, explaining to contemporary children the risky or fatiguing tasks depicted. Details such as Hine's way of determining children's height by measuring them against his own coat buttons add further depth and a personal touch to the already eloquent statements made by his thoughtfully composed black-and-white portraits. Also included are some of the photographer's other projects throughout his career. Readers will not only come to appreciate the impact of his ground-breaking work, but will also learn how one man dedicated and developed his skill and talents to bring about social reform.

Roger Sutton

SOURCE: A review of *Kids at Work: Lewis Hine and the Crusade against Child Labor,* in *Bulletin of the Center for Children's Books,* Vol. 48, No. 2, October, 1994, pp. 44-5.

Like Russell Freedman himself, child labor photographer Lewis Hine "knew that a picture can tell a powerful story," and his photographs not only depict the miseries of working children in the early decades of this century but also implicitly depict the humanity of the photographer himself, a balance equally achieved by Freedman's fluent text. Hine began his career in 1901 as a teacher at New York's Ethical Culture School, but soon became a roving photographer on behalf of child welfare advocates, joining the National Child Labor Committee full-time in 1908. His photographs, large and cleanly reproduced here, provided eloquent witness to a national scandal, showing children as young as three years hard at dangerous, dulling work in factories, mines, fisheries and farms. The portraits have dignity and poignancy, with children lined up against impossibly large machines, toting enormous sacks of produce or cotton, or sorting through bins of coal. The text gives the stories—Hine's as well as the larger social picture—behind the photos, including Hine's later projects photographing European war refugees, the construction of the Empire State Building, and the sad decline of his photographic reputation and death in poverty in 1940. Spaciously designed, the book moves easily between words and pictures and will invite thoughtful browsing as well as more concentrated study in history and photography curricula. While there are no notes, a bibliography and index add reference value.

Mary M. Burns

SOURCE: A review of *Kids at Work: Lewis Hine and the Crusade against Child Labor,* in *The Horn Book Magazine,* Vol. 70, No. 6, November-December, 1994, pp. 744-45.

They look at us from faces that seem to be much older than their years. Their clothes are ill-fitting; their posture that of adults—and, indeed, they are do-

ing adult work. These are the children who, before World War I, were laboring in America's factories and mines at substandard wages under substandard conditions. Among the early crusaders for reform was a young schoolteacher and photographer named Lewis Hine, who, in 1908, left his teaching position for a full-time job as an investigative photographer for the National Child Labor Committee, then conducting a major campaign against the exploitation of children. It is Lewis Hine's photographs that serve as a visual accompaniment to Freedman's interpretive, finely wrought, eminently readable text. The narrative not only documents the abuses of the times but also traces the chronology of Hine's development as a crusader, his personal struggles, his techniques for outwitting the owners and managers who wanted to conceal their inhuman practices, and his final years of poverty when, at the end of the Great Depression, he was forced to apply for public assistance. The account has about it the quality of a modern epic whose hero, although scorned by fortune and tried by adversity, triumphs as a visionary. As Freedman so succinctly comments: "With his box camera and his sympathetic eye, he made a dramatic difference in people's lives. In a real sense, the face of America never looked the same again." The penultimate chapter includes the "Declaration of Dependence," framed in 1913 by the National Child Labor Committee, which asserts the right of children to protection from dangerous labor practices, opportunity for education, and a chance to enjoy normal childhood activities. The final chapter offers a brief commentary on current conditions which need addressing—notably among migrant workers and recent immigrants. Freedman has always exhibited a sure sense for selecting details which bring history to life and which make it relevant as well as compelling. This portrait of Lewis Hine is no exception. Bibliography and index.

Alan M. McLeod

SOURCE: A review of *Kids at Work: Lewis Hine and the Crusade against Child Labor,* in *The ALAN Review,* Vol. 22, No. 2, Winter, 1995.

The subtitle for **Kids at Work: Lewis Hine and the Crusade Against Child Labor**—defines the "documentary" focus. Hine, a teacher-photographer, was so disturbed about child industrial labor that he became an investigative reporter. His photographs of children at work, sometimes children as young as three years old—working as newsboys, shrimp-pickers, and farmhands; laboring in cotton mills, coal mines and canneries—contributed to important changes in labor laws. The stark black-and-white pictures play an important role as well in Freedman's tracing the social reforms needed and Hine's contributions. The book should appeal to younger adolescents interested in photography, in social reform, or in understanding how life was different for many youths earlier in this century.

Celeste F. Klein

SOURCE: A review of *Kids at Work: Lewis Hine and the Crusade against Child Labor,* in *KLIATT,* Vol. 32, No. 4, July, 1998.

This is a useful book which accomplishes three things: a biography of Lewis Hine, a history of child labor in the U.S., and a photographic documentary. Hine graduated from high school in 1892 and found a job at which he worked thirteen hours a day, six days a week, for four dollars a week. Enrolling in the State Normal School in Oshkosh he met a teacher, Frank Manny, who became his mentor. When Manny went to New York as superintendent of the Ethical Culture School he asked Hine to join him on the faculty. Manny wanted Lewis to head a school camera club, so Hine got a $10 box camera and learned its use along with his students. First he photographed the new arrivals at Ellis Island. Then several child welfare groups commissioned him to document with pictures the abuses they were trying to correct. In 1908, the National Child Labor Committee offered him a full-time job in their efforts to outlaw child labor. This book shows the results of his efforts, with photos of children working in laundries, textile mills, cotton fields and other places. Especially heartbreaking are the pictures of small boys, black with coal dust, as they emerge from the mines; and little girls working in the spinning room of textile mills where they were valued for their small hands. Hine was threatened by owners, and also the police, as he tried to photograph the child laborers. He tried subterfuge to gain entry into factories, posing as a fire inspector or an insurance salesman. In 1912, thanks to Lewis Hine and the National Child Labor Committee, NCLC, the U.S. government established the Children's Bureau. During the Depression adults began to compete for the jobs held by children and labor

unions were increasingly powerful and demanded work for adults. However, it wasn't until 1938 that President Roosevelt signed the Fair Labor Standards Act which set minimum wages and hours for all workers and placed limitations on child labor. As a reporter who saw an exhibit of Hine's pictures wrote, "There has been no more convincing proof of the absolute necessity of child labor law . . . than these pictures showing the suffering, the degradation, the immoral influence, the utter lack of anything that is wholesome in the lives of these poor little wage earners." Sad to say, Lewis Hine died in poverty. After his death he began to be recognized as a great photographer and the pictures in this book attest to that fact. All who look at it will be shocked by what they see, but it is part of our history and a part that we must be reminded of.

THE LIFE AND DEATH OF CRAZY HORSE (1996)

Kirkus Reviews

SOURCE: A review of *The Life and Death of Crazy Horse,* in *Kirkus Reviews,* Vol. 64, April 15, 1996, p. 601.

A spectacular match: Freedman's tale of the great Oglala Sioux's career is coupled with 50 black-and-white pictographs done by a tribal historian. By all accounts, Crazy Horse was a strange, solitary, ascetic man, and he is still revered as much for his private generosity as for his military exploits. Freedman (**Kids at Work,** 1994, etc.) depicts him as a classic, mythic hero, describing with dash and drama the vision that shaped his reckless courage, his role in the Fetterman Fight, at the Little Big Horn, and in countless smaller engagements, his stubborn resistance to the war's changing tide, and the ambiguous circumstances of his death. Unlike Judith St. George (*Crazy Horse,* 1994), Freedman plays down his subject's bloodthirsty side, but both authors present balanced, convincing accounts of the prejudice, confusion, and simple incomprehension that fueled the Indian Wars, and reaffirm the central role that Crazy Horse played in them. As was true of Freedman's **Indian Winter** (1992), illustrations created not long after the events they depict give this a unique authority; Amos Bad Heart Bull (1869-1913) was a cousin of Crazy Horse, and his drawings, done in the 1890s, are based on Sioux witnesses' personal accounts.

Shirley Wilton

SOURCE: A review of *The Life and Death of Crazy Horse,* in *School Library Journal,* Vol. 42, No. 6, June, 1996, p. 156.

Gr 7 Up—An account of the Oglala Sioux leader's life, written with the attention to detail of a historian and the language of a storyteller. Freedman paints the famous warrior's story on a broad canvas, describing the forces (desire for farmland, gold, railroads) that brought increasing numbers of white settlers to the Indian lands. The divisions among and within the tribes in the face of the ever-growing problem are explained, as is Crazy Horse's adamant refusal to give in to either the threats or the treaty offers of the U.S. Army and the government. The climactic battle of the Little Big Horn is described and shown to be the last triumph of the Sioux before they were herded onto reservations, and the last great victory of Crazy Horse before he was pushed to surrender and face his own violent death. Judith St. George's *Crazy Horse* (Putnam's, 1994) tells very much the same story but adds more details of Indian tribal life and customs. Freedman's book is richer in historical background. His focus is on the conflict of two cultures, and in that conflict Crazy Horse plays the role of the tragic hero, resisting the inevitable, fighting for his people's freedom even when he knew the cause was lost. An impressive bibliography is appended. Black-and-white reproductions of Indian pictographs from a collection of drawings by a Sioux artist (Crazy Horse's cousin) decorate and lend authenticity to Freedman's story—a story that is readable and balanced, and one that illuminates an important chapter of American history.

Hazel Rochman

SOURCE: A review of *The Life and Death of Crazy Horse,* in *Booklist,* Vol. 92, Nos. 19-20, June 1, 1996, p. 1721.

Gr. 6-12. [Freedman's] biography of Crazy Horse is a bloody war story, filled with fighting, massacre, brave resistance, and raging grief; but Freedman tells it without sensationalism, true to the modest spirit of the great Oglala Sioux warrior. Crazy Horse was a quiet loner. Only in battle was he a leader of furious action. The details of the individual battles are here, the skirmishes, ambushes, and combat of the guerrilla war. What Freedman focuses on throughout, however, is Crazy Horse's role in the Sioux's independence struggle against the move to reservations. We see the events as Crazy Horse did the waves of new migrants trying to take his country, whites sweeping westward and slaughtering the buffalo, building the transcontinental railroad, and with the discovery of gold, trying to take even the sacred Black Hills of his people and force them into reservations. "The Indians wanted the whites to get out of their country and quit traveling through it." There's drama in the occasional switch to how the whites saw things: "the Indians stood in the way"; the U.S. Army had a "clear duty" to protect the advancing frontier for white miners, ranchers, and farmers. Freedman names the best sources, gathered from eyewitness accounts, some 50 years after the events. The book is beautifully designed, with thick paper, a haunting jacket painting by Ronald Himler, and remarkable drawings throughout from the picture history by tribal historian Amos Bad Heart Bull that show scenes of hunting, battle, courtship, and ceremony.

Publishers Weekly

SOURCE: A review of *The Life and Death of Crazy Horse,* in *Publishers Weekly,* Vol. 243, No. 25, June 17, 1996, p. 67.

This latest biography from a master of the genre draws on first-hand accounts of the life and personality of the great Lakota warrior Crazy Horse, combining them with a succinct but dramatic narration of the bloody conflict that ended only with the forced settlement of the last free Native American nation. Born around 1841 as a member of a freely ranging band, Crazy Horse died in 1877 as a captive of the U.S. Army. Quiet and reserved, "he wore no war paint, took no scalps, and refused to boast about his brave deeds," writes Freedman. But he was a revered leader in battles along the Oregon and Bozeman trails which culminated in the Battle of the Little Bighorn—as the Indians of the northern Plains fought an ultimately futile war to keep their independence. Illustrations are taken from the ledger book kept by Crazy Horse's cousin Amos Bad Heart Bull (1869-1913), the historian of the Oglala Sioux. Reproduced from black-and-white photographs made before the ledger book was buried with the artist's sister in 1947, in accordance with Sioux custom, the art is not as crisp and sharp as contemporary kids are used to. But along with the personal accounts the pictures effectively evoke life as Crazy Horse would have

▢ *MARTHA GRAHAM: A DANCER'S LIFE* (1998)

Hazel Rochman

SOURCE: A review of *Martha Graham: A Dancer's Life,* in *Booklist,* Vol. 94, No. 15, April, 1998, p. 1324.

Gr. 7-12. The subjects of Freedman's photo biographies range from his 1988 Newbery Medal-winning *Lincoln* and his two Newbery Honor Books, *Eleanor Roosevelt* (1993) and *The Wright Brothers* (1991), which was also *Booklist*'s Top of the List for youth nonfiction, to his stirring *The Life and Death of Crazy Horse,* a 1996 *Booklist* Editors' Choice. This is his first book about an artist, and, as always, he writes with eloquence and grace about the private person and her revolutionary public role. Martha Graham herself said that her life was her work, as dancer, teacher, and choreographer; and Freedman's focus is on how she created a thrilling new modern dance language that connected movement with emotion, how she made visible "all those feelings that you have inside you that you can't put words to." He connects her artistic breakthroughs with the social and cultural history of her time, the political and artistic rebellion that challenged the role of women and the formality of ballet. In discussing individual dances, he shows how her themes of the outsider and the lonely rebel changed to complex psychological portraits of people like Emily Brontë and Emily Dickinson. The electrifying black-and-white photographs are an integral part of every chapter: you read Freedman's lyrical description of a performance and feel you must see a picture of it; turn the page, and there is a photo of Graham in flaming action. Full documentation in chapter notes at the back shows the routes of Freedman's research: books, articles, and tapes that readers can search out, and also his own extensive personal interviews with those who knew and worked with Graham. Another great YA title that will appeal to adults as much as to teens.

Publishers Weekly

SOURCE: A review of *Martha Graham: A Dancer's Life,* in *Publishers Weekly,* Vol. 245, No. 14, April 6, 1998, p. 80.

Freedman (*Lincoln*; *Eleanor Roosevelt*; *Franklin Delano Roosevelt*) once again animates American history through biography; here he adds culture to the mix as he chronicles the inspiring life of legend-ary dancer Martha Graham. The venerable author hooks readers in immediately with his description of young Martha learning to move her body by watching a lion pace from one side of its cage to the other. Freedman then seamlessly charts the fiery, passionate Graham's rise from a 19-year-old "homely, overweight" dance student to principal dancer to teacher to the creator of modern dance.

The biography points up Graham's commitment to a "uniquely American style of dance," focusing on such works as *Frontier,* an homage to her ancestral roots, and *Appalachian Spring* for which she collaborated with composer Aaron Copland. Freedman acknowledges that the dancer's sources of inspiration and consolation came from other American artists: writer Emily Dickinson (the source of Graham's work *Acts of Light*) and composer Scott Joplin ("Maple Leaf Rag" was her last complete work), among them. Her passions were not circumscribed to her work), she also took stands on tough political issues, both in her dance (e.g., *Deep Song,* 1937, which "expressed her anguish over the brutal Spanish Civil War") and in her life—she refused to perform at the 1936 Olympic Games in Berlin ("How could I dance in Nazi Germany?"). But Freedman does not paint an unblemished picture. His abundant sources, including unpublished transcripts of an interview with Graham's longtime companion Louis Horst, as well as his own interviews with Graham's former dancers, colleagues and friends, make clear the shadow side of her passionate nature. What emerges from these pages is a multilayered view of a genius who danced and choreographed, and designed her own costumes and lighting, but who was also human—a woman who laughed and cried, hoped and feared, and who unflinchingly followed her dream. Stunning photographs arrayed chronologically demonstrate the dramatic changes Graham wrought upon dance as a discipline. Four at the close of the volume, showing Graham in what appear to be a dance sequence, are particularly spectacular. This outstanding biography speaks not only to dancers but to anyone interested in the arts, history or the American entrepreneurial spirit. Ages 10-up.

Kirkus Reviews

SOURCE: A review of *Martha Graham: A Dancer's Life,* in *Kirkus Reviews,* Vol. 66, April 15, 1998, p. 578.

In a biography as elegant as its subject, Freedman (*Out of Darkness,* 1997, etc.) delves into the life of the dance pioneer who not only revolutionized modern dance but married it with theater, music, literature, and art in a dazzling and emotional way. Graham began her serious dance study already too "old" (at age 19), according to prevailing standards; despite critics and a public who didn't initially understand her work, Graham was so fiercely dedicated to her art that she became one of the 20th century's most important influences on modern dance. Freedman discloses Graham's intensity in work and relationships, and explains her techniques and dances in lively, theatrical language; he doesn't canonize Graham, however, but portrays her as a passionate woman, with a fiery temperament, whose every aspect of life was reflected in her art. Extraordinary black-and-white photographs coalesce with the clear and stimulating chronicle of her life and art, until a complete picture of a genius emerges from the pages of this enlightening, liberating volume. Starred Review.

Marilyn Payne Phillips

SOURCE: A review of *Martha Graham: A Dancer's Life* in *School Library Journal,* Vol. 44, No. 5, May, 1998, p.154.

Gr 4 Up—The renowned dancer, choreographer, and teacher is a fascinating subject. Graham was a woman who defied the odds—she did not start dancing until she was 19, she did not have a traditional tall, lithe dancer's physique, and yet through sheer will power and perseverance, she became the most important name in modern dance. A living legend, she performed until she was 75, created 181 dances—the last at age 95. The personal cost of such fame was high indeed. She would be the first to admit that she lived to dance. Freedman has done an extraordinary job of conveying that passion and of presenting Graham's complex personality as viewed through multiple perspectives. It is evident through his careful notes and annotated bibliography that he did his research. As in his previous books, the format utilizes generous margins and a wealth of sharply reproduced black-and-white photographs depicting the many faces and poses of Graham dancing, teaching . . . always performing. This book has more detail and photographs than Trudy Garfunkel's *Letter to the World: The Life and Dances of Martha Graham* (Little, Brown, 1995). Recommend it to students looking for a great woman's biography, as well as to dance fans or, for that matter, any aspiring artists. A remarkable look at a remarkable talent.

Susan P. Bloom

SOURCE: A review of *Martha Graham: A Dancer's Life,* in *The Horn Book Magazine,* Vol. 74, No. 4, July-August, 1998, pp. 511-12.

Once again, preeminent biographer Russell Freedman proves the art of nonfiction. Inspired by Martha Graham, his graceful prose soars, capturing the spirit of the dancer. Mindful that Graham discarded the old vocabulary of dance to literally invent a new language of dance, "modern" dance as she alone conceived it, Freedman stretches to conceive a vocabulary that will complement her innovative artistry. Nowhere does the drama of Martha Graham's long and legendary life dim: even when the stage lights are not directly shining on her as performer, Freedman catches the passion of her dedication. His text opens with Graham's visits to the Central Park Zoo in New York, where she spent hours "fascinated by the elemental power of the lion's great padding steps, by the purity of its movements." His poetic words receive additional layering from Graham: "Finally, I learned how to walk that way . . . I learned from the lion the inevitability of return, the shifting of one's body." From beginning to end, Freedman underscores this daring dancer and choreographer's life with salient details, often in her own words. Other voices (her dancers; her lifelong friend and collaborator Louis Horst; her lover and husband Erick Hawkins) and stories from other important figures of the twentieth century with whom Graham interacted round out Freedman's account. Photographs of startling imagery further illuminate the finely honed text. Freedman concludes Graham's story with the only uncaptioned pictures in the book: four consecutive photos dramatically reveal dancer Graham realizing a single role in poses of emotional and physical spectacle; a fifth picture plays final tribute to the woman with a soul-searching portrait of remarkable thoughtfulness. No reader, whether interested in dance or not, will want to miss Graham's extraordinary story, Freedman's remarkable achievement.

Janet Mura

SOURCE: A review of *Martha Graham: A Dancer's Life,* in *VOYA,* Vol. 21, No. 3, August, 1998.

Martha Graham's name is recognized by almost anyone over the age of twenty and anyone who is into dance. She died in 1991, known as a dancer and choreographer who changed the face of modern dance in America and the world. Martha invented a new language and style for dance. She wanted to present body movements that expressed all of the emotions: love, anger, hate, joy, and all the passions that make up each of us. Her genius enabled her to connect the right moves to illustrate and make visible the feelings that are inside. In Pittsburgh in 1894, Martha was born to a father who was a doctor with an Irish background and a mother who could trace her ancestry back to the Mayflower. Martha had two younger sisters, Mary and Georgia. In 1908 the family moved to Santa Barbara where the three girls thrived. In 1911, Martha's life was changed by one event—seeing a performance of Ruth St. Denis. Modern dance was changed by Graham who still performed into her seventy-fifth year and created new and innovative dances until she died just short of her ninety-seventh birthday. This is a wonderful and warm biography about a difficult and dedicated woman. Photographs fill the pages, many of which have rarely, if ever, been seen. Martha's recollections combine with memories of her students, close friends, and family to create a portrait of an amazing woman. While she was not always likeable, her artistic sense shines in award-winning biographer Freedman's words. This well-written life story belongs in middle, junior, and high schools as well as public collections and wherever dance is loved.

Julie Grosmann

SOURCE: A review of *Martha Graham: A Dancer's Life,* in *Stone Soup,* Vol. 27, No. 5, May, 1999, p. 18.

When I first realized that **Martha Graham** was a biography, I didn't think it would be an interesting book. But after I got into the book, I realized how wrong I was. Martha Graham was a headstrong independent woman who, like me, was fully devoted to dance. She also made a major mark in dance history. In fact, I learned a lot of interesting choreography techniques from her that I can use in some of the dances that I choreograph.

I learned two very interesting things that she did. One is that if you read lots of different things, it will expand your imagination, so you will have more creative energy to use on creating dances. The other is watching people and animals to learn how they focus their energy and their movements, so that those movements can later be worked into dances.

I don't completely agree with Martha when she states that she doesn't think classical ballet shows enough emotion and drama. However, I'm glad Martha felt that way, because if she hadn't or wasn't as dedicated to dance as she was, dance would not be the way it is today. Although Martha and I don't completely agree on that topic, I found out that we are alike in many other ways.

Some of those ways are: we both enjoy dance, music, writing stories, plays and poems. We have also both been published. Martha and I are also alike in personal ways too. We are both very serious with our studies, especially dance. We also have the same kind of sense of humor, wicked and mischievous.

At first it was a little hard for me to think of Martha Graham as mischievous, especially after I read about her bad temper when things didn't go her way. It was a good thing her bad moods didn't stay long. If they had, her dance teacher Ted Shawn would have stayed mad at her for slamming his door so hard the window broke. If he had remained mad at her, she wouldn't have gotten her shot in *Xochitl.* I was very impressed that she got the part. It was a very hard dance role, and she mastered it just by watching other dancers perform it.

I was very surprised to learn that Martha liked Scott Joplin's "Maple Leaf Rag." In fact, the last dance she created when she was ninety-six years old was called "Maple Leaf Rag." This was a very big coincidence because we had just studied that song in my music class just before I read it in this book.

I also learned many interesting things about Martha Graham. One of those was that Bette Davis, Woody Allen, and Gerald Ford's wife Betty all studied with Martha. I was very impressed to learn that Martha created 181 dances in her life. Another good thing about the book was that the author, Russell Freedman, wrote the book wonderfully. I could easily imagine the scenery and people that surrounded Martha from his descriptions. I could easily imagine the pain Martha felt when her father died. I have read several biographies, but this one was definitely the best.

There was one thing I thought I definitely knew about Martha Graham: that she lived a long time ago. I was wrong. She died on April 1, 1991, when she was ninety-six years old. This was a wonderful, well-written book and I would recommend it to anyone who likes to dance or enjoys reading biographies. The book I thought I would hate I ended up loving.

📖 *BABE DIDRIKSON ZAHARIAS: THE MAKING OF A CHAMPION* (1999)

Randy Meyer

SOURCE: A review of *Babe Didrikson Zaharias: The Making of a Champion,* in *Booklist,* Vol. 95, No. 21, July, 1999, p. 1932.

Gr. 5-12. A phenomenal athlete, brash celebrity, and gender role rebel, Babe Didrikson Zaharias took an amateur woman's basketball team to new heights before embarking on a solo career as an Olympic athlete, track star, golfer, and entrepreneur. Children used to athletes who limit their focus to one sport will marvel at Babe's accomplishments. Freedman does a good job of tracing her rise from scrappy neighborhood games to stardom and gives readers a sense of the way she was worshipped on the playing field and vilified for her unladylike appearance (the taunt "muscle moll" was invented by a sportswriter to demean her). But something in his characterization seems flat. We do get a glimpse of her rocky marriage to wrestler-hustler George Zaharias, but there isn't much more about her personal life or the "intimate friendship" she enjoyed with Betty Dodd, a fellow golfer who lived with the Zahariases. This is an entertaining account of Babe's life in sports, but in the end, there are still some things that remain elusive. Black-and-white photographs, notes, and a selected bibliography.

Publishers Weekly

SOURCE: A review of *Babe Didrikson Zaharias: The Making of a Champion,* in *Publishers Weekly,* Vol. 246, No. 29, July 19, 1999, p. 196.

In another exemplary biography, Newbery Medalist Freedman (*Martha Graham*) turns to Mildred "Babe" Didrikson Zaharias (1911-1956), arguably the preeminent woman athlete of the 20th century. He pays ample attention to Babe's extraordinary achievements—e.g., her three world records in track and field at the 1932 Olympics; her record-setting golf career in the '40s and '50s—but his book's greatest strength lies in his portrait of the person behind the athlete, a portrait that hums with the energy and vibrancy of Babe herself. A bold tomboy Texan from a poor family, Babe saw sports as a way to earn recognition, respect and a living, something almost unheard of for a woman at the time. Using quotations from friends, rivals and Zaharias herself, as well as a bounty of period photographs, Freedman brings her irrepressible personality leaping from the page. At a golf championship in Scotland, she egged on the polite and quiet crowd to cheer for her; playing a bit part in the movie Pat and Mike, she obliged the screenwriters to change the script so she wouldn't have to lose to the Katharine Hepburn character. Freedman tiptoes around the issue of Zaharias's sexuality, especially when describing her troubled marriage to a former wrestler and her close association with another female athlete. By paying attention, however, to the times in which she lived, Freedman demonstrates Zaharias's role as a challenger not only of sporting records, but of cultural assumptions about class and gender as well. This celebratory work gives readers a chance to cheer Zaharias's legendary life. Ages 10-up.

Roger Sutton

SOURCE: A review of *Babe Didrikson Zaharias: The Making of a Champion,* in *The Horn Book Magazine,* Vol. 75, No. 5, September, 1999, p. 623.

Freedman's measured yet lively style captures the spirit of the great athlete, who seemed able to master any sport she chose. The book is at its best in the chapters about Babe's track-and-field triumphs; the later account of her golf career drags a bit. Aside from the odd silence regarding Babe's lesbianism (mention of which is relegated to an afterword, and there coyly), what's missing is a strong enough context to give today's young readers (most of whom will know Babe only as a name—if that) a sense of how this athlete's place in history goes beyond the playing field. Alone, though, her records are staggering, and Freedman's enthusiastic admiration provides enough reason to read. Plenty of black-and-white photos capture Babe's spirit and dashing good looks; the documentation—notes, bibliography, index—is impeccable.

Kirkus Reviews

SOURCE: A review of *Babe Didrikson Zaharias: The Making of a Champion,* in *Kirkus Reviews,* Vol. 67, No. 12, June 15, 1999, p. 963.

The best athlete of the 20th century may have been Babe Didrickson Zaharias, who appears in a vibrant biography that crushes any remaining myths about women in sports. Freedman (**Martha Graham,** 1998, etc.) makes clear that almost from Babe's birth in 1911, in an era in which women were barely accepted in sports, she displayed phenomenal athletic ability and determination to become a champion in every sport she played. She was so consumed by sports that she played baseball with boys who were glad to have her, and went on to win two gold medals and one silver medal at the 1932 Olympics, a performance that brought her an enduring national celebrity. Her colorful personality lights up the narrative at ev-ery turn and in every story, e.g., after fighting for the right to play golf against socialites who didn't want her, she became, arguably, the best golfer who ever lived. Even with her natural ability Babe still trained at an almost inhuman level. Her insistence on victory was matched by a love of life that sparkles through the book; her story, as told by Freedman and supported by a profusion of black-and-white photographs, leaves readers wondering what she could have done in a less restrictive era and who will follow in the path she blazed.

The following series published by the Gale Group contain further information on Freedman's life and career: *Authors and Artists for Young Adults,* **Vols. 4, 24;** *Contemporary Authors,* **Vols. 17-20 Revised;** *Contemporary Authors New Revision Series,* **Vols. 7, 23, 46, 81;** *Junior DISCovering Authors; Major Authors and Illustrators for Children and Young Adults; Something about the Author,* **Vols. 16, 71;** *The St. James Guide to Young Adult Writers.*

Leo Lionni
1910-1999

(Full name Leonard Lionni) Dutch-born American author/illustrator of picture books and author of nonfiction.

Major works include *Little Blue and Little Yellow* (1959), *Swimmy* (1963), *Frederick* (1967), *Alexander and the Wind-Up Mouse* (1969), *Cornelius* (1983).

For further information on Lionni's life and works, see *CLR,* Volume 7.

INTRODUCTION

Leo Lionni is best known for his lavishly illustrated children's books which usually contain subtle moral lessons and address such issues as rebellion, truth, individuality, perseverance, and resourcefulness. Often referred to as fables, Lionni's works are written in a lively tone that engages both children and adults. In 1964 he wrote, "I believe, in fact, that a good children's book should appeal to all people who have not completely lost their original joy and wonder in life." Using the natural world as his setting, Lionni has been highly praised for his illustrations and collages that offer "both pictorial richness and great economy of shape, line, and form," according to Lesley S. Potts of *Dictionary of Literary Biography.* Potts continued, "he remains a consummate artist whose greatest strength lies in creating images that tell a story with charm, elegance, and grace."

BIOGRAPHICAL INFORMATION

Lionni was born in Amsterdam, Holland, on May 5, 1910, the son of Louis and Elizabeth Grossouw Lionni. Early in his life, Lionni became determined to spend his adulthood as an artist. He began studying the works of famous artists at local museums, and as his formal education progressed, he became very skilled at drawing, especially from nature. From 1928 to 1930, he attended the University of Zurich, and shortly afterward opened his own advertising agency and began exhibiting his own paintings. In 1935, Lionni furthered his education by obtaining a doctorate in economics from the University of Genoa,

Italy. Immigrating to the United States in 1939, Lionni quickly established himself as a talented art director, painter, journalist, and educator. Most of his work centered on graphic design and painting until 1959—the year his first picture book was published. Created on a train trip to amuse his grandchildren, *Little Blue and Little Yellow* became a hit and thrust Lionni into a new career as a children's author and illustrator. From his initial work, Lionni went on to make more award-winning titles for children, including *Inch by Inch, Swimmy, Alexander and the Wind-Up Mouse, Cornelius,* and many more. About his children's books, Lionni has commented, "The fact is that I really don't make books for children at all. I make them for the part of us, of myself and of my friends, which has never changed, which is still a child."

MAJOR WORKS

Lionni's primary goal for his books was "to achieve a coherence between form and content which even the closest, most intimate co-operation between different people cannot reach." His first achievement toward this end was *Little Blue and Little Yellow.* Considered a classic by many critics, the picture book focuses on two colored shapes, one blue and one yellow, who are very good friends. One day the two shapes hug and meld together to form a single green shape. Looking different, the shapes become frustrated as their own parents no longer recognize them. The story examines their frustration until they are able to find a way to separate back into their respective colors. *Little Blue and Little Yellow* received rave reviews for its imaginative use of torn-paper collage illustration and its engaging plot speaking of change, camaraderie, and love. While it was hailed for its imaginative approach to social issues, it was also praised for its presentation of color theory.

Lionni's second book, *Inch by Inch,* also caught the attention of the public and critics alike. Lionni's fable describes the unconventional tactics an inchworm takes to avoid becoming his predators' next meal. He offers to measure his foes' legs, tails, and other body parts. While this task proves simple enough, his real challenge comes when a bird requests he measure the length of its call. The tale shows how the inchworm survives by its own wisdom and ingenuity. Again Lionni illustrates the tale with the colorful torn-paper collages that would soon become his trademark.

Shortly after *Inch by Inch,* Lionni published another book that impressed the critics as well as readers. *Swimmy* is a story of a fish who loses his siblings to hungry predators and finds an ingenious way to survive the treacherous waters. Upon finding another school of fish, he attempts to galvanize the group by convincing them to swim packed tightly together in the shape of a large fish to scare off predators. Many reviewers believe this story is a thinly veiled description of politics, in which Lionni had become interested at the time. In *Swimmy,* Lionni's torn-paper collage illustration technique transforms into expressively layered, soft-edged watercolor wash illustrations.

In 1967, four years after the publication of *Swimmy,* a new Lionni title, *Frederick,* which many believe is his most successful work, was released. *Frederick* is a fable about a young mouse who refuses to gather up food for the impending winter and instead spends much of his time basking in the sunshine, describing colors, and creating stories about the beautiful summer. While his peers initially ridicule him, he earns the respect of his fellow mice during the winter when they all long for the warm breezes and bright sunshine of summer. It is during this morose time that Frederick is able to entertain his fellow mice and brighten their spirits. Once again Lionni's fascination with the depiction of the natural world and his appreciation for the power of art prove to be engaging subject matter.

Lionni produced *Alexander and the Wind-Up Mouse* in 1969. In the story, the reader is introduced to Willy, a mechanical mouse toy, and Alexander, a common house mouse. Alexander longs to have the love and affection of the children of the house as Willy does. Forlorn Alexander wishes he were a mechanical mouse until Willy breaks and is thrown out in the trash. Quickly Alexander changes his mind and wishes only for Willy to become a real mouse so they can be companions. As Alexander's wish comes true the book ends happily. Lionni's plot echoes the power of love and the need to be true to oneself. Some critics believe Alexander's story is too simplified as compared to earlier Lionni works. Still others doubt the clarity of Lionni's illustrations, which in this book have risen to new heights of visual complexity.

Using his trademark collages, Lionni went on to create *Cornelius,* a story about a crocodile who enjoys learning and happens to walk upright. In the tale, Cornelius quickly becomes frustrated with his friends, who lack his enthusiasm, so he leaves his riverbed home for the jungle. There, he finds a monkey who hangs by his tail and stands on his head. At Cornelius's urging, the monkey instructs him in the proper way to perform these tricks. When Cornelius returns to the riverbed, his friends still reject his enthusiasm at his newfound skills. However, as Cornelius leaves to rejoin the monkey in the jungle, he notices his friends attempting in vain to perform the tricks he showed them. The tale illustrates the difference between followers and leaders. While the luxurious illustrations reflect Lionni's appreciation for the beauty and wonder of the natural world, critics have found the book's plot to be underdeveloped.

AWARDS

Lionni became an award-winning author/illustrator, often winning multiple awards for one title. In 1959, Lionni earned the *New York Times* Best Illustrated award for his first achievement, *Little Blue and Little Yellow;* he would go on to win the award two more times for *Swimmy* in 1967, and *Frederick* in 1968. Lionni was also honored several times with the Caldecott Honor Book award for *Inch by Inch, Swimmy, Frederick,* and *Alexander and the Wind-Up Mouse. Swimmy, Frederick, Alexander and the Wind-Up Mouse,* and his 1970 title *Fish Is Fish,* received American Library Association (ALA) Notable Book citations, and the George G. Stone Center for Children's Books presented Lionni with an award for his entire body of work in 1976.

AUTHOR COMMENTARY

Leo Lionni

SOURCE: "Me as in Mouse," in *Leo Lionni at the Library of Congress,* edited by Sybille A. Jagusch, Library of Congress, Washington, D.C., 1993, pp. 9-18.

As I stand here before you as an official guest of honor of the Children's Literature Center of the Library of Congress to help celebrate International Children's Book Day, I must confess that I always feel somewhat embarrassed when I am introduced as a children's book author. Not because I consider the making of picture books a minor art form and would prefer my name to be associated with more ponderous activities in the field of Art. Nor because I made my first book at the ripe old age of fifty. Nor because it happened as casually as it did.

My reluctance probably has its origin in my early childhood, when my first defiant answer to the question "What do you want to be when you grow up?" was "The bell of the trolley car." A few years later, and somewhat wiser, I came up with a more reasonable response: "I want to be an artist." That would still be my answer today.

At the time, we lived in Amsterdam, just a few steps from two of the most wonderful museums of the world, the Rijksmuseum and the Stedelijk. There I spent many a Sunday drawing from plaster casts of Greek sculptures and looking with awe not only at the paintings and drawings of Rembrandt and Velasquez but also at the abstract works of Mondriaan and Klee.

And then there were the copyists, with their gray smocks soiled with paint, an open paintbox at their feet, a palette in the left hand and a delicate brush in the other. Breathless, I would watch them as they moved slowly in front of their easels, performing, almost invisibly, stroke by stroke, the magic of duplication. They were the first real painters I had ever seen. It is surely from them that I learned to love the velvety scent of linseed oil and Venice turpentine, and to cock my head when weighing the success or failure of a touch of burnt umber. It was probably then, as I stood there spellbound, and like the artist, unaware of the people around me, that I discovered the creative delights of craftsmanship, and the pleasure of recognizing the solidity of one's lonely self in the midst of a crowd.

I learned about design by helping my Uncle Piet, who was a young architect, with menial drafting tasks. And at home I would listen, whether I wanted to or not, to my mother, an extraordinary soprano, practice a Mozart aria or a Schubert lied. Painting, sculpture, architecture, design, and music, old and new, all came under the same heading: Art. And I wanted to be an artist.

Today, as then, I am involved in all the arts. I paint, I sculpt, I design. I write. Much of it to the sound of Mozart and Schubert. What tempts, excites, and motivates me is the underlying unity of the arts, their many surprising connections and cross-references, and the central poetic charge they share.

Such an eclectic attitude may well seem to be dispersive. And indeed I sometimes wonder if it would not have been better to devote all my time and energies to one well-defined profession. But in retrospect I am happy to have lived so intensely my adventure with all the arts. Not to claim the status of a "real professional" in any one endeavor has been a small price to pay for the many benefits and pleasures of trespassing.

It now seems strange to me that my incursion into the open, sunny field of children's books happened when it did, late in life, for no art form benefits as much from the total experience in the arts as the picture book. No wonder that when I entered the field I knew that I was walking on familiar ground.

It happened in a most casual manner on a crowded commuter train from New York, where I worked, to Greenwich, Connecticut, where we lived. With me were my two restless grandchildren Annie and Pippo, who had come to spend the weekend with us. To keep them quiet and well behaved was not an easy job. After all the strategies of reasonable persuasion had failed, I had an idea. From the ad pages of *Life* magazine I tore a few small pieces of colored paper and improvised a story—the adventures of two round blobs of color, one blue, the other yellow, who were inseparable friends and who, when they embraced, became green. The children were glued to their seats, and after the happy end I had to start all over again. That evening at home I made a rough dummy.

My friend Fabio Coen, then children's book editor for Obolensky, Inc., saw **Little Blue and Little Yellow** when he came for dinner at our house the very next day, and decided then and there to have it published.

I had been lucky. The story had run smoothly out of my mind, as if it had been secretly maturing there for a long time. This happens often, I understand, with an "opera prima." It embodied many of the visual ideas I had been toying with throughout the years, such as the psychological implications of positioning images in space, and the flow of visual tensions that results from the way images are moved from page to page. The story was born complete, with a beginning, a development, a crisis, and a happy ending. And although I wasn't quite conscious of it at the time, it was a perfect metaphor for a child's search for indentity. Making children's books was as easy as child's play.

That was thirty years ago. Now Annie, an architect, is expecting a baby, and Pippo is a graphic designer in Paris. And I have just given birth to my thirtieth picture book.

Because of the instant success of **Little Blue and Little Yellow,** I expected Fabio to ask me to make another book, and I was enthusiastic when indeed he did. But when I sat down at my desk, I could produce no more than meaningless doodles. I began to toy with a "Little Blue Goes to the Zoo," but soon the crippling realization came to me that the very uniqueness of my first book precluded a sequel. Whatever I could think of had the flavor of a stale leftover. As I considered my options, it became clear that a new book would have to be totally different in theme, style, and technique. After much creative turmoil, I finally produced **On My Beach There Are Many Pebbles.**

On My Beach was different, all right. The illustrations were realistic pencil drawings of invented pebbles (letterpebbles, fishpebbles, peoplepebbles) that lay hidden among "real" pebbles on a beach. It had no story, not even the hint of a plot, let alone a metaphor. It was an elegant coffee-table book for children. I still consider it with pride to be one of my handsomest achievements, but it has little connection with the many books that were to characterize my career as an author of fables. Perhaps it wasn't a children's book at all.

In a way my third book, **Inch by Inch,** turned out to be my first, for unlike **Little Blue** and **On My Beach** it seems to have embodied all the qualities I later demanded of my work. It is a short animal fable told in words and images that are clear, simple, and memorable; it has a well-defined stylistic coherence between text and illustrations; its tone is light and humorous; and although it doesn't have an explicit moral, it invites search for meaning. I know that this is much to ask for, and in looking back at the body of my work I realize that perhaps I have failed more often than I have succeeded. It now is also increasingly clear to me that what characterized **Inch by Inch** was the simplicity and the strength of the idea that generated it. And it has become clear that making illustrated fables is not child's play.

What prompted me to invent this fable of an inchworm and a nightingale? Where did the idea come from? Did it come from the distant memories of my early youth in Amsterdam, when, on my way home from school through the Vondelpark, armed with an empty marmalade jar, I would collect woolly caterpillars (those most mysterious of insects) and later, spellbound, watch them weave their white cocoons? Or was it the nightingale that graced our Greenwich garden with the intricacies of its silver song while I was struggling with an idea for my next book? Or was I simply obeying a sudden, irrepressible urge to paint birds and foliage?

Where *do* ideas come from? Authors of children's books well know how frequently the question is asked. It implies the naive assumption that authors have the key to a bottomless reservoir of stories as yet untold, and that they possess a highly specialized mechanism to retrieve them.

Nothing could be further from the truth. To trap the incredibly complex mental process that shapes the development of a story from birth to full-fledged maturity is a hopeless task. As it moves forward from word to word, from image to image, from page to page, a story leaves but the vaguest traces of its tortuous itinerary, and at the end the glowing, solid reality of the finished work all but obliterates the long travail that brought it to its satisfying conclusion. Time and again have I tried to identify the thoughts, feelings, or events that triggered an "idea" into being. Of my thirty books, I have succeeded in tracing but a few to the possible circumstances of their birth. **Frederick, Swimmy,** and **Cornelius** are among these exceptions. They show how fortuitous and fragile those circumstances are, and how difficult it is to answer the question "Where do you get your ideas, Mr. Lionni?"

In the early sixties we were living in the hills above the small resort town of Lavagna on the Italian Riviera. The house, a pink stuccoed cube typical of the area, sat in the midst of terraced vineyards and dense olive groves, and from the windows the view embraced the spectacular Tigullio Bay with Sestri Levante to the east and Portofino to the west.

The studio was an adjacent reconverted barn. One sunny afternoon, on my way to work, I found myself face-to-face (or foot-to-face) with a very frightened little field mouse. When it saw me, it froze on its tiny feet. Then it jumped up and darted into the geraniums that flanked the flagstone path.

It was a warm day. The air was filled with the heavy scent of magnolias and orange blossoms and the monotonous sound of crickets. Far below in the hazy sunlight the ocean quivered slightly. I decided to take a nap.

As I lay on my couch, my thoughts began to meander in ever-widening circles. I woke up an hour or so later from a heavy sleep, incapable of moving. As I lay there motionless on my side, my eyes wandered along the shelves of my studio, which were filled not only with books but with hundreds of objects I had collected on my travels around the world. "How much nonsense," I thought. And I found myself saying (I still remember the words), "Once upon a time there was a little field mouse. All the other mice gathered nuts and berries for the winter ahead, while he collected pebbles. 'Why do you collect pebbles?' the others asked, annoyed. 'You never know. They may come in handy some day,' he answered mysteriously."

When I got up, I went about my business without giving that fantasy or my encounter with the mouse another thought. But I remembered them a few weeks later when I began working on the story of *Frederick,* which then seemed to have appeared from nowhere.

Way back in the early fifties we spent a month in Menemshah on Martha's Vineyard. One day I stood on a mooring in the little harbor waiting for a friend to pick me up with his boat when in the water below I saw a school of glittering minnows idly moving about. Suddenly, there was the roar of an outboard motor. Closing ranks, the minnows swiftly swerved around and like one big fish disappeared in the dark of the deeper water. They reappeared several years later at the surface of my memory as *Swimmy* and his friends.

Cornelius was born from a doodle I drew during a long and tedious telephone conversation. It is not surprising that it should have been the drawing of a lizard, because our garden is inhabited by hundreds of the playful little animals, who congregate in the warm hours of the day on the flagstones of the path to my studio. Absentmindedly, as I listened and talked, I drew one. It was standing on its hind legs like a miniature dinosaur. Without knowing why, I added a zigzag line to its back, and then when I finished the call, I threw the doodle into the wastepaper basket. But almost immediately I retrieved it, smoothed the wrinkles, and looked at it, letting my thoughts wander. Again, as with Frederick, words came to my mind, this time a title: "The Crocodile Who Walked Upright." It later became "Richard, the Upright Crocodile" and still later, when the text had been written, and the pictures drawn, simply *Cornelius.*

It would be nice to know how the little mouse on the path to my studio began collecting pebbles and later became Frederick, a poet who collects sunrays, colors, and words; how a school of fish became the friends of Swimmy, a political idealist; and how the doodle of a lizard grew into Cornelius, a crocodile who saw and changed the world because he walked upright. For better or for worse, the steps and leaps of the imagination escape the mechanics of our memory and our understanding. The little we *do* know is that somehow in the flow of thoughts that endlessly fill our minds, the artist learns to recognize, capture, and remember that which is useful to his purpose.

Now you may ask yourself why I titled this talk "*ME* as in Mouse?" The answer is simple: I wanted to stress the point that like all fiction, illustrated children's books are inevitably autobiography.

I have mentioned some minor incidents of my own life that have triggered the ideas for my fables. What I did not mention is the fact that without delving deep into the distant memories of their own childhoods, authors could not find the mood, the tone, the imagery that characterize their books. They could not create convincing protagonists were they not able to fully identify with their heroes, a quality they inherit from their early youth.

If, in that sense, Frederick, Cornelius, and all the others are *me,* then in the context of this gathering, Swimmy is perhaps the most pertinent example. Little by little, conditioned by the events of his life, he discovers the meaning of beauty as a life-force and finally assumes his role as the eye who sees for the others. "I'll be the eye," he says.

Like Swimmy, the creator of picture books for children has the responsibility to see for the others. He has the power and hence the mission to reveal beauty and meaning. A good picture book should have both.

Come to think of it, would "I as in Eye" have been a better title?

Leo Lionni

SOURCE: *Between Worlds: The Autobiography of Leo Lionni,* Alfred A. Knopf, 1997, pp. 231-32, 234.

Probably one of the most important events of 1963 was the arrival of the first copy of *Swimmy,* my fourth children's book. When I began unwrapping the package, my hands were so shaky that Nora took the package and the scissors I was brandishing, and in no time at all produced what in a single glance I recognized as my best book to date. I placed it with my three others, side by side against the wall, dragged the armchair to the center of the studio, and sat down.

The need to compare what I was doing now with what I had done before, and to recognize the direction in which my work was moving, was a habit I had inherited from Leon Karp. With my paintings it had become an interrogatory practice, but evaluating the continuity of content and style in the books required years. Since I had an agreement with my publishers not to do more than one book a year, this annual event had taken on an importance in my life that I would never have predicted. And, indeed, when I sat down to look at the four books, I was fascinated by the differences and the similarities.

The first thing that struck me was that no group of books by one author could possibly look as different one from another as these four. Defying all the rules for building a reputation, a personality, a trademark, they seemed to have very little in common. *Little Blue and Little Yellow* was the most aggressively modern and the least bookish of the four; it had broken all the rules and was a real invention. *On My Beach* did not look like a children's book at all and probably wasn't. Yet it contained many memories of my childhood vacations on the Mediterranean pebble beaches: the close-up look, the endless search for "special" pebbles with the discovery of hidden images and unusual shapes. Impressed by the success of *Little Blue,* Fabio had asked me to produce a comparable book for the following year. Logically my first efforts had been directed at *Little Blue Two,* but the more I tried to find a viable idea for a sequel, the more I realized that *Little Blue* was a unicum that should not be exploited or imitated. I decided that if I made more books, each one should have a character of its own. After toying with the tempting idea of Little Blue goes to the zoo (another identity quest), I decided to go in the exact opposite direction: black and white instead of color, drawings instead of collages, sharp-focus realism instead of abstract shapes, spreads instead of single-page illustrations. But while I was working on the drawings for *On My Beach Are Many Pebbles,* I had another idea which, because of its autobiographical implications, slipped to the foreground, the story of an inchworm, which became my second book, with the title *Inch by Inch.*

And now, with a slightly mysterious cover, low key in color and composition, here was *Swimmy,* my first real fable, which in no time became the role model for most of the books that were to follow. It contains all the principles that have guided my feelings, my hands, and my mind through my long career as a children's book author.

Swimmy was the book that for the first time led me to consider the making of books as, if not my main activity, one that was no less important than my painting and my newly discovered sculpture. In my relentless involvement in the invention of new forms and new ideas, I had never thoroughly examined what had made the old ones satisfying and successful, nor had I found enough distance from the process of making to realize how complex the production of these four books had been. The ethics of art not only as a pleasurable but as a useful activity was clearly the moving force in the book. The central moment is not so much Swimmy's idea of a large fish composed out of lots of tiny fish but his decision, forcefully stated, that "I will be the eye." Anyone who knew of my search for the social justification for making Art, for becoming or being an artist, would immediately have grasped what motivated Swimmy, the first embodiment of my alter ego, to tell his scared little friends to swim together like one big fish. "Each in his own place," Swimmy says, suddenly conscious of the ethical implications of his own place in the crowd. He had seen the image of the large fish in his mind. That was the gift he had received: to see.

Different as the four books were, they were linked by characteristics: the rhythm, the simplicity of the action, the logic of the sequencing and positioning of the protagonists on the page. All of these qualities had their origins in the hundreds of pages I had manipulated in putting together the many issues of *Fortune* that had been produced under my art direction. I must admit that even in an activity as new to me as the making of a children's book, in many ways I was a pro before I began, and I no longer feared an inability to maintain the variety, the originality, and above all the passion and the fun with which I had initiated this new profession. Foreign editions of the books began to multiply, and the mailman started bringing me a fan letter now and then.

For the first time in all my work, I found myself confronting a tangible audience. Along with the fan mail came invitations from schools, and these awakened in me a need and a desire to understand my audience. I found myself digging deeper and deeper into the memories of my childhood, and I learned to distinguish within myself that which was peculiar to my own feelings and experience and that which was universal to children everywhere. I became ever more conscious of the problems children face and the importance of the messages we send to them. It is often said—and I think somewhat too easily—that to write for children you must be the child, but the opposite is true. In writing for children you must step away and look at the child from the perspective of an adult.

Leo Lionni

SOURCE: "Leo Lionni," at *http://www.randomhouse. com/teachers/rc/rc_ab_lli.html,* November 9, 2000.

Of all the questions I have been asked as an author of children's books, the most frequent one, without doubt, has been "How do you get your ideas?" Most people seem to think that getting an idea is both mysterious and simple. Mysterious, because inspiration must come from a particular state of grace with which only the most gifted souls are blessed. Simple, because ideas are expected to drop into one's mind in words and pictures, ready to be transcribed and copied in the form of a book, complete with endpapers and cover. The word *get* expresses these expectations well. Yet nothing could be further from the truth.

It is true that, from time to time, from the endless flow of our mental imagery, there emerges unexpectedly something that, vague though it may be, seems to carry the promise of a form, a meaning, and, more important, an irresistible poetic charge. The sense of instant recognition with which we pull this image into the full light of our consciousness is the initial impulse of all creative acts. But, though it is important, it produces no more than the germ of an idea. Each book, at the birth of its creative history, has such a moment. Some are fortunate enough to have, from the outset, a strongly identified hero, one with an inescapable destiny. Others are blessed with a promising beginning, or perhaps with the vision of an ending (which means working backwards to a surprise opening). Others stem from a clearly articulated conflict situation. Sometimes, I must admit, the motivations of a book may be found in a sudden, unreasonable urge to draw a certain kind of crocodile. And it may even happen that in the dark of our minds there appears, out of nowhere, a constellation of words that has the bright, arrogant solidity of a title. Only last night I was jolted out of a near-slumber by the words the mouse that didn't exist. I am sure that,

temporarily tucked away in my memory, they will eventually become the title of a story for which as yet I have no idea.

To shape and sharpen the logic of a story, to tighten the flow of events, ultimately to define the idea in its totality, is much like a game of chess. In the light of overall strategy, each move is the result of doubts, proposals, and rejections, which inevitably bring to mind the successes or failures of previous experiences.

Inspirational raptures may happen, but most books are shaped through hard, disciplined work. Creative work, to be sure, because its ingredients come from the sphere of the imaginary. But the manipulation of these ingredients requires much more than mere inclination or talent. It is an intricate process in which the idea slowly takes form, by trial and error, through detours and side roads, which, were it not for the guidance of professional rigor, would lead the author into an inextricable labyrinth of alternatives.

And so, to the question "How do you get your ideas?" I am tempted to answer, unromantic though it may sound, "Hard work."

GENERAL COMMENTARY

Amanda Smith

SOURCE: "The Lively Art of Leo Lionni," in *Publishers Weekly,* Vol. 238, No. 16, April 5, 1991, pp. 118-19.

In his newest children's book, **Matthew's Dream,** Leo Leonni tells the story of one determined mouse's odyssey from child to artist. Rendered in his unique combination of painting and collage and told as a fable—the form that Lionni prefers—the book is particularly colorful and vivid, even more so than much of Lionni's previous work. That Lionni is a mature artist is clear: the distinguished roster of his earlier 33 volumes, which have garnered four Caldecott Honor awards, includes **Frederick, Swimmy, Alexander and the Wind-up Mouse, Inch by Inch,** and **Fish Is Fish.** Still it's surprising to discover that the lively creator of this new book is 80 years old.

Today Lionni, with his wife, Nora, whom he married 60 years ago, divides his time between a Manhattan apartment and the Tuscan countryside, where the couple lives in a 17th-century farm house. In Italy he has a separate studio; in New York he works in a large, light room in his apartment.

Lionni refers to himself as "an odd combination," and his own odyssey from child to artist was an unusually eclectic one. Dutch by birth, the son of a Jewish father and a half-Protestant, half-Catholic mother, Lionni was raised in Amsterdam, Brussels, Philadelphia, Genoa and Zurich, as his father's work—as diamond cutter, accountant and finally corporation manager—took the family from city to city and country to country. Lionni eventually became a graphic artist, but early on, he earned a doctorate in, of all things, economics.

In 1939, as the political climate worsened in Europe, Lionni and his own family—by then there were two sons—came to settle in America and Lionni began a highly successful career in graphic arts, working for a decade as art director for the advertising firm N. W. Ayer and subsequently as art director for *Fortune* magazine, receiving in 1984 the American Institute of Graphic Arts Gold Medal, the field's highest honor. He has been a painter, sculptor, photographer, filmmaker. His career as a children's writer and illustrator came late and almost by accident, when he was completely established as a professional. It began on a commuter train from New York to Greenwich, Conn., when, to entertain his restless grandchildren, Lionni tore scraps of paper from a magazine and gave them identities and stories—the inception of his first book for children, *Little Blue and Little Yellow.*

In *Matthew's Dream,* art is at the center of the mouse's life. So art is the core of all of Lionni's work. In terms of his overall career, when asked if any of it means more to him than anything else, Lionni replies, "I would say that painting is still perhaps the key. It's less tangible. Painting is really very mysterious." When speaking of the artists he admires, Lionni says, "I think it's impossible today not to have Picasso as a hero, a role model. If [today's artists] say no, I don't believe them. I love Bonnard because of his way of handling his brush and color. For each [aspect] you have a different role model. My heroes are here," Lionni says, and points out the art that graces his working space in New York, works by artists such as Giacometti, Calder, Klee, Moore.

Lionni is a citizen of the world with enormous appetite for experience. In previous years he spent several weeks each year with Spanish gypsies and learned flamenco guitar. Often his interests and passions have informed his children's books: the time he has spent in India, for instance, led eventually to *Tico and the Golden Wings.*

Lionni says his first 12 years in Amsterdam were among the most significant influences on his children's books. "I remember the sun shining. Every time I've gone to Holland since, the weather has been terrible most of the time. There must have been something in my childhood which makes me remember it that way. I believe I had a very happy childhood. I was privileged to be an only child, and I think it helped me to cope with loneliness, which is everybody's problem, I think, for the rest of my life. And also, I think, how to develop my imagination. What I remember has to do with what happened when I was alone, with my interest in nature, my interest in art, my going to the museum and drawing, my going out and hunting for small animals and keeping them in cages and aquariums and terrariums in my little room."

Subsequent years in America and Italy were pivotal as well. "When I came [to America] in 1939, I had this great advantage over a lot of other refugees. I had been to an American school for a year, so I spoke English fluently, and I knew all about baseball and football and the whole bit. I had no problem in being Americanized, which really takes a long time for a lot of foreigners. But I felt I was coming home."

In Italy he completed his schooling and his university degrees and began working; his first job was writing about modern architecture for the prestigious architecture magazine *Casabella.*

Lionni says that in making his children's books, he discovered a great deal about himself and came upon hidden metaphors he hadn't used intentionally. He cites the example of *Swimmy,* in which one little fish, who avoids being eaten, organizes other fish to mass together and look like a single large fish, so they will not be swallowed up by truly larger fish. "The obvious metaphor is 'in union there is strength,'" Lionni comments. "The one that I was not conscious of is the autobiographical part, that when Swimmy organizes the other fish to be altogether one fish, he says, 'And I'll be the eye'—that is, 'I'll be the artist. I'll see the others. I have experienced how beautiful the world can be, and I want to show this to you, because we can't live this way in darkness.' Which is a much more interesting and a much truer, less rhetorical metaphor than the apparent one. What it means is that there is a density in the very simple stories that I tell."

Lionni finds the role of the children's book in a child's life terrifically important. "I've become very conscious of it recently. I'm sure it's not original, but it suddenly struck me that when a child is four or five, he has lived four or five years in a totally chaotic verbal environment. The picture book is the first thing that gets into his head where he is confronted with a verbal structure. If it's a good book, it has a beginning, a middle and an end. It's the first time that he will say 'more, again' after the reading is over. Now he knows what the end and the beginning is—just think of what a complicated notion that is. Which means that he also has a notion of what's in between, so that he has a sense of whole. He's not conscious of it, but for the first time, he's faced with structure. That I think is an enormously convincing consideration on the importance of the picture book."

The fable is the form that Lionni most often uses in his children's books. "I would call the story that has no meaning or conclusion an open-ended structure, whereas the fable is a closed structure. It's like the classical Greek theatre."

Lionni is "enormously concerned with language. That's one of the things I'm passionate about." Once he has an idea that he is enthusiastic about, he can complete a children's book in a month, but he says that the writing takes more time than the art. "Writing takes me longer because the possibilities are so infinite always. You find yourself in this big word-ocean, whereas with pictures you find yourself in a small lake. But writing, you're thrown into this infinity of possibilities. Of course, it's infinite what can happen on a canvas, but conceptually it's only so much. But time and a piece of paper are really two different things. Language exists in time, whereas the picture is all there—one glance and it's over."

For a talk this month at the Texas Library Association's meeting, Lionni has prepared what he terms his "autobiography in terms of language. What happens when a child goes from one language to another? What happens to your own language, to your own interior monologue, how it develops? What happens if you don't know words when you learn a language and you have to speak? You invent words that people find very funny but that are sometimes very poetic, because poetry is very often born from necessity. I remember that I didn't know the word for weeds so I used to call them 'bad grass.'"

Lionni's tales for children are a fine marriage between language and art, and at their center are small heroic creatures of the natural world—fish, birds, frogs and, of course, mice. Lionni's mice are among his most endearing characters, charming, often mischievous creatures rendered in collage. "I prepare all the mice beforehand," Lionni says. "I have about 40 mice in **Matthew's Dream,** so I prepare 40 bodies, 80 ears, 40 tails. I have little cups with them in and I assemble them. By just changing the position of the arms and the body, you get the expression."

Lionni says of his current book, "That book, like many of my books, is an elaboration around a very small but to me important, central idea, and the central idea is that I tried to explain what art is in an almost Zensized capsule." As Matthew looks at the dusty attic in which he was raised, with its hodgepodge of newspaper and memorabilia, his mind suddenly conceives of it in the abstract, distilling the shapes he sees. "The way reality was and the way he sees it after his experience [of going to a museum and dreaming] I was very happy to have that idea, because I think it explains more about art and about modern art than an hour-long lecture," the artist observes.

Clearly, Lionni continues vitally into his ninth decade. In many ways, he does not recognize age: "The fact that I'm a great-grandfather—expecting twin great-grandchildren in June, furthermore—doesn't impress me or depress me particularly, but the idea that my son is a grandfather—that really gets me," he says with a chuckle.

Even at this age Lionni continues to grow and change as an artist. This book has brighter, more vivid colors than many of its predecessors. "My paintings have become much more colorful, too, happier and more upbeat. I had an existential crisis which affected me, and I realized that maybe about a year or year and a half after this, I had a need to renew everything I was doing and to be very vital and life-assertive. My whole painting style changed."

"I think I'm an enthusiastic person," Lionni says, "and if I can deliver some of that enthusiasm, that's good."

Kathleen Burke

SOURCE: "Notable Books for Children, 1997," in *Smithsonian,* Vol. 28, November, 1997, pp. 163-64.

One afternoon in 1959, as author-illustrator Leo Lionni describes that day, "a little miracle happened." Having boarded a commuter train bound from Manhattan for Connecticut, he faced the necessity of entertaining two fellow travelers, his 5-year-old grandson and 3-year-old granddaughter. As the youngsters vaulted from seat to seat, he recognized that "fast creative thinking" was in order.

Lionni, who was, in his late 40s, already an internationally recognized artist and graphic designer, had resigned recently from a ten-year interlude at Time, Inc.: for a decade, he had been the art director of *Fortune* magazine. So it was that he happened to be carrying in his briefcase an advance copy of *Life*. As he opened the magazine, he recalls, "a page with a design in blue, yellow, and green gave me an idea." "Wait," Lionni announced, "I'll tell you a story." Next, as he remembers, "I ripped the page out and tore it into small pieces. The children followed the proceedings with intense expectancy. I took a piece of blue paper and carefully tore it into small disks. Then I did the same with pieces of yellow and green paper. I put my briefcase on my knees to make a table, . . . placed the round pieces of colored paper onto the leather stage and improvised a story about the two colors."

The result of his efforts was his first picture book, *Little Blue and Little Yellow,* published within months by the firm MacDowell Obolensky. From that fortuitous beginning, Lionni has gone on to write and illustrate more than 30 picture books, which have sold millions of copies throughout the world and include four Caldecott Honor titles, *Inch by Inch, Frederick, Swimmy,* and *Alexander and the Wind-Up Mouse.* (A selection of his books, *Five Lionni Classics,* also is available on videocassette from Random House.).

Fortunately for Lionni fans, a handsome collection of his works, *Frederick's Fables: A Treasury of 16 Favorite Leo Lionni Stories,* has just been published by Knopf. The appearance of this compendium coincides with the release of Lionni's autobiography, *Between Worlds,* also from Knopf.

His memoir offers an excursion, in the company of a humane and literate guide, into the worlds that have shaped his protean career as an artist, designer, sculptor and children's book author. Lionni began drawing in his early childhood: he grew up in Amsterdam, a few blocks from the Rijksmuseum. "On many a Saturday morning," he writes, "while my schoolmates met in the park for a game of soccer, I would walk to the museum with a box of pencils, a small drawing board, sheets of paper, and a folding chair . . . . There

in the great hall, I would draw." He was also a passionate amateur naturalist-collector and a painstaking architect of elaborate terrariums.

In that garret of his childhood lay the sources of the magical books he would create. "Not so long ago," Lionni writes, "I suddenly realized that the dimensions of my children's books are exactly the same as those of my terrariums. I also discovered that the protagonists of my fables are the same frogs, mice, sticklebacks, turtles, snails, and butterflies that more than three-quarters of a century ago lived in my room. And even the paper landscapes they now inhabit are identical to the ones I used to build with real sand, pebbles, moss, and water."

Each of Lionni's books is imbued with a dreamy ardor, the glowing images and measured text paying homage to everyday beauties, to light and to life. In *Frederick,* for instance, an aspiring poet field mouse has stored away the memories of colors and the cadences of verse to sustain his family throughout a winter of cold and hunger. The little bird who is the central figure in *Tico and the Golden Wings* dispenses his gilded feathers to assuage loss: "I gave my golden feathers away," Tico explains, "and . . . I bought many presents: three new puppets for a poor puppeteer, a spinning wheel to spin the yarn for an old woman's shawl, a compass for a fisherman who got lost at sea. . . ." And the murine protagonist of *Alexander and the Wind-Up Mouse* ventures deep into an enchanted garden in order to transform and rescue a beloved friend. Lionni's heroes and heroines are, one and all, rooted in open-heartedness and generosity—traits that should amplify every child's sense of what is right with the world.

Today, Lionni, who spent his young manhood in Italy (he fled the Fascists for America in 1939), divides his time between a New York City apartment and a 17th-century farmhouse in Tuscany. Many of his children's books have taken shape on sunny afternoons in an Italian studio. In that world, where bees drone, geraniums bloom and lizards skitter across stone paths, Lionni's dreams have transmogrified into timeless picture stories.

Vivian Gussin Paley

SOURCE: "The Mouse That Roared," in *School Library Journal,* Vol. 46, No. 1, January, 2000, pp.46-9.

"Mrs. Paley? It's me, Reeny. Did you hear? Leo Lionni died. Grandma saw it in the newspaper. Isn't it awful? Remember that time in kindergarten? Remember Frederick?"

Reeny is a fifth grader now. But when she was in my kindergarten, she fell in love with a mouse named Frederick and made us think about him and his creator, as if nothing else mattered. From *Frederick,* we went on to *Tico and the Golden Wings, Cornelius,* and *Swimmy,* until we had read every Leo Lionni book in our school library—14 in all.

Though reading them was never enough. We talked them through and acted them out; we copied them onto huge posters that encircled the room and spilled out into the hallway.

Reeny called it "the time of Leo Lionni." But looking back, it seems like a dream.

"What will happen to Leo Lionni when we're gone?" the children had anguished, surveying their extravagant paintings on the walls. Our room had become a private sanctuary of Leo Lionni characters and landscapes known, we thought, only unto us. "Once upon a time, uh-huh uh-huh, there was a mouse named Frederick, uh-huh uh-huh," Reeny had chanted, crayoning the perfect shade of brown for Frederick and for herself. "This brown mouse I'm drawing is Frederick," she told us every day, and, "This brown girl that's dancing is me," she trilled on, taping the figures to the wall.

Remembering the events of that incredible year, my last in the classroom, it's hard to believe that five years have passed. "I'm so glad you called, Reeny. You were the first one I thought of when I read about Leo Lionni."

"And then you thought about Tico, right?" Who but Reeny would remember my disappointment in the fate of Leo Lionni's bird with the golden wings? How I longed for Tico to keep his remarkable gift instead of replacing each feather of gold with a black one to placate his jealous flock. Five-year-old Reeny understood my lament, even as she argued that Tico must conform or lose his friends.

Were Tico's friends just being mean? we had wondered. Or was it Tico who was selfish? Why didn't Frederick have to conform? He let his companions do the work while he dreamed of words and colors. And what of Cornelius? Was he simply a show-off or someone of exceptional vision?

Leo Lionni's animal fables pierced to the heart of what concerned us most: What is mine to decide and what decisions belong to the group? Why do fairness and friendship intersect in such puzzling ways, until we can hardly tell which course of action will make us happy? Is conformity required in order to be loved by the flock?

But do young children really ponder such matters? Uh-huh uh-huh, we discovered, indulging ourselves in the layers of meaning on every page. We could not simply read about Frederick and Tico and Swimmy and Cornelius; had this been the limit of our involvement, their secrets and ours would not have been uncovered. Leo Lionni understood this. "Study my illustrations and act out the words," he seemed to be telling us.

"Carve a path into each picture and into every character. Only then will my dilemmas become yours and yours become mine."

A quick perusal was never enough for us. We began with *Frederick,* reading the book over and over, acting out the story of a poet mouse and his somewhat ambivalent community, rehearsing their joys and sorrows until we could explain something new about ourselves to one another.

And, a week or so later, when we felt we could leave *Frederick,* the process would begin again with another book and then another. Before we knew what was happening, a whole year with Leo Lionni was a necessity, since every previous character had to comment on the doings of all those to come. We could no sooner put Leo Lionni away than dismiss a friend whom we were just beginning to understand.

A college professor of mine felt the same way about Plato, that a year was barely time enough to get to know the Socratic dialogues. If only we had been able to act them out, we might have reached the point where the chanting begins: Once upon a time, uh-huh uh-huh, there was a man named Socrates, uh-huh uh-huh.

Reeny breaks into my reverie. "I told Mrs. Ruperal-Sen about Leo Lionni. Did you know she's still the teacher in our old room? And guess what? Some of our posters are hanging up. She even put them in frames. Tico is there and Frederick and . . . " Reeny begins the delicious repetition of names, something we often did at the lunch table, tapping out the rhythm. "Fre-da-rick is number one, Tee-ee-co is number two, Swi-a-mee is number three. . . . "

Reeny pauses and takes a deep breath. "I miss Leo Lionni," she whispers. "I miss *us* with Leo Lionni."

"So do I." My eyes blink away the tears. "He was very old, you know. He'd been sick for a long time." There is no response. "Are you okay, Reeny?"

"I was just thinking," she says. "Frederick won't know about Leo Lionni. Of course not. The words and pictures, that's what he knows. That brown color, do you remember? And Frederick's eyes, the way they looked at you? And those stones, so soft and warm."

Her voice is soft and warm. I had forgotten how quickly Reeny was able to arrive at a new place and bring me with her. "How about Tico?" I say. "Has Tico ever forgiven Mr. Lionni for making him give away his golden feathers?"

"*Leo* Lionni," Reeny hastens to correct me. He was, of course, always Leo Lionni. No other name would do. "Here's what I think about Tico," Reeny tells me, as seriously as when she was in kindergarten. "Leo Lionni really did change his mind about Tico. That's why he wrote **Cornelius.** He lets him be completely different from the other crocodiles, standing up straight and all, even if they don't like it and are mean to him."

"Okay, but Tico is still in a bind."

"No wait!" she shouts into the phone. "No, see, like Cornelius gets hold of Tico and tells him not to be scared of what people say. You know, like, keep your golden wings, man, if that's what you want."

The Leo Lionni magic is still here. I am tempted to reveal to her that I wrote a book about the year of Leo Lionni, but decide against it. Let Reeny remember Leo Lionni in her own way. Let his characters continue to talk to her and to each other whenever she comes across them. They will always have something new to say to Reeny, her classmates, and to me. When you are lucky enough to spend a year getting to know certain people, they remain part of you forever.

However, I do tell Reeny one thing about Leo Lionni that makes her whoop with joy. "The year after our kindergarten class I met Leo Lionni."

"Really?" Reeny asks. "You talked to him, actually?"

"I told him that we were always wondering, in our class, which character *he* is, of all those he created. I said that most of us figured him to be Frederick, but a few decided he must be Cornelius."

"Did he tell you?" She is holding her breath, almost afraid to speak.

"I visited him in New York. He reached into a pile of his paperbacks and pulled out a copy of **Swimmy.** Then he took a brown crayon and circled Swimmy, a big circle with a line going down the page. At the end of the line he printed 'ME.' That's who Leo Lionni is."

"None of us thought Swimmy," Reeny declares. "But we should have, don't you see? Because we were like those other little fish. I mean, we surrounded him all the time. He took us everywhere with him. He made us like the big, big fish—together and stronger." She gives a triumphant laugh. "Yes, of course, he hasta be Swimmy."

Steven Heller

SOURCE: "Tribute: Leo Lionni, 1910-1999," in *Print,* Vol. 54, No. 3, May/June, 2000, pp. 26-30.

Shortly after Leo Lionni's 87th birthday in 1997, he lost the ability to work. And work is what kept Lionni alive. Despite having been diagnosed with Parkinson's disease 15 years earlier, he had continued to draw, paint, lecture, write, and play keyboard. At an age when younger men in better health had already retired, he was more determined than ever to practice his art. During those years, he created several children's books, designed huge iron sculptures, organized a major retrospective exhibition (with catalog), and wrote a critically admired memoir, **Between Worlds.**

When I last saw him, at his birthday celebration, which coincided with the publication of his memoir, he regaled his guests not with stories of the past, but with plans for the future. A few months later, the disease took over; two years later, in October 1999, he was gone.

Leonard "Leo" Lionni, one of the great graphic designers of the last century, was born in Holland in 1910. His father, an Italian Jew, was a master diamond-cutter; his Dutch-born mother was an opera singer. Lionni's Uncle Piet, an architect, gave him his first set of drafting tools, while two other uncles, both collectors of modern art, inspired him with their holdings. One of them, in fact, hung a Marc Chagall painting directly outside the boy's bedroom.

Lionni studied arts and crafts in primary school and was permitted to draw the plaster casts at the Rijksmuseum, where he was able to absorb Rembrandt,

Van Gogh, and Mondrian. He later studied architecture and music, which he enjoyed equally. About his passion for the arts, he poetically explained that they were "one big mood to me." At age 14, he briefly lived in Philadelphia, where his father had secured a job with the Atlantic Richfield Company. A year later, he moved to Genoa, Italy, where he attended a commercial high school and learned Italian. At 16, he met Nora Maffi; they were married two years later, a union that lasted 69 years.

Lionni attended the University of Genoa, where he received a doctoral degree in economics. But art was his passion. He began his career in Italy as a Futurist-inspired painter and as architecture critic for the magazine *Casabella*. F. T. Marinetti, leader of the Futurist movement, briefly took Lionni under his wing. It was also at this time that Lionni briefly began creating advertisements for Italian business concerns. But just prior to the start of World War II in 1939, he returned to Philadelphia, this time with his wife and two sons, to become a designer for N. W. Ayer under art director Charles Coiner.

Lionni's early jobs in the U.S. included art-directing advertisements for *Ladies' Home Journal*, Ford Motor Company, and Container Corporation of America; for the last he commissioned illustrations from artists like Willem de Kooning, Alexander Calder, and Fernand Leger. He also worked with a young Andy Warhol on ads for Regal Shoes.

In 1947, Lionni moved to New York, where he opened a small design office. One of his first assignments was art-directing *Fortune* magazine, the jewel in Henry Luce's publishing empire. "Once Luce asked me, 'Why can't *Fortune* be as good-looking as *Harper's Bazaar*?,'" he recalled. "My answer was obvious: 'Because businessmen are not as good-looking as fashion models.'" But Lionni not only altered the magazine's look through changes in format, he also gave unprecedented exposure to illustrators and painters, who created pictorial essays of places and events from around the globe. Moreover, mirroring his own career, he encouraged artists to "do things that they were not accustomed to doing."

As an editorial art director, Lionni eschewed flashy conceptual layouts; he preferred to keep his pages clean and simple. Century Schoolbook was his signature typeface because it was bold yet quiet. The neutral page allowed him to be expansive with art and photography. In fact, he did the photography for many photo essays himself. A magazine format, he felt, was a frame for individual expression—his own and the artists to whom he gave considerable license.

Lionni's other design projects during this period included consultation on the prototype for *Sports Illustrated*; the catalog for the Edward Steichen-curated photography exhibition "The Family of Man" at the Museum of Modern Art (still in print); and the American Pavilion at the 1958 Brussels World's Fair, which addressed the unsolved problems of American society. He was also graphic design consultant to Olivetti in Milan and MoMA in New York. And for a year and a half in 1955-56 he was art director/co-editor of *PRINT*, with editorial dominion over a unique miscellany in the magazine called "The Lion's Tail."

By his 50th birthday, Lionni realized that most of his life had been spent in the service of others. "Everything I had done was a happy compromise that I've never felt ashamed of in the least," he once said. But he was ready to leave the sinecure of Time-Life—and so, having always been a painter and sculptor, he resettled in Tuscany where he began to paint and sculpt huge fantasy plants in brass and iron (which were planted among the natural flora on his hillside property). He also sought a means to combine his applied and fine art into a single occupation. Surprisingly, he discovered that children's books were the perfect metier. Through this genre, he became internationally renowned.

Lionni created a slew of delightful characters, including Frederick, Swimmy, and Little Blue and Little Yellow. More importantly, he introduced a distinctly mature, introspective sensibility to children's literature, while at the same time never talking down to his audience. Such was his influence in the genre that a kindergarten teacher, Vivian Gussin Paley, wrote a book published in 1997 called *The Girl with the Brown Crayon*, about a year with her young students exploring the lessons of Lionni's creations. (Lionni knew nothing about the book until it appeared.)

His first children's book, **Little Blue and Little Yellow,** was the act of a grandfather anxious to quiet down his two rambunctious grandchildren during an hour-long train ride from New York City to his home in Greenwich, Connecticut. It was 1959 and Lionni, then art director of *Fortune*, took a copy of *Life* magazine from his briefcase, turned to a page dominated by the colors blue, yellow, and green, tore them into small circles, and improvised a story.

It was about two circles—Little Blue and Little Yellow—best friends who go hiking together. While playing hide-and-seek in a forest, they lose sight of each other, leading to frantic mutual searching. Then suddenly, behind a large tree, they are reunited. They hug, and in so doing, become Little Green. "The children were transfixed," Lionni recalled in his memoir, "and I noticed that the passengers who were sitting within hearing distance had put down their papers and were listening, too. So for their benefit I had Little Green go to the stock exchange, where he lost all his money. He broke out in yellow and blue tears, and when he was all tears he was Little Blue and Little Yellow again and their stock rose 12 points."

Lionni realized the story's potential and presented a more refined version to Fabio Coen, then the children's books editor for MacDowell Obolensky in New York, who agreed to publish it. "It would take more than one evening with Fabio before I could fully understand how much the simple little tale of two blobs of color would affect my soul, my mind, and my way of life," Lionni wrote about his new career.

In his books for children, Lionni found a key to unlocking decades of his own fears, joys, loves, and insecurities, and presented them through accessible animal metaphors. His children's books, for the most part, are windows into the far reaches of what he called "the soul." In fact, such books as *Little Blue and Little Yellow*; *Swimmy*; *Frederick*; *Nicolas, Where Have You Been?*, and *Matthew's Dream,* among his most popular and introspective, are surreptitious autobiographies. As the psychiatrist Bruno Bettelheim wrote in his introduction to *Frederick's Fables: A Treasury of 16 Favorite Leo Lionni Stories,* "It is the true genius of the artist which permits him to create picture images that convey much deeper meaning than what is overtly depicted."

His most reprinted book, *Swimmy,* is about a diminutive fish who bamboozles its enemy, a giant tuna, by organizing other smaller fish into the shape of a large one. When Swimmy says, "I will be the eye," it is clear that this is also a portrait of the artist as seer. "Anyone who knew of my search for the social justification for making art, for becoming or being an artist," explained Lionni in his memoir, "would immediately have grasped what motivated Swimmy, the first embodiment of my alter ego, to tell his scared little friends to swim together like one big fish." Swimmy's most memorable line in the book—"Each in his own place"—represents Lionni's awareness of the ethical implications of his own place in the society at large. "I think that's certainly the way Leo saw

his role as an artist, seeing for people," says Frances Foster, his editor for many years.

Lionni uses the children's fable to reveal his own and the world's moral complexities. One such, *Tillie and the Wall,* a book about seeing beyond impenetrable barriers, was published in Germany at the time the Berlin Wall came down—and indeed, sold very well there. Lionni was so excited by the potential of this book to impart worldlier ideas that he decided from then on that everything he did had to have some sort of social message. Like James Thurber, Dr. Seuss, and Maurice Sendak, he used the picture book as a kind of soapbox, reaching out to children and their parents alike.

In a review in *The New York Times Book Review* in May 1997, Bruce McCall lauded Lionni's memoir as the story of "a man with exquisitely fine-tuned creative imagination, a clear mind, perfect taste and mercilessly high standards." Lionni had been asked to illustrate this review with an original work, and although there were only a few hours during the day when his hand did not shake uncontrollably, he managed to complete the watercolor picture by deadline with time to spare.

On the night of his 87th birthday celebration, copies of Lionni's books lined the room where the party was held. They were proof to those of us in attendance that he had triumphed, if only temporarily, over the ravages of a relentless disease. But for Lionni they were less a capstone to a career than additional adornments to a lifetime of important work that he believed would continue indefinitely. On that evening, all of us there believed it, too.

TITLE COMMENTARY

CORNELIUS (1983)

Publishers Weekly

SOURCE: A review of *Cornelius*, in *Publishers Weekly,* Vol. 223, No. 13, April 1, 1983, p. 60.

When the crocodiles hatch from their eggs they crawl out onto the beach, but Cornelius exits and stands upright. It's obvious from the start that he's going to be different. He has a wide, crooked, friendly grin and many talents: he can see things very far away and has a talent for spying fish. Angry because his family isn't impressed, he storms off one day and meets a monkey in the jungle. Cornelius's new friend teaches him two tricks: to stand on his head and hang from a tree by his tail. Back home, his family just frowns and says, "So what?" when they see these new feats. But then Cornelius turns around to see them tumbling all over the ground trying to imitate his stunts. Lionni (author of four Caldecott Honor books) supplies colorful collages that are simple yet bold and dramatic. *Cornelius* is a heartwarming fable about an exceptional young fellow with a zest for learning and excelling, setting an example that finally jolts his family out of its scorn and ordinariness. (3-7)

WHO? (1983)

Publishers Weekly

SOURCE: A review of *Who?*, in *Publishers Weekly*, Vol. 224, No. 18, October 28, 1983, p. 70.

Lionni's wordless book is a brand-new idea, as one would expect from the honored artist and innovator. With its three companion volumes small board books, *Who?* contains "pictures to talk about," scintillating color creations in paint and collage, starring two of Lionni's familiar mice. The scenes pose questions but demand no correct answers. They are designed to amuse little children, stimulate their minds and invite thoughts on the illustrations' meanings. In the startoff title, the mice are seen venturing into the outside world for the first time and curious about creatures they meet. More fun and chances to use imagination are in *What?*

COLORS TO TALK ABOUT, LETTERS TO TALK ABOUT, NUMBERS TO TALK ABOUT, AND WORDS TO TALK ABOUT (1985)

Booklist

SOURCE: A review of *Colors to Talk About, Letters to Talk About, Numbers to Talk About,* and *Words to Talk About,* in *Booklist*, Vol. 81, No. 2, June 15, 1985, pp. 1458-59.

Ages 2-4. Lionni's distinctive mice frolic over the pages of these four sturdy board books, which have a fresh, open look and offer early learning opportuni-

ties in an attractive package. Because there is no text to speak of, except in *Words,* discussion will be an important factor in sharing these with toddlers. *Colors* features the mice in assorted shades, one color per page. *Letters* has the mice tumbling over and about the letters of the alphabet, as does *Numbers* (1 through 10). *Words* is the most complicated of the group, with Lionni offering a visual aid; the letters *c, a,* and *r* help form the body of an automobile. With proper adult or parental input, all should be effective; add these to the growing list of attractive baby and toddler books.

FREDERICK'S FABLES: A LEO LIONNI TREASURY OF FAVORITE STORIES (1985)

Publishers Weekly

SOURCE: A review of *Frederick's Fables: A Leo Lionni Treasury of Favorite Stories,* in *Publishers Weekly,* Vol. 228, No. 15, October 11, 1985, pp. 65, 68.

In an introduction by the eminent psychologist Bruno Bettelheim, parents are assured that picture books help little children to make sense of reality. He praises Lionni's "images which in one visual experience convey more than can be said in 1000 words." This is a collection of the artist's famous works, first published individually. Each economical, easily grasped tale is richly illustrated by the artist's color paintings and collages, emphasizing the meaning in the actions of the mouse Frederick and other lovable creatures. There are 13 stories, with variations on Lionni's central theme: the importance of gaining wisdom and of being, always, one's self without forgetting that everyone is part of society and responsible (like clever *Swimmy,* star of his own film) to all others. (3-8)

IT'S MINE! (1986)

Publishers Weekly

SOURCE: A review of *It's Mine!,* in *Publishers Weekly,* Vol. 229, No. 12, March 21, 1986, p. 87.

On an island in the middle of Rainbow Pond live three quarrelsome frogs, who can't seem to get the hang of sharing. They spend all their time bickering over whom the water, earth and air belong to. One day a large toad from the other side of the pond arrives to complain about the chronic shouts of "It's mine! It's mine! It's mine!" that shatter his peace. But the frogs pay him no heed, until a storm brings a flood. Only one rock remains above water, and the frogs take refuge there—sharing the only safe spot. As the water subsides they realize it isn't a rock they are huddled on—it is the toad. He has, of course, taught them the lesson they needed; from that day on they realize that everything around them is "ours." Characteristically, Lionni gets his message across through simple text and bright collage illustrations. Not an especially imaginative fable, but certainly an effective one. (3-6)

Bulletin of the Center for Children's Books

SOURCE: A review of *It's Mine!*, in *Bulletin of the Center for Children's Books*, Vol. 39, No. 8, April, 1986, p. 152.

Lionni has always been an effective creator of collage illustrations, and his use of color and composition is distinctively recognizable, with cool hues, contrasting shapes, and mottled or marble effects. His story is less impressive, being adequately told but laden less with originality than with didactic message. Three frogs argue about ownership of everything until a natural catastrophe brings them together and changes their competitive claims of "It's mine!" to a placid, communal, "It's ours!"

Ilene Cooper

SOURCE: A review of *It's Mine!*, in *Booklist*, Vol. 82, No. 17, May 1, 1986, p. 1314.

Ages 4-6. The three frogs who live on an island in Rainbow Pond—Milton, Rupert, and Lydia—quarrel all day long, frequently shouting "It's mine!" One day, a large mossy-colored toad comes to tell them that their bickering over silly things like who owns the air or sea must stop. But after the toad leaves, the fights and taunts begin again. Suddenly, a storm comes up, and their island begins sinking into the water. Soon they are all clinging to the one rock that is left. When the rain stops, they see they have been saved by sitting atop the toad. Grateful, the frogs realize that sharing is better than sniping at each other and that *mine* does not sound nearly as nice as *ours*. Adults may find this didactic, but for little ones new to the concept of sharing, this hits home. The attractive collage artwork, typically Lionni, is in appropriate shades of greens and browns with an oversize format that lends itself to story hours.

NICOLAS, WHERE HAVE YOU BEEN? (1987)

Publishers Weekly

SOURCE: A review of *Nicolas, Where Have You Been?*, in *Publishers Weekly*, Vol. 231, No. 18, May 8, 1987, p. 69.

When the field mice go to the berry patch, they can't find juicy red ones—the birds got there first, and this makes the mice mad. So mad, in fact, that they decide they don't like birds. And that opinion is reinforced when Nicolas is kidnapped, clasped in the claws of a big ugly bird. He struggles and falls into a nest with three little birds in it, and finds that he likes their stories and the red berries their mother brings for him. One day he wakes up alone; all his friends have flown away. He climbs down from his high residence, rejoins the other mice and tells them his story, and they agree: "One bad bird doesn't make a flock." Lionni's pristine work corresponds to the early reader's development. He creates a world of adventure and consequence from a wondrously minimal set of objects and words. Ages 3-8.

Betsy Hearne

SOURCE: A review of *Nicolas, Where Have You Been?*, in *Bulletin of the Center for Children's Books*, Vol. 40, No. 11, July-August, 1987, p. 214.

In what could best be described as an anti-war fable, Lionni depicts the adventures of a gray mouse, Nicolas, who protests the Great Meadow birds' appropriating all the best berries ("Down with the birds!"). Shortly thereafter, Nicolas is snatched up by a predatory bird, only to be dropped into the nest of a mother bird that feeds him along with her own brood. After the birds leave their nest, Nicolas returns to his own species with news of the birds' benevolence, which they prove by appearing with ripe berries ("One bad bird doesn't make a flock"). The book is beautifully designed and illustrated with Lionni's signature collage art, richly textured and vividly patterned. The story is more contrived than clever, but the dramatic graphics sustain the message better than lesser pictures might. Pages like the one where the angry mice imagine themselves killing birds against a black background render these compositions fresher than some of Lionni's other recent books, though the effect is ultimately didactic.

Mary Beth Burgoyne

SOURCE: A review of *Nicolas, Where Have You Been?*, in *School Library Journal*, Vol. 34, No. 1, September, 1987, p. 166.

K-Gr 3—The mice community is angered by the birds who continually pick the sweetest berries, while the mice are left with the unripened ones. When Nicolas goes in search of a berry patch unscathed by birds, he is snatched up by a large black bird, falls into a nest sheltering three baby birds, becomes friendly with them, and finally returns to his fellow mice, telling them of the good deeds of the bird family. The large white pages are filled with Lionni's marbleized, textured, and color paper collages. The green foliage provides a satisfying brightness to the grays, browns, and blacks. His mice and birds are well developed and multi-dimensional with their sharp-lined shapes and body parts. Facial expressions of anger and confusion are particularly effective. The text is composed of brief sentences that aptly support each page of action. The story is a little heavy-handed in its message (i.e., the final scene in which one mouse says, "One bad bird doesn't make a flock")—a saccharine ending to an otherwise delightful story. The book has potential for prompting classroom discussions.

📖 *SIX CROWS* (1988)

Publishers Weekly

SOURCE: A review of *Six Crows*, in *Publishers Weekly*, Vol. 233, No. 4, January 29, 1988, p. 429.

A war of scarecrows begins when a farmer tries to banish six crows from his wheatfield. He creates a horned, menacing figure; the crows fight back by building a giant, ugly bird to hover above the fields like a shadow. The owl intervenes and convinces both sides to talk peace. This moral tale eloquently depicts the pointlessness and futility of the ancient war of fear. As always, Lionni's characteristic primitive art and abstract forms appeal both to the naive perceptions of children and the universal sensitivity of all readers. Ages 3-7.

Booklist

SOURCE: A review of *Six Crows: A Fable,* in *Booklist,* Vol. 84, No. 19, June 1, 1988, p. 1676.

Ages 4-8. The art of compromise and the lesson that all creatures need each other are the concepts adroitly conveyed by renowned writer/illustrator Lionni in his latest fable. Set in a mountain valley where life's only annoyance is six noisy crows, Lionni's tale is told both through the sparingly worded text and the artist's signature collages, which boldly utilize most of the double-page spreads. As the farmer tries to frighten the crows away from his wheat field by building increasingly intimidating scarecrows, the creatures fight back by creating their own bird kite with bark and leaves, so ferocious looking that they soon have the farmer on the run. It is only when the wise old owl advises the adversaries to talk things out that the conflict is resolved to both parties' satisfaction. This enduring theme has a moral for young and old alike, making it a perfect choice for parents to share with their children.

Amy Spaulding

SOURCE: A review of *Six Crows,* in *School Library Journal,* Vol. 34, No. 10, June-July, 1988, p. 92.

PreS-Gr 2—Lionni's story about a farmer facing marauding crows teaches a lesson about making peace in the midst of escalating conflict. The farmer is enraged by six noisy crows who keep eating the wheat in his field, and he builds a scarecrow to frighten them off. The crows are disturbed, but not willing to give up, so they design a kite to scare off the monster. The farmer then builds a bigger and fiercer scarecrow, and the crows a fiercer kite. Meanwhile, the wheat is dying from neglect. A watching owl manages to bring the two sides together, and they work out a compromise. This brief, simple story works on a literal level as well as on a metaphoric one. It is illustrated with Lionni's usual handsome, colorful collages which project well for reading aloud to groups.

📖 *TILLIE AND THE WALL* (1989)

Publishers Weekly

SOURCE: A review of *Tillie and the Wall,* in *Publishers Weekly,* Vol. 235, No. 2, January 13, 1989, p. 88.

Some mice take the wall for granted, never speaking of it—in fact, never even seeing it. But for Tillie, a mouse who believes that the grass (and scenery) on the other side must be not only greener, but fantastic and beautiful, the lure of the wall proves impossible to ignore. When her glorious visions of the other side prove too much to bear, Tillie tunnels under. Her reception on the other side is a warm one—identical mice to the ones left behind greet her, and then follow her back home. There, she is a hero, and forever after the mice pass freely back and forth from one side to the other. The mice will look familiar to readers of Lionni's other works, but this story—like all his others—never falls to formula. His philosophical playfulness is in full force, and Tillie's visitation may be, after all, a circular one, with ambiguities to pore over and be delighted by. It's a journey worth repeating. Ages 3-7.

Martha Rosen

SOURCE: A review of *Tillie and the Wall,* in *School Library Journal,* Vol. 35, No. 8, April, 1989, pp. 85-6.

K-Gr2—It is reassuring to be in the company of Lionni's mice again. These inquisitive, clever animal characters prove once more the value of the fable as storytelling device, especially when it is simply told and beautifully illustrated. Tillie, one of a band of mice, is confined, not unhappily, to a meadow behind a long, high wall. Although there is companionship and plenty to eat, Tillie longs to discover the unknown world beyond the wall. In her reveries she creates an imaginary place peopled with fantastic creatures, giving Lionni an opportunity to display his coloristic artistry. It takes all of Tillie's determination and resourcefulness to overcome the complacency of her companions and eventually to find a way to the other side of the wall. The fact that Tillie is the youngest mouse, and a female, lends substance to the message that strength of character and leadership qualities will surface when a challenge arises. The simplicity of line and shape in the full-color collage illustrations enhance the mood of the text. This integration of art and prose, and the message that both convey, provide children with a superior picture book that can be enjoyed on several levels. Invite Tillie and her friends to join other Lionni favorites on the picture book shelves. As with Lionni's other books, this one should be a perennial favorite for primary grade story hours.

📖 *MATTHEW'S DREAM* (1991)

Kirkus Reviews

SOURCE: A review of *Matthew's Dream,* in *Kirkus Reviews,* Vol. 59, February 1, 1991, p. 183.

A classic Lionni mouse (torn paper, pink ears) visits a museum, dreams about entering the marvelous, varied paintings, and realizes that his destiny is to be an artist. The originality here is in the illustrations, where Lionni deliciously conveys the flavor of several other artists' styles ("One [painting] looked like crusts of pastry, but when he looked more carefully, a mouse emerged") without compromising the unity of his own. An attractive reiteration of an important theme.

Diane Roback and Richard Donahue

SOURCE: A review of *Matthew's Dream,* in *Publishers Weekly,* Vol. 238, No. 10, February 22, 1991, p. 220.

"A couple of mice lived in a dusty attic with their only child." This child is Matthew, and how he achieves success by pursuing his dream forms the basis for one of Lionni's most stylish and endearing works. One day Matthew—whose ambitions until now are "to see the world"—and his class go to the art museum, and Matthew's imagination is forever stirred. ("The world is all here, thought Matthew.") That night the little mouse dreams of swirling colors, and awakes knowing what he wants to be—a painter. With this decision, Matthew suddenly views his environs in a new light; his drab attic corner brightens, he hears new music in old surroundings. Matthew becomes a shining success—"He worked hard and painted large canvases filled with the shapes and colors of joy."

No less a success is the unique work in which this personable mouse stars. Lionni brings his own joyful shapes and colors into play here: his mice enchant in their simplicity; and poised against ample white space, his stunning collages irradiate the pages of this uplifting work. It is easy to see how this art can inspire Matthew—it will surely do the same for countless children. In a classic "less is more" mode, the text is direct yet abundantly meaningful—poetic without becoming sappy. In his gentle, understated—and ultimately moving—fashion, Lionni has spoken volumes about the artist, his world and his work. Ages 4-8.

Zena Sutherland

SOURCE: A review of *Matthew's Dream,* in *The Bulletin of the Center for Children's Books,* Vol. 44, No. 7, March, 1991, p. 169.

Gr. K-2. Bright, strong colors in a mixed-media (collage and paint) picture book tell the story of a mouse, the only child of a pair of attic-dwellers.

Taken to an art museum with his class, Matthew is entranced; later, back in the dusty attic, he realizes that the pictures he has seen have helped him find line and shape and color even in the attic. That's how Matthew becomes a painter and eventually gains fame. The handsome pictures and the enticing combination of an animal hero and an appreciation of artistic creativity has a strong appeal.

Anna Biagioni Hart

SOURCE: A review of *Matthew's Dream,* in *School Library Journal,* Vol. 37, No. 4, April, 1991, pp. 97-8.

K-Gr 3—A classy, classic Lionni mouse fable with themes like those in *Frederick* (1967) or *Geraldine, the Music Mouse* (1979, both Pantheon). Here, too, the joy, exuberance, and service of an artist's calling are made clear to the very young. A poor mouse couple lives in a dusty attic where they have great hopes for their only child. When they ask Matthew what he wants to be, however, he is uncertain—until the day his class goes on a field trip to the art museum. The paintings make a profound impression on him, and they clarify his vocation; he is to be an artist. In one memorable turn of a page readers see just what the tiny dreamer has seen, as Matthew's imagination transforms the dreary junk of his attic corner into a Picasso-like work of art. Both the torn paper collages and the reproductions of museum "*mouse*terpieces" in various painting styles invite children to look and look again. A strong, fine book by an illustrator who, like Matthew, paints canvases "filled with the shapes and colors of joy."

A BUSY YEAR (1992)

Kirkus Reviews

SOURCE: A review of *A Busy Year,* in *Kirkus Reviews,* Vol. 60, April 15, 1992, p. 547.

This tall, thin book opens to nearly square spreads that nicely accommodate collages of two mice and their friend, a fruit tree that talks. Each month, the mice notice how she changes—buds swell, blooms open, leaves fall—as they also learn about her needs (there's even a bit of drama when they put out a threatening fire). It's a genial tale, visually strong—Lionni, thrice a Caldecott Honor winner, has a sense of design that's unabated—but a bit weak on logic: the big, red fruit doesn't grow all summer; it just appears in September, ripe. Maybe the stork brought it. Still, nice.

Publishers Weekly

SOURCE: A review of *A Busy Year,* in *Publishers Weekly,* Vol. 239, No. 19, April 20, 1992, p. 54.

In this deceptively simple tale, Lionni characteristically hides a moral from which kids of all ages will profit. On New Year's Day, twin mice Willie and Winnie discover a "snowmouse" that appears to be holding a broom. But a voice announces, "I am not a broom. I am Woody the tree!" So begins a momentous friendship. The twins visit Woody each month and are thrilled when small buds and then leaves and blossoms appear on her branches. In June Woody confesses that she fears summertime, when people's carelessness with cigarettes and campfires causes many trees to die. Ready with a water hose, the twins protect their pal when a forest fire breaks out in July. After her leaves blow to the ground, the caring duo brings Christmas gifts to a cheerfully decorated Woody, and all are "happy and ready for another busy year." With Lionni's zingy, inimitable art, this tall, paper-over-board book is a welcome addition to his distinguished oeuvre. Ages 3-7.

Nancy Seiner

SOURCE: A review of *A Busy Year,* in *School Library Journal,* Vol. 38, No. 6, June, 1992, p. 98.

PreS—Once again, Lionni's mice discover some of nature's secrets. This time, a friendly tree teaches two young creatures about her annual cycle of growth, decline, and dormancy. On a snowy January first, Willie and Winnie mistake the bare branches for a snow-mouse's broom. They visit their friend monthly, seeing buds, then flowers, leaves, and finally fruit. In October, they mourn her loss of leaves. "'Don't worry,'" explains Woody. "'Next year I'll have new ones. You'll see!'" Only November's activities seem forced; the mice worry about a Christmas gift for the tree. In December, they decorate her boughs with festive colored balls and bring gifts of fertilizer and flower seeds. Illustrations are typical Lionni, with simplified collage figures of torn and cut papers, some plain and some patterned, placed against a background that changes color with the season. Although the tree remains rooted, the mice scurry about, climbing it to pick fruit, aiming a hose when it catches fire, and jumping to catch falling leaves. The lack of irrelevant background details makes the tree's changes clear and impressive. An enjoyable book that will help children become aware of the natural world around them.

Kay Weisman

SOURCE: A review of *A Busy Year,* in *Booklist,* Vol. 89, No. 1, September 1, 1992, p. 67.

Ages 3-6. Out for a walk in the January snow, mouse twins Willie and Winnie meet Woody, a talking tree. The three develop a rapport, and the twins visit their friend during each succeeding month. In May, Woody blossoms; the twins save her from a fire in July; in September, they harvest her juicy fruit; and, in December, they deliver Christmas gifts to Woody—manure, bulbs, and seeds. In the hands of a less capable illustrator, this might have become still another anthropomorphic season book. Fortunately, Lionni's appealing collages (done in a variety of color schemes appropriate to each month) make this an attractive choice that will be useful for story hours and popular with Lionni fans.

MR. McMOUSE (1992)

Kirkus Reviews

SOURCE: A review of *Mr. McMouse,* in *Kirkus Reviews,* Vol. 60, September 15, 1992, p. 1190.

When Timothy (a typical Lionni mouse) looks in the mirror, he's startled to see a stranger in black who looks a lot like a businessman with a tail. So he leaves his city home and sets out for the country, where the mice are afraid of him until friendly Spinny names him Mr. McMouse. It's explained that he'll have to take some teats if he wants a "field mouse license": berry-eating, running, and tree-climbing. He fails the first two, heroically saves Spinny when a cat interrupts the third, and is awarded an Honorary License. Lionni's collages are clean and handsomely composed, and his expressive figures are appealing, but the story here—beginning as a rather adult parable, then degenerating into formula—lacks direction. Still, it's told with style and good humor, while the art of this three-time Caldecott Honor winner is always of interest.

Publishers Weekly

SOURCE: A review of *Mr. McMouse,* in *Publishers Weekly,* Vol. 239, No. 47, October 26, 1992, p. 69.

Life as a happy city mouse ends abruptly for Timothy when he looks into the mirror one morning and sees "a strange creature dressed in black staring at

him." His brown ears and furry gray body have been replaced by a human-like form sporting a man's hat and coat; only a long tail links him to his original incarnation. Fleeing the city in panic, Timothy seeks refuge in a typically quixotic, Lionni-esque countryside adorned with marbleized trees and paisley boulders. A band of field mice, reassured by the hero's tail, dub him Mr. McMouse and offer membership in their group—if he can pass a battery of tests and earn a field mouse license. The artist's trademark cut paper collages colorfully and succinctly illustrate Timothy's quest, though unfortunately the narrative here is a minor one. This slight tale's opening, in particular, may confuse little ones—why does Timothy change, and exactly who or what does he become? Still, Lionni (*Swimmy*; *A Busy Year*) provides Timothy with a hero's ending and weaves a gentle message of self-awareness into this offbeat tale. Ages 2-6.

AN EXTRAORDINARY EGG (1994)

Kirkus Reviews

SOURCE: A review of *An Extraordinary Egg,* in *Kirkus Reviews,* Vol. 62, April 15, 1994, p. 559.

Jessica is a fancier of stones and pebbles, but her friends Marilyn and August, also frogs, don't share her enthusiasm until she turns up with what Marilyn, "who knew everything about everything," identifies as a "chicken egg." The little "chicken" that hatches is congenial and loves the water; once she even saves Jessica when she gets entangled in water weeds. Then the "chicken's" mother turns up, greeting her baby, accurately, as "my sweet little alligator." With the frogs urging them to visit soon, the alligators depart amiably, leaving the trio to laugh at the "chicken" who called her baby an alligator: "What a silly thing to say!" Lionni's mixed-media art (soft, delicately stylized settings in subtle colors, ample white space, appealing collage-like figures) is particularly felicitous, and kids will love identifying the little alligator and laughing at the frogs' mistakes. Just the thing to lighten up a picture-book hour. Starred Review.

Elizabeth Bush

SOURCE: A review of *An Extraordinary Egg,* in *The Bulletin of the Center for Children's Books,* Vol. 47, No. 10, June, 1994, pp. 326-27.

Jessica the frog is the latest addition to Lionni's gallery of pint-sized visionaries and adventurers. The eccentric in a frog trio on Pebble Island, Jessica is "always somewhere else." Naturally it is she who brings home a remarkable trophy from a day's exploration—a beautiful object, "round like the full moon on a midsummer's night." Marilyn arrogantly states, "It's an egg. A chicken egg." Deferring to Marilyn's reputation for superior wisdom, Jessica and August agree that the creature who breaks out of the shell is indeed a chicken, although viewers will plainly see it is an alligator. Jessica and the hatchling become inseparable friends until "little chicken" is reunited with her mother. Jessica reports to the frogs that mother chicken called her baby "my sweet little alligator," and the three friends can't control their laughter. Lionni's signature artwork—cool blue and gray palette, streamlined and bright-eyed animals—is comfortably familiar to old fans. And the broad humor of the simple fable should delight any child who enjoys being in on a joke.

Jane Marino

SOURCE: A review of *An Extraordinary Egg*, in *School Library Journal,* Vol. 40, No. 6, June, 1994, p. 109.

K-Gr 3—A fable about friendship with a touch of mistaken identity. One day Jessica, an adventuresome young frog, rolls home a "beautiful stone" to show her two froggy friends. Marilyn, who knows "everything about everything," states with absolute certainty that it's a chicken egg. So when an alligator hatches, the three frogs are surprised and delighted with how well their "chicken" can swim. When she saves Jessica from drowning in a tangle of weeds, the two become inseparable friends. One day, a bird lands to lead the alligator back to her mother; Jessica accepts this with equanimity. She is a heroine whose wonder at the world and loyalty to her friends rank her with such erstwhile heroes as Joyce's "Bently" and Dr. Seuss's "Horton." But while those two stalwarts protect and cherish their eggs before they hatch, most of this story centers on the relationship that develops after the little alligator springs from its shell. Lionni's understated text perfectly complements his signature illustrations, which are a skillful combination of collage, crayon, and watercolors. An *eggs*-traordinary treat from a master storyteller.

Carolyn Phelan

SOURCE: A review of *An Extraordinary Egg,* in *Booklist,* Vol. 90, Nos. 19-20, June 1, 1994, p. 1841.

Ages 4-7. Jessica the frog discovers an egg, which her frog friend Marilyn identifies as a chicken egg. A baby alligator hatches out, but the frogs continue to call it a chicken. When Jessica helps the "little chicken" find his mother, she's amused when the mother calls him "my sweet little alligator." It's not much of a story, but pre-schoolers who are old enough to know their alligators from their chickens will enjoy being in on the joke. Lionni's collages of cut papers, shaded with crayons or oil pastels, make distinctive double-page spreads that show up well at a distance, and the text is clearly written. A mildly appealing animal tale for Lionni fans.

LITTLE BLUE AND LITTLE YELLOW (REPRINT, 1995)

Carol Otis Hurst

SOURCE: A review of *Little Blue and Little Yellow,* in *Teaching PreK-8,* Vol. 26, No. 2, October, 1995, p. 80.

It's so nice to meet old friends again and this month, William Morrow has made that possible with the first paperback edition of **Little Blue and Little Yellow** by Leo Lionni (Mulberry, 1995). According to *Books in Print,* it never did go out of print in hardbound, but it sure has been well hidden! Now, at last, this simple story which may be a fable, or may be an allegory, or may be just a simple story of friendship between two blobs of color—is readily available.

Most of you know that the book was created when Leo Lionni was on a long train trip with two very bored grandchildren. They asked him to draw them a story, but the only paper he had was in the magazine he was reading, so he tore out circles of color from the magazine and manipulated them on the table top to tell a story. Hurray for ingenuity!

After everyone has enjoyed hearing the story, have the kids retell it in a variety of ways. For instance, the kids can try using plastic gels or circles of color from transparencies to tell the story on the overhead. Or, they can fill cupcake tins with tempera paint and use that for their retelling. They can even put the gels over flashlights and see Little Blue and Little Yellow take on the qualities of light. With a little imagination it can be a costumed drama.

Go from **Little Blue and Little Yellow** to other books of color, or if you want to dig a little deeper and talk about prejudice, racism or fears of being different, this one little book can set off a year of study.

📖 BETWEEN WORLDS: THE AUTOBIOGRAPHY OF LEO LIONNI (1997)

Publishers Weekly

SOURCE: A review of *Between Worlds: The Autobiography of Leo Lionni,* in *Publishers Weekly,* Vol. 244, No. 7, February 17, 1997, p. 202.

When at 49 (in 1959), Lionni resigned as design director for the Time Inc. magazine *Fortune,* an executive asked, "You mean to say that you are not happy here?" Lionni insisted that he was. "Then why are you leaving?" "Because," he explained, "I don't want to be that happy." Lionni did not want to remain in a vocational groove, even a lucrative one. Set free, he could divide his life between the milieu of his youth and the U.S., in which he found himself professionally, and practice all the arts in which he had already sampled success. Further, he could follow his imaginative illustrated book for children, **Little Blue and Little Yellow,** with a new one each year. (Some would be instant classics, selling in the millions in many languages.) Of Dutch and Italian Jewish ancestry—his family fled Italian fascism for America in 1939—he turned his gift for images and languages into rewarding careers in advertising, design, editing, writing and the plastic and graphic arts. Lionni developed the prewar "Never underestimate the power of a woman" advertising campaign and writes (in a book composed before Parkinson's disease limited the use of his fingers) with an ear for metaphor and an artist's vision that charm the reader from the start. Despite his apology, "My memory always seems to walk in when the show has already started," the reader encounters hard-to-forget relatives and friends here and experiences with Lionni his triumphs and tragedies. His narrative emphasizes the earlier years, for, Lionni writes, "The sixties, seventies, and eighties, once a future, are now zooming by, flickering like . . . abandoned railway stations in the void of night." Seventy-five photos and drawings, plus 24 pages in color illustrating his work in many media, add a visual dimension to the memoir.

Hazel Rochman

SOURCE: A review of *Between Worlds: The Autobiography of Leo Lionni,* in *Booklist,* Vol. 93, No. 13, March 1, 1997, p. 1103.

As a grandfather at age 49, Lionni first began writing and illustrating his children's fables, including his Caldecott Honor Books *Inch by Inch* (1960) and *Swimmy* (1963). He also had a long, illustrious career as a painter, sculptor, critic, and designer in art and commerce. The title of his modest, eloquent autobiography, published in his eighty-seventh year, refers to the many worlds he has spanned in work, time, and geography. Born in Holland, he left Europe on the eve of the Nazi invasion and became a naturalized U.S. citizen. He was art director for Ford, General Electric, and *Ladies' Home Journal;* he designed the book **Family of Man** (1955), designed *Sports Illustrated,* and much more. He includes many photos and pictures that show his work and his friendships with the famous artists of his time. Then in 1959, he quit his job at *Fortune* magazine and returned to Europe. His tone is upbeat, honest, unsentimental, reflecting the strength he finds in his displacement, whether he is an adult writing for children, a Bohemian artist in a gray flannel suit, or a European not quite comfortable on Madison Avenue.

Vivian Gussin Paley

SOURCE: A review of *Between Worlds: The Autobiography of Leo Lionni,* in *The Nation,* Vol. 264, No. 21, June 2, 1997, pp. 25-6.

"A child's world is a world of parts, of minutiae," Leo Lionni tells us early in his beautifully written memoir. "For children, still unaware of the weight of meaning, things exist for the mere pleasure of being what they are . . . . When for the first time from the top of a dune they see the ocean, they run to the water's edge to pick up a shell." Then, if the child grows up to become a Leo Lionni, artist and writer, art director and graphic designer extraordinaire, he will spend the rest of his life inventing new ways to take the measure and pleasure of the parts until their secrets are revealed to all of us.

For Lionni, nowhere have all these visions come together in closer harmony than in his stunningly illustrated animal fables, whose characters act out the great issues of life: those conflicts between self and community, between things as they are and that which must be changed. The author can no more avoid the "weight of meaning" in his fables than in **Between Worlds,** an account of his struggle to find place and purpose in his transition from the Old World to the New.

Lionni quickly establishes a direct path from that child on the beach to the maturing artist, looking at himself in countless mirrors to see who he has become. Such is the continuity he draws between his life and his art, I cannot help but imagine him as one or another of his own characters from inside the world of his fables.

Born in 1910 into an Amsterdam household of modest means but expansive good taste and talent, it was his great fortune to begin life at a time when it was still considered proper to grow up slowly, discovering the world first from the child's perspective. There was much to wonder about: The family enjoyed a variety of eccentricities and passions, adapting easily to new languages and cultures as they moved from city to city to improve their circumstances. His father, a diamond cutter and accountant of Italian-Jewish birth, was inclined toward the intellectual, and his mother, from a Dutch-Christian working-class family, was a gifted opera singer whose brothers filled the house with works of art.

Indeed, "the Chagall" that hung modestly next to little Leo's attic room had a lifelong effect upon him. "It was altogether another world," as he describes the painting, "where anything could happen and everything was unexpected—a noisy, busy world, close by and touchable. Perhaps it was the secret birthplace of all the stories I ever wrote, painted, or imagined."

But it is Lionni's next memory that strikes my teacherly soul: On the other side of "the Chagall" was my room, my ivory tower, the temple of my aloneness . . . the place where I made things happen. . . . For there, with the miraculous consent of my otherwise fastidious mother, I was allowed to gather and collect the abundant, varied, and often smelly evidence of my vehement passion for nature. It was there that I could observe, unobserved, the metamorphosis of seeds, caterpillars, and tadpoles, and study the etiology of white mice, orange-bellied salamanders, and gray-green sticklebacks. And it was there . . . I would empty my paper bag cornucopias of the driftwood sculptures, the shells, the carcasses of crabs, that I had patiently disentangled from the black garland of algae that lined the ebbing tides.

This then is where the creator of Swimmy and Frederick began, the secrets of Chagall mixing with those brought by the tides, and where he learned to draw at Uncle Piet's drafting table, absorbing the feeling of being an artist, a scientist and a maker of things. The world outside, however, was in political upheaval; individual and collective freedoms were embattled by the forces of fascism and fear. How does the artist who hates cruelty and domination preserve his "temple of aloneness" while responding to the call for action?

Against the backdrop of a Europe in turmoil, assaulted by the folly and fury of new ideologies nurtured in anger, the arts were frantically probing the new frontiers and the new alliances which our elders had envisaged and explored but barely exploited. . . . Everywhere I went I met people . . . who knew how to keep the embers of freedom burning.

His sympathies were with his friends in the underground, in the Communist Party and in splinter left-wing groups, but Italy and Holland were becoming too dangerous for Jews. By the time the Lionnis had escaped to America in 1939, the artist as a man of principle had been tested many times. "I probably owe it to my first encounters with the political realities of Fascism and Nazism that early in my adult life I reached the conviction that all human acts have social and political consequences." To express himself as a socially responsible artist became an overriding concern; to detect the point at which commercial success compromised aesthetic and democratic principles became his measuring stick.

And so we have the young immigrant in his first big job refusing to work on an advertisement that warned the reader of the evils of socialism. Surprisingly, he would be allowed to assert his beliefs and keep the job. No matter how often he rejected the conformity and conservatism of the marketplace, his work was sought after by advertising and publishing giants.

Even so, he became increasingly discontented. "I sensed that never again would I feel the joy that made me jump up and run to Mother yelling, 'Look what I made!' . . . I was longing for the lonely pebble in my hand, the wagging tail, the silent smile, the single stroke of blue." Then, riding on a train with his grandchildren, "a little miracle happened." To entertain the children he began tearing paper into splotches of color, telling a story as he went along. By the end of the day, the game had turned into his first book, *Little Blue and Little Yellow.* At nearly 50, Leo Lionni reinvented himself and went on to write and illustrate twenty-nine more celebrated works for children.

By the time *Swimmy* came along, Lionni was committed to his new role. "Here was *Swimmy,* my first real fable, which in no time became the role model for most of the books that were to follow. It contains all the principles that have guided my feelings, my hands, and my mind through my long career as a children's book author. *Swimmy* . . . led me to consider the making of books as, if not my main activity, one that was no less important than my painting and my newly discovered sculpture."

For a teacher who cannot imagine a classroom of young children without a dozen or more Leo Lionni books readily available for reading aloud, dramatizing and in every possible way absorbing the art-filled pages, our author had climbed the highest mountain.

"Because of my fables," he tells us, "I feel at ease in the worlds of the imaginary." This must be why children step so easily into the distinctive milieu of each of his characters. But perhaps it would be more accurate to say: Because the author feels so at home in the world of the imaginary he has been able to invent his fables. The connections to his own story are inescapable.

"All my fables have the classical structure, and as in Greek drama their protagonists wear the masks of their fates, from the very first gesture when the line of action begins to move inexorably through the pages." I no longer wonder which of his fictional protagonists is Lionni himself; clearly he has played each role in turn.

An autobiography that spans eighty-six years would appear to tell the final chapter, but Leo Lionni, though in fragile health, assures us there are yet new roles he can imagine for himself. This may be the key message of *Between Worlds*: With courage and imagination it is possible at any age to discover new shells on the beach and begin one's story again. We are all of us in some way Frederick, the poet mouse, sitting apart from the crowd, thinking our own thoughts and seeing our own images, in our temple of aloneness.

Roy R. Behrens

SOURCE: "The Lion's Tale," in *Print: America's Graphic Design Magazine*, Vol. 52, No. 1, January, 1998, pp. 28, 219.

At age 77, graphic designer and children's book author Leo Lionni was diagnosed with Parkinson's disease. He responded to the news with characteristic good humor. Because of his tremor, he explained, he would no longer be able to sign copies of his books, but his flamenco guitar playing had improved dramatically.

That wry, self-deprecating humor is also delightfully evident in the opening passage of Lionni's autobiography, in which he imagines his own birth: "It was the fifth of May, 1910, in a bungalow in Watergraafsmeer, a suburb of Amsterdam, when I was suddenly held high, shivering at the center of shifting lights and an explosion of sounds. It had been a hectic, scary day, but, in retrospect, a good one. Two fives and a ten—a small symmetry within the infinity of numbers. Two fives—my hands. Ten, my fingers. I would be making things."

Lionni's father was a diamond cutter, descended from Sephardic Jews; his mother, a non-Jew, was an operatic soprano. A precocious only child, he experienced early childhood as a melange of woeful and funny events: his taciturn grandfather's fondness for gin; the marriage of Uncle Jan to a prostitute from the brothel across the street, whose premarital pregnancy turned out to be a tumor; drawing lessons from his childhood hero, Uncle Piet, who was an architect, oarsman, and playboy; Uncle Willem's elaborate tax dodge of storing his art collection on the walls of relatives' homes, including significant pieces by Klee, Kandinsky, Chagall, Kokoschka, and Mondrian. These tragicomic characters performed before Lionni's eyes like creatures in a giant terrarium, not unlike the little collection of frogs, mice, sticklebacks, turtles, and snails that he kept in his own room. Of these memories, the least comic and most terrifying related to the time when Lionni was 12 and was left with his grandparents in Brussels while his parents emigrated to the U.S. Although he eventually joined them in Philadelphia, the abandonment was "a trauma violent enough to leave permanent scars."

When Lionni was 15, his family moved to Genoa, and Italian became his fifth language. A misfit in that country's school system, he was required to prepare for a career in economics, a subject in which he eventually earned a Ph.D. In 1922, Mussolini had gained control of the government, and while Lionni himself escaped persecution, he recalls street demonstrations by the Black Shirts, book burnings, and the internment of anti-Fascist politicians, such as Fabrizio Maffi, whose daughter Nora (to whom the book is dedicated) became Lionni's wife. In 1938, Lionni, a pregnant Nora, and their first son, Louis Manni (now an architect in Vermont), moved to Zurich and then to the U.S.

In America, Lionni fulfilled his destiny as a maker of things. Though he never formally trained as an artist, he had dabbled in art since childhood, and had worked briefly in Milan as an art director. After arriving in the U.S., where he remained from 1939 to 1960, he gradually became known as an influential art director and graphic designer. He worked initially with Charles Coiner at the N.W. Ayer advertising agency in Philadelphia, where his accounts included Container Corporation of America, Ford Motor Company, General Electric, and *Ladies' Home Journal.* Later, he moved to New York, where he art-directed *Fortune* magazine; designed the museum catalog for the celebrated "Family of Man" photography exhibition at the Museum of Modern Art; worked as design director for Olivetti of America; co-founded the Aspen Design Conference; designed *Sports Illustrated* magazine; and, in the late 1950s, was co-editor and art director of *PRINT,* for which he wrote a column, "The Lion's Tail."

In this vivid albeit fragmented memoir, we also learn about Lionni's impression of Josef Albers, who invited him to teach at the legendary Black Mountain College (where he "grossly overestimated the intellectual level and experience of the students"); the intimidation he faced, as a socialist, during the McCarthy era; his friendships with artists Saul Steinberg, Ben Shahn, Alexander Calder, and Robert Osborn; and the spells of self-doubt and discomfort he felt as an art director because of an internal struggle between two irreconcilable self-images, the impromptu Bohemian artist and the calculating advertising designer: "I hated my gray-flannel suit," he recalls, "my black Madison Avenue tie, my careful haircut."

The great watershed in Lionni's life (he calls it "a little miracle") took place in 1959, when he was 49 years old, as he and two grandchildren, Pippo and Annie, were riding on a commuter train from New York to Connecticut. To entertain the children, he improvised on his briefcase a children's story in which the only characters were abstract scraps of colored paper, torn spontaneously from a magazine. Titled **Little Blue and Little Yellow,** the story launched a new career for him as a prolific creator of children's books. He eventually wrote and illustrated 28, including such favorites as **Swimmy** and **Alexander**

and the Wind-Up Mouse. He and Nora moved back to Italy, where, for nearly four decades since, the range of his work has included drawing, painting, sculpture, printmaking, collage, mosaics, film animation, writing, traveling, and—yes—flamenco guitar.

Which worlds is Leo Lionni between? Judaism and Christianity, socialism and capitalism, business and art, reason and imagination. As the book concludes, he recalls the terrariums of his childhood and discovers a method by which to connect the two worlds of youth and old age: "Not long ago I suddenly realized that the dimensions of my children's books are exactly the same as those of my terrariums . . . . My miniature worlds, whether enclosed in yesterday's walls of glass or in today's cardboard covers, are surprisingly alike. Both are the orderly, predictable alternatives to a chaotic, unmanageable, terrifying universe."

Barbara Bader

SOURCE: A review of *Between Worlds: The Autobiography of Leo Lionni,* in *The Horn Book Magazine,* Vol. 74, No. 3, May-June, 1998, pp. 322-26.

Imagine a triptych. In the center is Leo Lionni's mouse poet Frederick, who soaks up the sun and thinks while the other mice busily store away food for the winter. But unlike Aesop's cautionary grasshopper, who idles away the summer in song and suffers in winter—"sing now and see what it will get you," says the censorious ant—Frederick makes good his claim to be doing work too: storing up colors and words that sustain the mice when their stores of food are gone.

On the left is the young Leo Lionni, naturalist and artist, creating in terrariums "elaborate fictions squeezed into the narrow dimensions of a miniaturized nature"—or, he realizes in later life, the dimensions of his picture books. "Both are the orderly, predictable alternatives to a chaotic, unmanageable, terrifying universe." And: assertions of self.

On the right is Reeny, a little black girl with a brown-like-me crayon in Vivian Paley's University of Chicago Laboratory School kindergarten, who discovers in Frederick—herself: "Because I'm always usually thinking 'bout colors and words the same like him."

Sheer coincidence has brought forth, simultaneously, Lionni's story of his long, inexhaustibly creative life as a graphic designer, art director, design impresario, and pure artist (painter, sculptor, photographer . . .), in which picture books are both incidental and crucial, and Paley's pinpoint narrative of a kindergarten year powered by Lionni picture books, the eighth of her celebrated tales out of school. The timing is accidental; not the reverberations.

Lionni's autobiography is deceptive. Only a handful of pages deal directly with the picture books, yet it takes a keen awareness of the picture books, perhaps, to discern in the iridescent crazy-guilt narrative an underlying, deeply personal story: the idyllic childhood abruptly sundered; the brilliant, captive career, the return, or flight, to pure creativity. There are, of course, signposts.

Leo Lionni was born in Amsterdam in 1910, the son of a Sephardic Jewish diamond cutter turned account—a number-cruncher with dash—and a true-to-life opera singer. Creating his own private worlds or mingling with his fascinating elders, the young Lionni begins his intense involvement with art. From Chagall's "Fiddler on the Roof," one version of which hangs outside his bedroom door, he makes up stories—"the ancestors, no doubt, of all the fables I was to dream, write, and illustrate . . . ." At the nearby Ryksmuseum, he feels the light and space of the Old Masters. The works of Kandinsky, Mondrian, Klee, and other masters of the Modernist Revolution hang on family walls. Then, suddenly, the glass shatters. His parents leave him, with his rich, detached Brussels grandparents, to revive his father's flagging career in America. And for the boy who knew he was going to be an artist, all certainty vanishes.

For the next seventeen years Lionni bounces from Brussels to Philadelphia to Genoa to Zurich to Milan. He masters five languages and multilingual thinking; makes two stabs at getting a business degree (being unqualified, by Italian standards, for university study); marries (happily ever after) at twenty-one, becomes a (delighted) father at twenty-two; threads his way among Italian Futurists, Fascists, and anti-Fascists; flirts with cinematography, essays a little architecture, finds the glimmering of a profession designing displays and exhibits for Motta, the confectioner known in the US for its pannetone . . . and early in 1939, with Hitler's troop massing, leaves for America with his portfolio, where, despite his originality, he lands a job at the big Philadelphia ad agency N.W. Ayer—as relieved as you may be upon reaching the end of this sentence.

At twenty-one, Lionni is eager "to sink my young, wounded roots into rich and generous American soil." He resumes his close involvement with art. In front of a traditional portrait in oils by his agency colleague Leon Karp, he rediscovers "the beauty of the act of painting." His own work moves in the direction, natural to him, of pictorial storytelling—in the fantastic vein of surrealist Max Ernst. At Ayer, in a chance act that gains him advertising immortality, he plucks from a wastebasket the line of copy "Never Underestimate the Power of a Woman," intended for the *Ladies' Home Journal,* and demonstrates that it can be illustrated. (A 1942 example: Hitler giving a straight-arm Nazi salute, the Statue of Liberty raising her torch.)

Thus launched, Lionni becomes art director for important accounts, most notably the enlightened Container Corporation of America—his opportunity to sign up some of America's most advanced artists, unite pure and applied art, and raise institutional advertising to new heights. New York, the capstone, beckons; but sight of a sea of cubicles at the giant J. Walter Thompson agency, with wrought iron gates like a zoo, puts him to flight. Not, however, back to Philadelphia and Ayer. "I began to hate myself for being an advertising man . . . I wanted my own studio, in New York."

There begins the period in Lionni's career, from 1948 to 1961, when he and a handful of other great creative talents remade American graphic design. Just about everyone remembers Lionni's catalog for the Family of Man exhibit; children's librarians may also recall his cover for *Going for a Walk with a Line.* He art-directed *Fortune,* part-time; launched Olivetti in America as a flagship of Italian design; founded and edited the stylish trade magazine, *Print;* chaired the First International Design Conference at Aspen, the beginning of Aspen as cultural mecca. And, already resolved to abandon commercial work and return to Europe, already thinking in metaphors and toying with positions in space, he constructed out of torn paper, on a train trip with his grandchildren, the story of *Little Blue and Little Yellow.*

The morning the book is scheduled to go on display at Brentano's on Fifth Avenue, Lionni takes the dawn train from Greenwich, waits intently for the store to open, waits in terror for a copy to be picked up, examined, and—ahhhhhhh—bought! "My heart was turning somersaults," writes the most celebrated designer in the world.

Inch by Inch, which followed, represents Lionni's farewell to all that—his escape, like the inchworm's, from pointless, imposed labor. Then came *On My Beach There Are Many Pebbles:* close-ups, with strange shapes and hidden images, softly crayoned in black and white. "A book," drawn from Lionni's childhood summers, "that didn't look like a children's book and probably wasn't."

"Right or wrong, that was the last of the trial runs." With *Swimmy,* "my first real fable," Lionni found himself—as a creator of children's books, as a person who was an artist:

> The central moment is not so much Swimmy's idea of a large fish composed of lots of tiny fish but his decision, forcefully stated, "I will be the eye." Anyone who knew of my search for the social justification for making art, for becoming an artist, would immediately have grasped what motivated Swimmy, the first embodiment of my alter ego, to tell his scared little friends to swim together like one big fish . . . . He had seen the image of the large fish in his mind. That was the gift he had received: to see.

For Lionni, the picture books exist between the two worlds of the autobiography's title, the worlds of pure and applied art. Or would it be more accurate to say that they straddle the world, and bridge them? "The rhythm, the simplicity of the action, the logic of the sequencing of the protagonists on the page" all originate, he recognizes, in the many issues of *Fortune* he designed. The picture-book fables, the return to childhood make-believe with adult insight and expertise, are an answer to his long-time ambivalence about the role of the artist.

Lionni's autobiography, it bears repeating, is an assemblage of portraits, scenes, and reflections, without a strong narrative spine, that begs for a chronology and an index. But he is a fine descriptive writer and raconteur, and so acute about art that a passing observation goes ping.

That Lionni himself found no single answer to the role of the artist, a class of kindergartners discovers.

"Guess what, guess what!" declares Reeny, the sparkplug of Vivian Paley's class. "That is Leo Lionni we doing."

And Reeny has just met Lionni's mouse poet Frederick, her alter ego. How Lionni picture-book fables expand to fill the kindergarten year, how every person becomes "a Leo Lionni somebody," how all comers are ensnared and myriad issues implicated, is the story, the big story, of Paley's small heady book.

Frederick, storing away thoughts of summer, declines to help his friends store away food. To Reeny's classmate Cory, Frederick is "mean." "That's not the same as mean. He's thinking," replies Reeny. "Anyway, those others is nicer but I still like Frederick. Look how his tail is, Cory . . . ."

But what of Tico, in Lionni's *Tico and the Golden Wings,* whose rejection by his friends has long disturbed Paley, as readers of her previous books know. If Frederick can think away the summer with impunity, why should wingless Tico be shunned when his wish for golden wings is granted? Poor Tico, poor Vivian Paley. Even Reeny, individualist Renny, would have Tico give away his golden feathers and settle for the black norm keep his friends. "Else he be too lonely." Conformity of loneliness, Paley adds: "The choice is his to make." As for Frederick, he just has different friends, says Reeny. "Tico didn't have that other kind of friend." But Cornelius, that's another story. Cornelius, the nonconforming crocodile who walks upright and stands on his head, turns his back on the other, belittling crocs, and opts for independence, come what may.

In each of the books, Paley observes, "there is a struggle between self and community; the conflict is acted out in a dozen different ways. Who do I feel most like, the reader is prompted to ask, a Tico, a Frederick, or a Cornelius? . . . And how will my friends react to the choices I make?"

Each Lionni book adds new characters, new relationships, and new layers of meaning. "Reeny really figured it out," says Paley's co-teacher, Nisha Ruparel-Sen. "She said you have to have a special problem to be in his book." Ruparel-Sen reads stories from the many-layered book of her childhood, the Ramayana: will Hanuman be a "Leo Lionni somebody" too?

Harriet Tubman is. Reeny's grandmother has come to school to celebrate her birthday, because both of her parents are working, and to tell a story. And seeing the children act out *Swimmy,* she decides to tell about Harriet Tubman—"a slave," who "escaped from the people who owned her, sort of the way Swimmy swam away from the big fish." And, like him, "she saved the other slaves." In choosing *Swimmy* as her birthday book, Reeny was sending a message of her own. "She knew I'd notice she's the only black girl in the class," says her grandmother, who'd prefer Reeny go to a neighborhood school, with more black children and teachers, so she can be another Harriet Tubman. But Reeny never stops thinking, and some days later she reminds her grandmother that Swimmy is the leader of red fish. "Red fish. That means a black fish could be the leader of another color fish."

A serendipitous experiment with five- and six-year-olds becomes an intellectual journey without end, not unlike the way Lionni has lived his life.

Additional coverage of Lionni's life and career is contained in the following sources published by the Gale Group: *Contemporary Authors,* **Vols. 53-56;** *Dictionary of Literary Biography,* **Vol. 61;** *Major Authors and Illustrators for Children and Young Adults; Something about the Author* **Vols. 8, 72.**

How to Use This Index

The main reference

> **Baum, L(yman) Frank**
> 1856-1919 .... **15**

lists all author entries in this and previous volumes of *Children's Literature Review*.

The cross-references

> See also CA 103; 108; DLB 22; JRDA;
> MAICYA; MTCW; SATA 18; TCLC 7

list all author entries in the following Gale biographical and literary sources:

AAYA = *Authors & Artists for Young Adults*
AITN = *Authors in the News*
BLC = *Black Literature Criticism*
BLCS = *Black Literature Criticism Supplement*
BW = *Black Writers*
CA = *Contemporary Authors*
CAAS = *Contemporary Authors Autobiography Series*
CABS = *Contemporary Authors Bibliographical Series*
CANR = *Contemporary Authors New Revision Series*
CAP = *Contemporary Authors Permanent Series*
CDALB = *Concise Dictionary of American Literary Biography*
CDBLB = *Concise Dictionary of British Literary Biography*
CLC = *Contemporary Literary Criticism*
CMLC = *Classical and Medieval Literature Criticism*
DA = *DISCovering Authors*
DAB = *DISCovering Authors: British*
DAC = *DISCovering Authors: Canadian*
DAM = *DISCovering Authors: Modules*
      DRAM: *Dramatists Module;* **MST:** *Most-Studied Authors Module;*
      MULT: *Multicultural Authors Module;* **NOV:** *Novelists Module;*
      POET: *Poets Module;* **POP:** *Popular Fiction and Genre Authors Module*
DC = *Drama Criticism*
DLB = *Dictionary of Literary Biography*
DLBD = *Dictionary of Literary Biography Documentary Series*
DLBY = *Dictionary of Literary Biography Yearbook*
HLC = *Hispanic Literature Criticism*
HLCS = *Hispanic Literature Criticism Supplement*
HW = *Hispanic Writers*
JRDA = *Junior DISCovering Authors*
LC = *Literature Criticism from 1400 to 1800*
MAICYA = *Major Authors and Illustrators for Children and Young Adults*
MTCW = *Major 20th-Century Writers*
NCLC = *Nineteenth-Century Literature Criticism*
NNAL = *Native North American Literature*
PC = *Poetry Criticism*
SAAS = *Something about the Author Autobiography Series*
SATA = *Something about the Author*
SSC = *Short Story Criticism*
TCLC = *Twentieth-Century Literary Criticism*
WLC = *World Literature Criticism, 1500 to the Present*
WLCS = *World Literature Criticism Supplement*
YABC = *Yesterday's Authors of Books for Children*

CLR Cumulative Author Index

Author Index

CLR Cumulative Nationality Index

AMERICAN

Aardema, Verna **17**
Aaseng, Nathan **54**
Adkins, Jan **7**
Adler, Irving **27**
Adoff, Arnold **7**
Alcott, Louisa May **1, 38**
Aldrich, Bess Streeter **70**
Alexander, Lloyd (Chudley) **1, 5, 48**
Aliki **9, 71**
Anderson, Poul (William) **58**
Angelou, Maya **53**
Anglund, Joan Walsh **1**
Armstrong, Jennifer **66**
Armstrong, William H(oward) **1**
Arnold, Caroline **61**
Arnosky, James Edward **15**
Aruego, Jose (Espiritu) **5**
Ashabranner, Brent (Kenneth) **28**
Asimov, Isaac **12**
Atwater, Florence (Hasseltine Carroll) **19**
Atwater, Richard (Tupper) **19**
Avi **24, 68**
Aylesworth, Thomas G(ibbons) **6**
Babbitt, Natalie (Zane Moore) **2, 53**
Bacon, Martha Sherman **3**
Ballard, Robert D(uane) **60**
Bang, Molly Garrett **8**
Baum, L(yman) Frank **15**
Baylor, Byrd **3**
Bellairs, John (A.) **37**
Bemelmans, Ludwig **6**
Benary-Isbert, Margot **12**
Bendick, Jeanne **5**
Berenstain, Jan(ice) **19**
Berenstain, Stan(ley) **19**
Berger, Melvin H. **32**
Bess, Clayton **39**
Bethancourt, T. Ernesto **3**
Block, Francesca Lia **33**
Blos, Joan W(insor) **18**
Blumberg, Rhoda **21**
Blume, Judy (Sussman) **2, 15, 69**
Bogart, Jo Ellen **59**
Bond, Nancy (Barbara) **11**
Bontemps, Arna(ud Wendell) **6**
Bova, Ben(jamin William) **3**
Boyd, Candy Dawson **50**
Brancato, Robin F(idler) **32**
Branley, Franklyn M(ansfield) **13**
Brett, Jan (Churchill) **27**
Bridgers, Sue Ellen **18**
Brink, Carol Ryrie **30**
Brooks, Bruce **25**
Brooks, Gwendolyn (Elizabeth) **27**
Brown, Marcia **12**
Brown, Marc (Tolon) **29**
Brown, Margaret Wise **10**
Bruchac, Joseph III **46**
Bryan, Ashley F. **18, 66**
Bunting, Eve **28, 56**
Burch, Robert J(oseph) **63**

Burnett, Frances (Eliza) Hodgson **24**
Burton, Virginia Lee **11**
Butler, Octavia E(stelle) **65**
Byars, Betsy (Cromer) **1, 16**
Caines, Jeannette (Franklin) **24**
Calhoun, Mary **42**
Cameron, Eleanor (Frances) **1**
Carle, Eric **10**
Carter, Alden R(ichardson) **22**
Cassedy, Sylvia **26**
Catalanotto, Peter **68**
Charlip, Remy **8**
Childress, Alice **14**
Choi, Sook Nyul **53**
Christopher, Matt(hew Frederick) **33**
Ciardi, John (Anthony) **19**
Clark, Ann Nolan **16**
Cleary, Beverly (Atlee Bunn) **2, 8**
Cleaver, Bill **6**
Cleaver, Vera (Allen) **6**
Clifton, (Thelma) Lucille **5**
Climo, Shirley **69**
Coatsworth, Elizabeth (Jane) **2**
Cobb, Vicki **2**
Cohen, Daniel (E.) **3, 43**
Cole, Brock **18**
Cole, Joanna **5, 40**
Collier, James L(incoln) **3**
Colum, Padraic **36**
Conford, Ellen **10, 71**
Conrad, Pam **18**
Cooney, Barbara **23**
Cooper, Floyd **60**
Corbett, Scott **1**
Corcoran, Barbara **50**
Cormier, Robert (Edmund) **12, 55**
Cox, Palmer **24**
Creech, Sharon **42**
Crews, Donald **7**
Crutcher, Chris(topher C.) **28**
Cummings, Pat (Marie) **48**
Curry, Jane L(ouise) **31**
Curtis, Christopher Paul **68**
Cushman, Karen **55**
Dalgliesh, Alice **62**
Danziger, Paula **20**
d'Aulaire, Edgar Parin **21**
d'Aulaire, Ingri (Mortenson Parin) **21**
Davis, Ossie **56**
Day, Alexandra **22**
de Angeli, Marguerite (Lofft) **1**
DeClements, Barthe **23**
DeJong, Meindert **1**
Denslow, W(illiam) W(allace) **15**
dePaola, Tomie **4, 24**
Diaz, David **65**
Dillon, Diane (Claire) **44**
Dillon, Leo **44**
Disch, Thomas M(ichael) **18**
Dixon, Franklin W. **61**
Dodge, Mary (Elizabeth) Mapes **62**
Domanska, Janina **40**
Donovan, John **3**

Dorris, Michael (Anthony) **58**
Dorros, Arthur (M.) **42**
Draper, Sharon M(ills) **57**
Dr. Seuss **1, 9, 53**
Duke, Kate **51**
Duncan, Lois **29**
Duvoisin, Roger Antoine **23**
Eager, Edward McMaken **43**
Ehlert, Lois (Jane) **28**
Emberley, Barbara A(nne) **5**
Emberley, Ed(ward Randolph) **5**
Engdahl, Sylvia Louise **2**
L'Engle, Madeleine (Camp Franklin) **1, 14, 57**
Enright, Elizabeth **4**
Epstein, Beryl (M. Williams) **26**
Epstein, Samuel **26**
Estes, Eleanor (Ruth) **2, 70**
Ets, Marie Hall **33**
Feelings, Muriel (Grey) **5**
Feelings, Tom **5, 58**
Ferry, Charles **34**
Field, Rachel (Lyman) **21**
Fisher, Aileen (Lucia) **49**
Fisher, Dorothy (Frances) Canfield **71,**
Fisher, Leonard Everett **18**
Fitzgerald, John D(ennis) **1**
Fitzhugh, Louise **1**
Flack, Marjorie **28**
Fleischman, (Albert) Sid(ney) **1, 15**
Fleischman, Paul **20, 66**
Forbes, Esther **27**
Foster, Genevieve Stump **7**
Fox, Paula **1, 44**
Freedman, Russell (Bruce) **20, 71**
Freeman, Don **30**
Fritz, Jean (Guttery) **2, 14**
Frost, Robert (Lee) **67**
Fujikawa, Gyo **25**
Gaberman, Judie Angell **33**
Gag, Wanda (Hazel) **4**
Gaines, Ernest J(ames) **62**
Galdone, Paul **16**
Gallant, Roy A(rthur) **30**
Gantos, Jack **18**
Garden, Nancy **51**
Gauch, Patricia Lee **56**
Geisel, Theodor Seuss **53**
George, Jean Craighead **1**
Gibbons, Gail **8**
Giblin, James Cross **29**
Giovanni, Nikki **6**
Glenn, Mel **51**
Glubok, Shirley (Astor) **1**
Goble, Paul **21**
Goffstein, (Marilyn) Brooke **3**
Gordon, Sheila **27**
Gorey, Edward (St. John) **36**
Graham, Lorenz (Bell) **10**
Gramatky, Hardie **22**
Greene, Bette **1**
Greene, Constance C(larke) **62**
Greenfield, Eloise **4, 38**

Taylor, Theodore **30**
Thomas, Ianthe **8**
Thomas, Joyce Carol **19**
Thompson, Julian F(rancis) **24**
Thompson, Kay **22**
Tobias, Tobi **4**
Tresselt, Alvin **30**
Tudor, Tasha **13**
Tunis, Edwin (Burdett) **2**
Twain, Mark **58, 60, 66**
Uchida, Yoshiko **6, 56**
Van Allsburg, Chris **5, 13**
Viorst, Judith **3**
Voigt, Cynthia **13, 48**
Waber, Bernard **55**
Walter, Mildred Pitts **15, 61**
Watson, Clyde **3**
Weiss, Harvey **4**
Wells, Rosemary **16, 69**
Wersba, Barbara **3**
White, E(lwyn) B(rooks) **1, 21**
White, Robb **3**
Whitney, Phyllis A(yame) **59**
Wibberley, Leonard (Patrick O'Connor) **3**
Wiesner, David **43**
Wiggin (Riggs), Kate Douglas (Smith) **52**
Wilder, Laura (Elizabeth) Ingalls **2**
Wilkinson, Brenda **20**
Willard, Nancy **5**
Williams, Barbara **48**
Williams, Garth (Montgomery) **57**
Williams, Jay **8**
Williams, Vera B. **9**
Williams-Garcia, Rita **36**
Willis, Connie **66**
Wisniewski, David **51**
Wojciechowska, Maia (Teresa) **1**
Wolff, Virginia Euwer **62**
Wood, Audrey **26**
Wood, Don **26**
Woodson, Jacqueline **49**
Worth, Valerie **21**
Yarbrough, Camille **29**
Yashima, Taro **4**
Yep, Laurence Michael **3, 17, 54**
Yolen, Jane (Hyatt) **4, 44**
Yorinks, Arthur **20**
Young, Ed (Tse-chun) **27**
Zelinsky, Paul O. **55**
Zim, Herbert S(pencer) **2**
Zindel, Paul **3, 45**
Zolotow, Charlotte S(hapiro) **2**

ANTIGUAN

Kincaid, Jamaica **63**

AUSTRALIAN

Baillie, Allan (Stuart) **49**
Baker, Jeannie **28**
Base, Graeme (Rowland) **22**
Brinsmead, H(esba) F(ay) **47**
Chapman, Jean **65**
Chauncy, Nan(cen Beryl Masterman) **6**
Clark, Mavis Thorpe **30**
Clarke, Judith **61**
Crew, Gary **42**
Fox, Mem **23**
Graham, Bob **31**
Hilton, Nette **25**
Jennings, Paul **40**
Kelleher, Victor (Michael Kitchener) **36**
Klein, Robin **21**
Lindsay, Norman Alfred William **8**
Marsden, John **34**
Mattingley, Christobel (Rosemary) **24**
Nix, Garth **68**
Ormerod, Jan(ette Louise) **20**
Ottley, Reginald Leslie **16**
Phipson, Joan **5**
Rodda, Emily **32**
Roughsey, Dick **41**

Rubinstein, Gillian (Margaret) **35**
Southall, Ivan (Francis) **2**
Spence, Eleanor (Rachel) **26**
Thiele, Colin (Milton) **27**
Travers, P(amela) L(yndon) **2**
Trezise, Percy (James) **41**
Wrightson, (Alice) Patricia **4, 14**

AUSTRIAN

Bemelmans, Ludwig **6**
Noestlinger, Christine **12**
Orgel, Doris **48**
Zwerger, Lisbeth **46**

BELGIAN

Herge **6**
Vincent, Gabrielle (a pseudonym) **13**

CANADIAN

Bedard, Michael **35**
Blades, Ann (Sager) **15**
Bogart, Jo Ellen **59**
Buffie, Margaret **39**
Burnford, Sheila (Philip Cochrane Every) **2**
Cameron, Eleanor (Frances) **1**
Cleaver, Elizabeth (Mrazik) **13**
Cox, Palmer **24**
Doyle, Brian **22**
Ellis, Sarah **42**
Gal, Laszlo **61**
Gay, Marie-Louise **27**
Godfrey, Martyn N. **57**
Grey Owl **32**
Haig-Brown, Roderick (Langmere) **31**
Harris, Christie (Lucy) Irwin **47**
Houston, James A(rchibald) **3**
Hudson, Jan **40**
Hughes, Monica (Ince) **9, 60**
Johnston, Julie **41**
Katz, Welwyn Winton **45**
Khalsa, Dayal Kaur **30**
Korman, Gordon (Richard) **25**
Kovalski, Maryann **34**
Kurelek, William **2**
Kushner, Donn (J.) **55**
Lee, Dennis (Beynon) **3**
Little, (Flora) Jean **4**
Lunn, Janet (Louise Swoboda) **18**
Mackay, Claire **43**
Major, Kevin (Gerald) **11**
Markoosie **23**
Matas, Carol **52**
Milne, Lorus J. **22**
Montgomery, L(ucy) M(aud) **8**
Mowat, Farley (McGill) **20**
Munsch, Robert N(orman) **19**
Oberman, Sheldon **54**
Pearson, Kit **26**
Poulin, Stephane **28**
Reid, Barbara **64**
Richler, Mordecai **17**
Roberts, Charles G(eorge) D(ouglas) **33**
Seton, Ernest (Evan) Thompson **59**
Smucker, Barbara (Claassen) **10**
Stren, Patti **5**
Taylor, Cora (Lorraine) **63**
Wallace, Ian **37**
Wynne-Jones, Tim(othy) **21, 58**
Yee, Paul (R.) **44**

CHILEAN

Krahn, Fernando **3**

CHINESE

Namioka, Lensey **48**
Young, Ed (Tse-chun) **27**

CUBAN

Ada, Alma Flor **62**

CZECH

Sasek, Miroslav **4**
Sis, Peter **45**

DANISH

Andersen, Hans Christian **6**
Bodker, Cecil **23**
Drescher, Henrik **20**
Haugaard, Erik Christian **11**
Minarik, Else Holmelund **33**
Nielsen, Kay (Rasmus) **16**

DUTCH

Biegel, Paul **27**
Bruna, Dick **7**
DeJong, Meindert **1**
Haar, Jaap ter **15**
Lionni, Leo(nard) **7, 71**
Reiss, Johanna (de Leeuw) **19**
Schmidt, Annie M. G. **22**
Spier, Peter (Edward) **5**

ENGLISH

Adams, Richard (George) **20**
Ahlberg, Allan **18**
Ahlberg, Janet **18**
Aiken, Joan (Delano) **1, 19**
Alcock, Vivien **26**
Allan, Mabel Esther **43**
Ardizzone, Edward (Jeffrey Irving) **3**
Arundel, Honor (Morfydd) **35**
Ashley, Bernard **4**
Awdry, Wilbert Vere **23**
Baker, Jeannie **28**
Banner, Angela **24**
Barklem, Jill **31**
Base, Graeme (Rowland) **22**
Bawden, Nina (Mary Mabey) **2, 51**
Bianco, Margery (Williams) **19**
Biro, Val **28**
Blake, Quentin (Saxby) **31**
Blake, William **52**
Blyton, Enid (Mary) **31**
Bond, (Thomas) Michael **1**
Boston, L(ucy) M(aria Wood) **3**
Breinburg, Petronella **31**
Briggs, Raymond Redvers **10**
Brooke, L(eonard) Leslie **20**
Browne, Anthony (Edward Tudor) **19**
Burnett, Frances (Eliza) Hodgson **24**
Burningham, John (Mackintosh) **9**
Burton, Hester (Wood-Hill) **1**
Caldecott, Randolph (J.) **14**
Carroll, Lewis **2, 18**
Causley, Charles (Stanley) **30**
Chauncy, Nan(cen Beryl Masterman) **6**
Christopher, John **2**
Clarke, Pauline **28**
Cooper, Susan (Mary) **4, 67**
Corbett, W(illiam) J(esse) **19**
Crane, Walter **56**
Cresswell, Helen **18**
Cross, Gillian (Clare) **28**
Crossley-Holland, Kevin (John William) **47**
Cruikshank, George **63**
Dahl, Roald **1, 7, 41**
Defoe, Daniel **61**
de la Mare, Walter (John) **23**
Dhondy, Farrukh **41**
Dickinson, Peter (Malcolm) **29**
Dodgson, Charles Lutwidge **2**
Doherty, Berlie **21**
Farjeon, Eleanor **34**
Farmer, Penelope (Jane) **8**
Fine, Anne **25**
Foreman, Michael **32**
French, Fiona **37**
Gardam, Jane **12**
Garfield, Leon **21**
Garner, Alan **20**

Nationality Index

CLR Cumulative Title Index

Title Index

Title Index

Title Index

Title Index

Title Index

Title Index

Title Index